PROTECTING CHILDREN FROM DANGER

Building Self-Reliance and Emergency Skills Without Fear

A LEARNING BY DOING BOOK
FOR PARENTS AND EDUCATORS

Bob Bishop
and Matt Thomas

North Atlantic Books
Berkeley, California

Protecting Children From Danger

Published by
North Atlantic Books
P.O. Box 12327
Berkeley, California 94701–9998

Illustrated by Paul Willis
Cover and book design by Paula Morrison
Typeset by Catherine Campaigne

Protecting Children From Danger is sponsored by The Society for the Study of Native Arts and Sciences, a nonprofit educational corporation whose goals are to develop an educational and cross-cultural perspective linking various scientific, social and artistic fields; to nurture a holistic view of arts, sciences, humanities, and healing; and to publish and distribute literature on the relationship of mind, body and nature.

Library of Congress Cataloging-in-Publication Data
Bishop, Bob, 1940–
    Protecting children from danger : building self-reliance and
emergency skills without fear : a learning by doing book for parents
and educators / Bob Bishop and Matt Thomas.
        p.   cm.
    Includes bibliographical references.
    ISBN 1-55643-159-7
    1. Safety education—United States. 2. Children's accidents—
United States—Prevention. 3. Child rearing—United States.
4. Self-defense for children—United States. I. Thomas, Matt.
II. Title.
HQ770.7.B57 1993
649'.1—dc20   93-5977
                                                               CIP

1   2   3   4   5   6   7   8   9   /   97   96   95   94   93

To our Children
Anders, Chorus, Cully, Johann, and Reyna
and to all children everywhere—
may we give them love and real wisdom to grow

Dear Parent/Educator,

Welcome to *Protecting Children from Danger*. This book is designed for parents and educators to teach children about personal safety through a systematic interactive learning process.

Although the exercises and games described in the book have been effective in the past, we make no guarantees or claims about the program or its effects. Therefore neither the authors nor P.O.L.O. International and its staff are liable for negligence resulting from your use of the materials in any way.

Please be considerate of the children you will be working with. Do not push them beyond their individual means or present the training program in a competitive spirit. The idea is to have fun while learning important skills that can be useful in future potentially dangerous situations.

The Authors
and P.O.L.O. International

TABLE OF CONTENTS

Foreword

Human infants are helpless at birth and they remain relatively dependent longer than other mammals. Many animals take their first steps almost immediately and become independent within a few days or weeks. The newborn porpoise swims instinctively to the surface for its first gulp of air. Soon after the young calf takes its first faltering steps, it is frolicking through the herd. Wolf cubs, blind at birth, are roughhousing in a few short weeks. In the animal kingdom maturity and self-reliance come quickly, or youngsters are certain to fall prey to the beasts that are their predators.

Some human beasts prey on children.

Our children need reassurance, confidence, and training to avoid not only human predators but more common dangers as well, such as household fires and other emergencies. Most of all, children fear being lost, cut off from the adults who protect them.

We cannot accompany our children everywhere, or protect them every moment. This book's practical wisdom empowers our children to take care of and protect themselves, a valuable gift and a concrete form of love. I feel that this book provides a valuable method for enhancing children's resourcefulness, confidence and self-esteem so they can avoid dangerous situations. But if danger finds them, well-informed and well-trained children can take the best possible course of action, guided by sound principles, to stay safe and stay alive.

Childhood is tough enough in the best of circumstances. I urge all parents and teachers to use this book to train children in sound and effective ways to confront life head-on with resourcefulness and confidence, so that one day they may enjoy their own children and pass on to them the life-saving, life-enhancing material presented in *Protecting Children from Danger.*

I know Bob Bishop and Matt Thomas personally. I know of their exceptional skills and training. The principles and practices they teach embody experience-based wisdom—what actually happens in the real world. Their combination of backgrounds and talents—both are educators and security professionals—makes a unique contribution to child safety and empowerment. *This book should be on every parent's bookshelf, and this knowledge in every child's mind and body.* This book can save lives. And even if our children never face a human abductor or other life-threatening danger, it will help them serve as a source of confidence and strength for others.

Dan Millman
Author of *Way of the Peaceful Warrior*
and *No Ordinary Moments*

Introduction

CHILDREN AND THE PROTECTIVE WARRIOR SPIRIT

THE "GOOD OLD DAYS"

The daily news bombards us with constant reminders of how dangerous the world has become for our children. It is difficult to remain aware without being overwhelmed by the appalling level of violence in our society today. As we nostalgically reflect on the safety and sanctity of earlier times, we are easily lulled into wishing for a return to the "good old days."

In reality, however, the good old days weren't so good. In fact, most advances in society have made the world much safer for children. Primarily because of increased public health measures, most children now reach adulthood. This has not always been the case. In the Middle Ages—not long ago in the scope of human history—one in ten mothers died in childbirth, and three of every four children died before age four. The Black Plague swept through Europe twice, killing two-thirds of the population.

Less than 150 years ago, adults and children in this country were sold into slavery to be physically and sexually abused. Many who weren't slaves were exploited in sweatshops and mines at the beginning of the Industrial Revolution.

1

Settlers in the western United States suffered tremendous hardships and worked from sunrise to sunset. Children worked alongside their parents. The work required of them to survive was often worse than slavery. Infant mortality everywhere was high. Physical abuse of children was condoned and even encouraged by religious leaders and educators who followed the dictum "Spare the rod and spoil the child." Although it was not openly discussed, sexual abuse proliferated. Young girls were sold to brothels. Child brides were often forced into loveless marriages. Wife-battering was commonplace and condoned to "keep women in their place."

This part of our history was rarely written about, but it was the reality of most of the population. Everyday life was not glorious or romantic by any standards. So much for the "good old days."

Even today, children in countries around the world die from famine or disease. Others are exploited in squalid sweatshops. Young girls are still sold or kidnapped into slavery. Prostitution and pornography rings continue to exploit young children. In dozens of countries throughout the world, women still have few rights.

Despite its numerous shortcomings, Western civilization has made life much safer for children in countless ways. And it continues to do so. For example, before the passage of mandatory seat belt laws in some states, thousands of children were injured or killed in automobile accidents every year. By simply buckling up, we save thousands of lives and have reduced injuries by an estimated 75 percent.

Each advance toward making life safer has been brought about through step-by-step changes created by people of conscience and action. These men and women are our inspiration.

THE PROTECTIVE WARRIOR SPIRIT: LEARNING FROM THE GREAT TRADITIONS

As security professionals and martial artists with years of experience, we, the authors, have each been responsible for the lives and safety of rich, famous, and controversial people. When we met early in 1989, our common interests and similar experiences fostered an immediate friendship. We had many discussions about the security concerns of our clients, which always included the protection and safety of their children. Our clients especially feared child abduction. As parents ourselves, we shared their concern for this unfortunately frequent and tragic occurrence.

We began to consider other matters that threatened our children and to examine where we were focusing our professional time and energy. We quickly realized that our combined abilities and backgrounds uniquely qualified us to create an educational program to teach children self-reliance and self-protection.

We have also been inspired by our studies of the martial arts and historical warrior traditions because of their applicability to contemporary life. With respect to self-protection, there is definitely no need to reinvent the wheel. Rather, we can adapt ancient traditions for maximum use in modern life by adding the expertise of new developments in the fields of personal protection and family safety.

Ancient traditions included principles of action, behavior, and moral precept. Body, mind, and spirit were highly trained and integrated. Individuals learned to stay healthy and balanced, and to function with great emotional and mental clarity in daily life. Living the warrior way produced outstanding men and women. *The ancient and true purpose of a warrior was to preserve and protect life.*

Consequently, many of the traditional warrior principles are useful in any time or place; certainly they are useful today in times of danger. The word "warrior," as used in this text, means a person trained in the skills of defending himself or herself and others from harm. Warriors are by no means to be confused with "war-mongers," or aggressive conquerors, or even with the majority of dedicated military professionals.

In fact, the protective warrior spirit is an integral part of every man and woman. In a higher sense it is that human longing or need for courage, commitment to purpose, selflessness, service to others, and the transcendence of all limitations.

As Richard Heckler writes in *In Search of the Warrior Spirit*, traditional warriors also often served a spiritual purpose, ". . . as strong a ceremonial function within society (engaging and placating natural forces, and challenging taboos in times of crisis) as they did a military one in confronting outsiders. These were warriors in the classical sense of power initiates and providers of security." (p. 106)

Recognition of the value of traditional warrior ways in modern times is not a new concept. Dan Millman's bestseller, *Way of the Peaceful Warrior,* and David Roger's *Fighting to Win,* translate historical principles and philosophies to effective use in modern business and everyday life. In a like manner, much of this book is based on traditional warrior principles. We also include from our own experience and training modern concepts used by military and security professionals to protect themselves and others in times of danger.

Each of us can be empowered by the protective warrior spirit, using the knowledge in this book to teach our children not only to protect themselves, but also to lead full and intense lives.

In sharing our knowledge of warrior traditions and our personal experiences, it is our goal to dispel some myths, to impart realistic danger-awareness skills, and to communicate ways of effectively responding to danger and emergency situations.

ASSESSING CURRENT DANGERS TO CHILDREN

Obviously it is not possible in any one book to consider all the dangers that face children, so we began to assess current dangers with some reservation. We found that the leading cause of death for children ages one through fourteen is accidental injury. The U.S. Department of Public Health estimates that more than eight thousand children are killed by accidents every year in the United States, and another fifty thousand are permanently disabled. It is further estimated that more than ninety percent of these accidents are preventable.

Sexual abuse by acquaintances is also a serious threat to children. This subject has received a great deal of attention in recent years. According to the *1953 Kinsey Report,* one out of every four women was sexually abused as a child. Although reported incidents are even higher today—one in three—this is very likely because, thanks to increased avenues of help and support, abuse is more likely to be reported today than it was forty years ago.

Despite the importance of these two subjects, we have chosen not to focus on either. There are many excellent texts on accident prevention and on sexual abuse, some of which are referenced in the bibliography.

This book concentrates on the dangers that we believe are the most frightening to parents and children: child abduction, encounters with strangers, getting lost, fire, home security, and pedestrian/motor vehicle safety. By learning effective action in response to these specific dangers, children become capable of dealing with emergency situations in general.

Child abduction is a frightening subject for anyone to consider. We have seen estimates exceeding one million incidents a year, mostly involving child snatching in custody disputes. Many of these incidents and the resulting trauma to children could be prevented by effective family counseling. Even more dangerous than parental abduction is child abduction by strangers. The National Center for Missing and Exploited Children estimates that over fifty thousand children disappear each year whose cases remain unsolved.

Although these statistics have been disputed by some public agencies and we personally think they are exaggerated to some degree, it is undeniable that our children face serious dangers in today's world. How can we help our children to prepare for and respond to these dangers? Our answers to this question shape our children's lives.

PARENTAL STRATEGIES FOR DEALING WITH DANGER

Parents usually adopt one of four basic strategies with respect to fear and perceived danger. The most common strategy, fueled by feelings of helplessness, is to *ignore the problem* and not do anything. The children of such parents survive primarily because of circumstances and luck.

The next most common strategy is for parents to *be overprotective*, attempting to shield their children from all danger. This results in limiting the child's activities and instilling fear of unfamiliar people and places. This may be justified when the child is very young, but over time this strategy becomes repressive and inhibits the development of self-reliance.

A third common strategy, explained by the belief that "only good things happen to good people," is to *pretend that danger does not exist.* Parents who use this approach believe that directing attention to dealing with negative events will actually attract them. This approach allows children more openness and freedom in their activities, but it also tends to make them naive and more at risk. Such children are not prepared to deal with dangerous situations. If a negative incident does occur, the after-effects can be even more traumatic for the child than the effects of living in the suppressive, fear-inducing environment of over-protection.

Stephen Covey, in his acclaimed personal management book *The Seven Habits of Highly Effective People,* talks about circles of influence and circles of concern. The circle of influence is that area in which people feel they can effect change. The circle of concern is that area in which people perceive problems and difficulties and dangers that can affect them. When people perceive that their circle of influence is much smaller than their circle of concern, and they focus their attention primarily on concern, they feel powerless and victimized.

Covey urges people to be proactive, to focus energy and attention on what one can actually affect and on how one can personally influence others. This foundation principle for personal effectiveness breaks the paradigm of feeling powerless.

From the protective warrior perspective, this is saying, "I will not be victimized by apparent circumstances, nor will I allow my loved ones to be. I will do whatever I can to become self-reliant in the face of danger, and I will help others to do likewise. Beyond that, I will not be concerned."

This brings us to the fourth strategy: for parents to *consciously build their children's self-esteem and to help them become as self-reliant as possible in the face of danger.* Of course, there are limitations of age and capacity to learn; but children are typically far more perceptive and able to learn than their parents realize. This fourth strategy is the focus of our children's educational program—and of this book.

In many ways, our own children became our teachers. We began instructing them in the subject matter of this book to see what they were capable of learning and retaining. They were so enthusiastic and attentive that their capacities and achievements not only met but far exceeded our expectations. In this text, we, the authors, are referred to as "Bob" or "Matt" wherever we wrote about personal experiences that we wanted to share with the reader.

One of the many incidents that validated our teaching approach happened when Matt's son Cully was just three years old. He surprised his nursery school teachers, and the police officers who came to his class to teach child safety, by demonstrating that he could dial 911 and that he knew his whole name, his parents' names, and his home address. He had been introduced to police officers in public places and had even visited a police station, so he already saw the police as people who would help him in times of trouble.

Another incident occurred one evening when Bob's son Chorus John was five years old. Chorus was at our home with his sitter, a young neighborhood girl. The girl decided to use a portable mixer to make brownies. Somehow she caught her fingers in the blades, trapping her hand. She screamed to Chorus for help. This was a real emergency!

Chorus ran to the phone, dialed 911, and told the police what had happened and where they were located. He then comforted the girl as best he could. The police arrived within minutes and rushed the girl to the hospital, where she was given emergency care. Fortunately, her hand healed completely.

After the incident, people expressed amazement at how calmly and effectively this young boy had handled the emergency. The police and hospital personnel asked how he knew what to do. He replied simply, "My dad taught me." Chorus only did what he had learned to do; it was no big deal to him.

Other parents began to request that we teach their children similar skills, and we saw the results duplicated again and again. We knew we were on to something.

These and other incidents increased our motivation to write this book for parents, educators, and anyone else who is concerned with the safety of children. Our motivation increased with each group of parents and children we trained. We firmly believe that if each of us is willing to devote time and energy to the professional principles and proven concepts of protection described in this book, our children can become capable of effective action in times of danger. They will naturally focus on being aware and self-reliant, rather than afraid.

This book provides a positive and unique approach to sensitive subject matter through the use of Western and Eastern learning principles, role models that children relate to easily, and creative experiential lessons for parents and educators to practice with children. The text includes both an educational methodology and a how-to guide, with the emphasis on learning by doing.

HOW TO USE THIS BOOK

Although this book was originally conceived as part of our child protection workshop, it has subsequently been developed for more universal application. It is a distillation of experience, research, and creative development. The concepts and principles discussed in the previous section are interwoven with guidelines for application throughout the text. Parents and educators will best gain an overall understanding of the subject matter and teaching approach by reading the book in its entirety before using with children.

LEARNING BY DOING EXERCISES

Children learn best by experience and only so much can be understood from reading a book. To maximize the benefits of this material, we suggest that parents spend time with their children, learning by doing what may be unfamiliar to them both.

The "Learning by Doing" exercises are significant in developing children's innate capabilities for self-reliance and appropriate response in dangerous situations. Each exercise is designed to build upon and complement principles developed in previous ones. Therefore exercises should be done with children in the order prescribed.

Another important reason for parents to learn by doing with their children is that once they see their children's capacity to respond in difficult situations, they can relax their own fears and concerns. Thus parents become more supportive of building their children's self-reliance.

Parents and educators will find that the use of workshops and other materials enhances and accelerates learning. (See "Workshops and Videotape Training Program" in Appendix A at the end of this book.)

The "Learning by Doing" exercises, for the most part, can easily be done by parents (or educators) with one or more children. However, some of the games and more elaborate exercises (like the fire drill) can best be done by more than one family cooperating to create an event. Attending a parent/child workshop led by a P.O.L.O. International certified instructor is also an excellent and enjoyable way to accomplish this.

Our children's safety depends entirely on us. It is with great pleasure that we offer this book, and our related workshops and videotape training programs, as tools to guide us on the path of providing safe and full lives for the children we love.

Bob Bishop
Matt Thomas
P.O.L.O. International

Chapter One

SELF-RELIANCE IS BEST

THE IMPORTANCE OF SELF-RELIANCE

Using our backgrounds in the traditional martial arts and in modern military and professional security, we have collectively provided training to thousands of people in criminal justice agencies and in private security. Some of the people we have trained may be the ones who respond when you call 911. In addition, we have provided professional protection for many individuals and families.

We love and cherish our own families, but though we are well qualified to protect them, we can't be there 24 hours a day, 365 days a year. They must be capable of protecting themselves.

We are often away from home teaching others. When the 1989 San Francisco earthquake struck, we were both teaching in Colorado. We couldn't fly home the next day. Our families were glad to see us, but everything was under control. Although it was a tragic disaster for many families in the Bay Area, we had been spared. We were grateful for the time we had spent with our families on psychological and practical preparation.

How can we prepare our children for emergencies? Being a responsible parent can seem overwhelming at times. Our society spends vast sums of money and time educating us, and we all spend considerable energy educating ourselves for our individual vocations. Unfortunately, however, the profession of being a parent is left mostly to chance—a few books and perhaps a couple of classes, usually just before the first child is born. By the time the second child comes along, who has time for more classes?

We hire professionals to educate our children and to care for them if they are sick or in trouble. If a child is lost in the woods, a veritable army of professionals and volunteers engages in a search and rescue effort. We rely on others in daily life, especially during emergencies, and our children rely on us most of the time—even when they tell us to go away.

Humans are a social species. Interaction and reliance on others is natural. However, we must be capable of self-reliance when others aren't around. In times of danger, we are often alone. Therefore, to truly protect our children, we must teach them self-reliance in avoiding or escaping from danger. This is asking a lot of children, but surprisingly enough, if their self-esteem is intact, they are often much easier to train than adults.

BUILDING A CHILD'S SELF-ESTEEM

There are some wonderful books on the value of self-esteem in children. In essence, self-esteem is the basis of emotional health for everyone—to feel loved for one's own sake.

As parents we love our children, but we need to communicate that love to them in ways that they understand. For example, when we leave for work in order to make money to support our families, our children would rather have us stay home to play with them. No matter how we explain the importance of work to the family's well being, a young child can perceive our leaving as abandonment. Even after we have spent the whole weekend with them, Monday morning can be difficult. Love must be communicated daily in our comings and goings in ways that they understand. When Matt's young son sent him off one day saying, "Go to work, Daddy, so you can buy me toys," he showed that he was starting to understand this concept. Not completely, but it was a beginning.

After feeling loved for one's own sake, the second principle of self-esteem is that children need to feel that they can handle themselves and their environment with competence. Our children's behavior in daily life reveals their self-image to us. How we react often reflects our own self-image.

Self-esteem is the basis for anyone's behavior during a crisis. How have we prepared our children? At one extreme, if we perceive them as completely inadequate in the face of danger, and they in turn mirror this attitude, then except for natural defense mechanisms, they are left tragically unprepared for danger or crisis. At the other extreme, they might feel unrealistically confident. However, given the opportunity to develop courage and experience success, they will expect to succeed. Changing our children's self-expectations in daily life is crucial to preparing them for emergencies.

Overprotection actually decreases children's self-esteem and forces them to withdraw from their own natural defense mechanisms. The more over-protective we are, the more they retreat into our shadows. The more we see them in our shadows, the more over-protective we become. This downward spiral ultimately limits growth and fosters resentment. Anyone with a teenager knows this spiral well.

Fortunately, children's self-images are constantly changing. They are very malleable, and if we change, they can change too. Like a polished mirror, we must reflect our children to themselves as lovable and competent in daily life and in times of crisis.

SELF-RELIANCE IN CRISIS SITUATIONS

If we stop to think about it, we actually make life-and-death decisions every day of our lives. We choose not to step into traffic. We refrain from touching hot stoves. We do not stick keys or forks into electrical sockets. But we have all experienced heart-stopping moments while teaching these "common sense" behaviors to our children.

We have been teaching our children to choose between life and death all along. We can adjust these standards so that self-reliance is developed in more difficult situations through a step-by-step process. But we must not set standards so high that our children aren't able to meet them. This can initiate a cycle of defeat and loss of self-confidence. We must constantly realign our goals with their capabilities. This continuous readjustment can provide extremely rewarding results—and more than a few delightful surprises.

One of the most important steps is learning to *respond to the individual needs of our children.* This requires that we listen to their words and, even more importantly, pay attention to their actions. As we demonstrate active listening and respectful responses, our children become more trusting and open with us. As a side benefit, children have wonderful imaginations; their openness can be a treasure chest of insight and joy.

Learning to be nonjudgmental during the teaching process is another key to building trust. It is also crucial to the learning process. It is most important not to withdraw approval when children fail to meet our expectations. Success requires that we remain enthusiastic, empathetic, and encouraging. All training processes have their ups and downs and their plateaus. As long as children feel safe about stepping backward, they will feel encouraged and secure enough to press forward again. Sometimes we'll be the ones who are running to catch up.

WESTERN LEARNING PRINCIPLES

In order to effectively teach children self-reliance, parents may need to develop some teaching skills themselves. We have found the following learning principles to be very effective in teaching both children and adults. We use the example of a child learning to walk to illustrate these principles.

ROLE MODELING OF BASIC BEHAVIORS

Most of us did not read books or attend classes to learn to teach our children to walk. Walking is a natural behavior, learned primarily by imitating others. Even children who aren't around others who walk will do so, although they walk much sooner by constantly observing others—their parents and even more importantly, their peers. Children may be quite content to crawl until they observe a playmate just a few months older walking. Immediately they will try to imitate the older child's behavior, and will be walking soon after.

Dealing with dangerous situations is also a learned behavior with an instinctual basis. Our ancestors had to learn specific behaviors to survive in addition to listening to their instincts. None of us would be around if they hadn't been successful. In teaching, it is important to introduce role models who will capture the imagination of our children, and for us to be parental role models as well. If children see us deal effectively with crises, they can do the same.

STEP-BY-STEP MASTERY OF TECHNIQUES

This is the foundation of any learning process. Each of us learned to walk step by step. Walking eventually leads to more complex skills like turning, running, jumping, leaping, or skipping. Later, walking becomes the basis of roller-skating, ice-skating, dancing, and skiing. Each of these complex skills develops from the first step.

In teaching our children to function under emergency conditions, we start with a simple first step and proceed from there. Often we return to the basics in order to master more complex movements.

POSITIVE REINFORCEMENT

This is not only the most enjoyable way to teach any skill, it is also the most successful. As our children look to us for approval, we must encourage each minor success. If we focus only on the final goal, we can become impatient and deprive them of well-deserved approval for the gradual progress they are making. This latter approach can impede learning.

In the step-by-step learning process, it is important to realize that for every two steps forward, there may often be a step backward. We all learn by our mistakes. An old Japanese proverb tells us, "Fall down seven times, rise up eight." When children learn to walk, they are nonjudgmental about themselves each time they fall. They might momentarily cry in frustration or pain, but soon they are up and tottering again. Though we may wince at each fall, we must remain nonjudgmental. We know that eventually they will walk. Patience and a positive attitude are the best ways to teach our children any skill.

PROGRESSIVE ADAPTATION OF SKILLS
TO DEAL WITH OBSTACLES

This is another integral part of the step-by-step process. When children learn to walk, we give them the most ideal environment possible—a level, carpeted area free of sharp objects. We don't introduce slopes, stairs, potholes, obstacles, or emergency stops on the first day. Each of these can be introduced after the basic skills are no longer challenging. After gradual adaptation and mastery, obstacles are seen as challenges that children seek rather than avoid. As adults, we retain this attitude. A hike in the mountains is a lot more enjoyable than a hike on a level track. Similarly, we introduce increasing levels of difficulty in dealing with emergencies as our children's skills develop.

SUCCESSFUL ACTION UNDER SIMULATED STRESS

This is the next step in preparing for emergencies. The first time we face a crisis, we can become strangers to ourselves. Our bodies produce adrenaline and significant physiological and psychological changes such as tunnel vision, rapid heart beat, time distortion, and the trembling of hands or legs.

As an example, all of us seem to have an innate fear of falling from a height. Can you remember your child's terror in looking down a slide for the first time? Young children usually reverse themselves on all fours and crawl backward down the slide the first time or two. But soon they are zipping down the slide, laughing with joy—and then they are looking for higher, longer, faster slides. Skiing is a multibillion-dollar industry based on the enjoyment people receive from mastering their fear of heights and enjoying the adrenaline rush of speed and controlled falling.

Children must become accustomed to their reactions in fearful situations. Their training must simulate danger enough to provoke an emotional reaction, yet still be safely under the control of responsible teachers, like you, the parents.

DEVELOPING REFLEXES

This is one of the last steps in learning. Effective action in times of danger needs to become automatic. Walking is a highly complex skill, but it quickly becomes a reflex. When we are out walking and encounter a curb, we don't become fearful about falling, think about the social consequences of falling, or worry about the physical damage that could result if we did fall. We simply adjust our stride and continue walking. Eventually, this is how we can respond to danger—exactly as we walk—reflexively.

EASTERN PRINCIPLES OF ACTION

Miyamoto Musashi was one of the greatest swordsmen of ancient Japan. After a lifetime of combat with the blade, he wrote a classic strategy and training book, *The Book of Five Rings*. In spite of the Teenage Mutant Ninja Turtles craze, we are not promoting the teaching of swordsmanship to children. However, an adaptation of Musashi's "Five Rings," or elemental principles, is most applicable in developing effective responses to danger. We continue with our example of learning to walk to illustrate this point.

EARTH

Being "grounded," or learning the basics, is the key to developing any skill. The child's first challenge in learning to walk lies in dealing with his or her relationship to the earth. A child learns to roll over, lift the head, crawl, climb, get up on two feet, and finally to take a step, embracing the earth many times along the way. Mastering basics is essential to true mastery of any skill.

WATER

Water flows around obstacles. When children begin to walk, they search for the easiest way to go around obstacles. Similarly, children cannot match the physical strength of an adult intent upon harming or abducting them. They must learn to flow around the adult's strength and find a weakness, just as water flows around obstacles.

FIRE

In learning to walk, children are driven by an "inner fire" that helps them to persist, despite numerous failures and the pain of falling. Fire inspires enthusiasm and energy. Fire also represents the passionate channeling of emotion as fuel in critical situations.

Human beings have survival instincts that have been developed over thousands of years. In times of danger, our bodies prepare us for fight or flight. In this society, most of us have been trained to handle our own uncomfortable feelings (fire) with denial and diversion. Unfortunately, when our lives are threatened, many of us continue to repress our anger, thus taking away one of our greatest natural defenses—fire. Before children can use fire in crisis situations, however, they must be taught how to control and direct it in daily life.

WIND

Teaching the principle of the wind is the most difficult because it is the most elusive. Although children don't have much experience in dealing with abstract principles, they can understand by example: They cannot hold their breath in their hands, but they can blow out a candle. In the face of danger, there are times to be elusive and times to become a hurricane.

VOID

This final principle has been called the "No-Mind Warrior State." This state can be thought of as reflexive action. When skills have been learned well, the conscious mind can cease to control, letting the body express its amazing wisdom to do what is needed. All of what we teach our children about action in times of danger must become reflexive, just like walking.

SUMMARY

- No matter how knowledgeable we adults are about emergency skills and self-protection, we can't always be there to protect our children.

- Building our children's capability for self-reliance is one of the best approaches to protecting them from danger.

- The ability to be self-reliant is based on self-esteem.

- We can nurture both self-esteem and self-reliance in our children by how we teach them.

- Western principles of learning and Eastern principles of action can be integrated to teach children effective skills in dangerous situations.

Chapter Two

FACING FEAR

OF CATS AND NINJAS

It's a warm summer afternoon. A small Siamese cat sleeps bliss-fully on the couch. Somehow, the Doberman puppy from next door has gotten into the house. Despite its youth, the dog already recognizes cats as things to chase and terrorize. The dog spots the sleeping cat, barks once, and charges toward the couch. Suddenly the cat is awake, all her senses heightened to peak awareness by the chemistry of perceived danger. Instead of an easy, unsuspecting target, the puppy meets a spitting, scratching ball of fury. After receiving a few rapid swipes across his face, he beats a hasty retreat with his tail between his legs. For a few minutes the cat maintains her ready state, but once she is satisfied that the danger is past, she resumes her after-noon snooze as if nothing had happened.

It's a dark night in a forest in ancient Japan. A young boy is hiding in the branches of a tall tree. He is trained in the ways of the ninja, and this night he is serving as a lookout. It is very dark and the sounds of wild things moving below keep him alert. He always keeps in mind the admonition of his master to "expect nothing and be ready for anything." He knows that when he feels afraid and there is no perceived danger, he must practice deep breathing to relax his mind and body. He does it well.

What the cat and the ninja youth have in common is a right relationship to fear. In both cases, fear is not to be viewed negatively simply because it doesn't feel good. It is to be recognized as a friend—simple body chemistry that releases adrenaline to mobilize the nervous system, heart, liver, and muscles to achieve rapid action in times of danger.

But what of the chronic fears and anxieties that plague us as modern men, women, and children? The answer seems to lie in understanding what is normal for us to fear and what is not, and then to develop our abilities to respond accordingly. One thing is clear in relation to children: Increasing their fear is not the way to teach them self-reliance. In fact, just the opposite is the case, even with respect to real danger.

NORMAL AND ABNORMAL FEARS IN CHILDREN

As children grow their experiences and boundaries expand as well, and it is only natural that new fears arise and old ones fall away. Schachter and McCauley discuss this matter in their book, *When Your Child is Afraid*. The book is designed to help parents understand their children's fears and to distinguish those fears that are normal and will be outgrown from those that are more serious and require professional assistance. It also suggests what to say and do to alleviate major fears in children of different ages.

Schachter and McCauley discuss fear as a primitive but complex emotion that is valuable when it helps us to mobilize our bodies and minds to respond to danger. They tell us that some fears are instinctive or part of our genetic heritage. Other fears, such as fear of strangers or anxiety over separation, are adaptive and help the child survive. Still others may evolve as a child attempts new skills, or develop in response to trauma produced by a situation or experience. The latter fears can become phobias if not properly handled. Phobias are fears that become chronic and cause a person to become dysfunctional.

Schachter and McCauley believe that fear is useful when it arouses individuals physically, helps them to adapt, and is innate or related to normal development. If treatment is necessary, they recommend a form of behavioral therapy in which the therapist accompanies the person and models appropriate behavior in a feared situation. Interestingly, this is one of the key learning principles we recommend to build self-reliance in children.

FEAR AND ILLUSION

Facing one's fear is a warrior principle that often leads us to discover that many of the things we fear most are not what they appear to be. Matt illustrates this point with an incident from his childhood:

> The *oni* (the Japanese version of "bogeymen" or "devils") first came to me when I was living in an orphanage during the occupation of Japan. Being three years old, I believed that these creatures with red eyes in green faces with long fangs and horns were real, rather than disguises worn by our caretakers to frighten us into submission. They beat me as they did my only friend Carlos, screaming that they would eat us because we were bad. When it was over, Carlos and I knew we had to run away before they returned. We crept into the caretakers' closet for extra clothing, as it was snowing outside. When we slid the door open, there were the *oni* ! Rather than flee, I bared my teeth at them while poor Carlos cried. The *oni* didn't move. They were just masks and cloaks! Pretty

soon we put the masks on and danced with each other, laughing through the tears.

I'm an adult now with a wife and three children. They all have beautiful smiles because they don't worry about the *oni*. Neither do I. Because I discovered the truth about the *oni*, I can live my life without crippling fear of them. So much of what we fear is illusion.

It is also true that much of what we fear is based in reality. Our fear can motivate us to act, but then we need to let it go. Psychological energy wasted on fear can be put to much better use.

BREATH AND LIFE: WORKING WITH FEAR AND OTHER EMOTIONS

All fear, when we really get down to it, is based on the fear that we won't survive; it is the fear of death. Ultimately, of course, every being that lives also dies. It is part of the natural chain of events for everyone. As Da Avabhasa says in his book *Easy Death,*

> The primary initiation that leads to human maturity is the confrontation with mortal fear. Only when the ultimate frustration that is death has been fully considered and felt and understood as a process, can the individual live without self-protective and self-destructive fears. (p. 108)

This book is a profound consideration of the process of death and spiritual practice in life. In it, Da Avabhasa considers fear from a point of view that we can make immediate use of. Remarkably, he discusses fear as ordinary but not necessarily natural, and certainly not something that requires "any great, profound, philosophical cycle of investigations of the universe." (p. 112) Instead, he says,

The alternative to fear is not some great answer that will ultimately prevent our being chronically and mortally afraid, which we all are, and which people are in general. Such knowledge is not even possible. The alternative is to recognize fear as an ordinary mechanism of the body beyond which we can, and should, in any moment Feel and Breathe. (p. 113)

In other words, since fear is body-based we can actually move beyond it through deep and balanced breathing.

In fact, the three primary negative emotions of fear, sorrow, and anger are characterized by imbalances in breathing. Fear is reflected by weak inhalations and exhalations, hardly breathing at all. Sorrow often results in jerky, nonrhythmic inhalations and weak exhalations. Anger is characterized by weak inhalations and forced, excessive exhalations. These patterns are described in an earlier book by Da Avabhasa, *Conscious Exercise and the Transcendental Sun* pp. 216–217), and also in Dan Millman's *The Warrior Athlete* (p. 70–91).

If you are afraid, breathe deeply with feeling and be sure to breathe equally in and out. If you are sorrowful, exhale strongly and be sure exhalation through the right nostril is full and clear. If you are angry, inhale deeply and be sure inhalation through the left nostril is full and clear.

Observe your breathing patterns over time and recognize your own patterns of reactivity. Then you can use the breath as a powerful but simple tool to balance your body and emotions.

FEAR AND THE WARRIOR SPIRIT

It is winter in a harbor town on the coast of Maine. A group of people fishing on a dock see a shark swimming nearby. In the excitement to observe the dangerous creature, a young boy is accidentally pushed into the icy water. The people on the dock are frozen with fear as the child sinks in the murky water and the shark heads in his direction. Almost without hesitation, a teenage girl plunges into the water, dives under, and grabs the boy, hauling him to safety just seconds before the shark reaches them both. Everyone praises the girl as a heroine—and she is—but she wonders why she was the only one to act while others stood by paralyzed by fear. She is a student of the martial arts, who has been fortunate enough to learn from a teacher who emphasized training of the warrior spirit.

The ancient warrior traditions—the Samurai of Japan, the Kshatreya of India, or Native Americans, like the Apaches—produced superb fighters who were highly skilled in the tactics and weapons of their times. The Samurai, for example, were masters of the sword and bow and horse, and they maintained themselves in excellent physical condition. However, they understood that training of the body was not enough. The spirit must be trained as well—not in a religious sense so much as in the recognition that in the midst of mortal danger a warrior must be present with complete emotional and mental clarity; otherwise he could be easily defeated despite his great skill in combat.

The Samurai understood that in times of mortal danger, a person can become a stranger to himself if he has never experienced the psychophysical changes that may occur: the adrenaline rush of fear, the extreme narrowing of perception that causes tunnel vision focused on the object of fear, the way that time seems to slow down, and the severe limitation of fine motor responses. Obviously, all this can drastically impede an individual's ability to respond as needed unless he or she is familiar with such effects and learns to function effectively despite them.

For this reason, the Samurai placed great emphasis on the "No-Mind Warrior State" and on the principles of action based on this theme. In *Fighting to Win*, David Rogers discusses these principles in relation to all of life. He calls this warrior state of mind *Mo Chi Chu*—acting (or moving ahead) without hesitation. Doing whatever is necessary in the moment.

To be in this state consistently requires the practice of the following principles.

FRONTAL KAMAE. The posture of facing an attack. Always face an attack or *any situation.* In other words, *Face Life. Accept Whatever Is Happening in Every Moment,* even if it is life-threatening. Before battle, American Indian warriors would often say to each other, "It is a good day to die, my brothers," fully accepting the potential reality of their own demise.

SONO-MAMA. See what is before you. See things *as they really are* without judgment or fear. *See Life.*

ZANTOTSU. Literally, close and strike. More generally, to take immediate committed action. *Engage Life* directly and forcefully if necessary.

AIKI. Engage without confrontation. Blend, harmonize, flow with the energy of the situation.

In other words, the warrior allows himself to feel his emotions fully in times of danger, recognizing them as a signal to be completely alert in the moment, accepting what is before him, perceiving clearly and taking whatever action is immediate and necessary.

A colleague of ours, Julio Toribio, Chief Instructor of Action Self Defense in Monterey, California, expresses these principles another way. From the standpoint of the modern security professional, he calls them "The Three A's":

• Awareness Yours! Know it! Your strengths and weaknesses, your tendency to become bored or distracted when you must be alert. Know yourself and what you tend to do in crisis situations.

- Assessment   Observe the scene clearly. See and hear what is happening completely.

- Action   Effective communication. Setting boundaries, running away, or defending oneself if required. Doing whatever is necessary in the moment danger arises—responding rather than reacting.

ADVENTURE AND ACCOMPLISHMENT

A proper relationship to our fears is important in our daily lives. If we are strong and courageous we are willing to take risks and have adventures, and to attempt to accomplish things that seem difficult or beyond our capabilities. Some people attempt difficult things, but when they fail they give up with an attitude of, "I'll never try that again. I learned my lesson that time." They become fearful, cautious, and limited in their participation in life.

Masaaki Hatsumi, the present-day grandmaster of *ninjutsu*, has written in *The Grandmaster's Book of Ninja Training,*

> People are far too afraid of all sorts of things in their lives. They fear for their health; they have fears about how strong they are; they fear for their safety, and so on. . . . Fear prevents people from doing so many things. They look after themselves far too well. If people would only not take so much care of themselves and have a little more confidence in themselves, a bit of courage—my own teacher used to say that if one had no courage, there was no hope—with courage anything can be accomplished. (p. 74)

Certainly we want our children to be aware of danger and not to take unnecessary risks, but just as certainly we want them to live full and strong and joyful lives. That is the legacy of the warrior spirit.

SUMMARY

- Fear can be accepted as a friend that warns us in times of danger.
- Increasing a child's fear is not a way to teach self-reliance.
- Fear is normal and useful if it arouses action, helps adaptation, or is related to normal development.
- Fear is not normal when it becomes chronic or obsessive, or when it causes dysfunctions physically or psychologically.
- Facing our fears allows us to go beyond them, often discovering that what we fear is illusion.
- Breath can be used to balance fear and other negative emotions.
- Principles of effective action in times of danger are based on:
  - Familiarity with the effects of fear.
  - Acceptance of the present moment.
  - Perceiving fully what is occurring.
  - Taking immediate and necessary action.
- A proper relationship to fear is essential for our children to live full and joyful lives.

LEARNING BY DOING

CLEARING THE AIR: COMMUNICATION BETWEEN PARENTS AND OTHER ADULTS

Objective: To get in touch with feelings and concerns for your children.

Materials: None.

Exercise:
Sit facing each other and communicate openly as follows:

- One person asks the other, "What are your greatest fears for the safety of your children?"
- The second person answers the question, speaking for three minutes without interruption.
- The person who asked the question then speaks for three minutes without interruption (in answer to the same question).
- Each person in turn summarizes for one minute.
- They can then share silent eye contact and a comforting hug.
- One person asks the other, "How do you convey your love to your children?"
- They repeat the speaking and summarizing cycle, ending with a hug.

This simple process can open up deep communication in a short time. When you are listening, truly listen. Don't leave the present moment to think about your reply. Soon you will find that your responses spring spontaneously from the heart.

DEEP BREATHING

Objective: To teach children to relax their emotions and restlessness through concentration on deep breathing.

Materials:
- A comfortable surface to lie on indoors, or outdoors in nice weather.
- Tape, CD, or record player to play soft instrumental background music.

Exercise:

This is a simple but very important exercise for children and adults. Concentration on deep abdominal breathing for a minute or so is a useful practice before beginning any focused activity and is common in most martial arts training. It is also useful in releasing negative emotions surrounding sensitive issues as discussed earlier in this chapter. Concentrated deep abdominal breathing balances our emotional state and allows us to become centered again.

Although there are many methods of concentrated breathing, one of the easiest ways to learn is to have your child place her hand on her belly so that she can feel it swell as she uses her diaphragm instead of her chest to breathe. As she does this, tell your child to:

- Count to three as she breathes through her nose.
- Hold her breath for three counts.
- Count to three as she exhales through her mouth.
- Hold her breath for three counts.
- Go back to the first step to begin the cycle anew.

Simple gentle stretches and joint rotations are also useful to release physical and emotional tension. A few minutes invested in stretching before concentrated activity helps to increase mental and emotional clarity.

FACING FEAR

Objectives:

- To understand children's fears by communicating with them verbally.
- To teach children about controlling fear through breathing.
- To accompany children through potentially frightening

but controlled circumstances and to model appropriate behavior.

Learning Your Children's Fears

Materials: None.

Exercise:

- When you are spending some quiet time with your children, ask them to tell you about the things they are most afraid of. Allow them to talk about anything, even if some of it seems silly or laughable or even disturbing to you. Encourage honesty. If they are shy about discussing such matters, you might start by telling them things that you are afraid of yourself. More than likely you will get some surprising responses.

- Talk to your children about fear being a "friend" that warns us in times of danger. Illustrate how someone who is afraid would probably breathe. Then show them how proper breathing (as described in "Breath and Life," earlier in this chapter) can lessen the "bad" feeling and allow them to take action. If possible, continue with the following exercise immediately.

Darkness

Fear of the dark is common among children, especially very young ones, and therefore it is a useful medium to work with, especially with respect to breathing.

Materials: None

Exercise:

- When it's dark outside, take your young child into a room and tell him that you are going to turn out all the lights and sit with him in the dark. You can do this any time in a room without windows. Make a game out of it. If he objects strenuously, you may have to work up to this. However, it is often enough to hold his hand and reassure him that you are not going to leave him alone. Allow him to feel afraid and to express himself.

- Remind your child of good breathing and how it gets rid of "bad" feelings.
  - Breathe in with strong inhalations and out with strong exhalations.
  - Have the child place his hand on your abdomen and encourage him to breathe in a similar manner.
  - Persist until he is able to relax and release the "bad" feeling.

- Repeat the exercise with you in the room but sitting some distance away from the child. See if he is able to do it as well without you touching him.

- If the child finds this exercise too stressful the first time, *gently* persist until you are successful. It may take several tries and you may have to go more slowly before the child is able to relax, depending on his age and the intensity of his fear of the dark.

Leap of Faith

Children often can't learn new activities until they learn to trust the person who is teaching them. This is especially true when physical skills are being taught that might be frightening to a child. Here is an exercise to instill trust in a child.

Leap of Faith

Location: A place where the surface is fairly soft—outdoors on the grass or sand, or indoors with carpets or athletic mats.

Materials: Objects of varying heights, from 1 foot to 4 or 5 feet in height, that you and your child can stand on.

Exercise:

- Have your child stand on an object that is one foot high and then jump off. Instruct her to raise her arms in front for balance, and to land on the balls of her feet with her knees slightly bent.

- Have her jump from increasingly higher objects until she reaches a height that makes her hesitate, or that you feel presents the danger of physical injury.

- Repeat the sequence a second time, only this time have her do each step with her eyes closed. Assure her that you will catch her so that she won't fall.

• If your child hesitates, get up on the object with her and jump together holding her hand; or you can get up on the object yourself and make the Leap of Faith with your eyes closed, allowing yourself to be helped by some other adult "spotting" for you. Then encourage the child to participate again until she has a basic sense of trust in you, or in whoever is teaching her the physical skill.

NOTE: In one of our P.O.L.O. workshops, we were doing this exercise with children and their parents. A five-year old girl was spotted incorrectly by an adult. The child was slightly bruised. She cried for a few moments, and then refused to participate in the exercise again. I (Bob) observed her for a short time and then went over to her. I asked her if she would like to jump with me holding hands. She nodded hesitantly, but agreed. We jumped together from a height of one foot. The other children applauded and the instructors praised her. Greatly encouraged by this small success, she asked to jump from greater heights, each time being rewarded by encouragement from everyone. She went on to participate in the workshop fully. This incident emphasized to us the importance of observing each child's response to a new learning experience and being sensitive to what is required to encourage confidence and success.

Chapter Three

FAMILY BONDING

PARENT TO CHILD AND PARENT TO PARENT

The strongest human bond is the bond between mother and child. This bond is universal and instinctive. For example, in studies that use pupillary response to measure positive and negative reactions, childless women, whether married or unmarried, have positive pupillary responses to pictures of children.

The father and child bond is a different story. Childless men, whether married or unmarried, generally have a negative pupillary response to pictures of children, while men who have children generally have a positive pupillary response. When the baby is first born, the father initially feels left out. When questioned, most new fathers insist that they bonded immediately with their baby. However, virtually every father that is questioned in depth will usually confess that he did not truly bond with his child at first. The men experienced feelings of jealousy or of being left out, along with feelings of tremendous responsibility or of being overwhelmed. At the same time, of course, they experienced feelings of elation, joy, and the warmth of fatherhood, along with the congratulations of their family, friends, colleagues, and acquaintances. The positive feelings are celebrated, while the negative ones are denied.

When mothers are questioned, at first they too deny any negative feelings toward their newborns. After trust is established, however, they usually confess that they sometimes felt overwhelmed and mourned the loss of freedom and the loss of romance with their husband, while still feeling the tremendous joys of motherhood.

The truth is, our children sometimes create negative feelings in us toward them and toward each other. Unless we as parents honestly address these issues in normal life, we can't expect to deal with them in times of crisis.

The love relationship between parents is most important in maintaining a family unit. If this bond dissolves, the family unit itself dissolves and then each parent individually has to take on the task of providing for their children's safety. When relationships are neglected because of other commitments, eventually the family unit deteriorates. Tremendous amounts of time are then needed to deal with the new parent/child problems. Therefore, to promote the bonding of the family unit, we need to begin with our relationship with our spouse.

The reestablishment of intimacy between parents is not the theme of this book; but when parental relationships break down, it's often the children who suffer the most. For example, most child abductions are by separated or divorced parents. Parents who set an example of emotional and mental intimacy and cooperation during normal times stand a better chance of functioning effectively in an emergency. Being side-by-side warriors in everyday life is a wonderful way to live.

PARENTAL AUTHORITY WITH LOVE AND UNDERSTANDING

The same process of emotional and mental intimacy can be the basis of a new relationship with our children. It's amazing to see how the cooperation between partners in the simulated emergencies described in the exercises can bring about cooperation in other aspects of parent-child relationships.

Simply because we brought our children into this world, we have a responsibility to guide them until they are mature enough to take full responsibility for themselves. Let's face it, that takes a long time, and our relationships go through tremendous changes!

The easiest and most efficient method of family government is a parental dictatorship. When the child asks why, the parent responds, "Because I say so!" Unfortunately, this response does not promote family bonding; nor does it help children learn to take responsibility for themselves.

It is important to be clear about the reasons for the rules we lay down, and we need to explain the consequences of violation of these rules in a way that the child can understand. On the other hand, the child often uses explanations as a negotiating tool to wear down parental objections.

If we remember our love for our children with every decision we make, and consistently demonstrate that love, the children can learn to understand our reasons. For example, wearing a seat belt is a necessary rule. The use of seat belts reduces injuries and fatalities as much as 75 percent. However, many children don't like being restrained. If we can't communicate with them, we just buckle them in. When Matt's son Cully was three years old and questioned the seat belt rule, Matt put his bicycle helmet on him and improvised an air bag out of his knockdown toy and pillows, put him in the seat without his seat belt, drove at five miles an hour down the driveway, and slammed on the brakes. Cully flew into the improvised airbag. He wasn't hurt—actually, he thought it was fun—but he definitely understood that if those pillows weren't there, he would be out of control and could get seriously hurt. The exercise was safe. They had fun. Cully learned a valuable lesson. For liability reasons we can't recommend that you do this exercise, but you can certainly think up your own ways of getting a point across without endangering your children.

Another one of Matt's sons, Anders, has not questioned the seat belt rule, so Matt hasn't done this exercise with him. Twice, when he wasn't paying attention because he was dealing with Cully or Johann, Matt forgot to buckle Anders into his car seat. Even though Anders was only two years old, he reminded Matt. Different children need different lessons at different times.

Another example is the age-old problem of a child hitting someone else. Sometimes parents hit their child to punish him for hitting a sibling. This stops the behavior temporarily, but all the child learns is that whoever is bigger gets to hit! A child who is restrained and sent to a corner learns that the consequence of hitting is the temporary loss of freedom. In the corner, the child has time to reflect on his behavior, and eventually stops hitting.

Establishing communication channels and practicing exercises in everyday life promote trust for parental authority that is the best preparation for a crisis.

Ask yourself if you allow your children as much responsibility as they are capable of assuming. Or are you just relating to them in the way that is most convenient for you? The Learning by Doing exercises in this book can initiate some interesting dialogues about safety.

RITUALS AND CEREMONIES

Communication requires structural formats. In the past, manners, rituals, and ceremonies were taught to facilitate communication, and in some cases we still use them to teach "proper behavior." Just as clubs and fraternities have their secret handshakes and rituals, families can develop their own bonding rituals. It may seem silly to us adults, but children really love making up "ceremonies."

The "pipe circle" was an important ritual for some of the American Indian cultures. In a large gathering, if everyone talked at once, nothing would get done. So the pipe was used as a symbol to indicate who had the floor; it was passed around until everyone had spoken. This ritual could be modified for a family gathering by using a timer and any "family object." Like Dumbo's magic feather, the object soon becomes unnecessary. The important thing is that the ritual encourages children to speak and parents to listen.

SUMMARY

- Family bonds between parents and children and between parents themselves are the basis for emotional intimacy that allow the family to act as a unit in times of danger.
- Family bonding helps children feel safe at home.
- It is important for parents to examine their family "government" and move toward a participatory style.
- Developing self-esteem and a sense of responsibility in children in everyday life is the best way to prepare them to take the initiative to act during emergencies.
- Family rituals and ceremonies are helpful in encouraging the bonding of family members.

LEARNING BY DOING

MAKING SYMBOLIC HEADBANDS

Animals and forces of nature have always been heroic and inspiring symbols of action, originating with ancient tribal warrior rites.

Objective: To inspire children's imaginations through positive identification with symbols of personal power.

Materials:

- A set of magic markers in assorted colors
- Cotton strips (6" to 24") made from a torn-up sheet or similar material
- Newspapers to cover floor and protect surfaces

Exercise:

- Guide children in the process of making personalized headbands that they will design and wear throughout the exercises.

- Ask the children to visualize what animals or forces of nature they see themselves as when they feel strong and powerful. Does she see herself as a lion or an eagle or a leopard? Does he see himself as lightning, thunder, a tornado, or a river?

- Have the children draw pictures, symbols, or names on the headbands, and wear them while they are doing some of the exercises in this book. Call them by the names they choose to inspire feelings of confidence.

FAMILY "PIPE CIRCLE"

Objective: To have children understand they have a voice in the family and that others listen and respect what they communicate

Materials: A symbolic object that can be passed easily from one or another.

Exercise:

- When it's a convenient time to meet with everyone in the family to discuss something of importance (like planning a vacation or some other positive subject), have everyone sit in a circle.

- Propose to the family that they are going to have a discussion the way American Indian tribal gatherings did, by passing a symbolic object to whoever wants to speak while everyone else listens.

- As long as that person holds the object, he or she is free to speak without interruption and everyone else should give the person their attention and really listen.

- Then the object is passes to another person who wants to speak, and so on.

- When everyone is heard, one family elder (father or mother) can summarize what has been said and make a proposal for everyone's agreement.

- Usually, you'll be surprised at how positive this can be for everyone who participates, and how it naturally draws the family closer together.

Chapter Four

FIRE AND OTHER DANGERS

AWARENESS AND THE
RECOGNITION OF DANGER

Proper awareness is the foundation for taking effective action in dangerous situations of any kind. If we are half asleep, we won't spot danger even though the signs are obvious. On the other hand, we don't want to walk around constantly on "red alert" either—our nervous systems couldn't take it. Fire fighters, soldiers who have been in combat, and law enforcement officers in high crime areas can certainly attest to this.

Jeff Cooper, a well-known shootist and combat firearms expert, has established a useful description of proper levels of awareness depending on the surroundings. He applies a color code to combat situations, but the principles are generally applicable whenever mental alertness is required.

Condition White: This is the level of awareness generally experienced by people when they arise in the morning. You're not really "with it" perhaps until you've had your first cup of coffee or juice. This level of awareness is appropriate only under the circumstances just described: in your own home. However, some people stay in "white" awareness throughout much of their lives, and this adds greatly to their potential for having an accident or being victimized.

Condition Yellow: A person is aware of his or her surroundings in specific terms. Information is being perceived and evaluated as you "scan" the environment and nearby activities. This is a relaxed, comfortable state. You are at ease but definitely aware of what is going on around you. You should be at this level of awareness as soon as you leave the safety of your home. Ask yourself if this is true of you and your children. Or do you stay in Condition White simply out of habit?

Condition Orange: This is where trusting your instincts comes into play. Your senses will guide you in most cases, but a little "reconnaissance" or "intelligence gathering" can go a long way if you are going somewhere unfamiliar. These terms may bring to mind military operations and clandestine activities, but they are simply ways of assessing the likelihood of something unpleasant occurring. Getting a little information about a place or an activity beforehand can be very useful. When you are in a foreign country, a new city, or any environment that you're not used to, you can easily be caught off guard. For example, someone visiting California for the first time may not be familiar with the extreme danger of fire during the summer months on the west coast. Or a visitor from Boston might not recognize a potentially dangerous neighborhood in Los Angeles simply because it doesn't look like the places that are dangerous back home. Trust your instincts by all means, but whenever possible gather some information beforehand.

FOREWARNED IS FOREARMED is definitely a warrior principle that anyone can use. Knowing when you should be in Condition Orange and looking for cues that may warn you of a possible threat is vital to your safety.

Condition Red: Danger is actually perceived. You recognize danger signs directly through your senses, or somehow your intuition warns you. At this point it is essential to take action, either by doing something directly or by changing what you were about to do. After an accident or a violent incident, people often indicate that they recognized the signs but didn't act on them. We often hear comments like the following:

"You know, I felt really funny when I checked into the hotel the night of the fire, but I just ignored it."

"There was something strange about the way he looked at me just before he attacked."

"I just knew something was wrong, the way that van was coming down the street so slowly, just before the shooting started."

People commonly refuse to trust their intuition because it may be inconvenient or they are unwilling to look foolish. Most of us are influenced by social conditioning that inhibits our intuition. However, you must learn to override these inhibitions. To protect yourself, *you must be aware, perceive, and act!* If you don't, you will find yourself in Condition Black.

Condition Black: *The action starts and you must deal with a potentially life-threatening situation.* Sometimes these situations are unavoidable, and you must simply face them; there is great uncertainty in life. More often than you might imagine, however, potentially dangerous situations can be neutralized by prior recognition and effective action.

In Condition Black you must be a warrior. You have no choice. Act without hesitation *(Mo Chi Chu),* bringing into place the Samurai principles discussed in Chapter Two: Face the situation completely, see what is occurring clearly, and bring to bear fully committed action to deal with the situation rapidly and effectively.

DANGER IS A WILD CARD! You never know when or where or how an emergency situation may arise, and there really aren't any "right answers" to how you should respond.

So much depends on circumstance. Therefore the real purpose of training and developing awareness skills is to provide ourselves and our children with what is needed to move from the "No-Mind Warrior State"—to be capable of spontaneous instinctive action, even in situations that are completely unfamiliar and for which we have no specific preparation. This must be our objective in teaching our children.

DANGER AWARENESS AND CHILDREN

Having established that a crucial step in effectively dealing with danger is to recognize it beforehand, we must teach our children to do likewise. However, children don't necessarily perceive the dangers that we do. Often what is obviously unsafe to us as adults seems harmless or goes unnoticed by children. The trick is to teach them what is dangerous in a way that they really *get*, without making them anxious or afraid.

We are constantly telling our children things like:

"That knife is sharp, don't play with it or you'll cut yourself."

"Stay away from matches, they'll burn you."

"Don't turn your back on the ocean because waves can knock you off your feet."

"How many times have I told you to stay out of the street, you could be hit by a car."

"Don't go near strangers or talk to them when I'm not around."

They should get it, right? But often they *don't!* Unless they actually perceive what being cut, or burned, or knocked off their feet really is, these experiences may only be concepts with either exaggerated meaning or none at all.

One very effective way of getting children to recognize danger is to allow them to experience what could harm them in small doses, under controlled circumstances.

Warriors train to simulate reality as closely as possible; but as parents we must take into account our own abilities as teachers. Are we sensitive to our own capabilities and those of our children, so that we don't put them into situations that could actually harm them for the sake of learning some lesson about danger? That would definitely be irresponsible.

With that in mind, however, we can share with you the learning experiences of Bob's son, Chorus:

Allowing him to fall into a swimming pool with his parents right there to pull him out (age two).

Letting him play by the ocean on a day when the surf was gentle, and allowing a small wave to knock him off his feet, with Bob right there to grab him (age three).

Letting him play with a small but sharp knife that he insisted he wouldn't cut himself with, until he did (age five).

Allowing him to light candles with a match until he inevitably burned his finger (age five).

Asking him to demonstrate what he would do if a stranger tried to grab him, then allowing him to initiate some "ninja turtle" moves that he and his friends were under the illusion would be effective, before Bob showed him how difficult it would be to defend himself against an adult without some very realistic training (age seven).

In each of these situations, everything was carefully controlled so the child was never actually in danger. However, he got the message loud and clear in each case, because he *bodily* experienced *why* he was told that certain things are dangerous. Needless to say, these lessons didn't have to be repeated; nor did they have to talk about them very much.

We can always be creative in how we teach our children about danger if we remember that they learn far less from what we tell them than from what they experience.

FIRE AND OTHER NATURAL
SOURCES OF DANGER

Every geographical area experiences dangerous phenomena. The very real dangers of earthquakes, fire, hurricanes, tidal waves, oceans and other bodies of water, tornadoes, extreme heat and cold, wild animals, and even erupting volcanoes are facts of life for people somewhere in North America. Each potential source of danger should be understood in terms of the following general principles:

- Ability to recognize the danger of the phenomenon as quickly as possible, especially if it occurs occasionally or periodically.
- Planning and preparation ahead of time so that each family member knows what to do to combat the danger or escape to safety.
- Realistic action drills performed often enough so that everyone remembers what to do if the emergency actually occurs.

Some of the procedures required may be very specific to the potential threat, but if these general principles are exercised with respect to one of the dangers, we can get a sense of what we might need to do in other emergencies.

Of all the dangers mentioned, fire is the most universal threat. It can occur almost anywhere, at any time, and it can be out of control before anyone is aware that it is happening. Statistics show that most people will experience at least three serious fires in their lifetime. The National Fire Protection Association says that seventy percent of all fatalities by fire occur in private residences, and many of those deaths could be prevented if the family had a simple fire escape plan.

The Learning by Doing section of this chapter focuses on emergency planning and realistic fire drills.

PUBLIC SAFETY OFFICERS AS ROLE MODELS

Fire fighters, forest rangers, paramedics, police officers, and other public safety officers have a wealth of knowledge about specific dangers and how to deal with them effectively. Make use of these people; they are a valuable resource!

In our P.O.L.O. workshops, we arrange for public safety professionals to visit. It's easy to do and their participation is invaluable.

Almost every local fire and police department has public relations personnel who are eager to find ways to demonstrate their value to the public, and to educate people about crime and fire prevention. You can arrange to have them visit your child's school or your church group or neighborhood association, and you can usually be fairly specific in what you would like them to demonstrate. The presentations are interesting, and the kids love it.

Also, many people are wary about making contact with fire fighting and law enforcement professionals. This attitude is often passed along to children; and even if it isn't, children tend to be intimidated by someone with a uniform or a gun. During such public relations programs the children (and their parents) begin to perceive that public safety officers are a valuable source of help to whom they can turn in times of danger.

Needless tragedies have actually occurred because children fled in terror from firefighters in self-contained breathing equipment who were trying to rescue them. Why? The children identified the firefighters with well known villains and bad guys in popular science fiction children's movies who looked or sounded similar. How to counter this unfortunate impression in children is discussed in the fire drill exercise.

At the very least, your children should become familiar with local police officers and with the emergency rescue personnel from your fire department. If there are Coast Guard personnel or forest rangers in your area, include them as well. You can arrange for a visit yourself, arrange for a group visit, or have public safety officers participate in a workshop training session as we do in ours.

Familiarization and friendliness with such people allows your children to see them as role models with valuable skills that they can use and emulate in emergency situations.

SUMMARY

- Proper awareness is the foundation for effective action in dangerous situations of all kinds.
- Lack of awareness greatly increases the potential for having an accident or being victimized.
- "Intelligence gathering" is simply assessing the likelihood of something occurring. Getting a little information ahead of time greatly increases your chances of avoiding potentially dangerous situations.
- Forewarned is forearmed is an important warrior principle.
- Be aware, perceive clearly, and act!
- In a life-threatening situation, you must be a warrior. You have no choice.
- Danger is a wild card. You never know where or when or how an emergency situation may arise.
- The primary objective of training and preparation is to develop the capacity for spontaneous, instinctive action in times of danger.

- Children don't necessarily perceive danger in the same way that adults do.

- Children learn far more from what they experience than from what we tell them. Therefore an effective way of getting children to recognize danger is to allow them to experience what could harm them in small doses, under controlled conditions.

- To deal effectively with potential danger, you must do the following: *Recognize* the danger before it occurs or in the early stages of development. *Plan and prepare* so that each family member knows what to do to escape or combat the danger. *Perform drills* so that everyone knows what to do in an emergency.

- Public safety officers have a wealth of knowledge about emergency situations. Make use of them.

- Becoming familiar and friendly with public safety officers allows children to overcome their shyness and perceive these professionals as true allies if help is needed.

LEARNING BY DOING

REALISTIC FIRE DRILL

Hundreds of children are badly injured or killed in domestic fires each year. Yet a simple understanding of emergency procedures and techniques could save many of them. The fact is, very few people actually know how to deal with fire danger—or any other emergency situation.

We consider emergency fire procedures to be among the most important aspects of safety training for both children and adults. Systematic training is necessary to instill confidence under a variety of conditions. We have developed a step-by-step training procedure that has been lauded by many public safety officials.

The fire drill is one of the few exercises in this book that requires a group larger than one family to do effectively. We suggest that several families get together in a home or at a local school.

The fire drill described here is typical of what we do in P.O.L.O. workshops, but it can be modified if you do it with a small group in a private home. You may want to eliminate the smoke generator, for the following reasons: 1. The "smoke," although harmless, makes the exercise so realistic that children can become afraid and refuse to participate if the step-by-step procedure is not strictly followed under the supervision of a trained P.O.L.O. instructor; and 2. The smoke usually has a slight odor and may leave some slight moisture residue. Although the effects are temporary and do not cause damage, you might not want to experience this in your own home.

Local firefighters are often invited to participate in P.O.L.O. workshops. Actual fire fighting professionals (or P.O.L.O. instructors dressed in fire fighting outfits) add a level of realism to this exercise that is hard to duplicate otherwise. In P.O.L.O. workshops we ask the firefighters to give a brief talk and to demonstrate the use of their rescue equipment before we do the drill. This allows the children to become comfortable with the officers. Who knows? They might even give each child a chance to use a real fire hose!

In P.O.L.O. workshops we always have a firefighter or a P.O.L.O. instructor put on the full "battle" outfit, including the SCBA (self-contained breathing apparatus) equipment. The children watch the firefighter put on each piece of equipment so they perceive that it is a real person wearing protection from fire, not a monster or bogeyman. You can request your local fire department to visit your children's school and give a similar demonstration.

P.O.L.O. International emphasizes the importance of this demonstration because (as we have already discussed briefly in this chapter) some recent films for children have depicted villains making sounds and wearing outfits easily associated with emergency SCBA equipment. Tragically, as a result of such association in real fire emergencies, children have actually panicked at the appearance of firefighters wearing SCBA equipment and fled from them into serious injury and occasionally death.

Objective: To simulate actual fire conditions so that children and parents can experience what it is like to function under such conditions.

Location: A large room with lighting control so it can be darkened.

Materials:

- Carpeting or exercise mats so that crawling exercises can be done comfortably.
- Smoke generator (optional). Commonly used by theatrical groups and available from home rental agencies and theatrical supply houses. Units are easy to use and put out a very effective quantity of nontoxic "smoke."
- Audio tape player and sound-effects tape with emergency fire noises.
- Large roll of brightly colored adhesive tape.

Discussion:

Discuss briefly the following basic facts about fire safety. (We have drawn these suggestions from information provided by the San Rafael, California Fire Department, the National Fire Protection Association and the National Safety Council.)

- Every home should be equipped with a smoke detector located so the parents can hear it even if their bedroom door is shut. Everyone in the family should know what the smoke detector sounds like when it goes off.

- Children should sleep with their doors closed, especially in large homes where they might be cut off from their parents by fire. Closed doors slow the spread of smoke and flame.

- If you suspect fire, test the door by touching it. If it is warm, use an alternate escape route. If it is cool, brace a shoulder against the door and open it slightly. If smoke and heat come in, slam the door shut and use an alternate escape route.

- If you are trapped in a room and unable to escape, keep the door closed and stuff the cracks with clothes or blankets to keep smoke out. If water is available, keep soaking the door and any of the walls that feel warm to the touch.

- When making your escape, small children should be lowered first before adults exit. Otherwise the children may panic and not follow you.

- *Tell children never to hide if there is a fire*—not under a bed or in the closet or anywhere. If they can't escape easily, they should wait by a window and signal for help with a flashlight or a bedsheet.

- Anyone who catches on fire should immediately stop, drop, and roll to put the flames out. Have everybody practice doing this as part of the exercise.

- More people are injured by smoke inhalation than by the actual flames. Heat and smoke rise, making it crucial to stay as low as possible while trying to reach safety. You and your children should learn to crawl effectively—it could save your lives.

Exercise:

The following description includes sound effects and smoke for the sake of completeness, although we have suggested modifying the drill in your private homes.

- Set up the room using either the mats or the colored tape to mark off a path to simulate hallways. There should be several right-angle turns and one or more dead ends. If you use a home for this exercise, make use of the layout of the dwelling. Have the smoke generator and the sound effects ready to roll.

- Adults and children should practice crawling on their bellies and on their backs "like a lizard or a snake." Practice slowly at first until everyone can crawl easily.

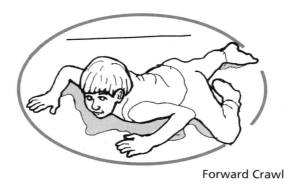

Forward Crawl

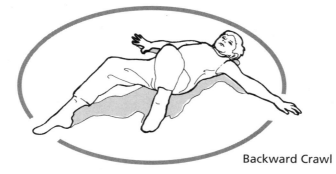

Backward Crawl

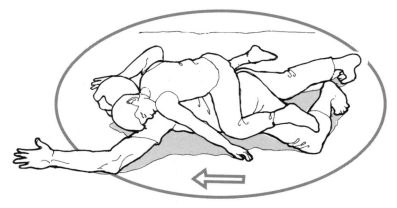

Forward Carry Crawl

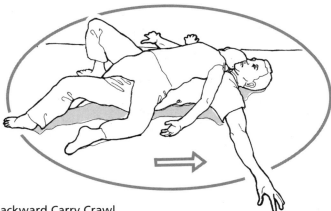

Backward Carry Crawl

Crawling is an important skill with respect to fire safety because
1. Smoke rises. Visibility and breathable air are usually found
closer to the floor. 2. People can carry someone unconscious
more easily in a crawling position than they can standing up.
Even relatively weak people using a back crawl can carry someone to safety.

- Once everyone is comfortable crawling slowly, speed things up by having them crawl as quickly as they are able along the marked "corridors." If some of the parents or children are unable to crawl because of a physical handicap, then encourage them to stoop as low as they can. No one should be made to feel inadequate because of a physical limitation.

- Parents and older children should then practice the crawling exercise carrying an "unconscious" child to safety on their backs and on their bellies. (Although it is physically easier for most adults to do the crawl/carry on their backs, we recommend that parents be familiar with both methods. See illustrations, pages 57–58.)

- Do this exercise with all the lights on, and no sound effects or smoke, until all the participants are comfortable doing it, especially the children.

- Introduce sound effects, then smoke, and finally darkness, *one element at a time.* As each element is added, make the crawling exercise a little more complicated. Use your imagination, but don't overdo it.

- In the "grand finale," each parent has to crawl through the darkness and smoke, with loud, realistic fire sounds and lots of shouting by everyone else, to reach a child. Then the parent must crawl back to "safety" carrying an "unconscious" child. As the parent-child team nears completion of the exercise, the "firefighter" with the full outfit can move in and assist the child in reaching safety. This imprints the image of the firefighter in the mind of the child as an ally in times of emergency.

You'll be amazed at how realistic this exercise will seem, and how well the children will perform. Usually, it's exciting and fun for everyone.

After the exercise it's important to sit in a circle and have each person tell what their experience was during the exercise and what they learned by doing it.

Be sure that everyone understands the following points:

- If you're not actually threatened by flame and smoke, staying in place may be the best thing you can do. Just because there's a fire doesn't mean that you have to move around and add to the confusion and panic. If you do need to move, learn to do so in a controlled manner no matter what everyone else may be doing.

- Learn to move (if you have to) by crawling or otherwise staying as low to the ground as possible. Be able to move quickly and to find your way by touch, since darkness and smoke will obstruct your vision.

- Firefighters are your allies and they will help you to the best of their ability. Listen to them and allow them to help you.

Optional Supplementary Exercise:

It is important to make simple emergency escape plans whenever you are away from home. As an extension of the fire drill exercise, you might take your children to a local hotel, preferably one with several stories, and have them do the following practices:

- Locate the nearest exit from the room that you are staying in. (This can be a "pretend" room, with the permission of the hotel management.)

- Count the number of doors from the exit to your room, then blindfold the children and have them crawl along the hallway, finding their way to the exit by feeling and counting the number of doors. With this procedure they can find their way even if darkness and smoke obstruct vision.

MOTOR VEHICLE PILLOW CRASH GAME

This is another exercise that is better done with more than one family participating. Four adults are needed to serve as simulated "cars."

Objective: To teach children the dangers of going into the street without looking to see if vehicles are coming.

Materials:

- A large play space, preferably carpeted or with exercise mats
- Several large pillows
- A soccer ball or any large ball of similar size
- A large roll of brightly colored tape

Exercise:

- With the colored tape, mark off a square space approximately 20' x 20' (or larger) in the center of the play space.
- Discuss traffic safety with the children. See what kind of a response you get, and whether they all have a clear understanding of the dangers of running into the street without looking. Tell them they will be playing a game to see if they really remember this danger.
- Choose any kind of game in which the participants throw or kick a ball back and forth. Soccer or basketball is fine, or any other game that absorbs their attention and interest. The games can increase in complexity as the exercise progresses.
- Station an adult with a large pillow at each corner of the area bounded by the tape. Tell the children to pretend that the boundaries of the square area are "streets" and that if

they run into the "street" they may be "hit by a car" (one of the adults will run at them and knock them down *gently* with a pillow).

• Have the adults participate in the game, shouting encouragement to the kids to play harder. They can shout, "run, get that ball, quick," especially when kids are near the edge of the square. The object is to raise the enthusiasm level and get the children to forget the "car danger." When a child actually crosses the boundary, he or she gets "hit by a car" and has to sit out for two minutes.

• Continue the exercise with increasing complexity until most or all of the children have crossed the boundaries and been "hit." At this point, they should be stopping at the boundaries consistently.

To summarize, the purpose of this exercise is to teach children by exposing them to simulated danger in controlled circumstances, and the goal of the game is by the end of play to have the children consistently staying inside the boundaries. Learning by bodily experience more easily develops an instinctive right response in children than any amount of telling them what they should do.

MEET A POLICE OFFICER

Objective: To overcome children's normal shyness or even fear of police officers or people in uniform. Adults can often benefit from this exercise as well.

Materials: None.

Exercise:

• When driving with your child, see how many police cars he can spot. Be sure to explain the difference when he mistakes a taxi or some other vehicle for a patrol car.

- Whenever you see someone in uniform, ask your child if he thinks that is a police officer. If the person isn't, explain why. Usually the most distinctive characteristic of police is that they carry a holstered gun. That is easy for small children to remember.

- Have your child speak to a police officer on the street, or take him to visit a police station and speak with police there. Tell him that if he is ever lost and needs help, one of the best people he can go to is a policeman or policewoman.

- Observe how your child responds in each situation and discuss your observations with him in a positive way.

Chapter Five

SAFE IN THE CASTLE

HOW SAFE ARE OUR HOMES?

Most of feel that our home is our castle, a refuge from the outside world. Most of the time this is true; but castles can be dangerous places as well. The truth is that most home accidents could be prevented by awareness, careful analysis, and logical accident-prevention measures.

For example, more children die each year in swimming pools than from firearms, even though the number of firearms is considerably greater than the number of swimming pools. Most people recognize that a gun is dangerous, so they take precautions; but most people see swimming pools as recreation, so they take fewer precautions.

There is no way that we can cover every type of home accident and its prevention in this book, but the checklists at the end of this chapter are quite comprehensive.

You can *start by touring your home with your children* to present the dangers of your home as though your children were visitors from another world. Look for places where accidents could happen or fires could start—electrical outlets that are overburdened with appliances, lack of fire extinguishers, the presence of toxic chemicals, and ways in which intruders could enter your home. Halfway through the house, try reversing the roles; your children can become the hosts and present potential dangers to you. This enjoyable exercise will teach them to start recognizing potential dangers on their own without becoming paranoid.

The good news is that you can easily correct most of the potential dangers you find in your home. This will give you and your children the confidence to tackle the next exercise, how to plan for a natural disaster.

Different parts of the country are subject to different natural disasters like earthquakes, floods, and tornadoes. If you have just moved into the area, find out from your local public safety department the most likely types of disasters and what your preparations should be. Be sure to include your children in the planning.

First figure out *a meeting point* and how everyone is going to get there. For example, if an earthquake strikes when the children are at school and the parents are at work, who will pick who up on the way home? If a parent can't make it to the school, what is the alternate plan?

Let your children pick their favorite canned foods and drinks. That way, when you rotate your stocks every two years the food won't go to waste. Teach them to use the camp stove and actually try eating what you store. One family I know purchased cases of expensive freeze-dried food only to find that none of their children would eat it.

Your preparations should *include emergency clothing and bedding.* If you anticipate leaving your home, pack your emergency gear in waterproof containers.

Anticipate personal hygiene and toilet needs. If you purchase a portapotty, be sure that everyone knows how to set it up and use it. It's important to flush all the chemicals out after practicing; some chemicals actually corrode the fittings, which could be a real disaster!

Organize some travel games and other pastimes, because there's often nothing to do but wait. Keeping children's minds occupied could make the psychological difference between surviving and going bonkers.

Spend a day "camping at home," using your emergency equipment. Then you can go to the store and get what you really need!

WHAT KIDS FEAR AT HOME

Burglars are the greatest perceived fear of most children. The movie *Home Alone* touched the hearts and pocketbooks of millions of children and parents. Matt's four- and six-year-old sons have watched the video over twenty-five times. Matt thought they were watching for the entertainment value, but it turned out that they were using it as a training film for a series of elaborate booby traps they built in the backyard, kitchen, laundry room, bathroom, and assorted bedrooms.

Another major fear of children is the fear of being lost. Being "lost" in your own home invokes even more of the following fears in three- to six-year-olds: fear of being alone, of abandonment, of the dark, of monsters, of noises, of bedwetting, of losing emotional control, of falling, and of being injured and not having a parent around.

For six- to twelve-year-olds, the following fears are added: fear of burglars and intruders, of kidnapping, of parental divorce, of sexual assault, of adoption, and of a natural disaster like a storm or an earthquake without the parents around.

It's amazing how many things children fear! We seem to have repressed our fears and then don't ask our children about their fears because we don't want to rediscover them in ourselves. Chapter Two elaborates on facing our fears.

No wonder *Home Alone* both scared and reassured so many

children and parents. The problem is, it's just a movie! Children know that in real life, they wouldn't stand a chance. They usually go back to denial about their fears and their parents just laugh the movie off. After all, it has a happy Hollywood ending.

When the sequel, *Home Alone 2, Lost in New York,* came out, my children, along with millions of others, started the cycle all over again. However, the two movies did spark conversations about home security, and revealed my children's fears about being left home alone. It's worth renting and watching with your children to open them up to doing the exercises at the end of this chapter.

In the meantime, you and your children can embark on the adventure of transforming your home into a castle.

In the olden days of fairy tales, knights, and princesses, kings and queens lived in castles with high walls, towers, moats, and drawbridges. Home intruders were around back then too! When the raiders came, the peasants abandoned their huts for the safety of the castle.

We think of our homes as our castles because we really don't have any other shelter to run to, and we may feel safer than people did in the old days. However, forty percent of attacks on women still occur in their own homes. On a personal level, statistics be damned, when a murderer or rapist is threatening us, we need the same security that our ancestors needed back then.

Let's face it, we the good guys are still prey for the bad guys. Like herd animals, we hope that the predators will eat others before they get to us. So for the most part, we take a few precautions and live in denial.

WHY PREVENTIVE MEASURES WORK

Prevention works because predators are lazy. The harder we make it for them to attack us, the more likely it is that they will pick on someone else.

There's a story about two hikers who encountered a ferocious grizzly bear. One hiker started to tighten his shoelaces. The other scoffed that a man can only run about twenty miles an hour, while a grizzly can top forty. "You can't outrun a grizzly," he told his companion. The other hiker replied, "I don't have to outrun the grizzly, I just have to outrun *you*."

Some people believe that if they get in trouble, they'll call 911 to solve their problems. Just as the peasants depended on the knights of old, we look to the police to ride to our rescue. We too call the police. In Matt's neighborhood, he trained the firearms and defensive tactics instructors, so the response time is less than two minutes. But even in the best of circumstances, he is still on his own for those two minutes.

Others aren't so lucky. Unfortunately, in one major city there is a ratio of one officer on patrol for every twenty thousand citizens. Approximately ten percent of the population have arrest records, so that leaves one officer for every two thousand criminals. Fortunately criminals are lazy and don't work full-time. Even so, in another major city more than 250,000 emergency calls received a busy signal and went unanswered.

In one highly publicized case, two women heard someone breaking in and called the police. The police arrived, knocked on the door, and didn't get an answer, so they left. The criminals raped and tortured the women at gunpoint for hours. When the victims tried to sue the police, the court ruled that the police were not obligated to help them.

Even if the police arrive in the nick of time, which is highly unlikely, are they really prepared to rescue you if the bad guys take you hostage? Matt has trained SWAT (Special Weapons and Tactics) teams and HRTs (Hostage Rescue Teams). He set up realistic training scenarios in which "hostages" sometimes didn't make it out "alive." In training, he tells his students that there are no mistakes, only learning experiences. In real life, it's not comforting to a hostage to become a learning experience.

Even the criminals who are caught and convicted are being released early due to overcrowding in the jails. People complain that it costs approximately $40,000 per year to keep a criminal locked up; but an average criminal causes about $400,000 per year in physical and personal damage. And the psychological damage is incalculable.

Instead of cursing the darkness, let's do something about it.

THE HOME SECURITY PLAN

Many police departments have a crime prevention officer who will come out to your home and make security suggestions. Use them if this service is available to you.

Regardless, consider the following cheap and easy security measures:

- Purchase alarm warning decals to scare off potential burglars (if they can read).

- Put up "Beware of the Dog" signs. Better yet, buy a huge dog dish and paint the name "Killer" on it. It doesn't matter if you have a toy poodle or no dog at all. Who says you can't lie to a criminal?

The rest of this chapter is about making sure that your child understands your home security plan.

Do your children know how to use a key? Do they know where your "hide-a-key" is hidden? Have you instructed them not to tell their friends? Do they put the key back after using it?

Do they know how to lock the doors and windows? Matt put inner bolts low in his house so that his children could reach them in the event of a fire. When Matt's son Cully was three, he saw a stranger by the back door. He smiled at the man, walked over to the door, locked the bolt, then ran for help. He explained that he fooled the stranger into thinking he was going to open the door. The "stranger," one of Matt's martial arts students, was impressed by the young boy's mental preparedness.

If you have a home alarm, do your children know how to turn it on and off? Do they know how to work the panic buttons? At age two, Cully pushed the silent alarm button at his grandparents' house. He was the only one who was happy to see all the policemen who responded, especially since the fine for a false alarm was $50.

Do your children know how to dial 911? Disconnect your phone and let them hit the numbers. Or if you have a speed dialer, mark the emergency button prominently so all they have to do is push it. When Matt's son Anders was three, he could call Matt at work just by pushing one button. He called once in a while, mostly just because he wanted to talk to Matt, although to him it was an emergency. When Cully was six, he caught Johann, age two, dialing 911 so he could talk to the nice fireman he saw on Sesame Street. Children definitely need to be taught when as well as how to use emergency communications.

If your police department has modern equipment to trace calls, all your child has to do is call for help and the dispatcher can read the address off the screen. When calling 911, teach children to leave the phone off the hook if they have to move because of danger. This allows more time for a call to be traced even without sophisticated equipment. Nevertheless, your child should be able to give your address. After practicing with them face to face, practice over the phone. This can be a game, but it is also a life-saving skill.

If you carry a beeper, put your beeper number on your speed dialer and make sure your children know the number. Drill them on proper procedure so they can do it easily.

Introduce your children to your neighbors. In some parts of the country this may seem obvious, but in other parts it isn't. Matt recalls living in a Los Angeles apartment for almost two years before he met his next-door neighbors.

Role-play with your children what to do when police arrive. A five-year-old child was hiding in a closet from the scary noises of a burglar. When the police arrived, he pointed his toy gun at the officers and was mistakenly shot. When an officer arrives, the response from behind cover should be "Thank God you're here!" This alerts the officer to the child's presence. The child should then wait for the police to ask him to come out, and show the palms of his empty hands.

Inappropriate responses are shining a bright light on the officers, dashing out from a hiding place toward them, and worst of all holding a weapon or improvised weapon that you or your child were going to use on the intruder. Role-play the correct responses first during the day and then at night. Have the child play the role of the officer and see how scary bright lights or sudden movements can be to officers investigating a dangerous situation.

After you've finished role-playing what to do when the police come, introduce role-playing what to do if an intruder comes. The order and step-by-step nature of the exercises are extremely important or children could become too frightened and not want to participate at all.

Have your children use the fire escape map of the house (see the Family Emergency Planning exercise at the end of this chapter) and discuss likely entry points for an intruder. Discuss ways to make those entries more difficult or noisy, like adding inner bolts or alarms, without making it impossible to escape in the event of a fire. Then make it a family project to implement the changes.

The next step is to figure out where your children should go if they see an intruder. Plan A might be for everyone to make a mad dash for the master bedroom. When everyone is in the room, an inner bolt could be locked on the reinforced master bedroom door and the family could wait for the police to arrive.

Plan B might be for the children to hide in prearranged places until the police arrive.

Of course, we don't call the police every time we hear a bump in the night. This sets up another dilemma. Every year over one million crimes are prevented and reported by armed citizens. How many are prevented and not reported? It is possible to be your own knight.

Just because you buy a piano, that doesn't make you a piano player. The same thinking applies to firearms. Parents who choose the option of arming themselves must get professional training in the use of firearms and flashlights, and then practice in their own home.

When Matt's son Cully was two, Matt woke up at three in the morning to strange sounds in the kitchen. He put on his police vest, gunbelt, and flashlight. Pistol in hand, he carefully started to investigate. First he checked his son's room. The crib was empty. Matt's heart jumped. In teaching gang suppression classes, he'd made some pretty nasty enemies. He wondered how they had bypassed his state-of-the-art alarm system to kidnap his firstborn!

Again he heard the sound in the kitchen. He flung open the door and flooded the kitchen with a 30,000-candlepower police flashlight. There was his two-year-old stealing cookies. Cully had figured out how to get out of his crib, so his first impulse was to get a snack.

With children in your home, it's important to figure out where they might be if there were a gunfight. Bullets can penetrate several walls in the average home. In addition, safe fields of fire require your children's knowledge and cooperation in staying still. This simulation might seem scary, but think of the alternatives!

SUMMARY

- Most people feel their home is safe, but this isn't necessarily true.
- The good news is that you can easily correct most of the dangers you find in your home.
- Many children have fears related to their homes, and some of those fears are very real.
- Very few families have any plans to deal with a natural disaster, fire, intruder, or other emergencies.
- Plans work. Include your children in the planning process.
- Preventive measures against intruders work because predators are usually lazy.
- Be sure to practice your emergency plans with your family. Include at least one night drill.
- Repeat drills periodically.
- Use the checklists at the end of this chapter in your planning and preparation.

LEARNING BY DOING

FAMILY EMERGENCY PLANNING

To a great extent, safety in the home depends upon mutual trust and sharing. Parents and children should work together to develop plans in case of home emergencies. By discussing potentially dangerous scenarios that may occur in the home, each family member learns that he or she is part of the whole and that all family members are responsible for the well being of the family unit. Confidence in each other's ability and support is necessary for everyone's safety and survival.

Objective: To understand how children perceive their home environment and to have them participate in planning what they should do if an emergency arises.

Materials:

- Large pieces of drawing paper
- Marker pens (several colors)
- Emergency checklists (following)

Exercise:

- Have your children draw a floor plan of your house or apartment. Have them draw all floors, including the basement. Help them to make the drawing as accurate as possible, but allow them to do as much as they can. Walk through your home with the children if necessary to get it right.

- Once you see that the children understand the configuration of the home, ask them to come up with plans for *what they would do in the following situations:*
  – A fire breaks out (suggest various locations in the home).

Refer to the Realistic Fire Drill exercise in Chapter Four.

– An earthquake (or other natural disaster that commonly occurs in your geographical location) actually happens.

– An intruder enters your house at night while you are
there (again, suggest various locations).

• The plans you develop with your children should be simple. *The objective is for each member of the family to independently exit the dwelling quickly and safely, or for you,
the parents, to unite quickly with the children and protect
them physically or lead them to safety.* Be sure to provide
a rapid, safe means of exiting upper-story windows, such
as a rope ladder. You should also *designate a meeting place
near your house.*

• This is a good time to have children practice learning the
emergency telephone number (911 in most urban areas
in North America), their last name, street address, nearest
intersecting street, their home telephone number, and the
name of their town or city. All children should be taught to
memorize these facts at a very early age—three or four
years old is not too young.

• Make copies of the following emergency checklists and
complete them with the children.

• *Practicing in your own home is essential.* We suggest you
go through the physical drills in the daytime and then
again at night. We also recommend that you repeat these
drills with your family periodically.

EMERGENCY CHECKLISTS

The following checklists are useful in completing the Family
Emergency Planning exercise. You can adapt them to your particular situation.

NATURAL DISASTER PREPAREDNESS CHECKLIST

PLANNING

❏ Consult the local FEMA (Federal Emergency Management Agency) office about natural disasters that could occur in your area.

❏ Make emergency plans with your children if you are all at home.

❏ Make emergency plans if any or all of you are away from home.

❏ Decide on a self-sufficiency time period, such as two weeks.

❏ Purchase and organize supplies for this period.

❏ Familiarize everyone in the family with the emergency supplies and equipment.

❏ Carefully store equipment in moisture-proof and rodent-proof containers.

MEDICAL SUPPLIES

❏ Large family first aid kit

❏ Prescription medicines for two weeks or longer

❏ Extra prescription glasses

❏ Emergency medications (non-prescription)

❏ Bee sting kit

SHELTER

❏ Sleeping gear for the coldest night

❏ Clothing for the coldest night

❏ Tent or temporary shelter

- [ ] Plastic sheeting to temporarily replace windows
- [ ] Wood and tools to support and attach plastic sheeting
- [ ] Flashlights with lots of extra batteries
- [ ] Candles or kerosene lanterns
- [ ] Battery-powered radio and/or TV with extra batteries
- [ ] CB radio and/or cellular phone with extra batteries

WATER, FOOD, AND SANITARY EQUIPMENT

- [ ] One gallon of water per person per day (more in the desert). Water should be treated for long-term storage.
- [ ] Food (have your children pick their own menus)
- [ ] Camp stove and extra fuel
- [ ] Garbage bags
- [ ] Toilet facilities (portapotty or shovel)
- [ ] Toilet supplies
- [ ] Diapers and wipes if needed

VEHICULAR

- [ ] Extra gasoline in safe-storage containers (Treat gas for long-term storage and rotate stock yearly.)

HOME EMERGENCY PREPAREDNESS CHECKLIST

FIRE

- [ ] Install or test smoke detectors (minimum of one close to the master bedroom so adults can hear it easily). Additional units can be located in:
  - [ ] Master bedroom
  - [ ] Children's rooms
  - [ ] Kitchen
  - [ ] Utility room or basement
  - [ ] Living room
  - [ ] Attic
  - [ ] Garage
- [ ] Establish evacuation plans
- [ ] Establish meeting point outside of house
- [ ] Test child's ability to exit via bedroom window
- [ ] Test everyone's crawl times via door exits
- [ ] Test everyone's ability to crawl out the door while holding their breath
- [ ] Hold daytime fire drill
- [ ] Hold nighttime fire drill

HOME INTRUSION

- [ ] Inspect home for ease of entry
- [ ] Put up security system decals (with or without an actual system)
- [ ] Install or test automatic external lights

- ❑ Install or test window locks
- ❑ Install or test deadbolts on doors
- ❑ Install or test phone in master bedroom (cellular if possible)
- ❑ Set up safe room where family can lock themselves in
  - ❑ Solid core door
  - ❑ Deadbolt
  - ❑ Peephole
- ❑ Install or test alarm system (optional)
- ❑ Call police to find out estimated response time
- ❑ Establish intruder defense plan
- ❑ Hold daytime drill
- ❑ Hold nighttime drill

AUTOMOBILE EMERGENCY KIT

PASSENGER COMPARTMENT

- [ ] Paper towels
- [ ] Road maps of areas you are (or will be) traveling in
- [ ] Hide-a-key (outside of car)
- [ ] Spare ignition keys (inside the car)
- [ ] Swiss Army knife
- [ ] Flashlight with extra batteries

TRUNK

- [ ] Minor tool kit
- [ ] Reflective vest
- [ ] Two cans of "run flat"
- [ ] Spare tire
- [ ] Jack and handle
- [ ] Tire lug wrench
- [ ] Road flares
- [ ] Jumper cables
- [ ] Spare fuses
- [ ] Tow rope
- [ ] Plastic garbage bags (for ground cloths)
- [ ] First aid kit
- [ ] Emergency blanket(s)
- [ ] CB radio or mobile phone (optional)
- [ ] Small army shovel

❏ Emergency fan-belt kit

PERSONAL ITEMS FOR EACH FAMILY MEMBER

❏ Comfortable walking shoes

❏ Rain gear (for an adult in order to walk for help)

❏ Clothing warm enough to spend a night in the car

❏ Water bottle (half a gallon)

❏ Energy snack foods for everyone

❏ Eating utensils

Chapter Six

BEING LOST, GETTING FOUND

BEING LOST OR MISSING: HOW IT HAPPENS

When a child is lost or missing, it's a terrifying time for everyone involved, especially for the child and his or her parents. Children get lost in a number of ways.

CHILDREN WANDER OFF
THROUGH THEIR OWN VOLITION

A child may wander off on her own and not realize that she is lost, while the parents, or whoever is responsible for the child, searches frantically for her. Or a child may wander off, then realize that he is lost and become panicked. Meanwhile the parents may be going about their business, oblivious to the fact that the child is no longer with them.

Usually, however, both adult and child realize the situation very quickly and begin a frantic search for each other.

In the case of young children, the cause for such an upsetting event is almost always the same: *parents or guardians become careless and distracted in public places, losing attention for the children they are with.* We can't really blame the children, even if we have done our best to impress upon them the importance of not wandering away. Children are naturally curious, and anything new and interesting attracts them like a magnet. It's not their job to stay by our side; it is ours as parents or responsible adults to keep them with us every minute.

However, we can teach our children some simple procedures and skills that will help them reunite with us quickly, and also know who they can safely turn to for help.

CHILDREN SOMETIMES RUN AWAY FROM HOME

Even young children sometimes run away from home if life has become too difficult for them. Usually, however, this is a problem with older children in the preteen or teenage years, when peers become a primary influence.

In Chapter Three we discussed the key importance of promoting family bonding and of nurturing children. Children who feel loved and supported at home rarely run away. When they do, it's usually a consequence of something being very wrong, often for quite some time. Love and support also help to neutralize the conditions that make a child easy prey for abductors.

BEHAVIORAL SIGNS OF POTENTIALLY RUNAWAY CHILDREN

The signs that a child is likely to run away are obvious. Every parent should be aware of them, since recognition will allow you to change the circumstances that are leading the child to desperation and the decision to leave home. Valuable information in this chapter on missing children (and child abduction in Chapter Eight) has been provided by Find Me, Inc. We gratefully acknowledge John and Louise Clinkscales for their permission to include these materials. Their dedicated work in helping parents to locate missing or runaway children was inspired by a loss of their own. We highly recommend their booklet "Blueprint for Action."

Growing isolation. The child spends an increasing amount of time alone, or tries to avoid family activities.

Sudden mood changes. The child exhibits sudden and unexplained mood changes that are not part of a usual pattern.

Reduced communication. Communication with the child is increasingly difficult.

Problems at school or work. The child is having serious problems at school or, if old enough for a part-time job, at work.

Family crisis. The child may be having difficulty adjusting to serious problems at home, such as extreme financial difficulty, divorce or serious conflict between parents, or a death in the family.

Unexplained money or phone calls. These can be signs of involvement with people and activities that the child doesn't want the parents to know about. They can also be preparations for running away.

Parental abuse or stack-blowing. If chronic in nature, such abuse can cause a child to want to get away from it all.

Abnormal sleeping patterns. This can be a sign of depression about a particular situation or about life in general. Running away is usually preceded by depression.

All families experience some of these warning signs from time to time, and that doesn't mean that a runaway is imminent. But like any warning signs, they should be heeded. Correcting potential problems is never a wasted effort, especially where children are concerned.

Sometimes a child will threaten to run away. *Do not ignore such a threat or make light of it.* Talk him or her through the situation. And whatever you do, *do not counter with threats or punishment.* If the child does run away, fear of punishment might prevent him or her from returning home.

CHILDREN ARE SOMETIMES ABDUCTED

Abduction is an all-too-frequent occurrence and one of the greatest fears of parents today. It is perpetrated most often in spousal disputes over child custody; a parent will take a child and disappear, perhaps forever. Even more frightening, however, are abductions by unknown persons for unknown reasons, which are often harmful, even deadly for the child. This tragedy occurs with alarming frequency.

In every case, an ounce of prevention is worth a pound of cure. Child abduction is so abhorrent that no caring parent even wants to think about it, and yet *by accepting that possibility and taking preventive measures, we can greatly minimize the possibility of it happening to our children.*

If you were a primitive parent living in the wilderness, you would have to accept and prepare for the possibility of your children being threatened by natural forces or wild animals. If you pretended that such dangers did not exist and failed to take preventive measures, your irresponsibility would significantly endanger your children. The times have changed, but parental responsibilities have not!

PREVENTING AND RESPONDING TO ABDUCTION

Communication and education are the most important keys to protecting your children. If you do it properly, you cannot tell a child too much. Openness and knowledge do not stimulate inappropriate action—ignorance and suppressed feelings do.

There are two general responses to the threat of abduction:

- Preparing ourselves and our children to recognize and neutralize the conditions that can lead to an abduction.

- Taking measures to assist in a recovery if an abduction or disappearance does occur.

PREPARING OURSELVES AND OUR CHILDREN

- Give love and support freely to your children, and make sure that they know this to be the case. Observe yourself to see if you abuse your child in any way, physically or verbally.

- Keep lines of communication open, even if circumstances sometimes make it difficult. Never belittle any fear your child has, whether real or imaginary. Also, listen when your child tells you that he or she does not want to be with someone. There could be valid reasons.

- Investigate any changes in your child's attitude or behavior. Watch for the warning signs just described, and respond immediately when conditions require action. Remember, an imaginary problem can have the same effect as a real one.

- Be involved in your children's activities, and know who they associate with. Make it clear to your child which homes and other places he or she may go to play or visit. Caution your child never to play in places where no one else is around.

- Notice if anyone pays undue attention to your child. If a youth director (church, scout, YMCA) or anyone else shows an unusual attachment to your child, try to determine the cause. It may be a harmless and natural affection, but sometimes it isn't at all. *A person so inclined could not have a better place to work from than an organized and accepted youth activity.*

- Teach your child about the deceptions used by sexual offenders and how to respond to them. It's not enough to warn children about "stranger danger" because many children are abducted by people they know, and abductors are very manipulative in breaking down children's defenses. They must learn the dangers of actions and situations regardless of who is involved. Chapter Eight, "Recognizing Bad Apples," covers the topic of child deception and manipulative strategies in depth.

- Do not put children's names on clothing, bicycles, or any other article that might allow a stranger to call them by name, thereby arousing curiosity and removing their normal sense of caution.

- Know your babysitter. Before you leave your child with anyone other than a trusted relative or friend, ask for references.

- Instruct your babysitter never to let a stranger into the house, no matter what the reason, and never to tell anyone on the telephone or at the door that he or she is the babysitter. This implies that the sitter and the children are alone.

- If for any reason your child is at home alone, instruct her not to let that fact be known to anyone who calls on the telephone or comes to the door.

- Never leave young children alone in public places, period! Not in cars, or shopping malls, or stores, or theaters, or at the beach, or anywhere you go with them. Don't let them go into public restrooms alone. Teach them to use the buddy system until they are old enough that it's no longer necessary. Keep young children in sight at all times, and instruct your babysitter to do so as well.

- When they are old enough to go out alone, practice with your children the ways that they may walk to and from school and their friends' houses. Teach them to seek assistance if anyone seems to be following them.

- Teach your children what to do if they get separated from you in a public place. They should go to a checkout counter or other location that you designate and wait there for you. They can tell someone in charge that they are lost, but they need to know who it's safe to ask for help. The Learning by Doing section at the end of this chapter describes some exercises that you can do with your children.

- Teach your child that if someone tries to take him somewhere, he should yell or scream, "This person is trying to take me away" or "This person is not my mother (or father)."

- Your children should know they must tell you immediately when the following situations occur:
  - Someone tries to take their picture without a reasonable explanation.
  - Someone tries to touch them in the areas covered by a bathing suit or asks to be touched in those areas.
  - Someone asks them to keep a special secret.

- Give your children permission to say *NO!* to adults. If it doesn't feel good or right, the child should not allow it—no matter who does it.

- Above all, teach these guidelines to your children in a normal, routine way. Ensure that fear is not a part of this important educational phase of your child's life.

MEASURES TO ASSIST IN RECOVERY

- Maintain records that would help to identify your child, such as photographs, fingerprints, and dental records. A very useful booklet for recording this information is *Kinder Passport*, by Jim and Jean Kahl, available from Securitec

Corp., 1126 70th Street, Suite S210, Milwaukee, WI 53214; telephone (414) 475–2345. The cost is $5.00, including postage and handling. Quantity discounts are available.

- Fingerprints can usually be obtained free from your local police or sheriff. If not, you can have your child finger-printed by the Department of Motor Vehicles for a nominal fee.

- Have current photographs of all members of the family available at all times, especially the children. The older a person is, the less current the picture needs to be. For preschoolers, the picture should be no more than three months old; for teenagers, no more than a year old.

- Brand your child's shoes with a woodburning kit. If possible, burn your telephone number into the soles of the shoes. The information will be left on dirt or mud surfaces, providing positive identification.

- Get everyone a passport. Once a passport has been issued it is difficult to get another for that person. A passport is easy to get, and desirable because often an abductor will attempt to take the child out of the country.

- Urge your child's school to verify an absence by telephoning the parent or guardian. A child who is abducted on the way to school may not be missed until he or she is due home.

- Ask a law enforcement official to speak to your local parents' group about actual cases of missing children in your area. Discuss ways that citizens can work with the police to locate missing children.

- Know the signs of an abducted child so you can help other parents find their own:
  – Most abducted children are under eight years old.

– Many show signs of abuse.
– Some are quite confused or vague, having been warned or threatened not to speak about their past.

• Know what kinds of parents abduct their own children:
– Usually male, between 21 and 31 years old.
– Has a past history of child and/or spouse abuse.
– Usually abducts the child for revenge against the spouse rather than believing it is in the best interest of the child.

• If you are divorced or separated and want to have your child with you:
– Know your former spouse's social security number, date of birth, assets and property owned, credit cards, and place of employment.
– Obtain legal custody of the child. If litigation is in process, require the other party to obtain court consent before leaving the jurisdiction with the child.
– Specify visitation rights as precisely as you can in the divorce papers. Know where your children will be taken.
– If your children are of school age, include in the custody order a provision to prohibit the transfer of school records without the approval of the custodial parent.
– Bonds of various types are also available to help ensure the return of the child. You may have to convince the court of the need.

GETTING FOUND: HOW TO MAKE IT HAPPEN

You can teach your children some simple skills so that they can facilitate being found if they are ever lost or abducted. These skills include orienting themselves to their location and knowing who they can safely ask for help.

• Be sure your child knows his or her full name, your name,

complete address including city and state, and your telephone number, including the area code.

- Teach your children to use the telephone to summon emergency help anywhere, usually by dialing 0 or 911. Drill them to stay on the line as long as they can to answer the dispatcher's questions. As mentioned previously, teach them to leave the phone off the hook if they have to end a call because of danger. This allows time for the call to be traced so the police can respond as quickly as possible.

- As a routine part of outings, practice with your children the awareness of landmarks, buildings, and other notable artifacts that could help them orient to their location.

- When your children are old enough to read, teach them how to use a town or city map. This is an extremely valuable skill, and it's fun to learn. (We'll save wilderness map reading until Chapter Seven.)

- Teach your child to *link up with the good guys and to get the help she needs,* whether it's just information or assistance in finding you, or real help in times of danger. Asking for help has four components: *who, where, what, and when.*

   You can't expect young children to "just ask anyone for help." They may be too shy or afraid to do so, and they often lack the ability to discriminate between people *who* would be helpful and those who might do them harm. Take them to various public places and point out *where* there are people they can safely approach, even though they are strangers. People behind counters in stores or at checkout stands in supermarkets are usually safe bets. So are people in uniforms, especially police officers or security guards with holstered guns. (Uniforms and badges can sometimes be phony, but such ruses are usually a threat only if the person approaches the child.)

- Teach your children that if they are lost or in trouble they should look for someone to help as soon as possible and not to wait until things get worse or they are panicking to seek assistance. *What* to ask for is obviously important as well. *Drill your children to ask for assistance directly and politely and not to make light of their predicament when they are in real danger.*

THE PARENTS' ROLE

Teaching your children such skills will certainly develop their self-reliance and help them to return home safely, but *in the case of abduction it may not be enough.* There is a lot of help available, but you, the parents, must know how to initiate the effort and keep the ball rolling. We suggest that parents prepare themselves for what they will have to do if such an unthinkable event actually happens.

Remember the warrior principles in times of danger: Face life no matter what is occurring; see the situation clearly; and take whatever immediate, committed action is necessary. These principles can help us to deal effectively with a real emergency, like the abduction of a child.

There is probably no situation that creates a more heartbreaking, helpless feeling than the disappearance of a child. If this tragedy should happen, you will need all the emotional support you can get to help you through the days, weeks, months, and possibly even years to come.

You must become actively involved in the efforts to find your missing child. Your task will probably be difficult, and it may be unsuccessful. This should not discourage you, but rather emphasize to you that *you must be willing to do everything you can as often as you can for as long as you can.*

When a child is missing, the earlier an investigation is started, the better the chance of finding the child quickly. If a report is not made immediately, the ability to follow fresh clues may be lost.

If the reason for the disappearance is unknown, the authorities will often assume that the disappearance was voluntary rather than due to foul play, and will give the search effort low priority. In such situations, the burden of the search will primarily be yours.

If your child is alive, the only way to effect a return (except for voluntary returns in the case of runaways) is to make contact with him or her. There are two basic approaches to try: Directly on a person-to-person basis—making contact with neighbors, friends, or anyone who may have heard or seen something and who might be able to provide information about your child; and indirectly through third parties, such as police, schools, and support groups.

Depending on the circumstances, you must decide which method to emphasize. If foul play is suspected, the police should be drawn in quickly. In any case, you should use both methods as much as possible.

FINDING A MISSING CHILD

- File a missing person report *immediately* with the local police or sheriff. Be completely truthful about the facts. You may need to take a critical look at relationships and conflicts within the family. Too often authorities are handicapped because they are not made aware of *all* circumstances that could have led to the disappearance.

- Know the limitations of working with local law enforcement agencies. It is sometimes difficult to get police help on weekends for non-emergency matters. Your missing child is definitely an emergency for you, but the police may treat it as routine unless foul play is suspected.

Departmental pride sometimes keeps local police from accepting outside help of any kind, even from other police agencies.

Nonjurisdictional police often cannot act without the request of jurisdictional police. In most cases, this includes the FBI.

- Ask local law enforcement authorities to fill out the form "Missing Persons Report and Request for NCIC Entry." This information will be entered in the Nationwide Crime Investigation Computer network. This form should *always* be completed when a child is missing. If the local authorities will not take the information, you have the right to go to the nearest FBI office and report the refusal. The law requires that the information be taken, and the law also gives parents and guardians the right to go directly to the FBI. If you still have a problem, contact your Congressional representative or senator.

- Ask local authorities to register your missing child with the State Department of Justice or other crime data computer banks in your area. Also check with your state bureau of investigation, through your local sheriff if necessary.

- If your child has been abducted by his or her natural parent, check with your local district attorney's office for advice and suggestions.

- Offer a reward in your local newspaper and have a reward poster printed. The poster should include a recent photograph, a description of the child, and a description of identifying marks, clothing, or mannerisms. Include a telephone number (usually police or sheriff) and an address (preferably a P.O. box number, to avoid crank calls and visits). Offer a reward for *verified* information on the whereabouts of your missing child.

- *Get as much publicity as you can.* Contact local newspapers and radio and TV stations. Such publicity greatly expands the public's awareness and increases the possibility for leads that will aid in the child's recovery.

- Check out any satanic or unusual groups that are active in your area. Go to local parks and other places where young people hang out. Show your missing child's picture around to see if you can get any leads.

- Check out all ideas and suspicions. Don't rule anything out, even if it appears "out of character." The mere fact that the child is missing (if foul play is not involved) is "out of character."

- Start a scrapbook. Use it as a source to keep yourself informed about what you and others have done.

- Keep a pencil and paper by the telephone to record anything you learn in conversations with the police, friends, your child's schoolmates, or anyone who calls with a lead. A tape recorder is also a good idea.

- If you decide to hire a private investigator, be careful to get a reputable one who comes highly recommended.

- Psychics have been effective in some cases where other methods have failed, but they are a long shot at best. In any case, do not pay a large amount of money for such services. The best do not cost the most.

- Check local morgues and hospitals. This may seem morbid, but it needs to be done.

- *Use the missing person network as much as you can.* Register your missing child with the National Center for Missing and Exploited Children. Send details to Action Agencies in the missing persons network in your area. Also get your child listed in the network's pictorial publications.

The following organizations provide valuable assistance and resources. They can also give you the names of other groups and individuals in the network who can assist you in your efforts.

National Center for Missing and Exploited Children
2101 Wilson Blvd., Suite 550
Arlington, VA 22201
Business (703) 235-3900, Hotline (800) 843-5678

Find Me, Inc. (John and Louise Clinkscales)
P.O. Box 1612
LaGrange, GA 30241
(706) 884-7419

Adam Walsh Child Resource Center
7812 Westminster Blvd.
Westminster, CA 92683
(714) 898-4802
(Centers also in Florida, New York, and South Carolina)

These organizations have valuable publications that expand on the information in this chapter. *Definitely* make use of them if the need arises.

Above all, *don't give up hope or efforts!* That's a warrior principle of the first order. The battle is not over until it's over!

If success comes and your missing child is found or returns voluntarily, you must show great compassion and love. If family problems contributed to the disappearance, they must be resolved. If you are unable to deal with the problem, seek professional counseling and assistance, or the situation is likely to repeat itself.

And finally, if success does not come, you must choose to go on with your life. No one can do that but you.

WHEN A CHILD COMES HOME

It is crucial to the recovery of a child who has been traumatized by an emergency situation or by the abuse of an adult that parents know what to do to help in the healing and recovery period.

A child who returns home after a trauma has essentially gone through a battle, so it's very important for that child to be cherished and loved and nurtured and integrated back into the family. A child who has been severely traumatized may need professional help to recover from the experience. Take your time in selecting a therapist, and be sure to choose one who you are sure understands trauma and has your child's best interests at heart.

Remember also that healing can take different forms and it may seem to take a very long time before your child is fully recovered.

EVERYDAY TRAUMAS

Not all childhood traumas are major, or even particularly obvious to us as parents. For example, if we knew that every day when we left work someone would be waiting outside the office who was going to punch us and throw us on the ground, we would consider that a major trauma. Yet this happens to children every day when they encounter schoolyard bullies, and sometimes the child who is being shoved around is afraid to tell anyone.

That's one reason it's important to spend time with our children and really listen to them. If your child seems upset, ask questions. Probe gently. Try to find out what's really going on. Listen intently, with real concern Then it's up to you to take appropriate action to protect your child.

As an example, Matt relates an incident involving one of his sons: Cully used to be teased by his schoolmates because his ears stick out. We thought of several things we could do to stop the teasing, or at least to make it less traumatic. First we got him a haircut that didn't accentuate his ears. And we talked about the problem. Matt explained that the people who made fun of him were showing their shallowness and ignorance, and that we can't let people like that have power over us emotionally. We also talked about how everybody's ears are different. We looked at different kinds of ears, on other people and in photographs. We went to a museum and examined paintings of ears. We read about how people in other cultures adorn their ears. And we looked at all kinds of earrings. Finally, Cully talked to the other children about how it hurt his feelings when they teased him; and Matt spoke to his teacher. The result of all of these actions was that Cully became less sensitive—and the other kids stopped teasing him.

By helping your children to deal with everyday minor traumas, you are actually training them to cope with a major trauma, should one occur, or even to prevent some traumas from happening in the first place.

Finally, it's important to help your child to continue to look at life in a positive way—to recognize that past pain doesn't have to extend into the present.

WHAT *NOT* TO DO WHEN A CHILD IS FOUND

In 1992, Bob experienced a humbling incident when his son was eight years old and apparently missing for a short period of time. He tells the story as follows:

My son Chorus was involved in an afterschool program at the community center near his school. I usually taught a jujutsu class for the boys in his group there on Monday afternoons.

This particular Monday had been a difficult day for me at the office. I arrived at the center to find the adult program leader in a worried state of mind. He told me that Chorus had been missing since leaving his school classroom several hours earlier.

I had recently been working on this chapter about missing children, and I immediately felt a pang of fear. However, I tried to remain calm, breathed deeply, and gathered together with the leader and the other boys. I asked each one if they knew where Chorus had gone. A couple of the boys said that he had come to the center for a few moments and then left. None of the boys knew where he had gone, and the leader said that he had checked every possible place that Chorus could be.

I began to panic. Despite many warnings to the contrary, my son had a habit of taking off without telling others. This was not the first time he had made me fearful by disappearing for a brief period. However, this was the longest time by far. I also began to feel anger toward the leader who, in my opinion, shouldn't have let this happen in the first place. As he felt my increasing anxiety, his own fear for Chorus's safety intensified. We were both beginning to panic.

I went to the phone to call the police with all sorts of terrible possibilities running through my head. Suddenly the leader called out to me: "Bob, I found him." I rushed over to the carpentry shop, where Chorus had been all along. But when I saw him, all the fear and anger I had felt became directed at him.

Instead of communicating my thankfulness for his safety, I created an unpleasant incident for everyone. I grabbed my son and yelled at him, "Where have you been? How many times have I told you not to go off without telling someone?" He said something cocky in reply and I really lost it. For the first time in his life, I hit him.

I slapped him in the face, not hard, but it so surprised him that he stepped back, tripping over his own feet. I then picked him up and yelled at him, "Don't you ever do that again, ever!" I'm sure it looked like I knocked him to the ground.

You can imagine the impression this made on those who witnessed my outburst. My actions were interpreted by teachers and children in all kinds of ways. One of the teachers even reported me to child protection services.

After the incident, I took my son and his friends into the center to teach jujutsu. Chorus was not allowed to participate, and the reason was explained to the other boys.

That evening I found my son in his room crying. I asked him why (as if I didn't know), and he said, "How would you feel if your dad hit you in the face?" It wasn't until that moment that I really felt the consequences of my actions. I had betrayed the sacred trust of my child that I would never harm him. In a moment of anger and fear I had struck him. He was far more hurt emotionally than he was physically.

I took him in my arms and we cried together for some time. I told him that I was very sorry. Despite the fact that he was wrong to go off without telling anyone, two wrongs don't make a right, and I should never have hit him. I apologized in a heartfelt way, and he forgave me for real. We've done a lot of good things together since then to make up for this incident. He doesn't go off without telling anyone, and I learned something of value from my mistake.

I went back to the center several days later to apologize and explain my actions to people who had witnessed the event. It was some time before the whole matter was brought to rest.

I sincerely hope that none of you who read this will have such an unpleasant experience or make a similar mistake when your child is found safe. Be grateful and loving, first. Discipline can come later if necessary.

SUMMARY

- Children often wander off in public places. This is almost always the fault of the parent or guardian who becomes careless or distracted and loses attention for the actions of the children.

- Children sometimes run away from home, although children who are loved and supported rarely run away. Parents should know the signs that usually precede running away, and immediately deal with the circumstances that are contributing to the possibility.

- Never ignore a child's threats to run away, and whatever you do, *do not* counter with threats of punishment, which could make the child afraid of returning.

- Some children are abducted by parents involved in custodial disputes and some by unknown persons for unknown reasons. *In any case, an ounce of prevention is worth the proverbial pound of cure.*

- Although no parent ever wants to think about his or her own child being abducted, *by accepting that possibility and taking preventive measures, the likelihood of such an occurrence can be greatly minimized.*

- There are two major types of preventive measures: preparing ourselves and our children to recognize and render ineffective the conditions that foster, cause, or make possible an abduction; and taking measures that would assist in a recovery if an abduction or disappearance does occur.

- Teach your children simple skills that will facilitate their being found if they are ever lost or abducted.

- Make sure that fear is not a part of this important educational phase of your child's life. Teach the preventive guidelines to your child in a normal, routine way.

- In the case of an actual abduction, the worst has definitely happened. You *must* be a warrior and *face* the situation. *See* what has happened and is happening. Then take continuous, committed *action* for as long as necessary.

- You must be willing to do everything you can, as often as you can, for as long as you must to have any chance of success.

- Use law enforcement agencies and the help that is available from the missing person network. Know your rights and insist upon them. Be discriminating about where you can best place your resources.

- *Never give up hope.*

- If success comes, and your missing child is found or returns home voluntarily, you must show great compassion and love.

- If success does not come, you must choose to go on with your life. No one can do that but you.

- Children who have been traumatized need to be integrated back into normal life in a caring, supportive way.

- Children who have been traumatized are likely to need professional help to recover.

- When you give children skills that inspire self-confidence, you are giving them the tools to recover from trauma.

LEARNING BY DOING

Most parents have had the frightening experience of becoming separated from their young children in a public place. The first three of the following exercises teach children the skills they need if they are lost in a public place.

FIRST TO CHECKSTAND ONE

Objective: To teach young children to go to a designated location if they get separated from their parents in a public place. (This exercise is for children younger than eight years old.)

Materials: None.

Exercise:

- Take the child to a local supermarket and tell him to find the way to checkstand one (or some such designated location) by himself. Make it a game—who can get there first, you or the child, without running?
- Watch from a distance as the child performs the exercise from several locations in the market without your help. Then tell her that if she ever gets separated from you, she should go to checkstand one and wait there for you. Assure her that you will always come there to meet her. Pretend to hide once and try it out to be sure she gets it.

SHOPPING MALL SCOUTS

Objective: To teach children to find designated meeting places in more complex situations.

Materials: None.

Exercise:

- This exercise should be done with more than one child, especially if they are young. The children should go in twos or threes to give them confidence and also because there is safety in numbers.

- Take the children to a large shopping center or department store and propose a game in which they are Indian scouts and have to find some landmark, which can be designated as the "fort" or anything else that might inspire their interest. (Your children might prefer the image of space explorers or ninjas.) Landmarks can be anything that is unique, like a fountain in a shopping center, or more mundane like the entrance to elevators or escalators in a large department store.

- Tell the children that they are to find their way to the designated location, and that if they get lost they are to ask directions *only* from people behind counters in stores (sales people).

- Let each child take the lead and do the exercise several times from different locations in the mall, making each successive time more difficult, and at least once causing the children to have to approach adults for help.

- When they have all succeeded, tell them that this is what they should do if they ever get lost or separated from you. *Thereafter, whenever you go to a public place, always designate a meeting location and remind the children what they should do if you get separated.*

SIMPLE MAP READING

Objective: To teach children who can read how to use to use a map to find their way.

Materials:

- A map of your neighborhood
- One or two highlighter pens
- A compass

Exercise:

- Obtain a map of your neighborhood or any nearby area where you would feel comfortable walking around with your child. (Sometimes maps are too complex and need to be simplified for learning use. If this is the case, enlarge the relevant portion of the map on a copy machine, or redraw the map to show only the main streets and landmarks.)

- Start by teaching your child how to read the simple map. Locate your own home and then choose a location somewhere away from the house, preferably in an area that your child is not familiar with. Plan two or more simple alternate routes that you can use to get there.

- Take your child to the street intersection nearest your house and show her how to use a compass to orient herself to the map and to her actual physical location. Then have her lead the way to the chosen destination using the compass, map, and street signs as references. Let her make mistakes and retrace her steps if necessary.

- Once she has successfully reached the initial destination, select other places for her to find, making each succeeding location more difficult to reach. Don't overdo it, especially the first time. Do this exercise several times with the child. End each session by having her find the way back home from the farthest location, if possible by a route she hasn't traveled before. Continue this exercise until the child seems capable of finding the way on her own if necessary.

TRAUMA AND PROBLEM SOLVING

Objective: To initiate a communication process dealing with children's experiences and minor traumas. This will set the stage for healthy recovery from future traumas, whether minor or major.

Materials: Notebook in which to write down the discussion topics and the solutions you come up with.

Exercise:

- Allow the child to voice his fears or worries about a problem that is currently on his mind.

- Tell the child about a similar problem you have had in the past. Put yourself back in that state of mind. What were your fears and worries? You may find that you have unresolved vestiges of those fears.

- With your child, think of some possible solutions to his problem. Write them down, affirming that the problem can soon be solved.

- Follow up the solutions with actions.

- Have a follow-up discussion a week or two later to discuss whether the proposed solutions have been effective. If not, continue the process until a solution can be found that works for the child.

Chapter Seven

WILDERNESS IS STILL WILD

WILDERNESS SAFETY

Camping is a wonderful, wholesome family bonding activity. Camping out in the wilderness is much safer than camping out in the city, where you might be mugged or arrested for vagrancy. Every year, millions of city and suburban families head out to blaze happy trails, mostly in asphalt-covered campsites, complete with barbecues, picnic tables, running water, and flush toilets.

Private campgrounds, county parks, state parks, and national parks all seem to have followed Joni Mitchell's line, "Pave paradise, put up a parking lot." You need to recognize that you are in a mobile, transient suburbia and act accordingly. The greatest dangers in campgrounds are the human criminals, not the bears! Unfortunately, the same rules for safety taught in the previous chapters apply in these campgrounds.

Those who want to go backpacking need permits, and reservations for campgrounds are sold months in advance, sight unseen. Few parents take young children backpacking, and those who do are either very experienced or very inexperienced campers.

Of the millions of Americans who go hunting every fall, most stay in motels, cabins, and campgrounds like the summer crowds. But due to the nature of their sport, they wander through the woods a lot on their own. Although hunters are usually better prepared, they still get lost, have accidents, and mostly don't get their game but have a good time anyway. For many young boys, their first hunting trip is the closest thing they'll ever have to a male rite of passage. Wilderness rules are especially important to them.

Sometimes motorists don't intend to go camping but their car breaks down in the middle of nowhere. Usually it's just annoying and inconvenient, but every year stranded motorists die of exposure because their car broke down or they got stuck in the middle of a snowstorm. Wilderness weather came to them!

Skiers obviously are out to have a good time. However, if they take a wrong turn late in the afternoon or have a bad fall on a remote run, they could find themselves in an emergency situation by nightfall.

Natural disasters also happen. In California, camping equipment is also an earthquake preparedness kit. In other parts of the country, you might store your gear in your tornado or hurricane shelter. If a storm knocks out your electricity, you can camp out in your living room.

BE PREPARED!

The first step in preparing for a camping trip is detailed planning. Include your children in this planning—they'll love it.

Although macho wilderness instructors have told Matt that all one needs is the right attitude and the right training, he noticed that they all had the best possible boots and knives, and that they were not standing in front of him naked. The right equipment can make camping a lot more comfortable. Purchasing equipment or dusting off your old gear can be an adventure that you can share with your children.

For example, Matt found out that mice in the garage had chewed through his trusty hiking boots and had made a nest in the toe. His three-year-old son added several new words to his vocabulary, and Daddy spent several minutes in the corner, because their house rule is equal punishment for bad behavior.

The most interesting thing the mice taught him was that his feet had grown wider—or the boots had shrunk— so that if the mice hadn't ruined them, he would have had a miserable time breaking them, or his feet, in again. The point is that you should carefully examine and test each piece of equipment. For example, dead batteries in a flashlight are no big deal at home; but when you're miles from the closest Seven-Eleven and you've just heard a bump in the night, the flashlight becomes crucial to your safety. When your children start asking you what's out there and you're fumbling with a flashlight that doesn't work, your parental competence rating takes a nose dive! In fact, each child should have his or her own flashlight and other personal emergency equipment.

EMERGENCY KITS

Savage beasts are not the greatest danger to humans in the wilderness. The biggest killer? The weather. This may not seem such an exciting subject; when Matt gives wilderness safety lectures, the members of the audience usually start squirming in their seats when he starts to talk about the weather. Boring! He can sense what they really want to hear—bear stories!

Like bears, the weather is actually neither our friend nor our enemy. It just is. Hot is hot, cold is cold, and whether or not we survive is irrelevant to the grand plan of nature. However, whether we or our children survive is *very* relevant to us.

In the wilderness, or even on an afternoon hike, how we relate to nature's changes determines our chances for survival.

When people set out for a hike the weather is usually fine—otherwise they stay indoors. How many of us have ever set off to hike during the middle of a thunderstorm at night? However, a balmy afternoon can easily turn into a wet, freezing night. If we are adequately prepared, it doesn't have to be a big deal. If we aren't prepared, our lives can be at stake. The simple solution? Whenever you are in a wilderness area, even on a day hike, carry a daypack containing warm clothes and a space blanket to help you live through a "dark and stormy night." The following sections will help you decide what your pack and your children's packs should contain. Don't leave camp without your daypack! The wilderness does not accept American Express.

Each of your children should have two packs—a belt pouch to wear in camp and a fanny pack to wear away from the campsite.

MEDIUM-SIZE BELT POUCH (4x6x3)

Contents:

- Loud whistle
- Signal mirror
- Mini-flashlight
- Space blanket
- Compass
- Swiss Army or Leatherman knife

Children should always wear their belt pouches when you're camping—you never know when they'll need a whistle or a knife.

The first item in the belt pouch (or worn around the neck) is a whistle. Giving a three-year-old a whistle might seem like insanity, but despite your perception of your children's decibel production levels, a child's voice can only be heard for about a hundred yards. They can go hoarse in a matter of minutes, and if there are any covering noises like running water or sound barriers like a forest, their range decreases tremendously. A whistle can be heard up to 400 yards, and a child can blow it intermittently for hours. The source of a whistle is also easier to locate than the source of a shout. SOS—three short toots, three long toots, three short toots—is a universal distress signal. Even three-year-olds can learn this signal, and they'll practice it for hours!

The next item the child should carry at all times is a signal mirror. A five-year-old can learn to signal with a mirror in five minutes. If an air search is needed, a signal mirror can be seen for miles. Like the whistle, the mirror can be worn around the neck or in the pouch.

A high-quality waterproof mini-flashlight is both a convenience and an emergency tool. Be sure that your child can operate the switch. Start with new batteries for every trip and bring lots of extras, because children love to play with their flashlights. Teach your children to signal SOS with the flashlight; this will save your ears from incessant whistling.

A good compass is essential once your child is old enough to use it. Small children often believe that if they follow the arrow it will lead them home. A ten-year-old can learn to use a topographical map and a compass. Orienteering games can actually be a lot of fun.

A Swiss Army knife is an extremely useful tool. Matt also likes the Leatherman because it has a pair of needlenose pliers. He never leaves home without a knife, even in the city, and he uses it four or five times a day. Giving a knife to a child is a serious rite of passage. Almost every person who has ever used a knife has cut themselves, but by teaching your children proper safety habits you can keep the cuts to a minimum. Matt let his sons use a Swiss Army knife in his presence when they were two and a half. The knife is a wonderful tool to teach responsibility.

FANNY PACK (5x10x5)

Contents:

- Clothing (polypropylene or wool, bright-colored, and warm)
- Waterproof matches
- Signal flares
- Water or electrolyte drink in canteen
- Water purification chemicals (liquid or tablet) or portable water filter
- High-energy food bars
- Insect repellent
- Bee sting kit
- Snake bite kit

In addition to their day-packs, children should wear their fanny packs whenever they leave the campsite. The packs should contain emergency spare clothing. Consider polypropylene for all emergency clothing. This modern synthetic fiber is one-third the weight of wool for equal insulation value. It pulls moisture away from the body so you don't get clammy. Polypropylene still insulates when wet and dries quickly. Thinsulite is even more efficient, but it is usually used in outerwear.

A silk or polypropylene balaclava (hood that also covers the face) can significantly decrease heat loss from the head, face, and neck. Polypropylene gloves or glove liners can keep your child's hands functioning in an emergency. Leather gloves are crucial for travel over rough terrain or at night. In a cold environment, the pack should contain a mini handwarmer as well. An extra pair of polypropylene socks is also important, preferably the new "blister prevention" socks. They work remarkably well.

A waterproof nylon (or Goretex if your budget can stand it) jacket and pants complete the clothing portion of the fanny pack.

Brightly colored clothes can also be used as a signaling device. The downside of bright colors is that they attract bees. Matt sometimes carries a mylar thermal suit, which is the lightest, warmest, and most reflective, but it's not suitable for hiking because it turns into an instant sauna if you exert yourself.

The belt pouch should also contain a space blanket. This lightweight miracle retains 90 percent of body heat, is radar-reflective, and can be visible for hundreds of yards on land and for miles from the air. In the desert, a space blanket can reflect the sun and keep you cooler by 10 to 20 degrees, and it can also be a rain and wind barrier.

Older children should carry waterproof matches to light a fire for cooking or signalling. You might also consider signal flares and other emergency equipment. The pocket flares are extremely dangerous because they fire a flare that burns at 5000 degrees 200 feet into the air. Smoke signals can also start forest fires. These signalling devices are easy to operate, but they are not toys. You need to judge the maturity of your children, and teach them fire safety in the woods.

Everyone, children and adults, should carry a canteen of water or an electrolyte supplement on day hikes. Matt swears by electrolyte drinks, although he usually dilutes them half and half with water. Teach your children that whenever they exert themselves, they should sip constantly. Your body can usually absorb about a quart of fluid every hour. However, during desert warfare exercises in the Sinai, Matt would go through five to seven *gallons* of Gatorade a day! The troops who were using water and salt tablets started cramping up by midafternoon. By the time you're thirsty, it's too late. When you are dehydrated, your reaction time and capacity to think clearly are severely retarded. Your judgment suffers, and you are liable to make errors that could be disastrous.

It's important to drink constantly during exertion in the winter too. Thirst is deceptive when you're cold. Even though you're surrounded by snow, the air can be almost as dry as it is in the desert. You lose a tremendous amount of moisture through the breath and sweat without realizing it. Also, you may experience cold-induced diuresis. (You pee a lot more and more often. Remember this when you bundle yourself or your child up for the snow!) When cross-country skiing, Matt uses an electrolyte replacement drink and disciplines himself to sip constantly.

Drinking water in the wilderness used not to be a problem, but these days even high mountain streams are often infected with giardia, also known as "backpacker's disease." The giardia organisms are resistant to chemical purification with halazone or iodine tablets and can survive brief periods of boiling, so water must either be boiled for more than 20 minutes or filtered through a ceramic filter like the one made by Katadyn. The filter weighs less than two pounds and can purify hundreds of gallons remarkably quickly. Matt has carried these filters all over the world. Their only drawback is the $250 price tag. However, once you are infected with giardia, the disease can go into remission, and often never be completely cured. So $250 is a cheap price to pay for your health and your children's health.

It's not really practical to expect a child to forage for food, but a couple of high-energy food bars and a canteen of water can make a big difference to a child who's lost in the woods overnight.

Insect repellent and bee sting and snake bite kits are discussed later in this chapter.

WILD THINGS

Americans are truly blessed with cultural diversity. We have been raised with the images of John Wayne and the macho cowboys of the Wild West, combined with the sentimental sweetness of Bambi and Yogi Bear. All of these modern myths are ridiculously unrealistic, yet they mold how we perceive the wilderness on an unconscious level. For example, a recent "nature" film perpetuates this Hollywood image by depicting bears as wonderful and hunters as horrible. In the film, an orphaned grizzly cub is raised by a gruff but kindly grandpa grizzly who teaches him to be the noble king of the forest bears, despite the evil hunters. In real life, instead of adopting the cute orphaned cub and showing him the ropes, grandpa grizzly would have had cub sushi for lunch.

BEARS!

It's simply a fact that the greatest danger to grizzly cubs is other grizzlies, even their own fathers! To a hungry bear—and bears are always hungry—protein is protein. Usually the bear will snack on organs, then cover the carcass to let it rot for a few days before returning for a ripe, smelly, decomposing feast. You may be recoiling a bit, but bears are neither good nor evil, they're just doing what bears have done for as long as there have been bears.

Matt's first experience with savage beasts was smelling the rotting-meat stench of rancid bear breath at 3 AM. He was a freshman at Stanford, so his first thought was, "That must have been one heck of a party!" Then the bear growled. He knew this was no hangover! The chill of reality sent cold shivers, followed by hot flashes, racing from his head to his toes and back again. He wished he were back in the dorm that he had been yearning to escape from, instead of zipped up helpless in a mummy bag in the middle of nowhere in Yosemite. Suddenly it dawned on him why they're called mummy bags!

Matt's second thought was that this couldn't be happening to him because, being an intellectual Stanford student, he had read all about bears. He had put his food in his stuff sacks and hung it in a tree. Unfortunately, he had left his toothpaste in his toilet kit, which even more unfortunately was next to his head. This bear smelled like he really needed that toothpaste, so when he drooled on Matt, he graciously let him have the whole kit. The way that bear chomped into that toothpaste would have made a great television ad!

Even though the bear seemed immense in the moonlight, the scientist in Matt recognized it as a two-year-old black bear. Punk "teenage" bears are the worst! They're big enough to be trouble, but they don't have the good sense of an adult. Also, they may still be hanging out with mom. Most bear attacks involve a mother with cubs or half-grown offspring. Momma bear still feels a need to protect them when they get into trouble—which, being "teenagers," is often. And it's even worse if mom has sent them packing. If they're out on their own, they may be somewhat inept at food gathering, as well as constantly frightened because wherever they are, they are in another adult bear's territory. The penalty for trespassing is a severe mauling or death. Life is not pleasant for "teenage" bears, so they are constantly scared, hungry, and ticked off. They take out their aggression on anything smaller than they are. Unfortunately, human beings fit in this category.

In this case, what finally drove the bear away was when he (or she—the scientist in Matt was not into examining bear gender at this time of morning) bit into a shaving cream can. What an ad for Gillette! The can ruptured with a loud pop and a glorious geyser of foam. The bear jumped stiff-legged on all fours, three feet straight up, and reversed directions in midair. Dan Millman, Matt's gymnastics coach, would have rated that leap a 9.5! Then he streaked off with a startled WOOF!!!, leaving behind a trail of steaming bear poop. Of course, Matt was running in the opposite direction, limited only by the constraints of his mummy bag. He would have thought it was impossible to run in a mummy bag, but the wilderness is full of enlightening experiences.

Needless to say, Matt took bear precautions very seriously after that—so seriously, in fact, that he was eventually hired by the Alaska branch of the U.S. Geological Survey to teach their annual bear defense course for fourteen years.

Bears evoke tremendous fear, far beyond the statistical odds of being attacked. Matt has encountered hundreds of bears in the woods and has never had a serious problem except for the first time. Matt has always been armed too, except for that first time. Because it's illegal to carry firearms in national parks, he avoids national parks.

Carrying a firearm and knowing how to use it are two different things. Firearms and children are always a potentially dangerous combination. If you are going to carry a firearm, you need expert training. Don't just carry a firearm as a good luck charm—if you carry it, know how to use it.

However, since firearms are not allowed in national parks or in many state parks and county parks, prevention is even more important. The first step is to ask a ranger to explain the bear situation at your camp. It's important to know what kind of bear you're likely to encounter. Black bears are found throughout the United States. Grizzlies are found only in a few Rocky Mountain states and Alaska. Their behaviors are quite different.

Black bears are usually shy and therefore unseen, especially in areas where they are hunted. However, they are extremely intelligent and adaptable, and if they learn to identify humans as a food source they become "problem bears." If you feed a bear, you are setting the stage for a negative bear-human encounter. Eventually the bear will have to be either tranquilized and relocated or killed.

Grizzlies feel that they own the forest. The answer to the question "Where does a 500-pound grizzly sit?" is "Anywhere it wants." In areas where grizzlies are hunted, they avoid humans. If they are habituated to humans, then for the most part they mind their own business if you mind yours. But if they learn to associate humans with food they too become "problem bears," but of a greater magnitude.

Most bear-human encounters are harmless and thrilling. However, almost ninety percent of recorded bear attacks involved mothers with cubs. In the rest of the attacks, it is possible that the sex of the bear was unknown or the cubs were hidden before the attack took place. If you see a mother and cubs, move to safety immediately!

If you encounter a bear unexpectedly, stop! Do not run—running can trigger a predator-prey response. Do not make direct eye contact, which can be interpreted as a territorial challenge. Look on the ground near your feet, keeping the bear in your peripheral vision. Back away slowly, turning your head slightly to check the ground behind you so you don't stumble.

To detect bears at night, one could set up a perimeter alarm using four mousetraps attached to tripwires. A hand-held marine or road flare can scare bears away temporarily. A marine fog horn or a high-intensity spotlight (over 100,000 foot-candles) may also drive them off. You may be able to frighten off a black bear by yelling and throwing rocks, but a grizzly is not likely to be impressed.

Cook your food and clean your utensils 50 to 100 yards from your sleeping area or tent. Also, be sure to put anything that might even smell like food in stuff sacks the same distance away from your tent.

If anyone in your party is menstruating, don't camp in bear country. In one test, this was the second most attractive scent to bears, after seal blubber.

In the few instances in which bears have attacked children with the intention of eating them, very little aside from a competent person with a firearm could have rescued the child. Matt's best advice is to keep small children out of bear country, or at least to watch them constantly.

Most experts agree that if you are attacked, you should curl into a fetal position with your hands behind your neck and play dead. This tactic may work in a territorial attack, but it requires supreme courage and presence of mind in a most dangerous circumstance.

BUGS

If you were foolish enough to stand outside naked in Alaska, you might get two thousand mosquito bites in an hour. There are some parts of Florida and Minnesota where the mosquitoes are just as thick. No, we weren't out there naked with a calculator! These figures are based on studies in which scientists had volunteers expose their hands for a few minutes to let themselves get bitten and then calculated total body surface area times the rate of bites. And no, we weren't some of those volunteers. Even we have our limits!

However, we have had our share of mosquito, chigger, ant, tick, flea, spider, horsefly, and centipede bites. We've also been stung by bees, hornets, and wasps. More people die from bee stings every year than from snakebites. If you or any member of your family is allergic to bee stings, consult your physician and get several bee sting kits. Be sure to note their expiration dates and replace them accordingly. An allergic person who isn't treated immediately can die within minutes of being stung.

There are dozens of insect repellents on the market. Matt prefers the military issue, Jungle Juice. It's cheap, and he has field-tested it on every continent except Antarctica. A mosquito net over a boonie hat is also a blessing in bug country.

In the Southwest, scorpions can be a problem, especially for children who go looking under rocks. Teach them not to overturn rocks, or to do it with a long stick.

Teach your children that when they put on their boots in the morning, they should hold them on the heel and then turn them upside down and shake them out. This is sound advice for any environment, but especially for the desert. When Matt was going through desert warfare training at Twenty-nine Palms in Southern California, he was still half asleep one morning when he shook out his boots as he did every morning, usually evoking laughter from his teammates. Even though it was a small scorpion that fell out, it made a *big* impression on Matt! He actually did an interesting little dance, since his first impulse was to step on the scorpion, but in midstrike his body realized that he was barefoot. Matt's boots were in his hands, and that scorpion had its stinger straight up. Amazing time distortions happen in the no-mind warrior state. Tap dancing took on a whole new meaning. Matt's martial arts shout certainly woke up his teammates. For the next few days they seemed to have nothing better to do than to creatively embellish their imitations of his protective reactions. By the time they were back on base, their performance on the dance floor had elevated this minor incident to a hysterical new art form, especially after drinking a few—you guessed it—"scorpions!"

Ticks are a serious problem in some areas. If not diagnosed and treated immediately, Lyme disease can be chronic and debilitating. Rocky Mountain spotted fever is a potentially fatal disease that is carried by ticks. Be sure to ask the rangers about local hazards and take appropriate protective measures, such as wearing a wide-brimmed hat, light-colored long-sleeved shirt (ticks show up better against light colors), and long pants. Matt usually wears high-top boots and ties his pants over his boots. After going through an infested area, he removes his clothing carefully and thoroughly inspects himself and his hiking partner for ticks. He combs his hair and inspects his clothing. A favorite hiding spot for ticks is in the shoelaces of boots.

In the South, the tiny mites called chiggers can be a big problem. Careful inspections and the use of an insecticide are highly recommended.

In some areas, leeches infest the waters. They secrete a local anesthetic so you don't even feel them attach. When Matt was forced to operate in a swampy jungle environment, he used to wear pantyhose. Initially he took a lot of flak from his teammates, but it works—leeches can't attach through pantyhose. These days, tight Lycra swimsuits are socially acceptable and serve the same function as pantyhose. So if you remotely suspect leeches and your children insist on going in the water, tight is right!

SNAKES

Even though more people die from bee stings every year than from snake bites, poisonous snakes occupy a place of particular horror in our psyches. By taking your children to the zoo or reading natural history books with them, you can teach them to recognize the poisonous snakes in your area and to learn their habits. For example, many snakes like to lie in the sun in the early morning in places that have southern exposure.

Local natural history is very important. For example, in California originally only 15 percent of the rattlesnakes would not rattle a warning. Human beings killed off those that rattled, and now in some areas almost 75 percent of the rattlesnakes don't rattle before they strike.

Colors and habits are also site-specific. Matt once saw a charcoal-gray rattlesnake in a pile of charcoal-gray granite just as he was stepping over it. It wasn't rattling! Matt thinks he set a new record for the broad jump. His girlfriend, who was behind him, accused him of running away, but he did come back and place his staff between her and the snake. *Then* it started rattling, and so did four or five others. That was chilling!

Snakes love abandoned buildings because mice love abandoned buildings. When Matt was moving out to a wilderness cabin, the local deputy told him that the last guy who lived there went out to his woodpile for some wood in the middle of the night and got bitten by a rattlesnake. It was two days before someone found him, and he lost his arm. Not the most pleasant welcome wagon story, but you can bet he watched that woodpile for any sign of movement. When Matt finds rattlesnakes out in the wilderness, he leaves them alone because they are part of the balance of nature. But around his campsite or cabin, he goes on snake patrol. If you do kill a rattlesnake, don't touch it right away. Even a severed head can bite reflexively for over an hour.

The moral is, if you have children in a rural environment, teach them to avoid snakes—but first have a snake hunt around your campsite. You should also have a snakebite kit with you at all times and know how to use it.

"TAME" WILD ANIMALS

Feral animals (usually cats and dogs that have been abandoned) and wild animals that have become accustomed to humans are also a hazard. When a hungry animal approaches, the temptation to feed it is great. However, these animals are extremely nervous, and a sudden movement could trigger a defensive bite. So when the camp beggars come, don't feed them. If your children insist on feeding them, make sure they keep a safe distance and throw the food to the animal.

Diseased animals are an attractive wilderness hazard to young children. Chipmunks or squirrels that let children pet them are probably sick, possibly even with rabies. Impress on your children the importance of staying away from any animal that lets you approach it.

DANGERS? YES, BUT IT'S STILL WORTH DOING

After thinking about all the dangers you might encounter when camping, you might wonder, why not stay home? If we were to list all of the dangers that we live with in an urban environment, which we avoid by simple common sense, we might all choose to "head for the hills."

When we learn safe practices in the wilderness, a whole new world opens to us. The beauty and the reverence for the life force that nature inspires weave a magic that lures us back. In the wilderness, just as in the city, knowledge is power. Having power allows us to relax and enjoy instead of being fearful.

This chapter provides only a brief introduction to the perils and wonders of the wilderness. There are many fine books that will help you and your children prepare to meet the challenges of the outdoors. We particularly recommend *Tom Brown's Field Guide to Nature and Survival for Children*, by Tom and Judy Brown (Berkeley Books, 1989).

SUMMARY

- Myths about the wilderness learned from cultural and media sources may need to be dispelled. Instead, both children and adults must understand the realities of the wild and the creatures who live there.

- Changes in weather can be life-threatening in the wilderness.

- The most dangerous animals in the wild, as in urban areas, are criminal human beings.

- For the most part, wild animals are enjoyable. But they are still wild and should be treated with respect.

- Besides being a nuisance, insects can be a serious health hazard.

- Preparation for the wild involves proper education and equipment as well as practical hands-on training.

LEARNING BY DOING

PREPARING FOR THE WILDERNESS:
THE WEEKEND OUTING

Objective: To include children in planning for a wilderness outing so they understand what it takes and feel more integrated into the event.

Materials: Pencil and paper.

Exercise:
Have a family meeting to discuss your camping trip. Have your children make checklists for:

- Emergency kits (two types discussed in text)
- Individual camping gear
- Group camping gear
- Food

Since preparation is at least half the fun, have your children accompany you to the army surplus store or to dig through your garage and attic to assemble the equipment.

Let each child pack his or her own personal gear, even though it may take twice as long and be incomplete.

Assign the preparation of each meal to a team and have that

team make up the menu, select the supplies, and prepare the assigned meal. This can result in outrageous meals as each team tries to outdo the others.

Have an overnight practice campout in your back yard. This can be a lot of fun—after doing this Matt's sons wanted to spend *every* night in the tent!

Purchase the items you suddenly find that you need desperately and put away the equipment you find you don't need.

At the next family meeting, pick a nearby camp site that has lots of activities for everyone. And be sure to pick an alternate activity in case the weather isn't good.

Happy trails!

INTRODUCTION TO NATURAL HISTORY

Objective: To prepare children for trips to the wilderness and to begin the learning experience before they go.

Materials: Books about wildlife and natural history.

Exercise:

There are many such fascinating books for all ages. They make wonderful bedtime reading for younger children, and older children enjoy exploring these books on their own.

A field trip to a zoo or a farm makes an enjoyable family outing. Instead of just looking at the animals, read up on their natural history before you go.

In California there are hundreds of local nature centers. These are well staffed, with charming and educational exhibits. Park rangers often put on nature shows and give informal lectures that can be a most useful source of information about your campsite.

MAP AND COMPASS READING
(EIGHT YEARS OR OLDER)

Objective: *To teach children the basics of finding their way in the outdoors.*

Materials:

- Compass
- Pencil and paper

Exercise:

Purchase an easy-to-use compass, preferably one with a straightforward instruction booklet.

Go to a local schoolyard (if you are allowed in after hours) or to a park, and teach your children to take bearings with the compass.

Learn to count paces over a known distance, such as a hundred-yard football field.

1. Measure off 10 yards.
2. Have your child count how many normal steps equal 10 yards.
3. Make a mark and go 30 yards true North.
2. Take a bearing of 90° and go 40 yards.
3. Take a bearing of 235° and go 50 yards.
4. Take reverse bearings and go back.

Make a map of the back yard and teach your children to triangulate to find their exact location.

Order topographic maps of a park in your area. Go to a copy store and enlarge the area in which you will be practicing. If a local park has enlarged topographic maps, even better. Then repeat the triangulation exercise in the park.

Drive your children to a semiwilderness park and have them use a map and compass to find their way to another location in the park.

Chapter Eight

RECOGNIZING BAD APPLES

DANGER AND THE "CRITICAL ONE PERCENT"

When children learn to exercise their own discrimination, they develop the confidence to distinguish between "Good Guys" and "Bad Guys." Remember the old sayings: "You can't tell a book by its cover," and "The bad guys don't always wear black hats." It's important for children to *recognize actions and situations that warn of danger rather than being taught to be wary of particular types of individuals.* Children are very literal, and when you use the word "stranger," they may think of someone who seems "strange" or makes them "feel funny" in some way. By learning the dangers of actions and situations, children can recognize similar degrees of danger, whether they come from a friend, acquaintance, or a stranger.

In order to understand the importance of children learning to recognize "bad apples," it is useful to look at the training and skills needed by personal protection professionals such as the members of the Secret Service, who protect the safety of prominent political figures, including the President of the United States.

About *95 percent* of protective service responsibility is management and planning. It is preventive in nature and is referred to as "hardening the target."

In this phase, intelligence gathering, planning, and advance work are the keys to overall effectiveness. This means assessing the potential threat, then setting up procedures, systems, and personnel to deal with potential danger to a client's person, family, and assets.

Another *four percent* of the job is the ability to respond effectively when confronted with difficult people or physical danger—the "sexy" skills dramatized in movies and on TV. This includes professional demeanor, effective communication in crisis situations, defensive tactics and the martial arts, use of firearms in combat, demolition search and identification, first-respondent medical skills, and the use of motor vehicles to escape and evade assailants.

However, the nature of personal attack (especially when planned or premeditated) is such that all of this is simply not enough.

Whether you consider seemingly random attacks on the streets by muggers, the strategic trickery of child molesters and abductors, or planned attacks by psychologically disturbed individuals, criminal "hit men," and politically or religiously motivated terrorists, there is usually a typical pattern that makes effective protection difficult.

Most importantly, those being attacked are usually taken by *surprise,* often when they are most *vulnerable.* The bad guys choose the time and place. They don't attack when the intended victim is in a strong position and help is at hand.

In addition, these incidents usually occur so *rapidly* that people under attack (and those who are there to provide protection) cannot react quickly enough to prevent the incident from occurring, and often someone is badly injured or killed.

These two factors obviously work to the great disadvantage of anyone attempting to protect themselves or others. However, warning signs usually appear in the faces and bodies of individuals who are planning to do harm, and inconsistencies occur in the flow of activities and environments that warn of impending danger.

The *critical one percent* of protective service is the ability to recognize these danger signs and to take immediate action that removes the advantage of surprise and neutralizes the impending attack. This is absolutely essential to the success of a protective operation. If a failure occurs in the *critical one percent,* no amount of planning and professional expertise is usually sufficient. Such awareness skills are strongly emphasized where Bob teaches at Executive Security International, North America's foremost school for professional bodyguards.

What does all this have to do with children? As we have stated earlier, *this book is about parents and children becoming aware and self-reliant rather than being afraid,* Proper awareness keeps us safe. As parents and educators, we can recognize situations that we should avoid and that we should teach our children to avoid as well. We must also acknowledge that our children are capable of recognizing danger signs and give them the training to do so without raising their fear.

With respect to developing awareness, what do we and our children share in common with protection professionals? What obstructs us all from using awareness effectively? Simply that *the use of awareness is a skill that must be developed and practiced* like any other good habit. And what works against us? Boredom on one side and distraction on the other.

Protection professionals often spend long hours in tedious situations where nothing is happening . . . boring . . . dullsville. But regardless of their inclination to space out, snooze, or read a book, they *must* maintain their alertness.

On the other hand, sometimes they are in exciting circumstances with lots of interesting activity going on, often involving beautiful, famous, and powerful people. Think how easy it would be to become distracted in such a situation. Again, despite their impulses, protection professionals must maintain their attention where it needs to be, This ability must be practiced and disciplined, Many planned assaults and street crimes like purse-snatching involve the use of existing or created distractions that engage the intended victim's attention.

An interesting exercise that we have used to develop this discipline of attention in bodyguard training is to take a training team (usually four people) to a movie that they have not seen and all agree they would really like to attend. Usually we choose an action movie with lots going on all the time. The team is instructed to escort the model "clients" into the theater and while the movie is showing never for a moment put their attention on the film. They are required to always observe the "clients" and what is happening around them. Try this sometime—it isn't an easy task by any means.

You can do similar exercises with your children to sharpen their ability to stay aware as described in the Learning by Doing section at the end of this chapter.

DECEPTION AND POTENTIAL DANGER

A good definition of deception is *the intentional misleading of one person by another without that first person's permission.* Actors, magicians, and poker players don't count, as we allow them to deceive us as part of acts or games that we enjoy participating in.

What we must be aware of are any *actions or words that attempt to mislead us.* From this perspective we can see that in some situations signs of deception can also be specific signs of danger. Many criminals attempt to deceive their intended victims by various means.

For example, an infamous serial killer prided himself on an

act he developed. He would pretend to be physically injured and in a lot of pain. That he was a charming and handsome young man made him even more dangerous. His targets were attractive, compassionate young women who he would lure into remote places where they would meet their demise. Once again, "bad guys don't always wear black."

You will probably never by conned by anyone you don't like or trust. Most con artists are successful because they either have a naturally charming persona or they work at developing one. You might even say it's part of the job description.

Bob teaches workshops on "Recognizing Danger and Deception" for criminal justice and security professionals and assault/rape prevention groups throughout North America. Participants in these workshops learn to look for specific signs in the faces and body language of deceptive individuals, and inconsistencies that happen in activities and environments that warn of potential deception and danger. For more information on this training contact P.O.L.O. International (see pages 169–170).

Much of the information on deception in these workshops is based on the work of Dr. Paul Ekman, considered to be one of the world's leading authorities on the subject. He has done research on nonverbal communication and deception for over 30 years. Paul and Bob collaborated to develop training programs that have been lauded by professionals in various occupations where recognition of danger or deception is of critical importance.

Even with good training and experience it's still not easy to spot what Ekman calls "natural performers." These individuals (approximately 5 percent of the population) are so convincing that signs of deception are not apparent. When natural performers lie, it's very difficult to detect, even for an expert.

There are basically two errors that can be made in detecting deception: believing a lie (accepting deception), and disbelieving the truth (rejecting innocence).

Obviously, we don't want to make the first error; we have discussed how dangerous this could be in some situations. We don't want to make the second error either, especially with friends and associates, because that could be damaging to relationships. Also, an atmosphere of distrust can develop around us that is not satisfying to anyone.

Just as we don't want to walk around being afraid, *we don't want to walk around being suspicious either.* The warrior way is to be aware and present without judgment. Remember the traditional warrior advice: "Expect nothing, be ready for anything."

DECEPTION AND CHILDREN

Recognition of deception is very important for the safety of children. It is true that sexual offenders who abduct and molest children sometimes take a child by force or threaten a child into submitting to them. However, more often than not, offenders see children as weak victims who can be manipulated easily, and usually they attempt to deceive children into accompanying them willingly.

Just as con artists and other criminals attempt to deceive adults by pretense, so offenders try to deceive children with all sorts of ruses.

Offenders may use a phony badge or uniform to impersonate authority, implying that the child has done something wrong and is required to accompany them somewhere. Common impersonations include police officers, park attendants and rangers, store detectives, and shopping mall security guards.

Often, offenders will initiate seemingly innocent contact with an intended victim. They may flatter children, or offer to give them something or to do some special activity with them.

One young boy in a shopping mall in Toronto was so enticed by an offender who offered to let him play a "really special" computer game that when his parents observed him walking off with the offender and called to him to come back, he ignored his parents and continued to walk away!

Offenders may also pretend to need help or assistance of some kind; or they may pretend that they know the child's parents and were sent to get the child for some very believable reason. The variations are numerous, and can be very effective.

Although adults can be taught to recognize deception in various ways, children usually cannot, and are much more easily deceived. However, we have found that children who are taught five simple principles and learn them well, can defeat attempted deception, regardless of who the perpetrator is or how clever the ruse.

FIVE PRINCIPLES FOR CHILDREN TO COUNTER POSSIBLE DECEPTION

1. Children should *never* go anywhere with anyone they don't know. Even if they *know* someone who asks them to go somewhere, they should always get their parent's permission before going.

2. Children should *never* take anything from anyone they don't know, *even something that belongs to them*. A good rule of thumb for children is to *always keep a distance of at least two arm lengths from adults they don't know.*

3. Have a *family password* that is known only to members of the family. Instruct children that they should never go with anyone who says "Your parents sent me to get you," unless the adult knows the password. *No exceptions!*

4. If an adult whom the child doesn't know asks for assis-

tance or help, *always get an adult to help him.* Adults who really need help can usually be helped much better by another adult.

5. If a child is approached by someone who seems to have a position of authority to tell a child what to do, the child should have another adult verify the credentials of that person (who may show a badge or be wearing a uniform) before complying. Most deceptions and impersonations can be uncovered in this way.

THE "WHAT IF. . .?" GAME

An effective way to learn these principles is a variation of the "What If. . .?" game that we have all played in some form with our children (and probably with our own parents as well). Just in case you don't remember, the game goes like this.

The parent asks the child *what* he or she would do if such and such a circumstance happened, and the child's response gives the parent information on what the child thinks and feels about a particular situation. The parent can then use the response to discuss the particular matter at hand with the child. Children often respond with "What If. . .?" questions of their own.

"What If . . .?" games can be used in a wide variety of learning situations. Educator Sherryll Kerns-Krazier in her *Safe Child Book* suggests this format when teaching children about personal safety. Other authorities do likewise, and we agree with them. However, when "What If. . .?" games are applied to situations that involve personal danger to children, it is important to remain sensitive to the child's fears. We continually observe that children do not learn well by intensifying their anxiety about anything that affects them directly, and they learn effective action much better when they act situations out, especially when their parents model appropriate responses.

Consequently, we recommend that "What If. . . ?" games be done generally in a role-playing mode, as discussed in the "Recognizing Bad Apples" exercise at the end of this chapter.

SUMMARY

- Children can learn to exercise their own discrimination and develop the self-confidence to distinguish between "Good Guys" and "Bad Guys."

- "Bad Guys don't always wear black hats," and children must learn to recognize actions and situations that warn of danger, rather than learning to fear strangers.

- Because of the nature of personal attack, the most important skill that anyone can have is the ability to recognize danger signs before the attack, and then take action to neutralize the intended attack. Protection professionals call this skill the *critical one percent*.

- This book is about parents and children being aware, not afraid or suspicious. Awareness must be developed and practiced like any other good habit.

- Boredom and distraction work against the effective use of awareness in many circumstances.

- Offenders use deception more often than force or threat to manipulate children into accompanying them willingly.

- Our working definition of deception is *the intentional misleading of one individual by another without that first person's permission.*

- Signs of deception can be signs of danger. Be aware of actions and words of others that attempt to mislead you about their real intentions.

- People are usually conned by people they like and trust. Even with good training in deception detection, people can be fooled by "natural performers."

- Deception and ruses used by offenders are clever and varied but can easily be countered in most cases, if children *learn and use* five simple principles of action.

- Learning these principles is best accomplished in a variation of the "What If. . . ?" game, in which parents role-model appropriate responses with their children.

LEARNING BY DOING

AWARENESS OF PEOPLE IN PUBLIC PLACES

Objective: To understand your children's perception of people they don't know.

Materials: None.

Exercise:

- Take the child to a shopping mall, a park, a zoo, or any crowded public place.

- Ask your child to watch the people and tell you if they notice anyone in particular. Who stands out in the crowd for them?

- When they pick someone, ask the child some questions about that person. Include questions like:
  - Do you think this is a nice person?
  - Is the person someone you would like to know?
  - How does this person make you feel?
  - How do you think you would feel if this person started talking to you?

- Don't ask leading questions about "being afraid" or "feeling funny" unless it is obvious from the child's response to a particular person that he or she is already experiencing that feeling.

- Note the child's response to people who are different in some way (race, culture, etc.) from your family, and his or her response to people who seem familiar because they are like those with whom you associate every day.

- Use the information you get to impress upon your children that they must observe the five principles with *anyone they don't know*, not just with people who seem different or strange in some way.

RECOGNIZING BAD APPLES: "WHAT IF. . .?"

The role-playing scenarios in this exercise are based on the experience of people we have spoken to; they illustrate deceptions that offenders may use. Even though children can easily be deceived by such offenders, we have found that children who are taught the five simple principles (described in the text) can easily counter possible deception.

Use your imagination to make up "What If. . .?" situations to role-play, and then model appropriate behavior that children can duplicate. Here are a few examples:

1. A woman approaches a child (legitimately—she is a friend of her mother), and says she's been sent by the mother to get the child. Mom's been hurt—she fell down and broke her leg. The child asks the woman for the family password. The woman responds correctly, and the child goes with her. (Principle 3.)

2. A store detective (phony) approaches a child and says he has been accused of shoplifting and must come along to talk to the "detective." The child refuses loudly, attracting the attention of a store employee, who asks for the

"detective's" credentials. (Principle 5) The offender beats a hasty retreat.

3. A man asks a child for directions to a gas station and assistance with getting some gas. The child enlists the aid of another adult. (Principle 4)

4. A woman (offender) entices a young boy to "come fly a kite" with her. The boy tells her that he can't take anything or go anywhere unless he asks his parents. (Principles 1 and 2)

Objectives:

- To illustrate "sneaky tricks" that offenders may use to manipulate children, and to model appropriate behavior in response.

- To give children confidence in exercising their own discrimination.

Materials:

- Costumes, hats, coats, sunglasses, and various play-acting props.

Exercise:

- Create "What If. . . ?" situations in which adults interact with children in various ways as illustrated in the above examples.

- In some situations an "offender" might attempt to manipulate a child into doing something with him or accompanying him somewhere.

- In other situations, the adult should genuinely communicate with the child.

- Vary the role-playing from positive to negative approaches so that children learn to use their discrimination as well as to recognize actions that should make them wary.

- In each scenario, have an adult model an appropriate response for the child to make. Repeat the scenario and have the child imitate the adult's response.

- Use enough scenarios so that children see in action *each of the five principles for countering deception described in the text* (pp 135–136).

Chapter Nine

RESISTANCE AND SELF-DEFENSE

THE PRINCIPLES OF ETHICAL SELF-DEFENSE

From the standpoint of ethical self-defense it is useful to consider the foundation principles of the Japanese martial art of Hakko Ryu Jujutsu (which Bob teaches). The foundation of this art is threefold: No Challenge, No Resistance, and No Injury. It is a powerful way to show respect for self and others, and is effective on many levels of providing personal protection.

No Challenge means that you must learn not to initiate or encourage conflict, either verbally or physically. Learn to respond rather than react to situations.

No Resistance means that if someone challenges you, or if someone attacks you verbally or physically, you do not resist that attack. You let it pass by, you move out of the way instead of confronting it. In this way, you create more options for resolving the conflict and for protecting yourself physically.

No Injury means that you do not use violence unnecessarily for self-protection. This includes not using words to offend or injure another. It also means not injuring someone needlessly in the process of protecting yourself physically. In reality you may in fact have to hurt someone who is trying to harm or kill you. *But there is no intention* to do so if it can be avoided.

In other words, these principles do not create a mindset that makes people more likely to use their anger or personal power wrongly.

The use of these three principles is important in developing a child's discrimination in the exercise of power, because they allow ethics to be used in action and in speech.

THE IMPORTANCE OF ETHICS

Teaching ethics is one of the most important ongoing responsibilities that parents have to their children.

Ethics are particularly important in conflict situations. At the center of teaching ethics are the concepts of self-respect and self-esteem, which give rise to the golden rule—do unto others as you would have them do unto you. The child must learn to respect others, and even to respect his or her opponent.

If you show respect for someone, no matter who he or she is, it will dramatically alter the way that person responds to you. If you respond to someone without respect, you actually escalate conflict. If you show respect, even if you are angry or don't like the person, you encourage resolution of conflict and usually get the cooperation that you want.

In terms of teaching our children ethics, it is important to examine our own sense of ethics. For example, if we are fearful or angry, but try to hide our emotions, our children will pick up on the fear or the anger. If we acknowledge that there are frightening situations, that anger is a real emotion that needs to be dealt with and expressed in a constructive manner, then when it comes to a conflict, these emotions can become a source of energy.

It's especially important for parents to teach their children to know whether or not a situation warrants resistance. If we teach a child effective resistance and self-defense, we don't want him using it against parents or teachers, unless the parent or teacher is doing something unethical. It's crucial to establish ethical boundaries, and to teach children to respect these first, and then to recognize when they are crossed.

Children have a tremendous capacity to learn and—if we actually listen to them—a tremendous capacity for telling us what their own fears and boundaries are. It's our job as parents to foster and develop this discrimination. Teach them the rules of society, and of the family, and of the school system. This is how society works and how we all get along with each other. Children must know that their personal feelings are important, but there are times when these feelings must be considered in terms of the larger society. For example, your child may feel like talking in the classroom, but it would be disruptive to the class if everyone could talk whenever they wanted to. Manners and etiquette are based on society's ways of teaching people respect for others.

Of course, different cultures have different manners. It's important for children to respect their own culture and its ways of doing things, and also to understand the boundaries of other cultural groups they have contact with.

Children's natural curiosity encourages them to test boundaries. Tell a child no and she'll try it again; tell her no again, and she'll try it again . . . about the third time you tell her, she sort of gets it. Testing those boundaries is just a natural part of growing up. That's why we should establish clear boundaries for our children.

Criminals also test boundaries, and children should understand that a breach of social customs can be an indication that boundaries are being tested. For example, in our culture it's not OK for a stranger to touch a child. If a stranger wants to touch, or even gets too close, it's important for the child to recognize that a breach is taking place. When the breach of etiquette starts, that's the time to start resistance. At the same time, of course, it's important for the child to understand that resistance is only to be used for self-protection. It's not to be used, for example, against another child, as a means of getting their way.

When Matt was a child in an orphanage in Japan, the older kids used to steal his food. He soon learned to fight them in order to keep food. His friend Carlos and he became quite a team, and they were able to defeat the worst bullies. But within a month, they became the bullies themselves and started stealing other kids' food, because no one was teaching them ethics. It's a natural thing for the oppressed to become the oppressors. Recognize that this can happen. Teach ethics along with resistance and self-defense.

One example of teaching ethics is with respect to toy weapons. In our society boys are encouraged by the media and by their peers to play with guns, swords, knives, bows and arrows. Even if they're not allowed to have those toys, they will make pretend weapons out of whatever is at hand. Girls for the most part are not encouraged to play with toy weapons; but when given the opportunity, they often enjoy it as much as the boys do.

We feel it is wrong to give play guns to children and let them shoot at each other or at adults. Even though most children have toy guns, we suggest they also have strict rules about using them. Only allow them to point toy guns at imaginary "bad guys," never at each other. If a child who comes to visit points a toy gun at them, they should be told, "That's not a polite thing to do." If this child persists, then your children should know to come and tell an adult.

There is one exception to the rule about pointing toy guns at another person. All kids love to squirt people with water guns. So we never allow our children to have squirt guns that look like real weapons. We let them play with the ones that are brightly colored plastic—pink or purple or bright yellow. That way there is no transference of identity to a real gun, because they're so obviously toys.

Of course, the idea is that the rule of never pointing a toy gun at a person carries over to never pointing a *real* gun. Weapons should always be kept in a safe place, but there's always the fear that a child might find them. A child might go to visit a friend whose parents keep a gun in the nightstand, and might find that gun and start playing with it. That's how tragedies occur. That's why it's so important for children to learn respect for firearms and the ethics of using weapons.

Another part of the teaching of ethics is the awareness that responsibility goes hand in hand with power; responsibility and ethics are integral to the right use of power. The use of knives is a good example, as kitchen knives are easily accessible in most homes. Matt's son Cully wanted a knife at a very early age. So when he was three years old Matt taught him to use a knife under his supervision. He could cut up vegetables for salads, and he could whittle things, but he could only do so under Matt's control. Cully became very responsible with a knife, and he never cut himself. As he grew, Cully was allowed to use a larger knife, but again he could only use it under Matt's supervision. When he demonstrated responsibility with the larger knife, Matt gave him a small, dull pocketknife that he could keep with him. The blade was less than an inch and a half long. Having a tool that he could control using was a significant boost to his self-confidence. But he recognizes that carrying that knife is a privilege, because he has learned the ethics that go along with it.

Games that teach the use of physical force and violence, games that use pretend weapons, are actually based on models of warfare. That's why the attainment of power must be continuously reinforced by ethics, manners, and responsibility. In a very real sense, as you teach a child self-protection, you enhance self-confidence, self-esteem, and the ability to be self-reliant; but you do it in a way that does not encourage the use of power wrongly in highly emotional circumstances.

As a child practices ethics, she recognizes that she is being ethical. It becomes a self-reinforcing constructive spiral; the more she demonstrates her ethical behavior the more privileges she gets, and the more responsibility she shows, the more ethical she will become. In this cycle, her self-esteem grows tremendously. This is true in confrontations, or in any situation that calls on the warrior spirit of courage and self-reliance.

In the summer of 1992, Bob took his seventeen-year-old daughter Reyna on an adventure trip to Colorado. In addition to several wonderful hikes, they went paragliding off Aspen Mountain, and did a class-five whitewater rafting trip on the Arkansas River with good friends Michael Kinsley and the Crum clan. Bruce Gordon, a world-class mountaineer (and Reyna's godfather) also introduced her to rock climbing on a very challenging slope near Independence Pass.

Reyna learned quickly in all of the potentially dangerous situations, moving beyond her fear. Of course, in all these activities she was under the control and supervision of experts. The training of the warrior spirit—basically, that courage to go beyond fear—doesn't always have to be taught in a conflict situation. Many games and other enjoyable activities can accomplish the same thing.

Once a child has learned to use ethics to discriminate, then he can learn how to resist an assailant. The first step in effective resistance is the sense of awareness that we discussed in Chapter Eight, the ability to recognize that something is wrong. The second step is the courage to take action, and the third step is having learned the tools to be effective.

EFFECTIVE RESISTANCE

In recognizing a potentially dangerous situation, teach children to remember that offenders are often cowards. People who attack children are cowardly. And if an assailant sees that his potential victim is aware and prepared to take action, it's very likely that he will flee.

For example, according to figures from the Department of Justice, if a woman who is attacked resists in any way, her assailant will flee about 50 percent of the time. Unfortunately, this gives rise to false confidence in how effective resistance can be. If the victim offers resistance and the attacker *doesn't* flee, then the likelihood of violence and injury to the victim rises to 80 percent.

That's why we emphasize *effective resistance*—so that if an assailant doesn't flee, the child is still able to take care of herself.

The use of *voice* is one of children's most effective forms of resistance, whether it's a cry for help or a challenge to the offender. First the child must learn to recognize which action is appropriate. For example, if there's no one around, it would be useless to call for help. In that case, the child should give verbal commands in a powerful way. Children can learn to speak from the diaphragm, so that the voice becomes lower in pitch. This is the human equivalent of a growl. When a dog that weighs only 35 pounds or so growls, most people back away. That snarl, that intensity, that ferocity can also be transmitted by a child.

Of course, we don't want our children to act like this under ordinary circumstances. But if a child is under attack, snarling and growling and pitching a low voice can actually be very frightening and even disorienting to an assailant. In this case it becomes easier to flee than to approach a growling, snarling kid. Also of importance is for the child to speak with a commanding voice rather than a whiny or pleading voice. The surprise element of the child barking commands like a drill instructor can be a powerful deterrent to a cowardly aggressor.

Another voice key is to speak in short, sharp commands. A person who is in crisis, in an emotionally unbalanced state, angry, or on an adrenaline high can only understand and remember sentences that contain about five simple words. Teach your child the Rule of Five—to use short sentences with only about five words and words with no more than five or six letters—for example, "I want you to stop." "You should stop right now." "Stop doing that." "Don't come any closer." These sentences clearly state the child's desires in relationship to the assailant.

EFFECTIVE FLIGHT

After voice, the next most powerful weapon in the child's arsenal is effective flight. The average adult can run faster than the average child, especially on a straightaway. But if the child has even a small lead, it will take a while for the adult to catch up with her. The child should try to flee to a place where there are adults. And he should be screaming all the way, something like, "Help, he's not my dad." If the attacker is getting too close, then the child should resort to zig-zagging, because children can shift direction faster than adults. She can also try to create obstacles, like running past a garbage can and tipping it over in front of the assailant.

Another possibility is for the child to climb a tree. The higher up the child is, the more visible he is to other adults who might intervene. Even more important, if the assailant also climbs the tree, the child is in a superior position in which he can use his feet against the assailant's hands. This is one place where the adult can't use his superior upper body strength against the child. The adult has to face the child's legs and feet, which can be formidable weapons.

Again, in evasive maneuvers it's important to keep yelling the whole time. Noise is a very effective deterrent.

Another effective evasive tactic is to crawl under a car. An adult who tries to get a child out from under a car might get stuck. Meanwhile, the child is kicking him in the hands and in the face.

Matt once had a small cat that was constantly terrorized by a big cat. His cat got in and out of the house through the dryer vent. One day Matt heard a horrible screeching and suddenly his cat came flying thought the dryer vent, followed by the big cat, who made it about halfway through and got stuck. His cat turned around and started swiping the bully across the nose, and the big cat was helpless; all he could do was screech and hiss. Finally he managed to back out of the dryer vent and run away. Like Matt's little cat, children should be alert to situations where their small size gives them an advantage.

Learning to move silently and hide effectively is another important skill. In most situations we do not recommend that children try to hide if someone seems threatening to them. If possible, they should run instead towards places where there are other people. There is definite safety in numbers, and in the presence of other people it is likely that children can get the help they need.

However, there may be a circumstance when no one is around and help is not available. In such situations, an ability to "escape and evade" may be the only alternative. Consequently, learning to move silently, to hide effectively, and to evade another while moving is an important skill to know. The "Learning by Doing" section contains several exercises to help develop this ability.

EFFECTIVE SELF-DEFENSE

But what if none of these evasive measures work and the child is cornered? How do we teach our children effective self-defense? Training in the martial arts is wonderful for developing children's strength, agility, and self-confidence, but this can also give the child a sense of confidence that isn't really warranted. The fact is that the average adult can easily overwhelm a young child. The way that kids fight other kids is very different from the way a kid would need to fight an adult. We believe that for a child to engage in serious combat, he or she must be trained professionally, in a step-by-step fashion that takes into account the individual child's readiness and ability.

However, one self-defense skill we do teach in our P.O.L.O. workshops is how to throw things as a deterrent to attackers. Everyone remembers the story of David and Goliath. We don't teach kids to use a sling, but we do teach them to pick up things to throw. In class we use tennis balls. In real life they could pick up rocks, or dirt, or sand, or throw whatever they already have in their hands. We teach them to throw the first object at the face of an assailant, to throw the second object at the body, and to hold onto the third object as a threat. The point is to make an assailant think, "Do I really want to attack this child who is throwing things at me?" Since child molesters are usually cowards, it's often easier for them to flee than to stand up to a determined child who is screaming and throwing things. (See "Tennis Ball Game" in the Learning by Doing section.)

If none of this works, and the child is under the control of the assailant, it is absolutely essential for the child not to give up, but to recognize that this is only a temporary setback. We call this *waiting for the opening*. And when the opening comes, the child needs to use surprise, distraction, and physical leverage simultaneously to escape. For example, if an abductor has the child in a car and pulls up to a stop light, the child can yank open the car door, scream, kick the abductor, and then quickly jump out. For such a strategy to work, the child must know how different types of car doors and locks work. This is something that parents can do with their children. *Whenever you're in a different car, make sure that your child understands the locking mechanism and how to get the door open quickly.*

In the gravest extreme, a child who is effectively trained is capable of causing injury to an assailant. But, if that child isn't equally grounded in ethics, he or she might cause serious physical injury to another child in a playground dispute. That's why it's the parents' responsibility to constantly emphasize the ethics of using superior power. A six-year-old child can deliver an incapacitating blow to the eyes, nose, or groin. But for children to effectively use physical force against an adult, they need professional training.

Matt offers training (separate from P.O.L.O. International's "Protecting Children from Danger" workshops) entitled "Model Mugging for Children" which is based on his years of teaching realistic self-defense to men and women. In this program children learn what really works in defense against adult "assailants" wearing protective gear. (For information write to Matt Thomas, Model Mugging, 859 N. Hollywood Way, Suite 127, Burbank, CA 91505).

We believe that the skills of realistic self-defense for children are best learned from a highly trained and certified instructor who will keep ethics foremost. If you decide your children need such training, choose an instructor carefully.

SUMMARY

- Children must have self-respect and also learn to respect others.

- Ethics, manners, and etiquette are ways of showing respect for others at home, at school, at play, and in society in general.

- Demonstrating respect for others increases the resolution of conflict. The three principles of demonstrating respect for others in self-protection are: no challenge, no resistance, and no injury.

- Ethics can and should be taught in various ways.

- Resistance in any form increases the chance for escape. But when resistance is not effective in causing an assailant to flee, the incidence of violence increases significantly.

- Children can be taught effective resistance through:
  - Recognition of danger
  - Setting boundaries
  - Learning to move evasively
  - Using voice and sound effectively
  - Using the principles of effective flight and evasion

- Effective flight discourages pursuit and is based on:
  - Lead time
  - Fleeing to other adults for help
  - Using objects and terrain as obstructions to pursuit
  - Changing direction frequently as pursuers get closer
  - Yelling or screaming all the way to draw attention
  - The use of heights or small spaces to deter pursuers—for example, climbing trees or crawling into small tight areas like drainage pipes or beneath automobiles

– Knowing how to move silently and hide effectively when necessary

- Martial arts are useful in building coordination, agility, and strength, but may give children a false confidence in their ability to protect themselves. The fact is that most children can be easily overcome by an adult.

- Effective self-defense for children must be taught with ethics foremost to avoid the misuse of personal power.

- Self-defense for children should be based on what can actually be effective for small individuals. In order of effectiveness and application, the child should:
  – Throw objects to deter, confuse, and delay an attacker
  – Use hands and feet to strike out and keep attackers away
  – Use surprise, distraction and physical leverage, or strikes with improvised weapons to escape grabs and holds
  – In the gravest extreme, resort to tactics that could seriously injure someone, such as strikes to the eyes, nose, groin, and other vulnerable parts of the body

- The use of physical force should be taught only by trained and certified instructors, who will keep ethics foremost. Choose carefully.

LEARNING BY DOING EXERCISES

RESISTANCE TRAINING

Do you remember when you were a child how difficult it was to say no to a grown-up? Even if you sensed a threatening situation, you were so conditioned that you would hesitate to even question an adult. Well, times have changed. We must teach our children to exercise their own authority, to know which adults to question and who to say "no" to.

Objectives:

- To teach children to say "No" to an adult when necessary.
- To learn to keep a safe distance when approached by someone they don't know.
- To learn what to yell if someone actually grabs them.

Materials: Several pillows or other objects that can be used as "obstacles."

Learning to Say "No!"

- Start with the children facing each other in pairs. Have one child say "yes" while the other says "no." Go back and forth (yes/no) with increasing volume and energy. After about half a minute, have children switch roles.
- Adults then replace one child in each pair as the "yes" person, being very forceful (verbally) with the child. The child continues to say "no."

Keeping a Safe Distance

- Practice setting boundaries. An adult approaches each child, and the child pretends the adult is someone he doesn't know. The rule of thumb for children is, *Always keep a distance of at least two arm lengths from adults they don't know.*
- An adult approaches the child, slowly at first and then quickly. The child steps back, keeping the optimum distance and yelling "no" as the adult persists in approaching.
- Place obstacles (pillows, etc.) in the patch of the retreating child so he must stay aware of his surroundings as he backs up.
- Finally, have the adult actually grab the child by the arm or pick him up and attempt to carry him. The child should

respond in a loud voice, *"No!" (or "Help!")* *"This person is not my father (or mother)!"* The child continues to yell until the adult lets go or someone comes to help.

Children should also know what to do if they are taken into a car against their will.

- If a child is taken into a car, she should roll the window down or pound on the window and continue to yell for help.

- If the car stops for a light, the child should quickly open the door while yelling for help, jump from the car, and run toward a place where other adults are. To facilitate this, children should become familiar with different cars and learn how to unlock the doors of as many as possible.

EVASION TRAINING

Objectives:

- To learn to move quietly on varied terrain (Stealth Movement).

- To perceive what is happening around one with senses other than seeing (Samurai Cat and Ninja Mice Game).

Stealth Movement

There are two basic stealth walking movements that can be learned easily:

Ninja Fox Walking

- Observe movement illustrated in figure. The basic technique is to lift one foot at a time while keeping all of one's weight on the other foot still on the ground.

- Each footstep should be placed slowly and carefully as follows to avoid any sound:

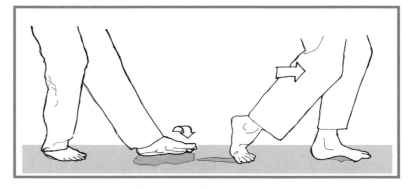

Ninja Fox Walking

- Place the outside edge of each moving foot on the ground first, then roll the foot slowly towards the inside (of the foot) as body weight is transferred from one foot to the other.
- Repeat the process slowly and deliberately with each step.
- Practice until it can be done without making a sound.

• Once children can do this easily, have them practice moving sideways and backwards with the same basic step.

Ninja Stork Walking (through shallow water)

This movement is a way to move through shallow water or large puddles silently.

• The movement is similar to the ground walking technique, except the lifted foot is brushed against the stationary leg (like a stork) to allow water to contact and run silently down (the stationary leg) instead of dripping noisily onto the water's surface. In this movement the toe of the moving foot should enter the water "like a blade" to avoid splashing.

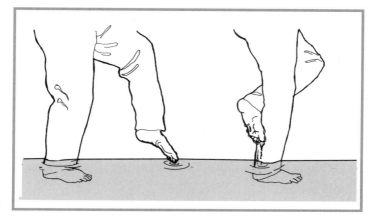

Ninja Stork Walking

This can be practiced in a simulated manner on dry ground or more effectively in shallow water or wading pools.

Samurai Cat and Ninja Mice Game

Materials:

- Blindfold (headband material can be used easily).
- Chalk (outside) or colored tape (inside) to mark off a bordered area (in the P.O.L.O. workshop we usually use an area approximately 12 feet x 24 feet for 6–10 children). The game works better inside, especially if the room can be darkened.

Exercise:

- Choose one child to be the Samurai "Cat." All the other children will be Ninja "Mice" at first. The "Cat" is blindfolded and spun around several times while the "Mice" position themselves wherever they choose within the boundaries.

- The "Cat" then tries to tag as many of the "Mice" as he or she can; while the "Mice" do their best to evade by moving SLOWLY and SILENTLY. Running is Not Allowed!

- Whenever the Cat says, "Cat! Cat!" the Mice must reply, "Mouse! Mouse!" (which obviously gives the blindfolded Cat a chance to locate and tag one or more of the Mice).

- Other than that, the Mice practice stealth movement and try to move as quietly as possible to evade the Cat and the Cat does his or her best to locate the Mice by sound or other "sixth" sense perception.

- If a Mouse goes outside the boundaries, he or she is automatically out.

- Each child should be given a chance at being the Cat until they tag at least one of the Mice. No competition, and be sure each child has a success.

What is most significant for parents (or educators) to do is stress the importance of moving slowly and quietly. Fast noisy movements more than once or twice during a time period and a Mouse is out. It's a game that children usually love playing, and really sharpens stealth movement skills.

HIDE-AND-SEEK FOR REAL

Objective: To teach children to hide effectively (and stay hidden) or evade someone while moving.

Materials: None (open space/outdoors required).

Exercise:

- One adult is chosen to play the role of a "bad guy" and will wear a disguise of some kind. Other adults will be "good guys" who ensure that safety is maintained and give helpful advice to the children in hiding during the game.

- Children are given an area with boundaries in which to hide. Then they are asked to find the best place they can to hide themselves (within the boundaries) and stay there until called to reveal their hiding place by one of the "good guys."

- Once they are hidden, the "bad guy" will try to find them. As the "bad guy" moves around he or she will say things like "I'm coming for you—I know where you are hiding—I see you now, I'm going to get you." (Offenders may do this in real situations to spook children into panic and leaving their hiding place if they believe what the offender says.)

- Children are instructed to remain completely still and completely silent *no matter what the "bad guy" says!*

- After the "bad guy" makes the rounds (and children are called from their hiding places) he tells the children who he was able to locate and who he wasn't. Praise and positive critique of the chosen hiding places should be given to the children.

- Children are then told to hide a second time, but during this round they are instructed to try to stay ahead (or go around) the stalking "bad guy" by moving stealthily from one hiding place to another. The objective is to get back to an agreed-upon location (goal) without being detected.

This exercise is usually great fun! Escape and evasion skills are learned easily and effectively. Be as creative as you want in instructing the children how to hide (using camouflage, covering themselves with leaves, sand, or whatever—it's up to you).

Note: the next figure shows one principle of observation from a hiding place—to look out from unexpected positions like close to the ground.

Wrong   Right

Observation from Hiding Places

Also indicate to children how crawling through tall grass or other vegetation can be detected by a trained observer watching the tops of the grass rather than scanning the area near the ground.

Caution: Because children might possibly pick places to hide which may not be safe, the area for this exercise should be chosen carefully and some hiding places (underneath cars or inside dumpsters, etc.) should be made "off limits" for the exercise, but still be considered as useful for a real situation.

SELF DEFENSE TRAINING (DETERRENCE)

Deterrence can be effective if one remembers that even warriors facing unfair odds knew how to throw things at their attackers to delay, confuse, and deter them while making a getaway. This is worth teaching children to do, as they can learn to do so quickly and effectively. Thus, the following exercise:

Tennis Ball Game

Objective: To teach children how to deter larger and aggressive individuals who may threaten them by throwing objects (any at hand) accurately.

Materials:

- Tennis balls (3–6 per child)
- Paper plates (3–4 per parent and child)
- Masking tape
- Magic marker
- Closed door (or wall) in a hallway

Exercise:

- Tape one paper plate on the door, waist high to your child.
- Tape the second plate on the door, waist high to you.
- Set the roll of tape 5–10 feet from the door.
- Using a gentle throw, hit the plate at your waist level with the ball (don't try to catch the ball as it returns).
- Have your child call out whether you hit or missed the plate.
- Have your child give you another ball.
- Repeat the first three steps.

- Have your child retrieve all three balls.

- Have your child gently throw the ball at their plate.

- Call out a hit or a miss. Be supportive either way.

- Give your child another ball.

- Repeat this for a total of three times.

- When the child can do it successfully, have them aim at your plate.

- When they can hit your plate, move the tape back three feet at a time.

- If they start missing, move the tape back to where they were hitting previously.

- Move their plate above your plate to your face level.

- Keep moving back so they don't get bored, or until they start to miss too often.

Once they have the skill to hit plates consistently in this manner, have them throw the balls as follows:

- Throw two balls quickly (one after another) at the target plates (adult face or waist level), then yell "stop" and hold the last ball ready to throw while backing up.

- If you have protective equipment for face, body, and groin, have the child practice throwing balls at you or another adult as they are approached in an aggressive manner.

Developing effective skills at this level usually comes quickly with some practice.

Caution: The potential for self-defense is obvious. *Children must be told emphatically to only use this skill for self-protection in emergencies.*

Afterword

LIVING WITH
STRENGTH AND JOY

We hope that your child will never need to use the emergency skills described in this book in a life-threatening situation. But these skills are also useful every day, with ordinary problems. Healthy self-esteem, the courage to take risks, a spirit of adventure—all of these help children to live intensely in the present moment.

Numerous books have been written about self-esteem—how it enhances learning, interactions with other children, and problem solving. The most important thing, though, is that the enhanced self-esteem allows a child to live with strength and joy rather than with fear. Self-esteem gives children the basis of courage, which is the ability to love themselves and others, to love life intensely, and to be willing to take risks.

Bravery is acting in a risky situation without knowing the consequences. And courage is knowing what the consequences are, but acting bravely anyway. The courage to live every day is tested every day—in starting a new homework project, taking up a new sport, moving to a new neighborhood, or making a new friend. All of these endeavors require a certain amount of courage, and the ability to look forward to life full of hopes and aspirations. The spirit of adventure allows us to explore as a baby explores, accepting ourselves, free of the fear of making mistakes. Without mistakes, we would never push our own boundaries. Mistakes are the process of learning.

Another way of teaching children courage is by teaching them to face their fears. Facing their fears in little ways allows them to face bigger fears. Small, everyday fears are often a block to action. By having the courage to face those fears every day, we can remove those blocks to action, opening the way to a life full of purpose and meaning.

Until enlightenment, no one is going to be completely happy all the time, and this book isn't about the keys to happiness or fulfillment. But in a way it is about living more intensely, rather than just letting life slip by. Every day can be an adventure in growth and learning. And every experience helps us understand the next experience.

We hope that this book has helped you to open new paths of communication with your children. By breaking the cycles of misunderstanding, lack of communication, and unpreparedness, we are giving our children an incredible gift, a gift that they will be able to pass on to their own children—the gift of preserving life, of enjoying life, of bringing the warrior spirit to everything they do.

Life is a process of ongoing learning. And when approached in the spirit of adventure, exploration, and mystery, life is the greatest school there is.

Appendix A

WORKSHOPS AND VIDEOTAPE TRAINING PROGRAM

We greatly appreciate your taking the time to read this book and to practice the exercises with your children. We hope you have found your time and effort to be well spent. We would like for you to know about our additional programs and materials to facilitate your children's learning.

"PROTECTING CHILDREN FROM DANGER" WORKSHOPS

Our workshops offer a dynamic and integrated parent-child learning experience that accelerates the process of developing self-reliance and teaching emergency skills to children.

These workshops are offered under the auspices of P.O.L.O. (Protecting Our Loved Ones) International. We offer programs for parents and children, and instructor classes for educators and others who are interested in being certified to teach these workshops.

VIDEO TRAINING PROGRAM

We also offer a complete videotape training program that illustrates most of the exercises and games in the Learning by Doing sections of this book. This program teaches educators and parents to use the material more effectively. The videotape training program includes the video, an adult/child workbook, and a unique child identification system.

If you are interested in obtaining further information about "Protecting Children from Danger" workshops or video training program, please contact us at P.O.L.O. International. (See page 170 for our locations in the United States and Canada.)

Appendix B

ABOUT P.O.L.O. INTERNATIONAL

P.O.L.O. (Protecting Our Loved Ones) International is an organization of educators and security professionals who provide training programs, media productions, and special services for protecting life and property. We offer a variety of programs that complement each other in a comprehensive and integrated manner.

Our public seminars and hands-on workshops have assisted parents, teachers, children, and men and women of all ages gaining the knowledge and understanding necessary to improve their self-esteem and protect their lives and property.

P.O.L.O. International also provides professional training for criminal justice, law enforcement, and security personnel, as well as offers consulting services to clients interested in personal protection and related security matters. P.O.L.O. International is closely affiliated with Executive Security International, North America's foremost school for professional bodyguards.

Our areas of expertise include child protection and kidnap prevention, awareness and communication training, behavioral psychology, crisis intervention, personnel protection, defensive tactics and the martial arts, as well as other disciplines related to personal safety and security.

Our inspiration comes from the traditional warrior purpose: to preserve and protect life. Our goal is to inspire the protective warrior spirit in everyone we teach.

In addition to our training programs, we offer the following:

- Instructor certification for the teaching of P.O.L.O. programs.
- Audiovisual production of educational materials and media projects.
- Marketing of educational materials and safety and security equipment.
- Special services (consulting, training, and operations).
  – Dignitary and Executive Protection
  – Kidnap Prevention
  – Emergency Preparedness
  – Self-Sufficiency

If you would like information on the range of programs and services we offer, please contact us. We welcome your inquiries.

P.O.L.O. International/USA
P.O. Box 150058
San Rafael, California 94915
(415) 453-9774

P.O.L.O. International/Canada
RR 5
Madoc, Ontario K0K2K0
(613) 395-3639

Bibliography

Arena, J. M., M.D. and M. B. Settle, Ph.D. *Child Safety Is No Accident.* New York: Berkeley Books, 1978.

Avabhasa, Da (Da Free John). *Conscious Exercise and the Transcendental Sun.* Clearlake, California: Dawn Horse Press, 1973. (phone: 1-800-524-4941)

―――. *Easy Death,* Revised Edition. Clearlake, California: Dawn Horse Press, 1992.

―――. *Look at the Sunlight Over the Water.* Clearlake, California: Dawn Horse Press, 1983.

Ayoob, M. *Gun Proof Your Children.* Concord, New Hampshire: Police Bookshelf, 1986. (Phone: 1–800–624–9049)

―――. *In the Gravest Extreme.* Concord, New Hampshire: Police Bookshelf, 1980.

―――. *The Truth About Self-Protection.* New York: Bantam Books, 1983.

Beal, M.D. *I Will Fight No More Forever: Chief Joseph and the Nez Percé War.* Seattle: University of Washington Press, 1963.

Berenstein, S. and J. Berenstein. *Berenstein Bears Learn About Strangers.* New York: Random House Books, 1985.

Bishop, R. L., and G. L. Peterson. "A Synthesis of Environmental Design Recommendations from the Visual Preferences of Children." Technical Report #2, Grant 5, R01-EC00301, U.S. Public Health Service (Sept. 1971).

Bolz, F. A. *How to Be a Hostage and Live.* Secaucus, New Jersey: Lyle Stuart, Inc., 1987.

Bosque, E., and S. Watson. *Safe and Sound.* New York: St. Martin's Press, 1988.

Briggs, D. C. *Your Child's Self-Esteem.* Garden City, New York: Doubleday & Company, 1970.

Brown, T., and J. Brown. *Tom Brown's Field Guide to Nature and Survival for Children.* New York: Berkley Books, 1989.

Clinkscales, J., and L. Clinkscales. "Blueprint for Action," La Grange, Georgia: Find Me, Inc., 1981

Covey, S. R. *The Seven Habits of Highly Effective People.* New York: Fireside Books, 1990.

Crum, T. F. *The Magic of Conflict.* New York: Simon & Schuster, 1987.

Ericksen, R. G. *How to Find Missing Persons.* Port Townsend, Washington: Loompanics Unlimited, 1984.

Ekman, P. *Telling Lies.* New York: W.W. Norton & Co., 1992.

———. *Why Kids Lie.* Charles Scribner & Sons, New York 1989.

Ekman, P., and W. V. Friesen. *Unmasking the Face.* Palo Alto, California: Consulting Psychologists Press, 1975.

Fritz, R. *The Path of Least Resistance.* New York: Fawcett-Columbine, 1989.

Hatsumi, M. *The Grandmaster's Book of Ninja Training.* Chicago: Contemporary Books, 1988.

Hechinger, G. *How to Raise a Street-Smart Child.* New York: Facts-on-File Publications, 1984.

Heckler, R. S. *In Search of the Warrior Spirit.* Berkeley: North Atlantic Books, 1990.

———. *The Anatomy of Change.* Boston: Shambhala Publications, 1984.

"HEW Statistics." In Barnett, H. L., M.D., and A. H. Einhorn, M.D. Pediatrics (14th Edition). New York: Appleton-Century-Croft, 1978.

Huchton, L. M. *Protect Your Child.* Englewood Cliffs, New Jersey: Prentice-Hall, Inc., 1985.

Hull, K. *Safe Passages.* Berkeley, California: Dawn Sign Press, 1986.

Hyams, J. *Zen in the Martial Arts.* Los Angeles, California: J. P. Tarcher, Inc., 1979.

Innosanto, D. *Absorb What Is Useful.* Los Angeles, California: Know Now Publishing Company, 1982.

Kim, A. *Ninja Secrets of Invisibility.* Boulder, Colorado: Palladin Press, 1983.

Kinsey, A. C., W. B. Pomeroy, L. E. Martin, and P. H. Gebhard. *Sexual Behavior in the Human Female.* W.B. Saunders 1953.

Kraizer, S. K. *The Safe Child Book.* New York: Dell Publishing Company, 1985.

Lowry, D. *Autumn Lightning.* Boston: Shambhala Publications, 1985.

Metzger, M., and C. P. Whittaker. *The Childproofing Checklist.* New York: Doubleday, 1988.

Millman, D. *No Ordinary Moments.* Tiburon, California: H. J. Kramer, 1992.

————. *The Warrior Athlete.* Wapole, New Hampshire: Still-point, 1979.

————. *Way of the Peaceful Warrior.* Tiburon, California: H. J. Kramer, 1980.

Musashi, M. *The Book of Five Rings.* Bantam Books, New York 1982.

National Fire Protection Association. "Sparky Meets E.D.I.T.H.," Quincy, Massachusetts 1978.

National Safety Council. "How to Survive a Hotel Fire," reprinted from *Family Safety,* Oakland, California: NSC/East Bay Chapter, Fall, 1979

Palumbo, D. G. *Secrets of Hakko Ryu Jujutsu.* Boulder, Colorado: Palladin Press, 1987.

Reed, W. *Ki: A Practical Guide for Westerners.* New York: Japan Publications, Inc., 1986.

Rogers, D. J. *Fighting to Win.* Garden City, New York: Doubleday & Co., 1984.

San Rafael Fire Department. "Home Preparedness" booklet, San Rafael, California: 1990.

Schachter, R., and C. S. McCauley. *When Your Child Is Afraid.* New York: Simon & Schuster, 1988.

Tohei, K. *Aikido in Daily Life.* Tokyo: Rikugei Publishing House, 1966.

Townley, R. *Safe and Sound.* New York: Simon & Schuster, 1985.

Trungpa, C. *Shambhala: The Sacred Path of the Warrior.* Boston: Shambhala Publications, 1984.

Tzu, S. *The Art of War.* (Translated by S. B. Griffith.) London: Oxford University Press, 1963.

Westbrook, A., and O. Ratti, *Aikido and the Dynamic Sphere.* Rutland, Vermont: Charles Tuttle & Co., 1970.

U. S. Army. *Military Leadership.* Field Manual 22–100, Washington, D.C.: 1983.

Yuzan, D. *Code of the Samurai.* (Translated by A. L. Sadler.) Rutland, Vermont: Charles Tuttle & Co., 1988.

Acknowledgments

From Both Authors

We gratefully acknowledge the people who helped to make this book a reality:

To Richard Grossinger, Sal Glynn, Lindy Hough and Jessie Woods of North Atlantic Books for their cooperation, support, and significant work in producing this book. To Perry Allen, Matt Barna, Paula Morrison and Paul Willis for illustrations and graphic design input. To Catherine Campaigne for typesetting the book.

To our friend, Dan Millman, for introducing us to each other, encouraging the completion of the project, and writing the foreword to this book. To Mary Tesoro for editing two chapters of an earlier manuscript. To Patrisha O'Sullivan and Brenda Phillips for secretarial/transcription work, and many useful suggestions. To John and Louise Clinkscales of Find Me, Inc., for providing valuable information on Missing Children and Child Abduction, and for allowing us to include this in the book. To Lisa Elliot, Rick Gibbins, Judith Hess, Rita Ornelas, Vince Ornelas, Susan Raczka, and Stephanie Samuels for their support of our workshop programs.

And lastly to Richard Pierce, Director of P.O.L.O. Productions, for his support and contribution to the overall project, and for his professional expertise in developing our videotape program.

From Bob

I gratefully acknowledge all those who, in one way or another, made my work on this project possible:

Firstly, to Sri Da Avabhasa. I am most grateful for his great wisdom teaching and presence in my life. And to the men, women, and children of the Free Daist Communion, who serve spiritual growth and human maturity.

To Susan, my love, for being there consistently, even during difficult times. To my mother, for her love and for never saying no when help was needed. To my father, and to Dotty, Joan, and Linda for love, patience and understanding. To the Hamanns, especially Charles and Peggy, and the entire Raczka family for their support.

To Matt, my co-author, for his friendship and inspiration as a creative and talented educator. To Paul Ekman, my mentor in the field of observational psychology, and to other friends at ESI who helped in my development as a security professional. To Robert Fritz for helping me to choose creation of this book for its own sake. To Ted Progler for counseling and consideration that led to the establishment of P.O.L.O. International, and to my former colleagues at EPA/Region IX, especially those from the old S&A division.

To my martial arts teachers and friends who taught me the ways of courage, good technique, and the warrior spirit: Jerry Bies, Hans Goto, Richard Heckler, Marshall Ho'O, Dan Innosanto, Wally Jay, Jerry Johnson, Rod Kobayashi, Rene Latosa, Greg Lee, Howard Lee, Gene Orro, Remy Presas, Dale Seago, Mark Sneller, Dennis Tatoian, Matt Thomas, and Julio Toribio.

To those in my life who have given love and lasting friendship: Barbara Axtell, Vince Battaglia, Dave Baumbach, Bob Casey, K. S. Chawla, Doug Childers, Cora Chun, Cathy Crum, Tom Crum, Bob Duggan, Rebecca Emch, Donna Gilcrease, Bruce Gordon, Ernie Halpert, Thomas Hirsch, Michael Kinsley, Bob Knight, Tony Konopka, William Kopiecki, Mary Beth Lufen, Kathleen Lustman, Matt Marx, Terry Patten, Lisa Pierce,

Richard Pierce, Steve Plocher, Jo Polito, Danny Poull, Gary Smith, and Mark Travis.

And lastly, to other friends, healers and teachers, not mentioned by name, who served me through illness and injury, and gave kindness, hospitality, and lessons along the way.

From Matt

I gratefully acknowledge all of the wonderful people in my life who helped to make this work possible:

To my family, Debra, Cully, Anders, and Johann, for their love, patience, and support.

To Bob Bishop, for his friendship, inspiration, professional expertise, wisdom, patience and true partnership.

To Denise Loveday, my business partner, co-instructor, co-author in other projects, co-producer, and acting partner.

To my birth mother, for loving me and caring for me long enough until she knew I would be safe.

To my parents, Anna and Joseph Thomas, for loving me, raising me, teaching me, and for bringing me to America.

To James, who became my older brother and early teacher, for protecting me and inspiring me.

To my many wonderful teachers: Beverly Kleinjan for inspiring me to academic and physical excellence and for opening my eyes to the world of literature and personal creativity; Gladys Katzman for encouraging me to think independently; Dan Millman, for teaching me to be a peaceful warrior and to teach with love, inspiration and joy, and for teaching me that there are no ordinary moments; Klaus Bensch for teaching me to think as a scientist, to "keep my b.s. detector in high gear at all times," for his faith in me to be my mentor throughout Stanford, and for his inspiration to use my academic knowledge for useful

purposes; Major Burbery, for teaching me that the purpose of a warrior is to preserve life and for introducing me to the academics of being a complete warrior in spirit, mind, and body and not just to be a soldier; Phillip Zimbardo for his work on cognitive dissonance; Albert Bandura for his work on Role Model learning; Karl Pribram for his work on the neurophysiology of learning; Collin Pittenridge for his work on animal communications; Carl Ebnother for his introduction to and exploration of the cutting edge of the science of mind and body; Ernst Hilgardt for his work on state conditioned learning; David Shapiro for his work on biofeedback as the key to long-term reflexive learning; Bud Winter for his work on optimal human performance by relaxing to win; Judy Brooks for teaching me to trust and acknowledge my intuitive self not only as an actor but as a teacher; Jerry Robinson for his work on optimal physical conditioning through Health for Life; Patrick Phair for his work in the Alexander Method; Stephen Young for opening the path to my own healing and for his work on relationships among fathers, sons, and brothers; Mary Allen for helping me come to terms with my own victimization by growing through it, and for her work on the fixative and transilient learning principles; Milton Katselas for his work using drama as a psychological learning tool; Bobbie Chance for her work on the intense personalization of roles to bring the role to life and the subsequent transformations in life; Lynn Phillips for his work on marketing and business in the real world; Greg Anton, Jim Hagen, Josh Henson, Alan Werthheimer, Howard Frumas, and Mark Fleischer for their legal counsel.

To many of my martial arts instructors but especially to my Shotokan sensei, Nishiyama, for the understanding of physical power; my Wing Chun sifu, Bill Paul, for integrating ethics and social purpose into my martial arts; my military Western warfare instructors who wish to remain anonymous, for their rig-

orous and realistic training; my kempo instructor, George Pega-low, for teaching me flexibility of styles, and our sensei, the "Father of Karate in America," Ed Parker, for his wisdom not only in the dojo but in the world of the politics of the martial arts, and for believing in me and encouraging me to grow into different arenas; my Thai kickboxing instructor, Joseph Milien, and our sifu, Carter Wong, for their work in realistic close quarters fighting; David Brown, Jeff and Kathy Adams, Danielle Evans, and Julio Toribio for demonstrating Aikido in daily life; Mike Alexander and a law enforcement instructor who wishes to remain anonymous, for their lessons on the criminal justice system and for the opportunities to train thousands of law enforcement officers; my Tibetan spiritual catalyst, Ron Lew, and Mark Wallach, for their work on anger management and Zen in the chaos; Mas Ayoob for his legal perspectives on real-istic martial arts; Paxton Quigley for teaching me about women's perspectives in realistic martial arts; Bob Duggan of ESI for his comprehensive wisdom on bodyguarding in the civilian world; Dale Seago for modernizing ninjutsu for the real world; Jim Mather for his wisdom on the business of the martial arts; my SOMBO instructor, Josh Henson, Joe Neely, president of SOM-BO USA, and the former head coach of the former Soviet Union, Alexandre Ionov, for opening the doors to one of the most comprehensive martial arts systems in the world; and last but by no means least, my son's karate instructor, Rob Alvelais, for inspiring my son to train in the martial arts.

To my teachers who taught me what not to be and my oppo-nents for showing me my shortcomings and weaknesses. Many lessons are learned the hard way.

To my many friends who have stood by me and helped me through the good times and bad.

Finally I wish to thank Lee Brandenberg, who gave me the portable computer that made writing this book possible.

About the Authors

Robert L. Bishop, Ph.D. (Bob)

Executive Director of P.O.L.O. International, an organization of educators and security professionals, Dr. Bishop leads seminars for corporate security and criminal justice professionals throughout the United States and Canada. His clients have included the California Department of Justice, and Board of Corrections, Municipal and Superior Court judges, trial lawyers, security management personnel from Fortune 500 companies, and a wide array of U.S. government, state, and municipal law enforcement agencies.

He is a member of the American Society of Law Enforcement Trainers, and the National Sheriffs' Association.

Bob is also the Seminar Program Director for Executive Security International. He teaches observational psychology and tactical communications as part of the Advanced Executive Protection Program at ESI. He was formerly an investigator for the U.S. Environmental Protection Agency, and was a founder of the Aspen Academy of Martial Arts. He is skilled in protection services, crisis intervention and negotiations, defensive tactics, and the martial arts. Bob holds a black belt in Hakko Ryu Jujutsu and is a certified instructor in the Filipino arts of Arnis and Escrima.

As a Peace Corps volunteer in India, Bob developed an educational program for science teachers that was duplicated throughout India and other South Asian countries. He graduated from CCNY with a degree in engineering. During his teens he spent time on the streets of New York City, where he learned first-hand lessons about fear and violence. He also learned the

value of loyalty among friends and family. These experiences greatly influenced his life and his interest in writing this book.

Dr. Bishop received his Ph.D. from Northwestern University, with research on the synthesis of design criteria from the individual perceptions of children. He is the author of numerous articles in scientific journals on environmental perception and nonverbal response.

He presently lives in northern California with his family.

Matthew J. Thomas, M.A. (Matt)

Matt Thomas was born of a Japanese mother and a Russian father during the occupation of Japan after World War II. He was adopted by American parents and came to the United States at an early age. As a young man he earned multiple-degree black belts in judo, karate, and kendo. He then went on to train in twenty additional styles of martial arts and was awarded a fourth degree black belt in the Russian art of Combat SOMBO.

Mr. Thomas founded Model Mugging in 1972. Widely hailed as the most effective women's self-defense program available, the training is now offered in major cities throughout the United States and Canada. Graduates who have used the program's physical techniques to stop an attack have either knocked out or disabled their assailants within a matter of seconds, as long as eight years after completing their training. The first Model Mugging course for men in 1989 was enthusiastically received by black-belt martial artists and law enforcement personnel, as well as beginners with no prior self-defense training.

Among the numerous courses Mr. Thomas has designed and taught for federal, state, and local government agencies and private corporations are Hostage Rescue Simulations for SWAT teams and the Bear Defense Course for the Alaska branch

of the U.S. Geological Survey. He has designed and implemented security procedures for multinational corporations and has provided executive protection for numerous private individuals.

Mr. Thomas received his bachelor's and master's degrees in biology from Stanford University, with honors. After attending Harvard Medical School for two years, he decided to pursue martial arts as a career. He also worked for several years as a stockbroker and international investment banker to finance his continuing martial arts training.

Presently Mr. Thomas works as an actor and technical advisor for the film industry with the Gersch Agency in Los Angeles and as a model with the STARS agency in San Francisco. He has three young sons, who are his main reasons for coauthoring this book.

Dead or Alive

"In the iconography of thrillers, a serial killer can be psychologically complex as well as gruesomely entertaining. But you can't beat a spree killer for raw action, and in *Dead or Alive* Michael McGarrity has produced a true monster in Craig Larson. . . . [McGarrity] knows the territory, which he portrays in a blunt, invigorating style that, even after a dozen books, still feels fresh." —Marilyn Stasio, *The New York Times Book Review*

"A taut and tidy thriller." —*The San Diego Union-Tribune*

"The book has the feel of a classic cowboy chase, with the good guys not quite catching up to the bad guy until the last pages."
—*Albuquerque Journal*

"Displays the author's usual fine sense of pace." —*Publishers Weekly*

"The story line is fast-paced and filled with much more blood than the usual Kerney whodunit and a strong sense of locale that would have pleased the late Tony Hillerman." —*Midwest Book Review*

Death Song

"McGarrity's dialogue is terse and natural, and the plot keeps moving forward. Given the climate of *Death Song*, McGarrity—who used to be deputy sheriff for Santa Fe County until turning crime novelist in the nineties—delivers maybe his most rugged, macho outing yet."
—*The Santa Fe New Mexican*

"McGarrity, a former deputy sheriff for Santa Fe County, writes convincingly about familial relationships, but his real forte is procedural detail: cops getting the job done by paying attention and grinding it out. . . . McGarrity brings back some of the noirish edge that distinguished Kerney's earlier outings. A solid effort from a reliable pro." —*Booklist*

"Gripping and well-crafted . . . confirms [McGarrity's] critical reputation as a superb writer of police procedural mysteries. . . . Former deputy sheriff McGarrity's complex characterizations and atmospheric settings combine with his richly detailed knowledge of police work, and the result—in this his latest and perhaps best Kevin Kerney novel—is top-notch entertainment." —*BookLoons*

continued . . .

"Michael McGarrity's well-received crime fiction relies on the melding of police procedures with a strong sense of place and sketched-out characters who resurface in his novels. . . . They are whodunits, New Mexico style."

—*Albuquerque Journal*

"A terrific police procedural with double the fun as father and son work together to solve the homicides. . . . Fans of the series know that Michael McGarrity always provides a strong New Mexico mystery; newcomers will seek the back list when retirement was a long way off for the hero."

—*Midwest Book Review*

Nothing but Trouble

"McGarrity combines a gift for tangled plots and great storytelling with realistic police procedures." —*Albuquerque Journal*

"I wish that more writers could churn out a novel as smoothly as Michael McGarrity. . . . His style is un-self-conscious; his protagonist is low-key; his narrative is layered but not overstuffed; his politics are subtle but discernible—and he's produced a well-crafted tale. . . . *Nothing but Trouble* feels nothing if not authentic. Setting, police procedure, filmmaking, even little current-event comments read as genuine." —*Tucson Weekly*

"McGarrity's trademark realism holds true . . . as does his smooth dialogue, and he shifts point of view seamlessly. . . . The Santa Fe–based best-selling author sure can make a locale come to life. . . . The Southwest has never looked better." —*The Santa Fe New Mexican*

Slow Kill

"McGarrity . . . [at] his most polished and involved. . . . Credit McGarrity for his ability to propel the reader into the next scene."

—*Albuquerque Journal*

"Combin[es] realistic police procedures with well-drawn characters . . . [a] crisply told story." —*USA Today*

"Trademark realism. . . . McGarrity [is] a master . . . imaginative, intelligent . . . another solidly built tale from McGarrity."

—*The Santa Fe New Mexican*

"[McGarrity] excels at detailing police procedures as well as creating a homespun, wry tone that suits setting and characters."

—*Publishers Weekly*

Also by Michael McGarrity

Tularosa

Mexican Hat

Serpent Gate

Hermit's Peak

The Judas Judge

Under the Color of Law

The Big Gamble

Everyone Dies

Slow Kill

Nothing but Trouble

Death Song

MICHAEL McGARRITY

DEAD OR ALIVE

A KEVIN KERNEY NOVEL

 NEW AMERICAN LIBRARY

New American Library
Published by New American Library, a division of
Penguin Group (USA) Inc., 375 Hudson Street,
New York, New York 10014, USA
Penguin Group (Canada), 90 Eglinton Avenue East, Suite 700, Toronto,
Ontario M4P 2Y3, Canada (a division of Pearson Penguin Canada Inc.)
Penguin Books Ltd., 80 Strand, London WC2R 0RL, England
Penguin Ireland, 25 St. Stephen's Green, Dublin 2,
Ireland (a division of Penguin Books Ltd.)
Penguin Group (Australia), 250 Camberwell Road, Camberwell, Victoria 3124,
Australia (a division of Pearson Australia Group Pty Ltd.)
Penguin Books India Pvt. Ltd., 11 Community Centre, Panchsheel Park,
New Delhi – 110 017, India
Penguin Group (NZ), 67 Apollo Drive, Rosedale, North Shore 0632,
New Zealand (a division of Pearson New Zealand Ltd.)
Penguin Books (South Africa) (Pty.) Ltd., 24 Sturdee Avenue,
Rosebank, Johannesburg 2196, South Africa

Penguin Books Ltd., Registered Offices:
80 Strand, London WC2R 0RL, England

Published by New American Library, a division of Penguin Group (USA) Inc.
Previously published in a Dutton edition.

First New American Library Printing, December 2009
10 9 8 7 6 5 4 3 2

 REGISTERED TRADEMARK—MARCA REGISTRADA

New American Library Trade Paperback ISBN: 978-0-451-22870-3

The Library of Congress has cataloged the hardcover edition of this title as follows:
McGarrity, Michael.
Dead or alive: a Kevin Kerney novel/Michael McGarrity.
p. cm.
ISBN 978-0-525-95081-3
1. Kerney, Kevin (Fictitious character)—Fiction. 2. Police—New Mexico—Santa Fe—Fiction.
3. Police chiefs—Fiction. 4. Santa Fe (N.M.)—Fiction. I. Title.
PS3563.C36359D42 2009b
813'.54—dc22   2009028134

Set in Sabon
Designed by Leonard Telesca

Printed in the United States of America

For Flynn Raven McGarrity

ACKNOWLEDGMENTS

Thanks go to Chief Rick Sinclair and Officer Mitch Sutton of the Springer Police Department; Officer Christopher Blake of the New Mexico State Police; Adriane DeSavorgnani of the United States Embassy, London; and Colonel Anita M. Domingo, United States Army attaché at the United States Embassy, London, who provided me with invaluable help during the research phase for the book.

A very special thanks to Ms. Angela Gill of Kent, England, a dear friend who served brilliantly as my research assistant during my fact-finding trip to London.

DEAD OR ALIVE

Chapter**One**

Craig Larson stood in the middle of the crowded Bernalillo County Detention Center recreation yard and listened in disbelief as a dumb-ass guard told him he was going to be transported immediately to a minimum security prison outside his hometown of Springer, New Mexico. As it sunk in, Larson wondered if he was just about to become one of the luckiest jailbirds in the whole frigging world. Speechless, he stood rooted to the ground, looking at the guard with his mouth open.

"Come on," the guard said. "Get moving."

Larson nodded agreeably and followed alongside the guard, who explained that he would be processed out and turned over to a Department of Corrections officer for the trip to Springer.

"Got any personal stuff in your cell?" the guard asked.

Larson shook his head. Convicted but not yet sentenced, Larson knew there was no way in hell he was supposed to be going to the minimum security facility. All he could figure was that some dip-shit jail employee or retarded court clerk had screwed up. If that was the case, maybe lady luck was smiling.

Larson had jumped bail on the day of his sentencing hearing just over a year ago, after being convicted of embezzling over two million dollars from the estate of an elderly art dealer he'd once worked for. He'd been a fugitive from justice until last month, when cops busted him in an apartment two blocks from the beach in Venice, California, where he'd been shacking up with a divorced, thirty-something schoolteacher with thick ankles and a willing disposition to please.

Extradited back to New Mexico and booked into the county lockup, Larson had cooled his heels for two days before his attorney, Terry Foster, showed up. When Larson told Foster he didn't like being in jail at all and asked if there was any way in hell he could make bail, the mouthpiece choked back a laugh.

Without attempting to hide his disdain, he told Larson that he faced additional counts for unlawful flight, and because of that the judge would most likely sentence him to the maximum time for his embezzlement conviction. With a touch of glee, Foster also noted that Larson's fugitive status for more than a year would probably put him in the super-max prison outside of Santa Fe with the hard-core, badass cons. Foster concluded the meeting by telling Larson to find another attorney.

Larson figured Foster was pissed at him because he'd never been paid. But he also believed Foster had given him the straight scoop, because it jibed with what the old jailbirds in the county lockup had been telling him.

Until the guard said he was being transferred to Springer, Larson had contemplated faking alcohol addiction and a suicide attempt to see if he could get sent to a rehab program rather than prison. He knew he wasn't the type to thrive in an iron-pumping, career-criminal, alpha-male penal institution.

Larson didn't think of himself as overly aggressive or cruel. As he saw it, using guile, charm, and smarts was a much better way to commit crimes than violence. He resorted to that only when absolutely necessary.

The embezzlement conviction was nothing more than a one-time misstep on his part. Fortunately, the investigators on the case had been as dumb as most cops. Otherwise he would probably be looking at life without parole on death row.

In the processing area, Larson saw enough of the paperwork in front of a bleary-eyed guard to learn that he had been mistaken for another inmate with the same name who was slated to do eighteen months at Springer for a hit-and-run DWI accident.

The guard looked like he'd been held over to work a second shift. He barely glanced at Larson as he processed him out. The state correctional officer cuffed Larson's hands behind his back and marched him to the sally port where an empty Department of Corrections van waited.

"Am I your only passenger today, Officer?" he asked as the guard pushed him into the passenger compartment behind the steel cage that protected the driver. The name tag on his uniform shirt read "D. Trujillo."

"You're it," Trujillo replied gruffly.

Larson immediately started thinking that a breakaway might be possible. How to make it happen was the question. "Could you handcuff me at the front rather than behind my back?" he asked. "My arms and wrists really start to hurt when I'm cuffed this way."

Trujillo thought about it. Larson was a middle-aged white guy with no priors who'd been convicted of nonviolent crimes. "Okay, step out of the vehicle."

Trujillo made the switch, put Larson back in the van, locked his feet to leg shackles bolted to the floorboards, closed the side door, and got behind the wheel.

The sally port door opened and sunlight poured into the dimly lit space. Larson did some mental calculating as Trujillo drove outside into the glare of a hot, cloudless July day. Springer was a good two hundred miles up the interstate from Albuquerque. The drive gave him about three hours to figure out how to persuade Trujillo to stop, unshackle him, and let him out of the van. Even then, how would he get away?

Trujillo packed a semiautomatic sidearm and had a shotgun in a rack attached to the dashboard within easy reach. Both weapons were formidable obstacles to any escape attempt.

Larson listened as Trujillo advised a radio dispatcher that he was under way, transporting one prisoner. He held his breath, half-expecting to hear Trujillo ordered back to the jail, but the radio remained silent. In a few minutes, they were beyond the perimeter of the jail grounds, cruising toward the interstate, and Larson started breathing easier.

"I get really, really car sick sitting in the back," he said.

"You can shit your pants and throw up all over yourself back there. Makes no matter to me," Trujillo replied. "I'll just crank up the air conditioner to get rid of the smell and hose down the inside of the vehicle after we get to Springer. I don't stop until we get there."

"You'd do that rather than let me puke outside?"

"Yeah," Trujillo said with a slight smile. "And if you puke on yourself, you'll get hosed down too."

"Wonderful," Larson replied. "I thought Springer was a boys' school for juvenile delinquents."

"It was, up until a couple of years ago," Trujillo answered as he drove the van onto the northbound I-25 on-ramp.

Trujillo looked like he was in his mid-fifties, which made him ten to twelve years older than Larson. He had a round head, cauliflower ears, pudgy cheeks, and didn't resemble any of the Trujillos that Larson had known in his youth. But he'd been away from his hometown for almost twenty-five years and how people looked back then was pretty much a dim memory.

Larson decided to probe. "Are you from Springer, Officer Trujillo?"

Trujillo shot him a hard glance in the rearview mirror. "I don't need you trying to make small talk with me."

Larson shrugged, smiled pleasantly, and looked out the window. In a few minutes, they would be on the outskirts of Albuquerque heading north. Assuming the identity mix-up at the jail stayed undiscovered, what could he do to get free?

He'd lied about getting carsick, but that ploy hadn't worked. Getting Trujillo to cuff his hands in front gave him more use of his hands and arms. But that would be of no advantage unless he got unshackled and out of the cage. Other than the puking idea, nothing came to him.

He turned away from the window to find Trujillo checking up on him in the rearview mirror, and the thought hit him that the man couldn't possibly be from Springer, a town of no more than thirteen hundred people. Unless he'd only just moved there, he would have seen the resemblance to Larson's identical twin brother, Kerry, who lived on a ranch five miles outside of town.

Larson smiled.

"What's so funny?" Trujillo asked.

"I just bet you're not from Springer," Larson said.

Trujillo grunted in reply.

"Come on," Larson prodded with an easy smile. "Am I right or am I wrong?"

Trujillo sighed. "I'm from Raton, okay? Now just shut up and let me drive."

"Whatever you say," Larson replied as he turned his head to look back out the window. Trujillo kept the van in the right-hand lane of the interstate, and a steady flow of vehicles, including big-rig trucks, passed them by. Larson leaned forward and glanced through the cage at the dashboard speedometer. Trujillo had the van cruising along at a safe and sane seventy miles per hour.

They reached a long stretch of open road and Larson told Trujillo he was getting really sick to his stomach.

"Like I said before," Trujillo replied, "go ahead and puke all over yourself. I ain't stopping."

Larson made a couple of gagging sounds, tried to look sour,

which wasn't all that difficult, leaned back, and closed his eyes. Unless lady luck dealt him a couple more good cards, he was doomed to ride all the way to Springer only to be sent right back to Albuquerque and then on to the super-max with the hard-core badasses after sentencing. The thought made him shudder.

Beyond Santa Fe the traffic thinned out considerably. In an attempt to wear Trujillo down, Larson complained again about being sick, but got no response. He stared at his shackled feet and wondered if he could yank his legs free, kick the cage apart, and wrap his cuffed hands around Trujillo's neck and strangle him without getting himself killed in a car wreck.

He pulled hard at a shackle with his leg. The steel ring bit into his ankle and made him wince.

Halfway between Santa Fe and Las Vegas, the van blew a rear tire and slewed wildly. Trujillo steered into a spin, got the van straightened out, and braked gradually as he pulled to the shoulder of the highway. He got out to inspect the damage, then called dispatch, gave his location, and reported the tire failure.

"Do you need assistance and backup at your twenty?" the dispatcher asked.

"Negative," Trujillo replied. He clipped the microphone to the dash and opened his door.

"Since we're stopped, will you let me out so I can throw up behind a tree?" Larson asked.

Trujillo eyed Larson through the cage. He would much rather not have the vehicle smelling of puke. "Okay."

He stepped out of the van, opened the sliding passenger door, unlocked the leg shackles, unbuckled Larson's seat belt, and motioned him out of the van. "Let's go. I'm right behind you."

Trujillo prodded Larson toward a big cedar tree near a wire fence twenty feet from the shoulder of the roadway. "Get it over with," he said, his hand resting on the butt of his holstered sidearm.

Larson dropped to his knees under a branch of the tree. He brought some bile up and spit it out as his hand reached for a small stick lying in the duff.

"Is that it?" Trujillo asked derisively, leaning over Larson's shoulder.

"Give me a minute," Larson said. He grasped the stick so that the end protruded from his closed palm, and with his head lowered, he gagged some more for effect and faked throwing up. He shivered, coughed, spit, and waited until he couldn't hear the sound of any cars on the interstate.

"Are you done?" Trujillo asked.

Larson nodded but stayed put, hoping Trujillo would step closer and look down to see whether or not he'd been faking it. Just as he lifted his head, Trujillo came closer, within striking distance. Larson uncoiled and sprang, jamming the stick into Trujillo's left eye. The stick protruding from his eyeball snapped off and Trujillo screamed as he hit the dirt.

Larson stepped back, kicked him hard in the balls, leaned down, and drove an elbow into Trujillo's left eye. He straddled Trujillo, snatched his semiautomatic from the holster, slapped the barrel against his head, and pulled the limp body out of sight of the roadway, just before a car whizzed by. He fished a key ring out of Trujillo's pants pocket, undid the handcuffs, and looked down. Blood poured from Trujillo's mangled eye but he was still alive.

Larson thought about finishing Trujillo off and decided against adding a murder charge to his sheet. He shed his orange jail jumpsuit, pulled Trujillo's pants off, then rolled him on his stomach and cuffed his hands behind his back.

The pants were way too big around the waist and about three inches too short. Larson cinched them tight with Trujillo's belt, tapped the officer one more time on the head with the semiautomatic to keep him unconscious, and set to work changing the flat tire on the van.

As Larson tightened the last lug nut on the spare, a voice over the radio inside the van asked Trujillo to report in. Larson got behind the wheel and keyed the microphone several times to make static noises, hoping it would sound like a radio transmission failure. Then he floored the accelerator and drove away.

There was an undeveloped rest stop a few miles farther up. Larson knew he needed to ditch the Department of Corrections vehicle as soon as possible and find new wheels. Hopefully, a trucker would be parked there for a mandatory rest break or some motorist who couldn't hold his water would be making a quick pit stop behind a tree.

The only vehicle at the rest stop was a Honda SUV. A young, good-looking woman in shorts and a halter top stood at the open tailgate at the back of the vehicle, changing a baby's diaper. Nearby, a young man walked a small dog on a leash near a tree.

Larson pulled in next to the Honda to shield it as much as possible from motorists passing by, ripped the microphone cord off the radio in the van, and jumped out. The young woman turned. The startled look on her pretty face turned to anger when he grabbed her around the neck, pressed the semiautomatic against her head, and told her not to move. The man walking the dog froze.

"Don't be stupid if you want this pretty lady to live," Larson called out. "Walk toward me."

The young man had dark, curly hair; scared eyes; and a face that looked like it hadn't been used yet. He dropped the leash and the yappy dog took off after a rabbit on the other side of the fence.

Larson cocked the hammer for effect. "Now," he ordered.

The man took a few cautious steps and stopped. "Don't hurt my wife and baby," he said anxiously, his voice cracking.

"Do as I say and you all might live." Larson backed up to the van, pulling the woman with him, and told her to open the side door. "Pick up your baby and bring it over here," he ordered the man.

Larson glanced at the naked infant. It was a girl, maybe six months old, lying on a dirty diaper that was soaked in gooey, mustard-colored, stinky shit.

The man came forward, picked up the baby, and walked toward Larson.

"Get in the vehicle and slide all the way over to the far side."

Cradling the baby in his arms, the young man climbed in the van and scooted across the seat.

Larson put the barrel of the handgun under the woman's right arm and pressed it against her breast. "Get in beside them," he ordered.

Flashing a look of pure hate, the woman climbed into the van. She wore a wedding band that matched the one on the man's ring finger.

"Give me your car keys," Larson said.

"They're in the ignition," the woman said before her husband could respond.

Larson smiled at her. She was the one who had the balls in the marriage. "If they're not in the ignition, I'll kill you all."

The man dropped his eyes, but the woman didn't even flinch. "Like I said," she replied, "they're in the ignition."

"Good." Larson pointed the semiautomatic at the man. "Toss me your cell phone."

Wordlessly, the man unclipped the phone from his belt and tossed it to Larson.

Larson ground it under his foot as he smiled at the woman, thinking she would probably be dynamite in bed if someone made her pay attention properly.

"See the sets of shackles at your feet." He pointed his handgun at the floorboard. "Lock them around your husband's ankles and then do the same to yourself."

The woman snapped on the shackles and then looked Larson squarely in the eye. "Please leave the door open. Otherwise it will get too hot in here for the baby."

Larson laughed. Even with a gun in her face, she'd scoped out the fact that a van for transporting convicts had passenger doors and windows that couldn't be opened from the inside. "You're a piece of work, sweetie, I'll give you that."

He got in the driver's seat, drove the van behind a large juniper tree where it was hidden from the interstate, cut the engine, turned his head, and looked at the young family through the cage.

"I should kill you all," Larson said.

"Please leave the doors and windows open," the woman said.

Larson grinned at the woman. "You say please, but you don't mean it. I should take you with me and teach you how to say it, honey."

The woman gave him the finger.

"That wasn't nice," Larson chided.

He took the shotgun from the dashboard rack and put it on the backseat of the Honda. Then he closed all the van doors and windows, locked the man, woman, and child inside, and drove away. Since he was almost halfway to Springer, he decided to stop in and see his twin brother, Kerry. He had a quick question to ask him.

•••

There weren't any good alternate routes to Springer so Larson stayed on the interstate, keeping an eye out for cops. He made it to the Springer exit without a problem and drove directly to find his brother, who worked on a ranch along a two-lane highway that looped through open range to the town of Cimarron, some thirty miles distant.

The ranch had once been independently owned, but now was part of a bigger spread controlled by a prominent New Mexico family with strong political connections.

Larson hadn't visited Kerry at the ranch for a good ten years, and he rattled the Honda along the ranch road that he remembered as being lined with large shade trees. Most of the trees were dead or stunted from drought.

He stopped in front of a cluster of barns, sheds, and corrals. Off in the distance on a small rise he could see the campus of the new prison where the Springer Boys' School once stood. For a moment Larson wondered if Officer Trujillo was dead and if the young couple and their baby would survive. He decided it really didn't matter and went looking for Kerry.

Larson's brother was a full-time mechanic for the horse and cattle outfit. Cowboying had been his passion from the time they first did it as a summer job in their early teens. Larson liked the riding-around part, but thought it was way too much work for way too little money. A bad fall off a horse had forced Kerry to change jobs, and since he was naturally good with his hands he became a mechanic.

One of the barns served as Kerry's garage. The doors were open and country music blared from a beat-up boom box on the hard-packed dirt floor inside. A ranch pickup truck on blocks had had its transmission yanked, and the cannibalized remains of two four-wheel ATVs were parked along the back wall.

Larson called out for his brother and got no answer. A grimy, long-sleeved denim shirt and a stained baseball cap hung on a peg near the doorway. Larson put the shirt on over his jail-issue T-shirt to hide the semiautomatic stuck under his belt, and checked the other barn and a nearby horse stable. There were horses in the corrals but the barn and stable were empty inside.

He walked down the winding lane to the dell where the ranch house and guest cottage were nestled under large cottonwoods. The rambling hacienda had a long portal on the back side with an expanse of lawn enclosed by a low adobe wall. A flagstone path wandered from a gate in the wall to the guest cottage.

The main house was used infrequently by the owners to put up visiting family members, friends, livestock buyers, and the occasional hunter who paid for the right to hunt big game on the ranch. Kerry got free rent in the cottage for looking after the place when nobody was in residence.

Drawn window shades and curtains and the absence of any vehicles in the circular driveway told Larson the house was most likely unoccupied.

A heavy-duty pickup truck was parked outside the guest cottage. Larson had sent his brother the money to buy it. Through the open windows he could hear the sound of a noontime television news broadcast from one of the Albuquerque stations.

Before Larson got to the front porch, Kerry slammed the screen door open, hooted, and gave him a bear hug.

"What the hell are you doing here?" he asked with a grin.

Larson grinned back. "Saying hello to you, younger brother."

Kerry had been born twenty-five minutes after Larson. Except for Kerry being a quarter-inch shorter, seeing him was like looking in a mirror. They had the same baby-fine brown hair, light brown eyes, nose with a crease right down the middle, and prominent chin with a small dimple.

Because of a difficult birth that cut off his oxygen supply, Kerry wasn't nearly as bright as he should have been. In school, he'd tested in the very low normal IQ range and had been put in the slow classes.

"How come you're wearing my old greasy shirt?" Kerry asked.

"Because I like it," Larson answered.

Kerry laughed and held the screen door open. "Come on inside."

The front room of the cottage was neat as a pin. An easy chair faced a flat-screen television that sat on a sturdy handmade stand. A framed photograph on the wall showed Larson and Kerry on horseback when they were kids.

"I need to know who you told that I was staying in Venice," Larson said as he joined Kerry in the adjacent kitchen. After getting busted, he'd learned that a Crime Stoppers tip out of New Mexico had led the cops to him. Only Kerry had known where he was staying.

"No one," Kerry answered quickly with a shake of his head. He pointed at a half-eaten sandwich on a plate. "You want me to make you a sandwich?"

"No thanks. Somebody knew, Kerry. You told somebody where I was hanging my hat."

Kerry looked down at his boots.

"Tell me who it was," Larson demanded.

"Lenny," Kerry replied slowly.

"I don't know anybody named Lenny."

"Lenny Hampson. Came here from Texas. He's good people. Does auto body repairs out of his garage at his house. Sometimes we get together and have a beer at Josie's. He heard about you and thinks you're really cool. I told him you were laying low in Venice, but I didn't give him your address or anything like that. I swear to it."

"I believe you, little brother. Did you tell anybody else?"

"Nope."

"You're sure?"

"Yep."

"Do you still have any of that money I sent you?"

Kerry nodded. "I paid cash for my truck like you told me, bought some tools and the new TV, and kept the rest for a rainy day."

"Let me have it," Lawson said, figuring Kerry had held on to a good ten thousand dollars. "I'll pay you back."

Kerry's smile faded.

"What is it?"

"I've been thinking about getting a new deer rifle."

"Keep what you need for that and loan me the rest," Larson said.

Kerry's smile returned. He took a flour jar from a cupboard shelf, pulled out three thick wads of twenties and fifties, counted out what he needed for the rifle, and handed Larson the rest.

Larson smiled approvingly. "That's perfect. Now, if I were to visit your friend Lenny, where would I find him?"

Kerry gave Larson directions to Lenny's house. It was right in town, off a highway that ran east to the Oklahoma state line.

"Let me borrow a set of clean clothes, younger brother," Larson said.

"You could use some fresh duds," Kerry replied with a chuckle. "I never saw you looking so grubby."

Larson washed up and picked out a pair of fresh blue jeans with razor-sharp creases, a long-sleeved cowboy shirt, and a pair of boots. Everything fit perfectly. In the front room he took one of Kerry's cowboy hats off a wall rack next to the door, pocketed the money, rolled up the clothes he'd been wearing and put them under his arm, stuck the sidearm in his waistband, and told Kerry that he had to get going. He stretched his free arm around his brother's shoulders, gave him a playful shake, and asked him not to tell anyone he'd stopped by for a visit.

Kerry made a zipped-lips motion with his fingers and smiled in his typical bland, gullible way.

"I'll call you from the road," Larson said. "Does Lenny have anybody working with him?"

"He sure don't."

Larson left his brother on the front porch, walked up the lane, got in the Honda, and drove away. It was time to find a new vehicle, and he knew just the man to help him make the switch.

The garage where Kerry's pal Lenny had his auto body repair shop was along an alley at the back of a house. Parked at the side of the garage were four cars with crumpled fenders, bashed-in front ends, or smashed door panels. Along the backyard fence, a sweet four-wheel-drive pickup with an off-road package was parallel parked.

The sound of a grinder on metal greeted Larson as he got out of the Honda. He spotted Lenny at the back of the garage, working on a rear rocker panel, and walked to him.

When Lenny looked up and saw Larson, he turned off the grinder, lowered his mask, and smiled. "What brings you by here in the middle of the day?" he asked. "You got some work for me?"

Larson had figured Lenny would mistake him for Kerry. He pulled out the semiautomatic and pointed it at Lenny's face. "You've got the wrong twin, my friend."

Lenny pushed his safety goggles up to his forehead and blinked hard. His face flushed red and he started to breathe rapidly. "What's the gun for?"

"You're kidding, right?" Larson said. Lenny was short. In fact you could call him stubby. He had big round eyes and a thick neck that made him look porky.

Lenny put the grinder down. "I don't even know you, mister."

Larson half-expected him to start stuttering like Porky Pig. "I'm going to kill you for calling Crime Stoppers on me."

"I did no such thing," Lenny blustered, almost stuttering.

"That's a lie, Lenny. Tell me one more lie and you're a dead man. Did you do it for the money?"

Lenny stared into Larson's eyes for a long moment and then slowly nodded. "Times are hard. I needed the cash. Ain't even got it yet."

Larson smiled. "That's better, Lenny. It's always good to tell the truth."

"Don't kill me."

"We'll see about that. How about we get in your truck and go for a ride."

"Take the truck, the keys are in it."

"I need a driver, Lenny. Is it gassed up?"

"I filled the tank yesterday."

"Excellent. Do a good job as my driver and I might let you live. But first, we need to bring that Honda in here and lock it in your garage. Let's go."

Larson kept Lenny company with the handgun aimed at his chest while the Honda got put away out of sight. In the pickup, Larson stowed the rolled-up clothes under the passenger seat with the shotgun and told Lenny to head east on the state highway toward the town of Clayton.

"Where are you taking me?" Lenny asked. He was sweating through his shirt.

"On a scenic country drive." Larson cranked up the air conditioner. "How long have you lived in Springer, Lenny?"

"Twelve years come this September. I got a wife and two teen-age kids. That's why I needed the money."

"Perfectly understandable," Larson said amiably. "Do you know the back roads around here?"

"Some," Lenny answered.

"Good. I'm gonna tell you what roads to take. If you get me to where I want to go, you may just live to spend that Crime Stoppers money on your wife and kids. You savvy?"

Lenny gulped and nodded.

About twenty-five miles outside of town, Larson directed Lenny to an unpaved county road that headed south. They followed it to a few miles north of the village of Roy, where it joined up with a two-lane state highway. Past the village a turnoff took them near the famous Bell Ranch and across the Canadian River.

They were traveling in the least populated area of New Mexico, where cows outnumbered the people and traffic was almost nonexistent. A few miles beyond the small Hispanic settlement of Trementia, Larson ordered Lenny off the pavement onto a country road that wandered through a vast basin peppered with red-rock mesas. When the country road turned into a seldom-used ranch road, Lenny's pickup truck with the off-road option package handled the washouts, deep ruts, and boulders without difficulty.

Ten miles beyond the cutoff to the ranch headquarters, Larson ordered Lenny to stop the truck. "Get out," he said when Lenny killed the engine.

"What are you going to do?" Lenny asked in a shaky voice.

The bright afternoon sun bounced off the hood of the truck. It was getting on to the hottest time of the day. There were few clouds in the sky and virtually no shade on the parched basin. Heat waves rising from the ground distorted Larson's view of a few nearby stray cows that had raised their heads at the sound of the truck.

Larson waved the gun at Lenny. "Out."

Lenny scrambled out of the truck.

Larson slid behind the wheel and opened the driver's-side window. "It's ten miles back to the ranch headquarters cutoff and about twelve miles to Santa Rosa. You get to pick which way you want to go."

"Don't leave me out here without water," Lenny pleaded.

"If you'd rather, I'll shoot you now and leave you for the buzzards."

Lenny shook his head. "Don't do that."

"My brother likes your company, Lenny, that's the only reason you're still alive. Buy him a beer when you get that Crime Stoppers check."

Lenny nodded, lowered his eyes, and looked away.

Larson closed the window and drove off. The dust kicked up by the rear tires momentarily obscured Lenny as he stood at the side of the road. Larson thought about backing up and shooting Lenny just to be on the safe side, and he braked the truck to a stop. Through the rearview mirror he saw Lenny take off like a jackrabbit at a dead run cross-country.

He drove on, calculating it would take Lenny a good four or five hours to reach civilization on foot and get to a telephone, if he didn't die from dehydration first. He would have to ditch the truck and find another ride, but he had more than enough time to get to Santa Fe before then.

Larson pressed the accelerator and bounced the truck over some big rocks. If he remembered correctly, he had about another mile of rough road before it smoothed out.

• • •

Larson hadn't eaten since breakfast, and it was getting on toward late afternoon. In Santa Rosa, a town that catered to travelers on Interstate 40, a major east-west highway, he stopped, loaded up on snack food and soft drinks, and continued westbound. Traffic was fairly light and the big rigs pushed along at eighty miles an hour or more, only slowing to form convoys in the right-hand lane on the long hill climbs. Most of the passenger cars that passed him were from out of state.

Larson knew the route was heavily patrolled by state police, so he kept his speed at the posted limit and fell in behind a rancher in a big old diesel truck pulling a horse trailer. He tensed up when a black-and-white patrol car came at him traveling in the opposite direction, but it kept going and soon disappeared from sight.

He got off the interstate at the Clines Corner exit and headed north toward Santa Fe. He'd started the day in Albuquerque and was about to make almost a complete circle and end it in Santa Fe. There was no one behind him until he reached the White Lakes turnoff, when headlights appeared in his rearview mirror, coming up fast. He cut his speed in case it was a cop, and was quickly overtaken and passed by a black SUV with Texas plates.

Another set of headlights soon appeared in his rearview mirror, and Larson winced when the car closed and he saw the emergency light bar on the roof and the telltale spotlight mounted on the driver's-side door. On a straight stretch of pavement, Larson slowed slightly to give the cop car a chance to pass, but it hung back. He tried again at the next passing zone but still the cop stayed behind him.

Larson's mind started racing. If Trujillo had survived and the young family had been rescued, that would put the cops on to the Department of Corrections van and the Honda, but not Lenny's truck. Had some cowboy with a cell phone on his way back to the ranch picked up Lenny in the desert and called the cops? He groaned in disgust at himself. He should have killed them all.

He checked the rearview mirror, trying to see if the cop was talking on his radio, but he couldn't make anything out. If it was a tail and the cop had called for backup, somewhere up ahead there was sure to be a swarm of police blocking the highway. He decided to get off the pavement to see what the cop would do.

He crossed the bridge that spanned the railroad tracks near the village of Lamy, flashed his turn signal, and made a left onto a ranch road. He drove slowly for a quarter mile, constantly checking the rearview mirror for any sign of the cop car. The road behind remained empty, but that didn't mean anything.

Where the ranch road divided, he took the right fork, which dipped into a canyon and rose toward a house that sat on the crest. He topped out to find a truck and small SUV parked in front of the house. A horse barn with a corral stood about a quarter mile across a grassy field, and dirt tracks traveled up a small hill toward a big piñon tree. In the canyon below there was no cop car or sign of dust kicked up by tires.

Larson decided to switch vehicles. He pulled to a stop, honked the horn, got out, and rang the front doorbell. After waiting a minute, he rang again. When nobody answered, he checked the SUV and truck, only to find them locked.

Larson figured the ranch belonged to one of those rich easterners who liked to play part-time cowboy while the wife shopped Santa Fe. He smashed a glass patio door with the handgun and went looking for car keys. He snatched them from a wall rack in the mudroom just off the kitchen and came outside just as a pickup truck came down the dirt track.

He stuck the car keys in his pocket, hid the weapon behind his leg, and waved as the truck skidded to a stop. A perturbed-looking cowboy in his twenties piled out.

"What are you doing here?" the young man demanded.

"I just stopped by to visit and found that patio door busted," Larson said, bluffing.

"Hogwash. I was here twenty minutes ago and everything was okay."

"Well, it ain't okay now," Larson replied as he brought the handgun up and shot the cowboy twice in the chest.

The man coughed, clutched his chest, and collapsed to his knees. Blood stained his shirt and hands as he fell forward on his face.

Larson stepped up and turned the man over. This one was dead. Now for sure he'd be facing a murder one charge if he got caught.

He got into the SUV and drove back to the fork in the road where the vast Galisteo Basin spread out before him. The other branch of the road paralleled a broad, sandy arroyo. Should he return the way he'd come or take a chance on finding another outlet?

He decided to find another way to Santa Fe. If necessary, he'd drive cross-country and bust through fences. Once he got to Santa Fe, he'd leave the SUV in the mall parking lot at the south end of the city, take a bus downtown, and walk to Jeannie Cooper's South Capitol apartment.

He'd given her a hefty sum of money to keep something for him and now he needed to collect it.

Chapter Two

Jeannie Cooper rented a small one-bedroom apartment on a dead-end street in Santa Fe within shouting distance of the state capitol. Larson's knock at the door went unanswered. From a small enclosed patio at the rear of the apartment, he peered through the kitchen window. There was no movement inside.

Larson figured breaking in to search for the property he'd left with Jeannie would not be wise. He had ditched the SUV and was on foot. Without transportation, making a quick getaway if he had to would be impossible. He settled into an old lawn chair on the patio, out of sight from any nearby nosy neighbors, and waited for Jeannie to come home.

Larson had met Jeannie when he'd been working for Melvin and Viola Bedford as their personal assistant. He'd carefully murdered the elderly couple one at a time over a two-year period while embezzling money from their estate. He'd blown most of it on women and vacations at luxury resorts, and had even spent a few bucks on Jeannie, an employee of the landscape company that maintained the grounds at the Bedford residence. As far as Larson knew, she was still watering flowers, pruning shrubs, and pulling weeds for a living.

She was also manic-depressive, what the shrinks called bipolar. When she was up, she could be great fun. But when her dark moods hit, she became self-destructive and impossible to deal with.

Around dusk, the sound of a vehicle pulling into the parking space at the front of the apartment building brought Larson to his feet. He intercepted Jeannie as she unlocked her front door and turned the doorknob.

She looked at him with wide-eyed surprise. "Craig. I thought you were in jail. That's what the paper said."

Larson pushed the door open and put a hand on her back to hurry her inside. "I'm out on bail. I need that strongbox I left with you."

He turned on the ceiling light and looked around the small, tidy living room. A shipshape apartment meant that Jeannie was probably stabilized on her medication and neither manic nor depressed.

"What strongbox?" Jeannie asked.

"Don't give me that crap." Larson pushed her down on the couch. "You know what I'm talking about. I gave you a box of papers to keep for me."

Jeannie gave him a belligerent look. "I don't have anything that belongs to you."

Larson stared at her. When Jeannie got stubborn, she completely shut down, and he didn't have time to wait her out. Better play nice. He sat next to her, sighed, and said, "Maybe I'm mistaken, but I thought for sure I'd left a strongbox with you for safekeeping."

Jeannie smiled tentatively. "Not that I remember."

Larson patted Jeannie's hand. "I guess my legal problem has my head all screwed up," he said as an apology. "I still can't believe I was convicted of a crime I didn't commit."

He'd left Jeannie a locked strongbox supposedly containing his important personal and family papers. In fact, it held over two hundred thousand dollars in jewelry Larson had stolen from Viola Bedford after he'd murdered her, a year before he'd killed her husband, Melvin.

He had erased the jewelry from the inventory of property

owned by the Bedfords and destroyed the paper trail. Since Melvin and Viola had no living heirs, the jewelry was now clean as a whistle, and Larson had been counting on it to go into deep hiding.

Jeannie relaxed a bit. "After you jumped bail, a cop came to ask if I knew where you were. He said they knew you'd murdered Melvin and Viola but just couldn't prove it."

"Those assholes," Larson said. "They make stuff up all the time to scare people and get them to talk. You don't believe that crap, do you?"

"I didn't used to," Jeannie said, "until you came into my apartment, put your hands on me, and called me a liar."

"I'm really sorry, Jeannie." Larson flashed a warm smile. "But like I said, I've been through a meat grinder with these trumped-up charges the cops laid on me and the bullshit conviction." He shook his head sadly. "Now you tell me they're accusing me of murder. It all makes me a little crazy."

Jeannie squeezed Larson's hand. "That's okay, I forgive you."

"Thanks. Are you doing okay?"

"Most of the time," Jeannie replied. "I've been taking vitamins, some natural supplements, eating strictly vegetarian, and not drinking alcohol. It's helping."

"You look great," Larson said with conviction. He'd always liked her looks. Jeannie was tall, had a tiny waist, round, inviting hips, perky breasts, and big, blue, slightly wild-looking eyes.

She laughed and looked down at her grimy hands and dirty fingernails. "Yeah, I just bet I do. I'm tired and grubby."

"Still digging in the dirt for a living?" Larson asked.

Jeannie's eyes lit up. "Yep, but now I'm working for myself. I started my own landscape business this spring, and I've been putting in twelve-hour days ever since."

"Really?" Larson knew Jeannie had no money. She got by on her hourly wages and the occasional small check from her father, a retired postal worker who lived somewhere back east.

That meant she must have started her new business by dipping into the jewelry he'd left with her. He gave her a hard look.

"What?" Jeannie said, flinching at the meanness in Larson's gaze.

He grabbed her neck and squeezed. "You sold my jewelry, didn't you, bitch?"

Jeannie choked and turned red.

Larson squeezed harder. "Didn't you?"

Jeannie's fingers clawed at Larson's hand.

"Tell me or you're dead."

Jeannie's eyes welled with tears as she nodded.

Larson eased off on the chokehold a little and Jeannie gasped for air.

"I only sold some of it," she gasped. "Just what I needed to get my business started."

"Where's the strongbox?"

"Let go of me and I'll get it."

Larson squeezed Jeannie's neck and lifted her off the couch, until her feet dangled in the air. "Let's go get it together. Where?"

Jeannie pointed at the small, adjacent galley kitchen.

Larson marched her into the kitchen, released his grip, and pointed the semiautomatic at her. "Get it for me," he ordered.

She opened the cupboard under the sink, reached in, and pulled out the box. "Here."

The box had been pried open. Half the jewelry was gone, but his brother's wallet with his driver's license was still inside. Larson had stolen it from Kerry two years ago and it was still current.

He didn't doubt for a minute that Jeannie had looked inside the wallet, and that was bad news for her. He'd planned to make a clean getaway by assuming his brother's identity, and that meant nobody could know about it, at least not for a day or two.

He put the wallet in his back pocket. "How much did you get for the jewelry you sold?" he asked.

"Twenty thousand."

"You got ripped off. Now tell me where you keep the prescription meds you hoard for those rainy days when you want to kill yourself."

"I don't have any," Jeannie replied. "I'm not suicidal anymore."

Larson had heard her rap before and knew she'd overdosed at least twice after proclaiming she was never going to try to kill herself again. "Don't make me hurt you," he said.

"I told you I'm using vitamins and natural supplements now."

He forced the barrel of the handgun into her cheek and twisted it.

Jeannie blinked and started crying.

"Where are the drugs, Jeannie?"

She took a coffee canister out of the pantry and dumped a large stash of barbiturates on the kitchen counter.

Larson smiled. "Time for you to get mellow."

Jeannie shook her head. "Don't you do that to me."

Larson raked the gun barrel across her nose. "Don't you tell me what to do, bitch."

He took her into the living room, sat with her on the couch, and started forcing pills down her throat until she was too out of it to care. He kept force-feeding her the pills, slapping her to keep her awake. Finally, she passed out.

Larson stayed with her until her breathing slowed and then stopped. He checked for a pulse to make sure she was dead, found a travel bag in the bedroom closet, packed it with the strongbox, the handgun, and the money Kerry had given him, wiped his fingerprints from every surface inside the apartment he'd touched, and let himself out.

Because of the damage he had done to her face, Jeannie's death probably wouldn't go down as a suicide, but at this point he didn't care one way or the other. He had almost ten grand in cash, over a hundred thousand in jewelry he could convert into a sizable amount of money, and the use of his twin brother's identity. That would give him some running room if he could get out of Santa Fe quietly.

He decided to take the shuttle bus that ran from the downtown Santa Fe hotels to the Albuquerque airport. Once in the city, he'd find a place to crash and figure out his next step.

Lieutenant Clayton Istee of the Lincoln County Sheriff's Office finished his shift and hurried home to pick up Grace and the kids, who were packed and ready to start a ten-day vacation in Santa Fe. At the house, he parked his patrol vehicle and changed into civvies while Grace, Wendell, and Hannah loaded luggage and a picnic dinner Grace had fixed into the family sedan.

They locked up the house and started out from the Mescalero Apache Reservation in high spirits. Wendell told "knock-knock" jokes that made Hannah giggle and Clayton groan, until Grace told him to save the next joke for later. After the children settled down, Grace read out loud from a travel guide about some of the interesting things to do and see in northern New Mexico.

They could afford to vacation in pricey Santa Fe because they were staying at the ranch outside of the city owned by Clayton's father, Kevin Kerney, who had recently retired as chief of the Santa Fe Police Department. Kerney was now living in London,

England, with his wife, Colonel Sara Brannon, who was a military attaché at the U.S. Embassy, and their young son Patrick.

It was a three-year assignment for Sara, who planned to retire from the army at the end of her tour of duty, when the family would return to Santa Fe. Until that time, they hoped to make at least yearly trips back home. In their absence, the ranch was being looked after by Jack and Irene Burke, friends who ranched nearby, and their son, Riley, who was Kerney's partner in a cutting horse breeding enterprise.

Kerney had given Clayton a set of keys to the ranch with instructions to stay there as much as he liked while the family was overseas. Clayton hadn't planned on taking Kerney up on the offer so soon, but his boss, Sheriff Paul Hewitt, had assigned him to take a two-day seminar on advanced interrogation techniques at the New Mexico Law Enforcement Academy and ordered him to burn a week of leave before showing his face at work again. So for the first two days of the Istee family vacation, Grace and the kids would be on their own while Clayton attended the seminar.

Halfway into the road trip, late afternoon turned into evening and Clayton pulled off at a roadside picnic table on the lightly traveled two-lane highway. Grace served up a spread of homemade fried chicken, potato salad, and double chocolate brownies, and the family ate dinner in the cool of the gathering darkness without one vehicle passing by the whole time they were there.

Back in the car, the children fell silent and soon nodded off. It was pitch dark by the time they left the highway and rattled over the cattle guard and ruts in the dirt-and-gravel road that led to Kerney's ranch southeast of the state capital. The motion jarred Wendell and Hannah awake.

"Are we there yet?" Wendell asked in a sleepy voice.

"Almost," Grace answered.

"I need the bathroom," Wendell said.

"Can you hold your water for a few minutes?" Clayton asked.

Wendell shook his head. "I need to go really bad."

"Me too," Hannah said.

"Okay."

Clayton slowed to a stop and everyone piled out. Wendell relieved himself at the side of the road while Grace took Hannah in search of some privacy behind a tree. Above, at the lip of the canyon where Kerney's ranch house sat, a small pack of coyotes screeched, chattered, howled, and snapped. The commotion lasted a long minute.

"Are they hunting something?" Wendell asked his father.

"I think they may have caught their prey."

"How can you tell?"

"From the sound of it. Now they're fighting over the kill."

"Maybe we'll get to see it," Wendell said.

"Maybe."

With everyone back in the car, Clayton drove through the canyon and up the hill.

"Grandfather's house is just ahead," Clayton said.

"Can we see Grandfather's horses?" Hannah asked as the headlights briefly illuminated the horse barn across the wide pasture.

"In the morning," Grace replied.

Clayton wheeled into the driveway, and the headlights of the sedan froze a pack of coyotes surrounding a form lying on the ground in front of the house. The animals turned toward the sound, their eyes glistening in the reflected light.

"What is that?" Grace asked as she tensed up.

Clayton braked to a stop. "I'm not sure."

"That's a body out there," Grace said.

"We're too far away to tell what it is."

"A body?" Wendell asked. He unbuckled his seat belt and hung over the back of the front seat. "Where?"

Clayton backed up quickly, killed the headlights and engine, reached across Grace, and grabbed a flashlight from the glove box. "Everybody stay here."

"If that's a body, you have to take us away from here right now," Grace insisted.

Clayton touched Grace gently on the arm. Her demand was not unreasonable. It was especially important to avoid ghost sickness with children, and doubly important to protect them from being taken by the dead, who often wanted company to travel to the other world.

"I will, but not yet," he said.

"*Now*, Clayton."

"You know I can't do that." Clayton got out of the car and looked at Grace through the open window. "Stay here and keep the children with you."

"Let me go with you, Dad," Wendell pleaded.

"Stay in the car with your mother."

Wendell sulked and slumped against the backseat of the sedan.

"Stay put, sweetie," Clayton said to Hannah.

"Can I sit with Mother?" Hannah asked.

"Go ahead."

She climbed into the front seat and sat on Grace's lap.

As Clayton approached the coyotes, he picked up some rocks and started pelting them. The animals, three adults and a juvenile, backed off a few yards and then held their ground. He reached the body lying faceup and looked at it. Not much had been eaten, but the man's face was a mess, and some feeding had been done where the man's shirt had been shredded around the chest and two entry bullet wounds were visible.

He knelt down and moved the body just enough to pluck a wallet from a back pocket of the blue jeans. The dead man was Riley Burke, Kerney's neighbor and partner. He took a quick look around. Three pickup trucks were parked in the driveway. One belonged to Kerney, one probably to Riley Burke, and the third had a magnetic sign on the driver's door that read "Lenny's Auto Body Shop," followed by a phone number.

He returned to the sedan, opened the trunk, and pulled out an old wool blanket he kept there for emergencies.

"Who is it?" Grace asked.

"Not now," Clayton replied. Wendell was wide-eyed and standing bolt upright in the backseat. Hannah was frozen on Grace's lap. "I'll tell you more later."

He walked back to the body, covered it, and dialed 911 on his cell phone. While he waited for dispatch to pick up, he swung the flashlight beam in an arc to keep the coyotes at bay, their eyes flashing back at him in the night.

Clayton quickly identified himself when dispatch answered, gave his location, reported the dead body, and asked to be put through to New Mexico State Police Chief Andy Baca.

"Please identify yourself again and repeat your location," the dispatcher said after a brief pause.

"I'm Lieutenant Clayton Istee with the Lincoln County Sheriff's Office," he repeated forcefully, "and I am at Kevin Kerney's ranch outside Santa Fe. There is a dead man who appears to have been shot twice in the chest. I need state police officers and a forensic team sent to my twenty right now, and ask Chief Baca to call me on my cell phone immediately. Have you got all that?"

"Affirmative. Did you ID the body?"

"I did and it is not, repeat not, Chief Kerney."

"Ten-four. I'll call Chief Baca and have him contact you."

"Roger that. Do you need directions to my twenty?"

"Negative. I have a sergeant responding and more officers will be on the way shortly. ETA is under twenty minutes."

"Ten-four."

Clayton disconnected and heard the beeping sound of another cell phone coming from the pickup truck parked next to Riley Burke's body. He retrieved it and saw on the screen that Riley had missed six calls, the earliest five hours ago, the latest within the half hour. He wondered why no one had come looking for him, especially with his parents and wife living so close by.

From the driveway came the sound of the sedan's engine turning over, followed by horn-honking. He put some rocks on the four corners of the blanket covering Riley's body to keep the coyotes away and walked back to the car. Grace sat behind the wheel.

"I can't stay here with the children waiting for you," she said. "We're leaving. I'll get a room in town for the night and call you to let you know where we are."

Clayton nodded. "I may be here for some time."

"The week is ruined," Grace whispered.

"Don't think that way." He watched Grace turn the car around and drive down the road before returning to the ranch house. The coyotes had closed in on the body. Clayton chased them off before they could do additional damage, and they snarled in protest.

Chief Baca's call came as Clayton was about to use the house key Kerney had given him to make a quick tour of the ranch house.

"Dispatch says the dead man is not, I repeat not, Kerney," Andy said. "Is that true?"

"Affirmative," Clayton replied, as he noticed that Sara's SUV was not parked in the driveway. Perhaps it was in the garage or stored in the horse barn. "The deceased is Riley Burke."

"Damn," Andy said. "That's going to make Kerney very angry."

"I know it," Clayton said as he jiggled the front doorknob and found it locked. He walked through the enclosed courtyard to the glass patio door to the kitchen and saw that it had been smashed. The pattern of glass fragments on the floor suggested it had been broken from the outside in order to gain entry.

"And you think it's a homicide?" Andy asked.

"No doubt about it, Chief." Clayton stepped back from the debris so as not to contaminate evidence at the point of entry. "There's a broken kitchen patio door that suggests a home invasion. I'm going to go through the front door and take a quick look around."

"Be careful," Andy said. "I'm about to leave my house for your twenty. See you when I get there."

"Roger that, Chief."

Inside the house Clayton turned on the exterior lights to keep the coyotes at bay. The front room and adjoining library appeared untouched. The television and stereo system hadn't been taken, nor had any of the art on the wall been removed. In the master bedroom there was no sign of a burglar's quick search through the dressers for jewelry and other valuables.

The absence of disarray made Clayton question the motive for the break-in. Or had Riley Burke's arrival kept the killer from looting the house?

He checked the truck with the Lenny's Auto Body Shop magnetic sign on the door and found it was registered to a Leonard Hampson who resided in Springer. He phoned the information to dispatch and watched the coyotes yip and yap at him for being kept away from the fresh kill while he waited for the state police to arrive.

Sergeant Russell Thorpe, shift commander for New Mexico State Police District One, ran north on I-25 with lights and siren. As a

rookie officer, Thorpe had worked with Kerney, who'd been deputy state police chief at the time before taking over as top cop at
the Santa Fe Police Department. Several years later, Russell had
teamed up with Clayton Istee and Ramona Pino, an SFPD detective, on a case that involved the discovery of a graveyard outside of the town of Socorro where a serial killer had buried his
victims.

The unearthing of the crime scene was directly connected to
the hunt for another killer who'd plotted the murder of Chief
Kerney and his entire family, including Clayton, his wife, and his
children. Fortunately, Clayton had put the man down for good
before he could accomplish his bloodletting.

Russell knew that if Clayton Istee said the dead man at Kerney's ranch was a homicide victim, you could take it to the bank.
He was one hell of a fine investigator.

According to dispatch, Clayton had reported that it wasn't
Kerney lying in the driveway at the ranch. Word had it Kerney
was living large in London while his wife pulled a gravy tour as
the U.S. Army military attaché at the embassy. It was good to
know that he hadn't been killed on a brief visit home.

So who was the dead guy? A caretaker hired to look after the
place? A neighbor? Some wandering vagrant? And why had he
been killed?

Thorpe knew that about 90 percent of murder victims knew
their killers, which meant investigators usually had a good pool
of potential suspects to target. The small percentage of random
murders, killings by strangers, and murders that occurred during
the commission of other crimes could be much more difficult to
work because of the absence of any links to the victims.

He wondered if this homicide might have something to do
with the bizarre sequence of events that had started earlier in the
day when a correctional officer had been brutally attacked by a
convicted felon, sent by mistake to the state prison in Springer.

Every cop in the state was on high alert for Craig Larson, who had so far nearly killed the correctional officer, almost suffocated a young family locked inside a Department of Corrections van, and left a man to fry in the blistering hot desert grasslands outside of Santa Rosa.

Thorpe's radio kept him updated as he barreled down Lamy Hill to the ranch road turnoff, and word came to him that one of the vehicles parked at the ranch belonged to Lenny Hampson, the man who been kidnapped by Larson in Springer and dumped in the desert.

Dispatch also reported that two homicide agents were en route about ten minutes behind him, a forensic team was rolling with the same ETA, and of equal interest, Chief Baca was on his way to the crime scene.

On the ranch road, he rolled his front windows down, cut the siren, switched off the emergency lights, and pushed the unit hard through the canyon and up the crest. A waning half-moon had just risen, giving just enough light to outline the structure of the horse barn a quarter mile away. The outside lights of the ranch house flooded the porch, courtyard, and parking area in front of the house.

Through the open windows Thorpe could hear horses whinnying and coyotes barking. He flashed his headlights as he approached the house. Clayton Istee stood near a covered form on the ground, waving both hands over his head. Thorpe announced his arrival to dispatch, dismounted his unit, and hurried over to Clayton.

"Look who they sent me," Clayton said with a smile as he shook Russell's hand.

"I heard you made lieutenant," Thorpe replied, grinning back.

Clayton glanced at the three stripes on Russell's uniform shirtsleeves. "Yeah, and now you're a sergeant."

"How about that? Who's the victim?"

"Riley Burke." Clayton flipped off the blanket covering the body.

Thorpe stared down at Riley Burke, took in some air, and let it out slowly through his nose. "I know him slightly, met his wife and his parents on several occasions. They're Kerney's neighbors."

Clayton nodded. "This wasn't a burglary. A patio door was smashed from the outside to gain entry but nothing inside the house appears to have been taken."

Thorpe pointed at the truck with the auto body sign. "I'm not surprised. Two hours ago, the registered owner of that truck, Lenny Hampson, stumbled half-dead into a gas station on the outskirts of Santa Rosa and told the local cops that a fugitive named Craig Larson had dumped him in the desert without food or drink."

Clayton's eyes widened. Before he'd gone off duty, he'd heard about Larson's attack on the correctional officer and the theft of the Honda from the young couple with the baby, but the kidnapping was new information.

"That, I didn't know about," he said. "Larson may have come here to switch vehicles. There are fresh tire tracks that could be from the SUV Kerney's wife, Sara Brannon, drives. It's a red Jeep and it's not in the garage. I haven't checked the horse barn."

"Would you mind staying with the body while I take a peek inside the horse barn?" Thorpe asked.

"Actually I do mind, but I'll do it anyway because you're a friend."

"Don't you like dead bodies?" Thorpe asked as he started for his unit.

"Not really," Clayton replied. "By the way, there are six

missed calls on Riley's cell phone, some hours old. I'm guessing his wife and parents are away, otherwise they would have come looking and found him."

Thorpe stopped in his tracks and turned back to Clayton. "You're right. Where's his phone?"

"On the seat of his truck."

"Will you check Riley's contact list on the phone against the missed calls while I go look for the Jeep?"

"Not a problem," Clayton replied.

Thorpe got in his unit and drove toward the horse barn. Clayton retrieved the phone and quickly discovered that the missed calls were indeed from Riley's wife and parents. He put Riley's phone on the hood of the truck and used his own phone to call his boss at home and brief him on Riley Burke's murder and the tie-in to the manhunt for Craig Larson.

"Who's on scene with you?" Sheriff Paul Hewitt asked when Clayton finished.

"A state police sergeant, Russell Thorpe. He's solid. More personnel are on the way, including Chief Baca."

"Do you want in on the investigation?"

Clayton hesitated. State law gave blanket statewide jurisdiction both to sheriff's officers and the New Mexico State Police. Clayton could rightfully work the case if Hewitt gave him the authority to do so.

"Well?" Hewitt asked.

"That's up to you, Sheriff."

"And I say no," Hewitt replied. "I want you to take that academy course I've already spent taxpayer money for you to attend and then go on vacation. Understood?"

"Affirmative."

"Have you talked to Kerney?"

"Not yet," Clayton replied.

"Better do it soon," Hewitt advised. "Five will get you ten, once he learns about the murder, he'll book the next available flight home."

"I wouldn't bet against it."

"Keep me informed."

"Ten-four."

Russell Thorpe came back with news that Sara's SUV was nowhere to be found, and that he'd asked dispatch to issue a BOLO on the missing Jeep.

Clayton told him the missed calls on Burke's phone were indeed from Riley's wife and parents.

"Why don't you break the news to them," Russell suggested as he searched inside Lenny Hampson's truck.

"This isn't my case, Russell."

"I know that."

Clayton looked at the phone he'd placed on the hood of Riley's truck. Riley had been murdered on Kerney's doorstep, probably because he'd been looking after the place the way a good neighbor should. More than that, Riley was Kerney's business partner, and his parents had sold Kerney his land at a fair price after turning away other offers from well-heeled easterners who wanted to play cowboy in Santa Fe. The Burkes deserved to hear of the tragedy and their loss from a member of Kerney's family, which meant Clayton needed to make the calls. Kerney would expect no less. He picked up the phone.

"You haven't told me what brought you up to Santa Fe," Russell said, as he held up the Department of Corrections shotgun he'd found under the seat.

"I start a two-day law enforcement academy course tomorrow and then we were planning to stay over at the ranch for a family vacation."

"Grace and the children came with you?" Thorpe made sure

the chamber was empty and the safety was on before putting the shotgun on the hood of Hampson's truck.

"Yeah. Grace is checking us into a motel for the night."

"You actually believe you can be a cop and have any kind of normal family life?"

"Silly of me, isn't it? But I am starting to doubt it."

Clayton made the calls, first to Riley's wife and then to his parents, and they took the news hard. After he finished, he told Thorpe that the Burkes had gone down to Roswell to attend a cattle auction and Riley was to have joined them earlier in the evening.

"This sucks," Russell said.

"Murder usually does," Clayton replied, watching a string of flashing emergency lights top out on the crest of the canyon. He counted five approaching vehicles.

Russell stepped off to meet the lead car and Clayton's cell rang with an incoming call from Grace. She told him what motel she'd checked into with the children and asked when he'd be able to join them.

"I don't know how long I'll be," Clayton said, "so don't wait up for me."

"Who died?" Grace asked in a whisper.

In the background Clayton could hear the sound of a children's television show. "Riley Burke, shot twice in the chest."

"Oh dear."

The incoming vehicles parked behind Thorpe's unit. In the darkness Clayton couldn't make out the people exiting their units. "Gotta go," he said.

"If you're not here in the morning," Grace said, "I'm driving the children back home to Mescalero."

The line went dead. Clayton was just about to call Grace back when Russell Thorpe approached with Chief Andy Baca of the New Mexico State Police.

"Hello, Lieutenant," Andy Baca said, offering his hand. "Why don't you and the sergeant bring me up to speed?"

The report of the suspicious, unattended death of a woman named Jeannie Cooper brought Lieutenant Ramona Pino, commander of the Santa Fe Police Department Violent Crimes Unit, out on a hot and unusually muggy July night. She drove up Cerrillos Road toward the South Capitol neighborhood, listening to the secure channel traffic of the personnel handling the homicide at Kevin Kerney's ranch and searching for the red Jeep Craig Larson had stolen.

She stopped at a dead-end lane just off Paseo De Peralta, a street that looped around the historic Santa Fe downtown area. At the end of the lane, Officer Dennis Gavin stood in the glare of his squad car's headlights talking to a chunky older woman wearing a halter top, shorts, and flip-flops.

Pino approached and Gavin interrupted his interview to introduce her to Sally Newcomb, a friend of the victim who'd called the police after discovering the dead woman in her apartment. Newcomb had a blocky jaw and square face that matched her chunky body.

"According to Ms. Newcomb, her friend Jeannie Cooper has a history of suicidal behavior," Officer Gavin said. "She just finished telling me that she became worried when Jeannie didn't answer her phone. Ms. Newcomb came over, saw her truck, and knocked on the door. When she didn't get an answer, she let herself in with a spare house key she knew Ms. Cooper kept hidden under a rock and discovered the body."

"I see," Ramona replied. She looked at Newcomb, who appeared genuinely distraught. She glanced up at Gavin to get a read as to whether or not he was buying the woman's story.

At six-three Gavin towered over Pino. He gave her a slight nod to signal he thought Newcomb was on the level.

Ramona nodded in return, asked Newcomb to continue giving her statement to Officer Gavin, walked toward the open apartment door, and paused to look around before entering. Once a single-family residence, the building sat behind an electrical power substation that fronted Paseo De Peralta, within steps of some of the fanciest and most expensive art galleries in town. But it was a world apart from the high-end condos and multimillion-dollar homes of nearby Garcia Street and Acequia Madre.

The stucco was cracked and the wooden frames of the old-fashioned casement windows needed a coat of paint. The porch sagged beneath a rusted tin roof that covered the four doors to the separate apartments.

A row of mailboxes stood at the front of a gravel walkway that led to the apartments, and the front yard was packed dirt used as parking spaces that butted up to the porch. Cooper's apartment, an end unit, had a privacy fence that enclosed a small patio at the back. Using her flashlight, Ramona checked the patio, the front door, and the exterior windows for any visible signs of forced entry and found none.

Inside the apartment, Jeannie Cooper's body was sprawled on the couch, eyes closed, mouth open, one arm dangling over the side of the couch, the other positioned on the armrest above her head. Ramona looked at the fresh bruises and marks on the face, the red strangulation marks around the neck, and the discoloration at the corners of the mouth that suggested the woman's mouth had been forced open. She bent over and gently opened the mouth and saw several pills at the back of the throat.

She stepped back, keyed her handheld radio, advised the shift captain on duty of the ten-zero-one—her fifth homicide of the year—and called out the crime scene unit, her two on-duty detectives, and the medical investigator.

Back outside, Officer Gavin waited at his unit with Sally Newcomb. He gave Ramona the microcassette containing Newcomb's tape-recorded witness statement.

Ramona pocketed the cassette and asked Newcomb to stay with Officer Gavin until the detectives arrived and they could ask her about Jeannie Cooper's personal life.

Newcomb's expression turned somber. "Do you think she was murdered?"

"We have to look at all the possibilities."

"I saw the marks on her face, but I just thought that Jeannie had mutilated herself again," Newcomb said. "She always does that when she gets depressed. And besides, as far as a personal life goes she hasn't had one since she started her own landscaping company in the spring."

Ramona smiled. "That's exactly the kind of information that could be very helpful to us."

Radio traffic on her handheld told Ramona that the detectives and crime scene unit were five minutes out. She used the time to start questioning the residents in the other apartments. Two hours later, she had a homicide with no witnesses, no apparent motive, and no suspects. She huddled with her two detectives, Beatty and Olivas, while the MI and crime scene techs finished up inside the apartment.

"We could expand the canvass," Beatty said, "but I don't think it would do any good."

"Agreed," Ramona said, "although I think come morning we should talk to the business owners in the neighborhood to find out if they saw anyone hanging around in the late afternoon."

"I'll do it," Olivas said, sounding dour, which was more his prevailing outlook on life than an attitude in need of adjustment.

"Okay." Ramona handed Beatty a notebook she'd found in Cooper's truck. "There's a list of her clients and jobs in there. Make some calls and talk to the people she has been working for."

Beatty, a thick-set, middle-aged man who suffered from serious allergies, sniffled and nodded. "Sally Newcomb told me who Cooper used to work for." He consulted his notes. "His name is Daniel Peck. Owns a company called Milagro Landscaping. I found his home phone number and address in the telephone directory."

"I'll talk to him," Ramona said.

Beatty rattled off Peck's phone number and address.

Ramona wrote them on her notepad. "Did Newcomb know if Cooper was seeing anyone six months to a year ago?"

Beatty put his finger to his nose and sniffled. "She doesn't think there was anybody special, and she couldn't give me any names of who Cooper had seen in the past. But then, I got the feeling from Newcomb that she may have been interested in reeling Cooper in for herself."

"Interesting," Ramona said. "Note that in your narrative, so we can follow up on it if need be." She nodded toward the apartment. "This homicide has some wrinkles, but by the way the murder was committed, I don't think jealousy or lust was the motive. The perp forced the pills down Cooper's throat, which suggests he was angry at her for some reason."

"Are you thinking the perp is male?" Beatty asked.

"The bruise marks on Cooper's neck suggest that," Ramona replied.

"For a female, Newcomb has large hands," Beatty noted.

"I'm not ruling her out," Ramona said. "The sloppy attempt made to mask the killing as a suicide tells me that the killer knew the victim. I'd like both of you to take another look inside the apartment. Find me something that will link the victim to a suspect—a romantic entanglement, an illicit relationship, a conflict with a neighbor, former colleague, or ex-lover—whatever. You know the routine."

"Maybe we'll find some love letters or a diary containing revealing and damaging tidbits," Olivas said as he started toward the apartment.

"You really think so?" Beatty asked with sarcastic enthusiasm as he caught up with his partner.

"Nah," Olivas grumbled. "Nothing is that easy."

Pino flipped open her cell phone, dialed Daniel Peck's number, and got his answering machine. She left a message, went to her unit, and drove to Peck's residence, a post–World War Two pueblo-style house in the Casa Solana neighborhood, which had been the site of a Japanese-American internment camp during the war.

Lights were on inside the house, so Ramona parked and rang the bell. A deeply tanned man in his early fifties with short-cut gray hair answered. He wore a short-sleeved V-neck undershirt that revealed a Marine Corps tattoo on his left forearm. He had pleasant features and crinkly blue eyes.

Ramona flashed her shield and ID. "Daniel Peck?"

"That's right."

"I'm Lieutenant Pino and I need to ask you some questions about Jeannie Cooper."

"I haven't seen her since she quit working for me to start her own business. Did she overdose and get taken to the emergency room again?"

"No, she's dead."

Peck looked stunned. "She finally went and did it."

"No, she was murdered."

"Murdered?"

"It appears that way."

"Poor Jeannie," Peck said with a sigh. "She was such a gentle, lost soul, except when she got too manic or too down in the dumps. Then you must be looking for Craig Larson, right?"

"Why do you say that?" Pino asked.

"Because I've been watching the TV news story about his escape today from that prison guard he almost killed. My company did landscape and garden maintenance at the Bedford estate. Jeannie and Larson had a thing going right up to the time he went to trial for embezzling all that money."

"You know that for a fact?"

Peck nodded. "I saw it with my own eyes, and Jeannie told me all about it."

"What reason would he have to kill Jeannie?"

"You've got me," Peck answered.

There was no way Peck could know about the murder of Riley Burke at Kevin Kerney's ranch or the discovery of the abandoned pickup truck Larson had used to abduct Lenny Hampson from his Springer auto body repair shop. Ramona doubted he was deflecting suspicion from himself. Still, she needed to rule him out as a suspect.

"Can you account for your time since about four this afternoon, Mr. Peck?" she asked.

"You bet I can, Lieutenant. I kept a six-man crew working at a landscaping installation job until six-thirty and then went directly from there to a chapter meeting of Veterans for Peace."

"I'll probably want to talk to you again."

"Maybe we can have that talk over a drink, Lieutenant." Peck took out his wallet and gave Ramona a business card. "Once you've cleared me as a suspect, that is. I've been told that I clean up nicely. Best to call me on my cell phone."

"I'll do that, Mr. Peck," Ramona said stiffly.

She headed back to the Cooper crime scene. If Peck's hunch about Craig Larson was right, he might still be in the city. By radio, Ramona put the word out to intensify the search for Larson.

Russell Thorpe immediately responded to her advisory and asked for a back-channel update. Ramona filled him in on the connection between Larson and her murder victim.

"My, my, he's been a busy boy today," Russell said.

"It's not confirmed that he's the perp."

"Did you find the red Jeep?"

"Negative," Pino replied.

"Is your victim's vehicle missing?" Thorpe asked.

"Negative."

"Interesting," Thorpe said. "Let's debrief when you wrap up your preliminary."

"Ten-four, your place or mine?"

"At Chief Baca's ten-nineteen."

"Affirmative."

It was going to be a long night, and although Ramona stayed focused on the tasks ahead, she couldn't help wondering if Daniel Peck's unexpected come-on had been sincere or just a ration of BS.

Craig Larson spent a nervous couple of hours waiting for the last shuttle of the night to the Albuquerque airport. He killed the time in the small Santa Fe river park that paralleled East Alameda, where he could keep an eye out for the arrival of the bus at the hotel across the street. When it showed up, he hurried across Old Santa Fe Trail and joined the half dozen tourists waiting to board. Once on board, he found a seat away from the rest of the passengers and pretended to sleep.

At the Albuquerque airport, Larson went inside, used the lavatory, went back outside, and took a courtesy bus to the airport parking lot on Yale Boulevard. After getting off at a row in the back of the lot, he waited until the driver left on another run to the terminal before slipping through the entrance gate when the attendant wasn't looking.

He hoofed it along Yale Boulevard to Central Avenue, a good two-mile walk, tensing up when spurts of traffic passed him on the roadway, thinking for sure some gung-ho cop would stop and want to question him about walking along the street late at night. He made it to Central Avenue, where Yale dead-ended. At a nearby all-night drugstore, he bought a local paper, some snack food, and a drink, and walked up Central to the next city bus stop. A sign posted at the bus stop told him he'd arrived ten minutes before the last run of the night.

While he waited, he chewed on the snacks, washed them down with soda, and thought about what he would do after he checked into a cheap motel on East Central where nobody would remember his face or care what name he used as long as he paid cash and didn't cause any trouble. First, take a hot shower to wash the grime off; second, get some sleep; third, find a good greasy spoon in the morning for a big breakfast; and finally, look in the newspaper for a car to buy from a private party.

That was as far as Larson wanted to take it for the night. It had been an exhausting day.

ChapterThree

At ten minutes after two in the morning, Russell Thorpe dropped Clayton off at the budget motel on Cerrillos Road where Grace had rented a room. Clayton got a key from a drowsy front desk clerk and quietly unlocked the door to find Wendell and Hannah asleep in one of the double beds and Grace fully dressed sitting wide awake in a chair at a small table by the window. Grace put a finger to her lips, picked up the keys to the sedan, and motioned for Clayton to join her outside.

They sat in the car with the windows open, cooled by a slight breeze. There was just enough illumination from the parking lot lights for Clayton to see that his wife wasn't happy.

"Well?" Grace asked. She avoided looking at Clayton, her eyes glued on the door to their room.

"I'm not canceling our vacation, if that's what you're worried about. Sheriff Hewitt ordered me to have nothing more to do with the investigation after tonight, and that's fine with me." He glanced at his wristwatch. "I'm due in class at the academy in a little under seven hours."

"What took you so long tonight?"

"I had to break the news to Riley's wife, Lynette, and his parents, brief the state police chief, call Kerney in London, give a statement to the investigating officers, and talk to a city detective about another homicide by the same perpetrator."

"And that took you hours and hours?"

"Yes, sometimes it does," Clayton replied. "I don't want to argue with you about this at two in the morning."

"What did Kerney say when you spoke to him?"

"He's very angry and upset. He's leaving for Santa Fe as soon as he can get a flight out. He wants us to stay at the ranch as planned."

"Are Sara and Patrick coming with him?"

"No," Clayton answered. "He'll let me know later in the day when he's due to arrive." Grace still hadn't looked at him—not a good sign. "How are the children doing?"

Grace sighed. "They were completely hyper until exhaustion set in and they couldn't keep their eyes open for another second. I'm not sure I want to take them back to the ranch so soon after what they saw."

"They didn't *see* anything," Clayton replied.

"They're *children,*" Grace shot back.

"And the best thing we can do for them right now is not make a big deal about what happened at the ranch. If we stay away, it will only make them think that we fear this death, and that would be wrong for us to do. Riley Burke's wife and family will help him travel from this world to the next, so there is no witchery or ghost sickness to worry about."

Grace looked at her husband. He'd made a valid point. She'd been thinking purely as an Apache, which wasn't completely necessary for her to do. After all, this was a situation where Mescalero rituals didn't really apply.

"You're right," she said. "Have the police finished their work at the ranch?"

Clayton nodded. "Except for a broken patio door, everything has been put right. Chief Baca assigned a patrol officer to keep an eye on the place until we show up. I told him we'd be there around eight."

"You were sure I'd go back?" Grace asked.

"Not really. But I figured if you did want to return to Mescalero with the children, I'd have to stay behind to complete the academy course, get the broken patio door fixed, and look after the place until Kerney arrived."

"You'll go with us to the ranch before you start your class?" Grace asked.

Clayton smiled. "Absolutely, but if I'm going to be worth a plugged nickel, I'd better get some shut-eye."

Grace leaned over and kissed Clayton's cheek. "You look tired."

"I am," Clayton said as he pulled her close for a hug.

Grace tucked her head against Clayton's chest. "All of us should wear something black tomorrow."

Clayton nodded. Black helped to protect the living from the dead who might want company on their journey. "Of course," he said. "Let's get some sleep."

Kerney had gotten the call from Clayton at six A.M. London time just as he was rousing Patrick out of bed. The two of them had been on their own for the last two nights while Sara was at a Royal Army base in the Midlands.

The news of Riley Burke's murder had stunned him into silence. He had liked Riley immensely, trusted him completely, and had come to rely upon him as the driving force in their partnership to raise, train, and sell world-class competition cutting horses. He had seen a good bit of his younger self in Riley. Both had been ranch-raised, loved the land, and grew up dreaming of making a livelihood as ranchers like their parents and grandparents before them. Kerney's parents had lost their ranch when the government took it over to expand White Sands Missile Range in the Tularosa

Basin in south-central New Mexico, while Riley's parents had managed to hang on to most of their Galisteo Basin property in spite of the financial ups and downs of cattle ranching.

Kerney had worked side by side with Riley long enough to know that if Patrick grew up anything like him, he would be about as proud as a father could get.

As he fixed breakfast, Kerney didn't say a word to Patrick about Riley's death. Over the course of the last few months the family had been in Santa Fe, Riley had spent a lot of time at the ranch working with the horses, and Patrick had become quite fond of him, often tagging along at his heels asking endless questions that Riley handled graciously. During those months, Riley and his wife, Lynette, had come to dinner at the ranch several times and the friendship among all of them had deepened.

Breakfast over, Patrick washed his face and hands, brushed his teeth, combed his hair, and dressed for preschool. In the drizzle that seemed to be a permanent fixture of the London cityscape, Kerney walked with Patrick through the streets of Knightsbridge to the school, which was housed in a Georgian mansion.

Patrick was still adjusting to living in London, and Kerney wasn't all that much ahead of him. The city was a marvelous place, vibrant, chock full of things to do and see, and they hadn't even scratched the surface. But what father and son both loved best was those afternoons after school when they hurried to the Knightsbridge station, took the tube to Lancaster Gate, walked a few short blocks to Bathurst Mews, and rented horses to ride in Hyde Park.

Tucked on a cobblestone lane in an upscale neighborhood, the mews was a hidden-away combination of stables and small houses converted from stables. Before Kerney and Patrick were allowed to ride in the park without an escort, both had had to show that they were proficient on horseback, which they demonstrated with ease for the certified riding instructor, who'd voiced serious doubts about Patrick's ability to handle the spirited pony he'd picked out.

At the school, Kerney gave Patrick a hug, turned him loose, and watched as he skirted the group of children who had already arrived in favor of a quiet corner where storybooks were arranged on a row of low shelves. According to the school's director, Patrick had to be urged to join in group activities and play, and Kerney was beginning to worry some about his usually very gregarious son. When he turned four in a few months, he'd attend a nearby private junior school with an excellent reputation that charged a hefty quarterly tuition. His curriculum as a beginning student in what was called the Small School Department, for children ages four to six, would include English, mathematics, reading, and handwriting, along with exposure to history, geography, French, art, music, religious studies, and sports.

It was a far cry from the early education Kerney had received at the elementary school in Truth or Consequences, New Mexico, when he was growing up on the west slope of the San Andres Mountains near the White Sands Missile Range boundary. He hoped time would help Patrick adjust to his new school and surroundings.

Kerney walked home, his thoughts returning to the murder of Riley Burke. Although it wasn't logical, he felt partially responsible for Riley's death. If he hadn't asked him to look after the ranch, the young man might be alive today. Kerney knew it made no sense to feel that way, since their partnership required Riley to be at the ranch routinely to care for, exercise, and train the cutting horses. Still, guilt gnawed at him.

He needed to get back to Santa Fe as soon as possible, both to pay his respects and to give whatever support he could to Jack and Irene and Riley's wife, Lynette. But before he could book a flight, he had to let Sara know what had happened, and he had to arrange for a nanny to care for Patrick until Sara returned from southeastern England the day after tomorrow. Fortunately, there was a housing board at the U.S. Embassy that could speedily secure the services of a nanny on short notice.

Kerney stopped in front of the house the U.S. government had leased for them. He'd been amazed to learn they were not required to pay rent or utilities for the property. Instead, Sara's housing allowance went into a special government pool used to lease quarters for all U.S. personnel living in the UK.

The house they'd been assigned was part of a nineteenth-century mansion block that came with its own private communal gardens accessed through a locked gate. A redbrick building with tall casement windows, it had a steep pitched roof, a tall brick chimney, and a completely updated interior on three floors. On the open market, the house would easily rent for much more than what an army colonel could afford under any circumstance.

In the living room—what the Brits called the lounge—Kerney called Sara's cell phone, got her voice mail, left a message about Riley Burke's murder, and started checking the Internet for available flights. It was the height of the tourist season and every outgoing flight to the States was fully booked until tomorrow, and even then only business-class tickets were available.

He made a reservation on the earliest flight out of Heathrow, and arranged through the embassy for a nanny to take care of Patrick until Sara returned. He was about to call Clayton when Sara called.

"What terrible news," she said. "What else do you know about it?"

"Not much," Kerney replied. "Clayton said Riley was shot twice in the chest at close range and that the perp was an escaped fugitive. Clayton, Grace, and the kids discovered Riley's body at our front door."

"Wendell and Hannah saw Riley's body?"

"Of that I'm not sure."

"Grace surely wouldn't have allowed it. I'll call her as soon as I can. When are you leaving for Santa Fe?"

"You know me too well," he said. He gave Sara his flight information and told her he'd arranged for a nanny until her return to London. "I'm meeting with the nanny early this afternoon. If she's not suitable, I'll asked the embassy to refer another."

"Have you told Patrick that Riley is dead?" Sara asked.

"I don't have the heart to do it."

"Best leave it to me. When will you be back?"

"I don't know. Sometime soon after the funeral services, I would guess. In a week at the most."

"Don't raise my hopes with false promises," Sara said.

"What does that mean?"

"It means that unless this homicide is solved quickly, I don't see you walking away from hunting down Riley's murderer. You don't have that kind of temperament."

"I'm not a law enforcement officer anymore."

"I'm sure Andy Baca will gladly correct that minor technicality."

"I'll keep that in mind. Lynette, Jack, and Irene deserve to have Riley's killer caught—"

"Dead or alive," Sara said.

"My sentiments exactly," Kerney said.

"When the funeral services are set, let me know right away. If I can wrangle emergency leave, Patrick and I will fly over. We should all be there to pay our respects."

"I'd like that. So would the Burke family."

"It's all about family, Kerney. Give my boy big kisses and hugs for me."

"I'll do it."

Before calling Clayton, Kerney spoke first to his old friend Andy Baca at the New Mexico State Police.

"Have you caught the dirtbag?" he asked when Andy came on the line.

Andy snorted in disgust. "Not yet. He seems to have gone to ground."

"Can you break away from the office, drive to Albuquerque, and pick me up when I arrive?"

"Of course I can, I'm the chief. Give me the particulars."

Kerney read off his flight number and arrival time and Andy said, "I'll see you then."

Kerney's call to Clayton went unanswered, so he left a message on his voice mail, went upstairs to the master bedroom, and started packing for his flight the next day.

Although Riley Burke's murder was more than enough motivation to return to Santa Fe, Kerney knew his eagerness to leave also came from the feeling of being a total outsider in London and among the families of the military officers and enlisted personnel assigned to the embassy. It was a small, tight-knit group, and none of them, including the civilian support staff, knew what to make of the only male spouse in the crowd, not to mention one who was an ex–police chief to boot.

He was beginning to doubt his ability to be a retired, stay-at-home parent in London over the next thirty-four months and counting, and he felt shitty about his deteriorating attitude. Sara and Patrick deserved better.

After preschool in the afternoon, Kerney had promised Patrick a boat ride on the Regent's Canal and then a visit to the London Zoo. Until then he would surf the Internet to see what he could learn about the investigation into Riley Burke's murder. By now, there had to be news reports about it. He sat at the desk in a small upstairs bedroom that he'd outfitted as a home office and powered up the laptop.

•••

Among her many duties as the U.S. Army military attaché at the U.S. Embassy to the Court of St. James's, Sara was responsible for overseeing the activities of forty-plus army personnel detached on special liaison duty with British Army units throughout the United Kingdom. For the past two days, she'd been touring bases in the southern part of the country, working her way back toward London. Last night, she'd stayed over at the Winchester Army Training Regiment base in order to make an early morning meeting with a U.S. Army intelligence captain who was briefing the Brits about the latest top-secret version of a battlefield imagery system.

It was her first out-of-town trip since landing behind her desk at the embassy two months ago, and although she missed Patrick and Kerney, she was enjoying the break from being office-bound or scrambling from one meeting to the next with Ministry of Defence command staff and planners.

The job demanded long hours to keep up with all that needed her attention. Fortunately, her boss, the senior military attaché, Rear Admiral Thomas Lincoln Foley, was supportive and helpful.

Her meeting with the captain went well, and after a tour of the training facilities and the campus, she went back to her quarters, packed, consulted her road map for the next leg of her tour, a briefing at an armored corps garrison, and left the post.

As she drove through the cathedral city of Winchester, she let her thoughts return to the murder of Riley Burke. Her first impulse after hearing the news from Kerney was to hunt down and shoot the murderer herself, and she'd all but told Kerney to do exactly that.

Sara wondered if Iraq had turned her into one of the walking wounded who'd survived combat but lost their moral compass.

Dead or alive. She'd both said it and meant it, especially the dead part.

In Iraq, she had been shot at and wounded, and she had killed and wounded the enemy in return. She had watched young soldiers die in firefights, examined strewn bloody body parts of civilians blown up by suicide bombers, witnessed soldiers burned alive in Humvees, and seen women and children gunned down by errant fire in skirmishes, until she no longer reacted to the carnage.

She had finished her tour in a cold rage about war, killing, politicians who sacrificed others at no risk to themselves, and the gutless generals who told the politicians whatever they wanted to hear. She came home emotionally numb, disinterested in most of what happened around her, and feeling estranged from a country that seemed untouched by the war. Only Patrick and Kerney truly mattered, and even with them she occasionally shut down.

Until Iraq, she had always bounced back. Even after her Gulf War One tour, she'd returned home without suffering any long-lasting ill effects. She knew she had post-traumatic stress disorder, and after months of trying and failing to cope with it on her own, she'd finally made an appointment to see a shrink.

Going into therapy put a stopper on any future advancement in the military. But she'd reached 0-6, bird colonel, before anyone else in her West Point class, had a job that rarely led to stars on the collar, and planned to retire at the end of the three-year embassy tour of duty, so it really didn't matter.

Still a little uneasy driving on the left side of the road, Sara entered the motorway traffic, got up to speed quickly, and zipped along with the insane English motorists who seemed to enjoy playing their own version of Formula 1 and World Rally drivers on public roadways.

She looked down at her hands gripping the steering wheel and realized they were shaking, and that it didn't have a thing to do with driving on the left side of the road with the crazy Brits on the motorway.

After a long, hard sleep, Craig Larson woke up refreshed, turned on the motel room television, and surfed through the early morning news broadcasts. His photograph and the Crime Stoppers toll-free number were being shown on every channel. One station had a camera crew at Jeannie's house, another had a team at the rest stop where he'd taken the young family's SUV and locked them in the Department of Corrections van, and a third was interviewing Lenny Hampson with "Exclusive Breaking News" scrolling across the bottom of the screen. They were all playing up his brutality big-time and repeating a warning that "escaped fugitive Craig Larson is armed and dangerous."

Larson found it interesting that Lenny Hampson had walked out of the desert, the young couple and their baby hadn't died from heat exhaustion, and the Department of Corrections screw had survived, although he was in intensive care. That meant out of seven people, he'd killed only two: Jeannie and the young cowboy at the ranch, whose names hadn't been released to the press. That didn't seem an unreasonable number. He could have easily killed them all.

He wondered why TV news wasn't showing the crime scene at the ranch where he'd shot the cowboy. Probably the rich owner didn't want the publicity.

With his photograph on the television and probably in every newspaper statewide, his plans to have a big breakfast at a nearby diner, study the paper to find a car to buy from a private party, and use his twin brother's identity would have to be changed.

He opened the window curtains and scanned the half dozen

parked cars within his line of sight for out-of-state license plates. There was a blue Chevrolet from Oklahoma parked on the left, two spaces down from his room.

He tucked the semiautomatic in his waistband, concealed it with his shirttail, and stepped outside. The motel was an L-shaped building with the office close to the street, under a big neon sign. There were no maid carts on the walkway that bordered the rooms and nobody going to or from the vehicles in the lot.

He walked down to the room where the Chevy with the Okie plates was parked, and knocked on the door.

"What is it?" a man's voice asked.

Larson smiled at the peephole. "Management. We've got a report of a gas leak in one of the rooms, so we're doing a safety check of all the wall heaters. It's probably nothing."

"There's no gas smell in here."

Larson widened his smile and shrugged his shoulders. "Like I said, it's probably nothing, but I've got to check. Fire marshal rules, you know."

"Okay. Give me a minute."

The man who opened the door was in his fifties, with rounded shoulders, a gut that hung over his belt, and a puffy face.

Larson nodded politely as he stepped inside the room. "Hope I'm not disturbing the missus."

"There is no missus," the man replied. "Hurry it up, will ya."

"Sure thing." Larson walked to the wall heater, took off the vent plate, and pretended to inspect it. "Just passing through?" he asked over his shoulder as he twisted the gas valve a couple of times for effect.

"Heading home to Tulsa," the man replied as he moved toward Larson.

"Nice town, I hear," Larson said as he turned and coldcocked the man with the butt of the semiautomatic.

The man hit the floor facedown with a thud.

With his finger on the trigger, Larson stood over the unconscious man debating whether to shoot him in the back of the head or not. If he hadn't let all those other people live yesterday, maybe the cops wouldn't be so hot on his trail and his face all over the television.

He decided not to shoot him. The motel walls were paper thin, and even if he used a pillow to muffle the sound, a gunshot could still attract unwanted attention. He straddled the man's body, bent down, and with both hands, broke his neck. The snap sounded good.

Larson pulled a wallet from the dead man's pocket and took the credit cards, three hundred and twenty-two dollars in cash, and a driver's license issued to Bertram Roach. Larson wondered if people had called him Bertie.

In Roach's luggage, he found five hundred dollars in traveler's checks in a side pocket, and a loaded, nickel-plated .38-caliber pistol under two sets of clean clothes. He set aside the fresh shirts, dumped the remaining contents on the bed, pawed through them, and didn't find anything else useful.

The keys to Roach's blue Chevy were on the nightstand. He scooped them up, got Roach's toilet kit from the bathroom, put it into the empty suitcase along with the clean shirts and the pistol, hung a Do Not Disturb sign on the doorknob, and went back to his room. He packed quickly, paused for a moment at the window to make sure the coast was clear, hurried to the Chevy, and drove away.

Checkout time at the motel was noon, so Larson figured he had a good four hours before anyone would be looking for Bertie Roach from Tulsa, Oklahoma. Bertie Roach. Bertie Cockroach. *La cucaracha.* Larson hummed a few bars of the melody.

On the visor was a pair of sunglasses. Larson put them on,

feeling pretty good about the start of his day. He now had wheels that would get him out of the city without drawing any attention, and the rest of the morning to head down the road before the cops started looking for the *cucaracha*'s vehicle.

Larson's stomach grumbled as he cruised up Central Avenue searching for a fast-food joint with a drive-through window.

In his early fifties, born and raised in the town of Carrizozo, the Lincoln County seat, Paul Hewitt had been in law enforcement for slightly over thirty years. He'd started out as a patrol officer in Roswell and worked there for five years before transferring to the Alamogordo PD, where he rose to the rank of captain before retiring. After returning to Carrizozo, Hewitt ran for sheriff, got elected in a close race, ran for reelection four years later, and won by a wide margin. Limited to two consecutive terms, he was stepping down in January. This time he'd promised his wife, Linda, his retirement would be permanent.

Both of them were longtime horse owners who loved camping, trail riding, fly-fishing, and backpacking. With two children raised and launched, they planned to spend a good deal of time fishing in New Mexico's mountain lakes and streams, riding the high country, and hiking the wilderness while they were still fit and young enough to enjoy it.

But that was next year, after winter had passed and they'd returned from two weeks at a Mexican beach resort where they would celebrate their twenty-fifth wedding anniversary. Today, Paul Hewitt was filling in on patrol while Clayton Istee was away at training and taking annual leave for the rest of the week.

A small department, the Lincoln County Sheriff's Office had only a few sworn personnel to patrol a county larger than Delaware and Rhode Island combined and then some. When first elected, Hewitt had pledged to the voters that his department would provide round-the-clock coverage. Although at times he was stretched thin by officer vacancies, family emergencies, and mandatory training and annual leave requirements, he'd managed to keep that promise, mostly by going out and pulling patrol shifts himself.

Hewitt actually enjoyed working patrol when the occasion arose. It got him back in touch with the rigors of the day-to-day grind his deputies faced and the law enforcement issues and needs that mattered most to his constituents. It also gave him an opportunity to connect with the residents of some of the smaller settlements and villages scattered throughout the county, which often got overlooked until something bad happened.

With three decades of policing under his belt, Hewitt was alert and watchful by second nature as he cruised the county roads in and around the settlements of Tinnie, Hondo, San Patricio, and Glencoe. It had been a quiet morning. He'd stopped several tourists on state highways for speeding, and because he was driving an unmarked, slick-top unit, he issued verbal warnings to them instead of tickets. He'd helped a young woman on her way to work change a flat tire, made a close patrol of several neighborhoods in the fast-growing residential community of Alto, outside of Ruidoso, where some recent burglaries had occurred, and taken a coffee break at a roadside diner owned by a buddy who'd once been a fellow officer in the Alamogordo PD.

Back in his vehicle, which had everything but official police markings and an emergency light bar on the roof, Hewitt drove a long loop that took him from Lincoln to Fort Stanton and on to Capitan, before heading back toward Carrizozo. Traffic had been light all morning, with an occasional big rig on the main east-west, north-south roadways, a few recreational vehicles slowly navigating the climb through the hills to the mesa behind Fort Stanton, and some of the rural folks on their way to town.

Throughout the morning he'd paid close attention to state police radio traffic, listening for an update on the status of the dragnet for Craig Larson. Although Larson had subsequently killed two people, there had been no confirmed sightings of him since he kidnapped the owner of a Springer auto body shop, left him in the desert, and stole his truck.

Hewitt parked on the shoulder of the highway a few miles north of Carrizozo, near the White Oaks turnoff, checked in with dispatch, asked if there were any updates on Larson, and got a negative reply. He was about to start up the road to the old mining town, which was trying to reinvent itself as an arts and crafts center and tourist attraction, when a blue Chevy with Oklahoma plates flew by.

Hewitt's radar clocked the vehicle at 85 in a 55-mph zone, way above his tolerance level for speeders. He swung around and followed the Chevy, closed the gap, and called dispatch.

"This is S.O. One," Hewitt said. "I got a blue Chevy with Oklahoma plates traveling south at a high rate of speed on Highway 54 past the White Oaks turnoff. Requesting wants and warrants." He read off the license plate information.

"Ten-four, S.O. One. Stand by."

"Ask Carrizozo PD to assist in making a traffic stop," Hewitt added. He needed a uniformed officer in a marked unit to write the citation in order to make it stick in court.

"Ten-four."

Less than a mile outside of the town limits, the Chevy slowed. Hewitt came up behind the driver unannounced just as Carrizozo Police Chief Oscar Quinones's unit came into view with emergency lights flashing.

Hewitt hit the switch to the emergency lights mounted in the grill of his unit and gave a short siren blast to get the driver's attention. He was close enough to see the driver's head snap in the direction of the rearview mirror. But instead of slowing and pulling off the highway, the driver accelerated, swerved into the oncoming traffic lane to pass a slower moving vehicle, and headed right for Oscar's police cruiser. Quinones turned sharply to avoid the crash and his vehicle left the pavement, slammed into a guardrail, and nose-dived into an arroyo.

Hewitt tried to contact Oscar by radio as he gave chase. At the town limits the driver blew through the traffic light, made a wide turn on U.S. 380 heading west, and accelerated around a tractor-trailer pulling out from a gas station at the intersection. Hewitt stayed on the Chevy's tail and tried reaching Quinones again with no luck. He told dispatch to send first responders and emergency personnel to Oscar's twenty ASAP, and requested backup assistance from any and all available units.

Hewitt sat right on the Chevy's rear bumper, with his speedometer at 110 mph. The Chevy veered over the centerline, forcing oncoming traffic off the pavement. Hewitt eased off, hoping the driver would move back into his lane, but instead the driver braked hard, spun the Chevy around in a tight one-eighty, and came at him head-on.

Paul cursed and turned to avoid the impact, but the Chevy swerved and torpedoed into the side of his unit. Side and front air bags deployed, metal crunched, buckled, and squealed. The unit tilted up on two wheels, did a complete flip, and landed right-side-up with a bone-shaking jolt.

Stunned and shaken, Hewitt reached for the seat-belt latch, but it was wedged tight against the mangled door. He reached for the glove box, found the pocketknife he always kept there, cut through the seat-belt webbing, and was about to scramble out the passenger door when a shadow in the rear window made him reach for his sidearm and duck. Glass shattered with the booming retort of a large-caliber handgun. Hewitt freed his weapon and tried to plaster himself against the floorboard under the steering wheel, which proved impossible.

The sharp sounds of gunfire continued, the rounds tearing into the Plexiglas-and-metal cage behind the seat back. Hewitt opened the passenger door and scrambled out just as something hit him like a sledgehammer in the back of his neck. In an instant, a shock wave of searing pain ran through his body before he passed out.

Still somewhat groggy from the Chevy's impact with the unmarked police cruiser, Larson threw the empty handgun away when he saw the unconscious cop with a bullet hole just below his neck lying half-in, half-out of the vehicle. He grabbed the cop under the arms, pulled him the rest of the way out of the vehicle, and flipped him over on his back. He looked dead, but even if he wasn't, it didn't matter. In fact, nothing much mattered to Larson anymore.

From the corner of his eye he saw an older woman in blue jeans and a Western shirt climb out of a pickup truck parked on the other side of the highway and hurry toward him. From inside the wrecked police vehicle he could hear the dispatcher on the radio talking in "ten"codes.

Larson reached down, grabbed the .45 semiautomatic from the cop's hand, turned, and from a distance of ten feet, blew the woman away. He snatched the badge clipped to the cop's belt, paused to pick up the keys the woman had dropped in the dirt, and gave her a quick look. Spurts of blood running out of the hole in her chest told him she was as good as dead.

He could hear the sound of a vehicle approaching a bend in the road a quarter mile distant. He ran to the wrecked Chevy, grabbed his stuff, hurried to the woman's truck, and drove away before the car showed up in the rearview mirror.

All he could do now, Larson decided, was run and hide, until his luck or the money ran out and he couldn't go any farther. It wasn't much of an option, but it was still a hell of a lot better than spending the rest of his life in solitary confinement, or being executed by injection.

Larson eased the truck over to the shoulder of the highway and rolled to a stop when he saw two cop cars racing at him with lights flashing and sirens wailing. They passed by without slowing, and Larson continued on his way, traveling back toward Carrizozo, thinking he needed to find a place to hide out, and soon.

Kevin Kerney arrived in Albuquerque to find Andy Baca at the terminal gate in his state police uniform with his four stars on his collars. They shook hands and started down the long corridor toward the public waiting area behind the security screening checkpoint. Kerney's plane out of Chicago was the last flight of the night, and except for the footsteps of the passengers hurrying toward baggage claim and the exits, the terminal was quiet and empty.

"How's Paul Hewitt?" Kerney asked. When he'd last spoken to Clayton, Hewitt was out of surgery, still unconscious, and in critical condition. "Has he pulled through?"

"Barely," Andy replied.

"Meaning?"

"He's permanently paralyzed from the neck down."

Kerney stopped in his tracks as the color drained from his face. "What?"

"He's conscious, in full possession of his faculties, and a quadriplegic." Andy gave Kerney a minute to collect himself and said, "Did you check any luggage?"

Kerney shook his head and started moving again. "I've got a closet full of everything I need at the ranch. Are Clayton and his family still there?"

"No, they're back home in Lincoln County. Paul's number-two man retired two months ago and moved to Arizona. The job has been vacant ever since, but this morning Paul appointed Clayton to be his chief deputy."

"Good choice," Kerney said. "Clayton can handle the job. Have you spoken to Paul directly?"

Andy nodded. "I saw him earlier in the evening at University Hospital. He said that with Clayton's help he's going to serve out his term in office. He's trying to be positive, but it isn't easy on him or Linda. The doctors say he won't be going home for a while. They want to get him started on a physical therapy program before he's released."

"What about Larson? Have you found him? Last I heard, he was the prime suspect in Paul's shooting."

Andy shook his head. "We've lost his trail again, but we do know for certain that he shot Paul and killed the woman who stopped at the crash site. His fingerprints were on the weapon found at the scene and all over the blue Chevy."

Andy stepped around two women who'd stopped in front of him to hug and greet each other. "By the way, the semiautomatic he used on Paul is also the weapon he used to kill Riley Burke. He used Hewitt's gun to kill the woman, Janette Evans, a rancher's widow, aged sixty-eight."

"What else can you tell me?" Kerney asked.

"We traced the stolen blue Chevy that Larson crashed into Paul's unit to a man from Oklahoma named Bertram Roach. The Albuquerque Police Department found his body in a cheap motel room on East Central Avenue. The night clerk at the motel—it's one of those fleabag establishments used by hookers, pimps, and their johns—gave them a positive ID on Larson as a paying guest."

They were outside in the dry, cool high desert night where Andy's unmarked unit was parked at the curb, hazard lights flashing.

Kerney took a deep breath and knew he was back home. He looked at Andy over the roof of the vehicle. "How many people has this guy killed?"

"Four so far that we know about. A couple more of his victims could easily have died."

"And he just tossed his murder weapon when he ran out of ammo, took Paul's sidearm, iced a lady who stopped to help, and stole her truck?"

"Affirmative. This dirtbag just doesn't give a shit."

Kerney opened the passenger door. "Let's go."

"Where to?"

"The ranch. I need to take care of the horses and get some shut-eye before I pay my respects to Riley's wife and parents in the morning. And then I have to check in with Clayton and Grace, let Sara know what's happening, and come back down to Albuquerque to see Paul and talk to Linda."

"And after that?"

"If Larson hasn't been captured by the time we bury Riley Burke, I want a commission card and a shield."

Andy opened the driver's-side door. "I figured as much."

ChapterFour

Long before dawn, Kerney was back in the horse barn finishing up the chores he'd started the night before after arriving at the ranch. He mucked out stalls, laid down fresh straw, cleaned water troughs, put out feed, shoveled fresh manure from the paddocks, and curried the horses.

Every good cowboy and rancher knew that grooming horses wasn't done to make them look pretty, but to stimulate a healthy coat and treat any small cuts and sores that would otherwise go unnoticed. The process also included inspecting and cleaning hoofs and checking for thrush, a fungus infection.

Although he enjoyed the pleasure of being close to the animals and the satisfying routine of caring for them, it didn't keep him from worrying about Riley's young wife and parents. They had to be devastated at their loss and struggling hard to accept it, and he wondered what he could do to ease their pain and assuage his own sense of guilt about Riley's murder.

As a cop who over the years had delivered the news of sudden death to many grieving families, Kerney knew that words of sympathy, no matter how heartfelt, seldom gave relief. Surely there was something more tangible he could do for the family. He just didn't know what would be acceptable to them.

Jack and Irene Burke, like many other small ranchers, were land rich and cash poor, and Riley and Lynette had brought more in the way of shared hopes and energy to their young marriage than tangible assets. Should he sell the horses and give the proceeds to Lynette as her share of Riley's half equity in the partnership? Would Lynette, an excellent horse trainer in her own right and Riley's unpaid assistant, be willing to step into Riley's shoes and take over as Kerney's partner? Or would it be too painful for her to work day in and day out at the very place where Riley had been randomly gunned down?

He had left for London secure in the knowledge that the partnership was in good hands. But now there was no way without help that he could keep the cutting horse enterprise going and live full-time with Sara and Patrick in England. Maybe it would be best to sell the stock, give the proceeds to Lynette Burke, find a reliable live-in caretaker for the ranch, and wait until Sara retired before trying again to operate the ranch as a business. He decided to hold off on making any decisions until he knew what Lynette wanted to do.

He finished scraping his stud horse Comeuppance's hoofs and turned him loose by himself in a large paddock near the barn. Like any stallion, he would attack the geldings and try to drive them away or kill them if given the opportunity.

On a selfish level, Kerney didn't like the idea of getting rid of the stock and dissolving the business. He would then have no legitimate reason other than plain homesickness to make frequent trips back to the ranch.

By sunup the horses were watered, fed, groomed, and inspected. He saddled Hondo, and with the exception of Comeuppance, he trailed the stock up the hill behind the ranch house into the fenced north pasture. He watched them for a while against the backdrop of the morning sun cascading over the slightly misty Sangre de Cristo Mountains. The geldings pranced and high-stepped while Patrick's pony, Pablito, cantered off in the direction of the windmill. Sara's favorite gelding, Gipsy, a bald-faced, dark sorrel, trotted back to the gate, snorted, and shook his head as if to signal his displeasure that Hondo couldn't join him. Then he kicked up his heels and galloped away.

The fun of being back at the ranch made him feel guilty all over again about Riley's murder. He dismounted, unsaddled Hondo, and turned him loose in the pasture with Gipsy and the other stock. As he walked down the hill with saddle and bridle slung over his shoulder, he wondered what in the hell he could do about any of it.

After breakfast, Kerney cleaned himself up, called Jack Burke, and asked if he could pay a visit. Usually a man of unbridled enthusiasm, Jack sounded emotionally numb and dispirited as he told Kerney to stop by anytime.

Kerney said he was on his way and disconnected quickly to avoid blurting out anything about Riley's death or Jack's loss. He still had no idea what he might say, only that he needed to say it in person.

The Burkes lived on a ranch road fifteen minutes from Kerney's place, in a two-hundred-year-old hacienda sheltered by ancient cottonwoods at the edge of a broad, sandy arroyo. Kerney felt a sudden sense of dismay when he saw Riley's pickup truck parked in front of the small, enclosed yard that bordered the nearby foreman's cottage where Riley and Lynette had set up housekeeping.

Jack greeted Kerney on the steps of the screened hacienda porch, shook his outstretched hand, and explained that Irene and Lynette were meeting with the pastor of their church to discuss the services for Riley.

"I'm sorry I've missed them," he said.

Jack nodded listlessly as he ushered Kerney into the living room and gestured at the couch next to his favorite easy chair.

Kerney sat, waited for Jack to settle himself, and asked, "Have the services been set?"

"Not yet," Jack replied. "We're still arranging for family to come in. Mine from Deming and Lordsburg, Irene's from Texas, Riley's cousins from Spokane and Boise, and Lynette's parents from Wyoming. It takes a while to get everybody together."

"I don't have any words for you, Jack."

Burke held up his hand to stop Kerney. "That's good, because there aren't any, and they all ring hollow in my ears anyhow. Soon, we'll gather to celebrate Riley's life. You, Sara, and Patrick have to join us."

Kerney nodded affirmatively. Last night on the telephone, Sara told him her boss, the admiral, had approved her leave request, and she was ready to book a flight as soon as Kerney gave her the date for the funeral. "We'll all be there."

"Good," Jack replied, gazing down at his tightly clasped hands in his lap. "Good," he said again, the word barely audible. He tried to brighten. "How is Patrick?"

"He's fine, Jack."

"Good. That's good."

For a long time, Kerney sat in silence with his friend, imagining how horrible it must feel to lose a son who'd grown into such a fine young man. Jack wasn't crying or blinking back tears, but he was tensed up tight, every muscle in his hands, arms, face, and neck bunched and corded, a thousand-yard stare in his eyes.

Kerney wanted to tell Jack to let go, give in to the grief, and have a gut-wrenching cry, but he didn't say a word. Instead, he remained seated and unmoving on the couch for a long, uneasy time until Jack rose, excused himself, walked down the hallway to the bedroom he'd shared with Irene for over thirty years, and closed the door behind him.

Kerney waited awhile for Jack to return. When he didn't come back, he quietly let himself out. He drove home with a great sadness pressing down on him.

• • •

After shooting the cop and the old lady on the highway outside Carrizozo, Craig Larson was camped out no more than thirty miles away in some mountains off a seldom-used Forest Service road.

He didn't know much about Lincoln County, and he'd been anxious to get off the pavement as soon as possible in case a swarm of cops was converging on him. After passing through the village of Capitan, he left the highway for a well-maintained dirt-and-gravel road that ran directly toward some northerly mountains. For several miles he traveled through grassy rangeland before gradually ascending toward what appeared to be a mountain gap. Soon he was driving through woodlands and he felt safe enough to stop and see what exactly there was in the truck.

There were grocery bags on the floor in front of the passenger seat that he hadn't had a chance to look into and others in the truck bed. He pawed through them and found an assortment of canned goods, coffee and other supplies, two large jars of spaghetti sauce, ground beef, eggs, carrots, potatoes, a large bag of apples, cheese, crackers, four gallon jugs of water, and basic toiletries including soap, shampoo, and women's disposable razors. According to the sales receipt the woman had purchased them at an Albuquerque discount supermarket several hours before he'd shot her dead. The nice timing gave him a chuckle. What a bummer if he'd offed her before she'd done his shopping for him.

There were two old canvas tarps folded under the bench seat of the truck and a first aid kit with one of those shiny fold-up space-age emergency blankets that were supposed to keep you warm and did a fairly good job of it. There was also a shovel for digging out the truck if it got stuck. Apparently, the old biddy believed in being prepared.

The only thing she hadn't provided was a mess kit. He'd have to improvise and empty some cans to cook in. It would be a sin to waste the fresh meat and eggs.

He drove through the forest and half a mile on, he came to a side road with a partially open gate. A wooden sign attached to the gate read "1 Peter 2:24."

Larson wondered what in the hell that scripture passage said. He guessed some kindhearted Christians had a mountain ranch down that road. Maybe he could take them hostage and use their place as a hideaway until the heat cooled off.

He decided to do nothing and lie low for a while. He drove on and the road soon turned into a rough, narrow, seldom-used track that cut through a dense forest. About two miles beyond the gate, Larson found himself deep in the woods with no signs of any human habitation, no more gates, no additional side roads, and no hiking trails. His only reference point had been a faded Forest Service marker that told him what road he was on, but he didn't have a clue if it traversed the mountains, joined up with another Forest Service road, or simply petered out into a dead end somewhere up ahead.

He slowed to a stop and thought over his situation. If he went deeper into the mountains only to reach a dead end, the cops could box him in if they picked up his trail, and he'd have no chance of eluding capture on foot. Even if there wasn't a dead end up ahead, the fuel gauge on the truck was showing about an eighth of a tank, which meant he might be forced to hike out of the mountains even if the cops were nowhere around.

Larson reflected on the gate with the scripture sign. Maybe St. Peter was telling him it might be necessary to slaughter a few Christians. It would be a sin to waste that opportunity, he thought, and laughed long and hard at the repetition of the words in his mind. He turned the steering wheel and drove deep into the woods, until he was out of sight of any vehicles that might pass by.

He walked back to the road, scuffed out the tire tracks with his boots and a stick, and kicked duff over them to hide any sign that could lead someone to the truck. Then he set up camp using the truck as a shelter. He shoveled pine needles in the truck bed and covered them with one of the canvas tarps, stretched the other tarp across the bed, tied it taut with some rope he found in the glove box, and put some small dead and down twigs and small branches over the tarp to keep it from flapping in the wind.

Larson tilted the driver's-side mirror and looked at his face. His beard was growing in nicely, and he figured if he let it grow and shaved his head, the combination might give him a reasonably good disguise. He started to hack away at his hair with the small pair of scissors from the first aid kit and soon realized it would take a while to get it cropped short enough to shave. With nothing better to do, he kept clipping until his fingers got sore and his empty stomach started grumbling. He got into the truck, sat down on the passenger seat, opened a can of tuna fish and wolfed it down, grinning at himself in the visor mirror. Already he looked different with his hair cut short.

He threw the empty tuna fish can into the trees, got back out of the truck, and started to work with the scissors again. When his hair was short enough, he took a disposable razor out of the pack, splashed some water on his head, lathered up, and started shaving the rest of it off.

By his second morning in the mountains, Craig Larson had an itchy head from a dozen or so small razor cuts, as well as a twitch to get moving. Not once had he heard a vehicle on the road since he'd arrived. A horse and rider had passed by late the first morning, but by the time Larson reached the road, they were out of sight.

He was pretty sure the cops had no idea where he was. With

the truck's radio turned down real low, he'd listened to the news just enough to learn that Paul Hewitt, the sheriff he'd shot, was a paralyzed cripple, and the old lady he'd killed, Janette Evans, a former Lincoln County clerk, had been loved and respected by all. Supposedly, every cop and concerned citizen in the state was looking for lovable Janette's truck.

Larson decided to leave the truck where he'd hidden it, walk back to the "Bible Gate," and have a look around before figuring out his next move. He followed the forest road down the mountain until he got close enough to see the gate and then hiked through the woods paralleling the side road, expecting to come upon either a small ranch in a clearing or a vacation cabin in the woods. Instead, he encountered a large riding ring filled with teenage girls and boys on horseback, cantering in circles under the watchful eye of a wrangler.

From behind a tree, Larson watched for a minute. The girls looked quite tasty in the saddle as they bounced and jiggled. He moved past a barn, several stables, and a couple of equipment sheds. Beyond them, he found an enormous log lodge with a pitched shingled roof and a modern-looking building with a vaulted, needle-point roof. A number of railroad cars placed next to Old West–style false-front buildings lined several lanes near the lodge and the vaulted-roof building, which Larson figured might be a church. He wasn't sure what the false-front buildings and railroad cars were used for, but guessed they might be housing quarters for guests.

He stayed in the trees and out of sight, but moved close enough to read a sign nailed to a post in front of the vaulted-roof structure, which told him it was the worship center. He'd entered some holy-roller summer Bible camp.

Off to one side of the worship center was a compound Larson took to be staff housing. Under a stand of leafy trees, some cabin-size houses and several larger ranch-style residences were partially hidden by evergreen junipers. Laundry hung on clotheslines, toys for toddlers filled small porches, swings and slides stood in backyards, and dogs yipped and yapped behind chicken-wire fences.

Larson retreated and the barking dogs fell quiet as he made his way back to the forest road and started hiking up the mountain toward the truck. Since slaughtering a couple of Christians to hide out at a remote mountain ranch was no longer an option, he would have to rethink his plans.

The image of those teenage girls so sweet and pretty on horseback stuck in his mind. Maybe he should kidnap one of them, steal a vehicle, and just find another hiding place where he could enjoy some female company until things quieted down.

Chief Deputy Clayton Istee of the Lincoln County S.O. saturated his jurisdiction with every available resource in an attempt to find and capture Craig Larson. All sworn department personnel were called back to duty, including one deputy who willingly cut short his vacation in California and flew home to join the manhunt. All municipal and city police officers eagerly joined in, as did district state police personnel, game and fish officers, Forest Service and Bureau of Land Management officers, several New Mexico livestock inspectors, and dozens of local volunteers who were enraged about the murder of Janette Evans and the paralyzing injury to Paul Hewitt.

Even Sergeant Rudy Aldrich of the Lincoln County S.O., who was also the Republican Party candidate for sheriff in the November general election, had managed to set aside partisan politics for the time being and give his full attention to the manhunt.

Several area ranchers with private planes were flying aerial reconnaissance missions with volunteer spotters over the vast tracts of open range and the thousands of square miles of remote high country. Sheriff's posse reserve officers were out on horseback riding into remote canyons, through large, dense cactus flats, and up dry arroyos and draws looking for any sign of recent foot or vehicle passage.

Clayton ran the manhunt from his unit. As time allowed, he knocked on doors in rural areas to ask if anyone had seen Janette Evans's truck, backed up officers doing searches of abandoned or vacant properties, and spelled officers for breaks at the various roadblocks set up around the county. With each passing hour the odds of catching Larson decreased, and the continued massive effort to find him was based solely on a hope and a prayer that he might have gone to ground in Lincoln County.

An hour before dusk on the third day of the search, Clayton stopped at the diner on Capitan's main drag, got a container of coffee to go, returned to his unit, and went over a computer printout that showed all the rural locations that had been canvassed so far. On the slight chance that a hint of Larson's whereabouts might have been missed during the first go-round, Clayton had ordered another heavy concentration of close patrols in areas with remote ranches, vacation cabins, or second homes, at all forest campgrounds, at mountain trailheads, and along river bottomland, especially near Fort Stanton, where there were caves that could be used to hide out.

He'd divided the county into sectors to be covered, and assigned all but one to his deputies. He had taken the Fort Stanton area for himself, and had just spent the last four hours tromping along the Bonita River searching the caves.

Before driving home for dinner—it would be the first meal with the family since Paul Hewitt had been shot and Janette Evans killed—he decide to check the Twin Pines Adventure Bible

Camp at the base of the Capitan Mountains. He finished his coffee, drove east on Highway 380 to the county road turnoff, and made his way along the rolling, juniper-studded rangeland to the Bible camp.

When Clayton had first joined the Lincoln County S.O. as a patrol deputy, he'd made it a point to introduce himself to as many rural residents as possible during his work shifts. After his initial visit to the Bible camp, he'd looked up the citation posted on the gate and found that it basically said that Jesus had suffered on the cross to give mankind the opportunity to live a righteous life healed from sin.

A nominal Christian like most Apaches, Clayton wasn't all that comfortable with the notion of a single, all-powerful deity. The traditional religion of the Mescalero was a personal, family, and tribal matter, not a theology to spread hither and yon.

The camp had been quite an eye-opener for Clayton. It operated year-round, but summer was the busy season, when teenagers came to ride horses, shoot rifles, mountain bike, backpack, rock climb, play volleyball, work out in the gym, study the scriptures, and engage in Christian fellowship.

He parked at the camp director's house just as a spirited group of laughing teenagers came down the lane on their way to the worship center. He crossed the porch, knocked on the front door, and watched as the kids passed by, clowning, screeching, and teasing each other in the private world that adolescents inhabit.

The camp director, Reverend Gaylord Wardle, a soft-spoken, middle-aged man with a big, benevolent smile that Clayton had instantly mistrusted at their first meeting, opened the door. He greeted Clayton warmly.

"We're keeping a close watch on our flock," Wardle added before Clayton could speak. "We're doing head counts four times a day. No campers are allowed to leave the ranch unsupervised.

All are present and accounted for, and we've posted the photographs of the fugitive that another officer dropped off to us in every ranch building."

"That's very good," Clayton said. "Have you or your staff encountered any strangers on the county road?"

Wardle shook his head. "There has been virtually no traffic. With that murderer still at large I think people are afraid to be out in the mountains on their own, away from civilization. The only vehicles we've seen have belonged to the Forest Service or the neighboring ranches."

"Call 911 immediately if anyone unknown to you, your staff, or the campers shows up here unannounced."

"Wouldn't that be overreacting a bit?" Wardle asked. "After all, we do have photographs of the culprit."

"Appearances can be easily altered," Clayton countered.

Wardle stroked his chin. "Yes, of course. I didn't think of that."

Clayton stepped off the porch. "Thank you for your time."

"Of course. Each day at prayer we ask Jesus to protect all the men and women in law enforcement who are working so hard night and day to keep us safe. Thank you so much for all that you do. Are you any closer to capturing this madman?"

"Not yet," Clayton replied with a wave as he walked toward his unit.

He drove slowly through camp and out the open gate. On the county road he stopped, got out of his unit, and in the glare of the headlights took a close look at the surface of the road. It had rained in the mountains recently, just enough to wash away evidence of any vehicles traveling into the forest. But there was a set of fresh footprints on the road along with a set of hoofprints headed toward Capitan Gap.

He got a flashlight from his unit and followed the footprints a few yards past the gate, where the tracks left the road and cut through the woods parallel to the Bible camp access road. He got the local phone directory from his unit, paged through it, and dialed Gaylord Wardle's phone number on his cell phone.

"Are you patrolling the access road to the camp?" Clayton asked when Wardle answered.

"Yes," Wardle replied. "I've assigned nighttime sentry duty to several of my young-adult counselors, just to keep an eye on things, and we're also locking the gate at lights-out."

"Have you armed the counselors?" Clayton asked, hoping Wardle hadn't been that stupid.

"Yes, with .22 rifles, but for their own protection only. Not to worry, they're all National Rifle Association certified instructors."

Clayton had no legal authority to order Wardle to disarm his counselors, but that didn't stop him from offering some unsolicited advice. "To avoid a tragic accident, I suggest you lock up all your firearms, Mr. Wardle, including the twenty-twos your sentries are carrying."

"These young men are certified instructors," Wardle repeated in a bit of a huff, "and at Twin Pines we teach and practice the right to bear arms."

"That is your right," Clayton replied. "But your gun-toting counselors probably won't be much of a match for a killer on the run with nothing to lose."

"I appreciate your concern," Wardle said icily. "Good-bye."

Clayton disconnected, sat in his unit, and studied the computer printout of all the canvasses and field searches that had been conducted since the start of the manhunt. A sheriff's posse member had traversed part of the Capitan wilderness area on horseback, passed through the gap, followed the four-wheel-drive trail to Seven Cabins Canyon, and then ridden cross-county to hook up with the Summit Trail that led to Capitan Peak before doubling back to check the only campground in the area, along Spring Creek.

There had been no sightings of anyone, but Clayton knew a regiment of searchers on foot and horseback could easily miss a person who didn't want to be found in the vast expanse of forest and wilderness in Lincoln County. Although the Forest Service had removed all back-country hikers from the Capitan Mountains wilderness area, and was routinely checking all access points into federal land, Clayton made a note to have a deputy do a daily drive-by of the Bible camp starting tomorrow. Given limited resources, that was the best that could be done. He put the printout aside and started for the Rez, eagerly anticipating a home-cooked dinner with his family.

Clayton got home just as Grace, Wendell, and Hannah were sitting down to eat. They waited for him while he locked his sidearm in the gun case, washed up, filled his plate with barbecue short ribs and potato salad, and joined them at the table.

During dinner, the children dominated the conversation. Wendell, who attended the Boys & Girls Club several afternoons a week during summer vacation, talked with great excitement about disassembling an old computer that had been donated to the technology class at the club and learning all about what went into making the machine work.

Hannah, who attended a morning arts and crafts program run by volunteers, was having a grand time learning basket making and enlarging her Apache language skills at the same time, which was a requirement for participating. On the table in front of her was a small traylike basket, no more than four inches in circumference, done in the traditional star motif with four tapered points.

"What do you have there?" Clayton asked.

"My teacher said it is well balanced," Hannah said modestly.

Clayton raised an eyebrow. To the Mescalero, balance was essential to the circle of life, a key concept in the Apache worldview. His daughter's work had been highly praised. "Did she?" he asked.

Hannah nodded solemnly and held the basket out to her father. "It's for you."

Clayton wiped his mouth, took the basket from his daughter's outstretched hand, and carefully inspected it. Hannah had used split yucca leaves to weave her basket, and for a girl not yet six years old, the workmanship was darn good.

Hannah kicked her feet against the rung of her chair and kept her eyes glued to her father's face as she waited for his reaction.

"It is well balanced," Clayton finally said, speaking in the Apache language. "My daughter is too generous with her gift."

Hannah beamed delightedly.

After dinner, Clayton summoned up enough energy to shoot some baskets with Wendell at the hoop he'd installed over the garage door. Under the glare of exterior lights, Wendell faked, dribbled, and ran circles around Clayton, firing layups, jumpers, and hook shots at the basket with reckless abandon.

Taller than the boys on the Rez his age, Wendell had sprouted at least another inch since summer recess and was showing signs of becoming quite a good athlete. He had quickness, speed, and excellent hand-eye coordination. Clayton, who had lettered in cross-country track and basketball in high school, looked forward to the time when he could watch his son compete and cheer him on.

When bedtime came, he tucked the children in and then joined Grace on the couch in the living room.

"Did Wendell question you about the manhunt for Riley Burke's killer?" she asked.

"No. Why?"

"He's been telling Hannah that you're going to catch and scalp the man who murdered Grandfather Kerney's friend and shot the sheriff."

Clayton grinned. "Why, that little Apache savage. Where did he get that notion?"

"It's not funny, Clayton. I don't like him scaring his little sister. Hannah was very troubled by what he said."

"I'll talk to him."

"Are you going back out tonight?"

"I should."

"You've given every officer in the department a night off except yourself."

Clayton sighed. "I keep seeing Paul Hewitt lying in his hospital bed staring up at me, unable to move. The look in his eyes haunts me. I just don't want to stop until I catch the scumbag."

"And scalp him," Grace added.

"That too."

"I hope you know that you're not going to remain the chief deputy next January when the new sheriff takes office."

Clayton nodded. Touting similar clean sweep positions, both candidates had long ago made known their selections for the chief deputy job. If elected, the Republican candidate, Sergeant Rudy Aldrich, planned to appoint a police officer crony from another department, and his Democratic opponent, the Capitan police chief, had tapped a retired state police captain for the job.

"It may happen sooner than that," he said. "I've heard that the chairman of the county commission is going to call for a vote to have the state revoke Paul's police officer certification based on his permanent incapacity to serve. If that happens, the sheriff's position will be considered vacated, and since the majority of commissioners are Republicans, they'll probably appoint Aldrich as interim sheriff to give him a leg up in the general election."

"I can't believe they'd do that."

"Dirty politics in the sheriff's office have been a part of Lincoln County since the days of Billy the Kid."

"Would you be willing to stay with the department as a lieutenant under Aldrich?"

Clayton covered a long yawn with his hand. "I couldn't work for him. He's an autocratic backstabber and not very bright."

Grace stood, reached down, and caressed Clayton's cheek. "Why don't you get some sleep?"

"The roadblocks come down tomorrow. I need to get back out there and make the rounds."

"Rest first."

Clayton stretched out on the couch. "Maybe a short nap. Wake me in an hour."

Grace squeezed Clayton's hand. "Okay."

Ten minutes later she returned from the kitchen to find Clayton on his side sleeping soundly. She had no intention of waking him. Hopefully, he would sleep undisturbed throughout the night. She picked up the book she was reading from the coffee table, turned out the lights, and went quietly down the hall to check on the children before retiring to the bedroom.

Gregory Dennis Cuddy had attended the Twin Pines Bible Camp for the first time at the age of fourteen. Since then, he'd come back eight consecutive summers. In his third year, he'd joined the staff as a peer counselor. Having just graduated with a bachelor's degree in religious education from Ross Wentworth Bible College, a private evangelical institution in Brownwood, Texas, Greg was now the youth minister assisting Reverend Wardle and teaching Bible study twice a day.

An East Texas boy who loved to fish and hunt and excelled at sports, Greg had been a high school football star. But when a knee injury ended his athletic career, he took it as a sign from God to enter the ministry. In the fall, he would begin his studies for a master's in theology.

At six feet and two hundred and ten pounds, Greg Cuddy was every mother's dream of how a grown son should look. He was the all-American boy with light brown hair, an athletic physique, strong masculine features, and a rich baritone voice that would serve him well from the pulpit.

As a teenager, Greg had seriously considered a career as a forest ranger or a game and fish officer, but the call to preach the word of Jesus had been too strong for him to resist. However, he knew that he wouldn't be happy with the sedentary life of a church-bound minister. He had already decided that once he had his master's degree in hand and was fully ordained, he would serve Jesus as a career navy chaplain in the Marine Corps.

In addition to his role as youth minister, Greg also supervised the Twin Pines adventure program and served as the camp's riflery instructor and range master. When word came that the local sheriff had been shot, the woman who'd stopped to help had been murdered, and the killer was on the loose in the county, Reverend Wardle had naturally put Greg in charge of camp security.

Greg enthusiastically instituted a head-count policy, had campers team up in a buddy system so no one went anywhere alone, and assigned the staff to a rotating nighttime sentry duty schedule.

Tonight was his turn to pull a shift. After lights-out, he went to the armory and retrieved the lever-action .22 Marlin model 1897cb his parents had given him on his fourteenth birthday, loaded it, and made a walking tour of the campus before driving a staff pickup down to the gate to make sure it was locked.

After finding everything secure, he sat in the truck with the windows open, the motor and lights off, and let his mind wander. The last several days had been a rush for Greg. He liked the feeling of being in charge of camp security. It was kind of like being sheriff of Twin Pines. He liked the buzz that came from doing something that seemed a little dangerous. The idea of putting it on the line to protect others appealed to the image he had of himself as a natural born leader.

Now he was thinking that maybe he should delay graduate school in the fall, put off becoming a full-fledged minister for the time being, and enlist in the Marine Corps. With a tour of duty under his belt as a jarhead, surely he would be more accepted by other Marines once he became a navy chaplain.

Above the murmur of a slight breeze in the treetops, he heard some twigs snap in the underbrush. He stiffened, clutched the stock of his Marlin, and listened intently to the ensuing silence for a while before relaxing and taking a deep breath.

Wildlife abounded in these mountains. It could have been a deer, a coyote, a porcupine, maybe even a black bear or a mountain lion, although the big cats were rarely seen.

As Greg put the Marlin aside and reached to switch on the engine, a burning pain exploded inside his brain, a flash of white light burst in front of his eyes, and his head hit the steering wheel.

Craig Larson opened the door to the Bible camp pickup and in the glow of the interior dome light looked at the slumped form of the young man he'd coldcocked with the butt of the Lincoln County sheriff's handgun. On the bench seat next to him was a sweet-looking lever-action .22 rifle. Larson reached across the kid and grabbed the rifle. It was fully loaded with .22 long cartridges, a nice addition to his arsenal.

He decided not to kill the kid right away. He'd left behind too many bodies—alive and dead—that had kept the cops on his heels and within striking distance. Of course, until the last several days, he'd been in such a big hurry to get away from the cops there had been no time to even think about properly disposing of the bodies.

He tapped the kid on the back of the head to make sure he stayed unconscious for a while, wrestled his limp body to the passenger side of the cab, searched his pockets, and found a key that unlocked the gate barring the road. He got the bundle of money and jewelry he'd stashed under a pine tree, along with the pistol he'd lifted from Roach's luggage at the Albuquerque motel, slid behind the wheel, fired up the truck engine, and looked over at the cross dangling from a chain around the kid's neck.

Larson chuckled as he closed the driver's-side door and drove through the open gate. He'd come down the mountain to steal a vehicle from the Bible camp so he could get moving again, and the Christians—God love them—had made it so damn easy. *Praise Jesus*.

As he drove, Larson reviewed in his mind the route he'd selected from a state highway map in the old lady's truck. He knew from the radio news broadcasts that the cops had thrown up roadblocks around the county, and although he didn't know exactly where they had their checkpoints, he figured he was bound to run into one of them at the junction to U.S. 70, a major east-west highway up ahead.

Larson's plan was to travel east for a spell before heading north. He glanced over at the inert form of Gregory Dennis Cuddy, who, according to his driver's license, wasn't going to get to celebrate his upcoming twenty-third birthday. The kid, who had unwittingly supplied Larson with transportation and a loaded rifle, might still be of service. The Texas state line was only a few hours away. Why not dump Cuddy's body—Kid Cuddy, Larson decided to call him—on a Texas highway before traveling back into New Mexico and heading north? That might get the cops swarming to a place where Larson wouldn't be.

It was a worthy idea, but first Larson had to find out if he had a roadblock to contend with, and if so how to get around it. Although the Bible camp pickup truck probably wouldn't raise suspicion, and Larson looked quite different with a shaved head and the start of a beard, he wasn't about to just drive up to the roadblock and try to bluff his way through.

He stayed within the speed limit on a road with no other traffic, passing through the historic village of Lincoln, where few lights were on in the inhabited houses that fronted the highway. Beyond Lincoln the road was fairly straight with gentle curves every now and then, but he still kept a light foot on the accelerator. As the hills on either side of the highway receded, he came around a long, easy bend and caught sight of flashing emergency lights in the distance.

He slowed just as the truck headlights illuminated a real estate sign at a driveway offering a horse ranch for sale, turned in, quickly drove off the gravel lane, and parked the truck under some trees in a pasture that bordered a riverbed. He killed the lights and engine, and waited for his eyes to adjust to the darkness. Across the way stood a house and horse barn accessed by a wooden plank bridge that spanned the river. Everything appeared dark and quiet.

Larson reached over and felt Kid Cuddy's neck for a pulse, found it, and tapped him on the skull for good measure, to keep him knocked out.

Kid Cuddy, the knocked-out king, Larson thought with a smile. *Kid Cuddy, down and out for the count. Soon to be that way permanently.*

Larson had no idea where his heightened sense of humor had come from, but he was enjoying it immensely. He switched off the dome light to keep the cab dark when he got out of the truck, picked up the Marlin, stuck the semiautomatic in his belt, and started walking down the shoulder of the highway toward the flashing emergency lights, a short quarter mile distant.

When he was close enough to take a good look, he crouched down in some bushes and shaded his eyes from the flashing lights. He spotted one officer sitting in a black-and-white state police patrol car parked diagonally facing his direction. Orange cones and road flares placed across the pavement served as barriers to stop traffic.

Larson could see the cop clearly. He had a clipboard resting on the steering wheel and was writing something down under the bright glare of a halogen task light. Larson moved closer, until he was no more than fifty yards away, and waited a good five minutes to make sure there wasn't a second cop somewhere off in the bushes taking a dump. The cop's driver's-side window was open and Larson could hear the low sounds of sporadic radio traffic.

Larson had grown up in northeast New Mexico hunting rabbits, rodents, and varmints with a .22 as a kid, before moving on to larger animals and more powerful weapons. At a range of fifty yards on a still night with a clear target and a sweet rifle loaded with long rounds, one good head shot was all he needed to take the cop out.

Larson patted the rifle, silently thanked Kid Cuddy for his Christian generosity in providing him with such a fine weapon, brought the stock to his shoulder, held his breath, sighted down the barrel, and gently squeezed the trigger, thinking this was *really* going to piss all the other cops off.

• • •

Out of the corner of his eye from his hospital bed in the partially darkened room, Paul Hewitt could see his wife sleeping in the chair, her head resting against a pillow supplied by the night nurse. He'd married Linda almost twenty-five years ago and she was still his girl.

Small-boned and only five foot three, she managed to seem taller. Paul attributed it to her slender legs, narrow waist, and long neck, which gave the appearance of height. She wore her dark brown hair long, and he loved it when she wrapped it in a French twist and used her grandmother's hairpins to hold it in place.

Soon after they married, Paul had asked Linda to agree to an end-of-life power of attorney stipulating that in case of a catastrophic injury or terminal illness he was not to be placed on life support. At the time, he'd joked about having "Do not resuscitate" tattooed across his chest. Linda had countered his power of attorney with one of her own, stipulating the same conditions.

A man who loved life, Paul longed for death. Below the neck he felt nothing, not even the sensation of his diaphragm moving as he took a breath and slowly exhaled. He was angry at Craig Larson for not killing him and for inflicting a cruel and horrible burden on Linda. He closed his eyes.

Because he was a cop, and a good one at that, Paul knew how to ask questions and get people talking. Fortunately, the spinal cord injury had not caused aphasia, so over the past two days he'd chatted with doctors, nurses, physical therapists, nursing aides, and medical students about his condition. What he'd learned was depressing and disheartening. Physical therapy would consist of someone else moving his arms and legs to keep his muscles from atrophying. He would have to be turned in his bed to avoid sores. He would require laxatives and enemas in order to have bowel movements, would be forced to wear a bag to defecate into and a urinary device to piss into. He would have to be wiped and cleaned, washed and dressed, hoisted and lifted, fed and shaved. Because of his injury, he would now and forever be susceptible to bouts of pneumonia, bone fractures, urinary tract infections, cardiovascular disease, pulmonary embolisms, and a host of other complications.

Linda, as his primary caregiver, would require support, possibly therapy, certainly some regular relief from the stress of looking after her husband. Couples counseling was considered essential to deal with the initial and ongoing trauma of both living as a quadriplegic *and* living with one.

The miracle of modern medicine that had kept Paul Hewitt alive was a crock of shit.

He opened his eyes. Linda was standing over him, smiling.

"Kill me," he said.

Her eyes widened in shock. "Don't say that."

"Find someone who will."

"Never."

"Get me a lawyer."

"What for?" Linda asked.

"I want a divorce," Paul said, shutting his eyes to block out the sight of his wife's face.

ChapterFive

Officer Leroy Alfred Ordonez's body sat upright behind the steering wheel of the state police black-and-white, his head resting against the seat back. His right eye and mouth were open and there was a hole where his left eye used to be. A gooey blood stream from the wound had trickled down his cheek, coagulated on his uniform shirt, and dribbled on the clipboard lying in his lap. The size of the entry wound and apparent absence of an exit hole indicated that the killer had used a small-caliber weapon, probably a .22, most likely a rifle.

Clayton swallowed hard and stepped away from the black-and-white. Flashing emergency lights hurled brilliant colors into a midnight sky. Behind him, Gene Walcott, the only Lincoln County deputy on roving patrol duty, walked up the highway with a flashlight looking for evidence the killer might have left. In front of him, Captain Steve Ramsey, the district state police commander, stood with another officer viewing a laptop computer monitor Ramsey had placed on the hood of his unit.

Clayton glanced back at Ordonez's body. Some time back, after four seasons playing Minor League Baseball, Leroy had returned home to Ruidoso. He'd worked construction for a time before attending the state police academy and graduating first in his class. Leroy liked to joke that he could have made the big leagues if he had only learned to hit sliders, field grounders cleanly, and run the bases without being thrown out.

When their shifts coincided and time allowed, Clayton and Leroy met for coffee or a meal break. Although they never socialized much away from the job, Clayton considered Leroy a friend. At home on his refrigerator was an invitation to attend Leroy's upcoming marriage to Kathleen Ann Pennington. Grace had circled the date on their calendar and begun searching for a wedding gift. Now a gift wouldn't be necessary.

Clayton looked away from Leroy. He'd bottled up the image of a paralyzed Paul Hewitt staring at him from his hospital bed, and now he had to clear his mind of Leroy Ordonez. He walked over to see what Steve Ramsey had discovered on the video taken by the camera in Leroy's unit. Ramsey shifted his large frame to one side so Clayton could look at the laptop monitor, and pointed at the frozen image of a blurry, washed-out pickup truck.

"The killer was driving this truck," he said, looking down at Clayton from his six-foot-six height. "It's the only vehicle that passed through the roadblock around the time of the shooting. The driver blasted through the orange cones without stopping. We can't make out anything inside of the cab."

Clayton leaned forward for a closer look. What appeared as a blob on the passenger's-side door might be a magnetic business sign or a logo. "Can you zoom in on the passenger's-side door?"

"Until the lab can enhance the video, this is the best picture quality we have right now," Ramsey replied.

"Go back a few frames," Clayton said.

The officer operating the laptop did as Clayton asked and froze the image again. The passenger's-side door showed two slightly distinct but very wavy horizontal lines.

"Those lines could be nothing more than shadows," Ramsey said.

"Can you zoom out?" Clayton asked.

"It's a late-model Ford," Ramsey offered as his officer made the adjustment. "Probably a four-wheel-drive F-150."

"That's a Twin Pines Bible Camp pickup truck," Clayton said, flipping open his cell phone.

"Are you sure?" Ramsey asked.

"Let's make sure," Clayton said as he pulled up Gaylord Wardle's phone number from the recently dialed list of calls on his cell phone and pressed Send. After twelve long rings, Wardle picked up.

"Where are the camp's pickup trucks usually parked?" Clayton asked Wardle after he'd quickly identified himself.

"At the maintenance building. Why?"

"What are the makes and models?"

"We have three Ford F-150s, four-by-fours. They're a couple years old. Why?"

"One may have been stolen. Go to the maintenance building right now, find out if a vehicle is missing, and call me back immediately." Clayton rattled off his cell phone number.

Five minutes later a very upset Wardle called back to say a truck was gone and the camp's youth minister, Greg Cuddy, who was supposed to be on security patrol, was nowhere to be found.

Clayton calmed Wardle down enough to get a description of Gregory Cuddy and a license plate number for the truck. "Wake up everyone at the camp and do a head count," he ordered Wardle. "We need to know if anyone else is missing. I'll be there as soon as possible."

"Is a head count at this time of night absolutely necessary?" Wardle demanded.

"Either you do it, or I will," Clayton replied.

"All right," Wardle replied without enthusiasm.

Clayton disconnected, filled in Ramsey on what he'd learned, corralled Deputy Walcott, and told him to stop searching for evidence and follow him to the Bible camp. He got in his unit, switched on his emergency lights, and drove away. As the crime scene faded in Clayton's rearview mirror, a dispatcher issued a five-state regional BOLO on the truck, citing an officer down and the possible abduction of one Gregory Cuddy.

Back at the roadblock, not a word had been spoken about the impact of Leroy's death on the men who'd found him. In order to cope, every officer at the crime scene had wiped away all personal feelings. Grief would have to wait. Anger would have to wait. The shrinks called it depersonalization, but to Clayton and the others it was simply an issue of their own emotional survival.

According to the time and date stamp on the video, the cop killer had a good ninety-minute head start in the middle of the night, when there were few if any officers patrolling highways, and absolutely none roaming the many unpaved rural country roads of southeastern New Mexico and West Texas. It would take a miracle to catch him before daybreak, and chances of a capture after that weren't much better. He could be long gone before a dragnet could be launched.

Clayton had no doubt the killer was Craig Larson, but he had to prove it before he could announce it. With the speedometer hovering at ninety-five miles an hour and the emergency lights of his deputy a hundred yards behind him, Clayton raced down the highway.

In his hurry to go home, had he missed something during his visit to the Bible camp? Just thinking that made Clayton wince. He also wondered what would have happened if Grace had woken him when he'd asked her to. Would he have been at the roadblock with Ordonez when Larson arrived? Would his presence have been enough to make Larson turn around and find another route? Or would he also be dead with a bullet in his head?

As he drove the winding road through the hills west of Lincoln, he slowed, concentrated on the road, and tried not to think about all the maybes. Yet he felt negligent. When he turned onto the gravel country road, the dust from his wheels partially obscured the lights of Walcott's unit. In front of the open Twin Pines gate, Clayton stopped, got out, and took a look around with his flashlight while Deputy Walcott waited at the side of the road.

He quickly spotted very recent tire tracks and two sets of fresh footprints. One set matched those he'd seen earlier in the day and thought belonged to somebody from the camp. But as he followed them up the county road away from the gate, he began to have doubts.

He dropped down and looked at them more closely. The prints looked similar to a set he'd seen at Kerney's ranch, next to Riley Burke's lifeless body. Had his lack of sleep made him miss the connection earlier?

On the access road inside the gate, he took another careful look. Tread marks and footprints told him a vehicle had stopped, the driver had left the vehicle, walked to the gate, and returned. Additionally, he found more footprints similar to those of Larson's that came out of the woods, traveled around the back of the vehicle to approximately the driver's door, and stopped. There both sets of prints were partially obliterated, but the set that had come out of the woods continued on to the gate before returning to the truck.

Clayton picked a distinct clean impression of each of the footprints, made a quick measurement to determine shoe sizes, and took digital photographs, before proceeding to Gaylord Wardle's residence with Walcott following in his unit. He slowed to a stop in front of Wardle's house, to find him standing under the front porch light, a .22 rifle cradled in his arms.

Clayton had Walcott stand fast, approached Wardle, told him

to put the weapon down, and asked if anyone other than Cuddy was missing.

"No," Wardle said as he rested the rifle against the porch railing. "We've checked everyone twice. Only Gregory is unaccounted for."

"You're sure?"

"Absolutely." Wardle looked past Clayton at Deputy Walcott, who was waiting next to his unit. "I have a lot of very upset young people here. Can't you spare more officers for their protection?"

"Just keep everyone inside until we tell you it's safe, and you'll all be fine," Clayton said.

"How long will that be?" Wardle asked.

"Until we tell you it is safe," Clayton repeated, fast losing patience with the man. He reached out and picked up the rifle. "Yours?"

Wardle nodded.

It was a lever-action. Clayton emptied it, the rounds clattering onto the wooden porch deck. "Do you have a gun cabinet?"

Wardle nodded again.

He handed the weapon to Wardle. "Lock it up, call everyone at the camp who owns any kind of firearm, and tell them to empty their weapons and put them away. I don't want to see any civilians carrying, and I want an inventory of every gun in your armory as well as those that are in private hands as soon as you can get it to me."

Red faced with anger, Wardle opened his mouth to speak but Clayton cut him off.

"I don't need a lecture on your constitutional right to bear arms, Reverend Wardle. A state policeman has been shot dead, and the weapon the killer used may have come from Twin Pines."

"Oh, my," Wardle said. "First the sheriff and now this. Of course, we'll do everything you ask."

"Excellent. Where are Cuddy's quarters?"

Wardle gave Clayton directions, and handed him a master key that would open the front door.

Clayton thanked Wardle, left him on the porch, rejoined Deputy Walcott, gave him the key, and pointed him toward Cuddy's rooms. "I doubt Cuddy was abducted from his rooms, but check anyway. Let me know what size shoe he wears. Call me by radio."

"What's that going to tell us?" Walcott asked.

"I found two sets of footprints by the gate, and only one of them is a nine and a half. That's Larson's shoe size. The other print is a size ten and a half. If that's what Cuddy wears, you can bet we're not going to find his body here."

"How can you be sure?"

"Because the driver of the camp pickup was attacked at the gate while in his vehicle." Clayton handed Walcott the digital camera. "Do a quick search and then take this camera to Captain Ramsey."

Clayton climbed into his unit. "Tell him the last four images are of the footprints by the Bible camp gate. Have him download them to his laptop, transmit them to the state police crime lab computer, and ask if they can match them to any of the footprint evidence found at Larson's known crime scenes."

"Where are you headed off to?" Walcott asked.

"I'm going to see where Larson's footprints on the Forest Service road take me."

Clayton left the Bible camp and drove slowly up the forest road, using his unit's spotlight to follow the plainly visible footprints. If they were Larson's footprints, Clayton figured he must have planned to steal a vehicle at Twin Pines. No attempt had been made to hide the tracks on the way down the mountain.

Where the road turned rocky, Clayton dismounted his unit and walked, scanning for partial prints, broken twigs, scuff marks, trampled grass, or crushed leaves. Born and raised in the mountains of Mescalero, taught to hunt and read sign by his Apache uncles, Clayton was one of the best trackers in the state. As a police officer on the Rez, he'd chased and caught poachers and illegal trespassers, and taught his knowledge and skills to officers throughout the southern part of the state.

He was a good half mile away from his unit when the beam of his flashlight picked up a shoe partial next to an old hoofprint impression at the side of the road. He dropped down for a closer look and found some fairly fresh, broken tiny juniper twigs and evidence that tire tracks had been brushed away.

Clayton stepped off into the undergrowth and quickly found more tire tracks that led him directly to Janette Evans's truck and Larson's improvised campsite.

He felt no sense of accomplishment as he called it in. If he'd followed the trail hours ago instead of going home for dinner and a nap, maybe Ordonez wouldn't be dead, the youth minister wouldn't be at the very least kidnapped, and Larson wouldn't still be at large.

It made him physically sick to think about it.

Without pushing it too hard, Craig Larson made good time to the Texas state line. A dozen miles farther on, he passed through the dark and shuttered town of Plains, where the water tank, the tallest structure in the village, pierced the night sky. On the outskirts of town, he pulled off the pavement on the eastbound side of the highway and glanced over at his passenger. Kid Cuddy, the KO'd Kid, hadn't budged an inch since Larson had coldcocked him before gunning down the cop at the roadblock with a perfect head shot. He checked the kid for a pulse, couldn't find one, and glared at the body in disappointment. The KO'd Kid had up and died on him, spoiling all the fun.

Larson hauled the kid's muscular body out of the truck, started to drag it into some tall weeds, changed his mind, and instead propped it against a nearby utility pole where it wouldn't be missed come daylight. He hoped when the cops arrived they would concentrate their search to the east, but if not, so be it.

He turned the truck around, drove back to Plains, and headed north on a state road that would get him a good distance away from Kid Cuddy before Larson crossed back into New Mexico. The two-lane highway was empty, and except for some oil pump-jacks casting shadows from a dim quarter moon on a flat prairie, and a few pieces of farm machinery sitting in irrigated fields, the land was empty as well. In the several small villages Larson passed through, there was absolutely nobody out on the streets and no sign of life in the houses fronting the main drag.

He let his mind wander back to those tasty-looking teenage Christian girls he'd seen at the Bible camp, bouncing and jiggling on their horses. It got him hungry for a woman, and he decided that he'd be really pissed off at himself if he let the cops shoot and kill him before he got some girly action. He grinned at the anticipation of some good sex and a running gunfight with the cops.

At three in the morning, just south of Muleshoe, Texas, the dial to the gas gauge quivered at the empty line. Larson slowed way down, hoping he could make it to town and find a twenty-four-hour convenience store or a gas station where he could fill up. In town, on a tacky-looking street named West American Boulevard, he drove past an open stop-and-rob twice before he spotted the exterior surveillance cameras pointed at the parking spaces in front of the entrance and at the gas pumps. He made a turn onto a side street, pulled to the curb, and considered what to do next.

The pickup truck had two pine trees and the name of the Bible camp painted on both doors, which was going to make it far too easy to spot once the cops started seriously looking for it. Better to ditch the pickup now and get new wheels. An older-model Toyota sedan at the side of the convenience store probably belonged to the clerk on duty. He decided to make an even trade, the Ford pickup for the Toyota, whether the clerk liked it or not.

He sat and watched traffic on West American Boulevard for five minutes and only two cars passed by. If the trend held, that would give him adequate time to do what he had in mind. If not, he would just have to deal with whatever came along. He drove to the store, parked at one of the pumps, stuck the semiautomatic in his waistband at the small of his back, went inside, smiled at an overweight Mexican man behind the counter, and handed him some money.

"Fill up on pump one," he said genially.

The bored clerk grunted, put the money next to the cash register, and turned on the gas pump.

"Is that your Toyota outside?" Larson asked.

"It's my sister's car," the clerk answered in a thick Mexican accent, looking at Larson with a bit more interest.

"But you're driving it, right?"

"Yeah."

Larson pointed the semiautomatic at the Mexican's head. "Give me the car keys," he said.

With a shaking hand, the clerk hastily fished the keys out of his pocket and dropped them on the counter. "Take it," he said. "Take anything you want."

"Thanks." Larson scooped up the keys. "Is there gas in it?"

"I just filled the tank."

"That's great," Larson replied as he squeezed off a round. The Mexican's head snapped back from the impact of the bullet as blood speckled the packs of cigarettes in the rack on the wall.

Larson jumped the counter, pushed the Mexican out of the way, grabbed a pack of smokes from the rack, a disposable lighter from the counter, and the cash he'd given the Mexican. He went outside to the Toyota and fired up the engine; the gas gauge read full. He left the motor running, hurried to the gas pump, got his stuff out of the cab, and hosed down the pickup with gasoline. As the vapor fumes filled the air, he spewed a full stream of regular unleaded toward the store entrance and watched it seep under the glass doors. He dropped the hose on the ground, went to the Toyota, backed away from the store, and lit a cigarette. When the gasoline oozed within range, he flicked the cigarette through the open window, floored the Toyota, and pushed it to the limit down the street.

The fireball explosion that followed rocked the small car, lit up the night sky, and threw debris onto the roadway. Larson smiled in satisfaction. It was just like in the movies. He made a U-turn so he could get a better look at the fire. The pickup truck and store were masked by a wall of flames.

It was gonna be a hell of a mess once the fire was extinguished. It would probably take the cops days before they could piece any evidence together. By then, he would be settled in someplace where he could hunker down for a while and find a woman to party with.

Larson hadn't felt so good since the day he decided to murder Melvin and Viola Bedford. Back then, he thought he was doing it for the money, but now he realized that he just flat-out enjoyed killing people.

The New Mexico State Police helicopter carrying Captain Steve Ramsey and Clayton Istee touched down on the highway east of Plains, Texas, just as the sun on the eastern horizon began to

light up the prairie. Yellow crime scene tape enclosed a body resting against an electric utility pole, roadblocks had been set up in
both directions of the highway, and a small team of police officers was searching the area.

Ducking under the chopper's rotors, Clayton and Steve Ramsey hurried over to a thin man wearing a ten-gallon cowboy hat
and a Western-cut sport coat, with a sheriff's badge hanging from
a lanyard around his neck, and introduced themselves.

"Brownlow Clauson, Yoakum County Sheriff. Folks call me
Brownie," the man said, shaking hands with each of them. He
pointed at the dead young man. "Got the photo y'all sent and it
looks to me that there's your missing boy. An oil field crew getting an early start spotted the body about four this morning."

"What else can you tell us?" Steve Ramsey asked.

"Cause of death appears to have been blunt trauma to the
head. The boy got bashed at least three times. There are no other
visible wounds on the body. Time of death is probably no more
than four to six hours. 'Course, we won't have anything defini-
tive until the autopsy."

"Have you found any hard evidence?" Clayton asked.

"Just footprints and tire tracks so far." Clauson led them to
some evidence cones placed on the soft shoulder of the highway.

Clayton bent down for a look. "That's our man," he said as
he recognized both the footprints and tire treads, "and he's still
driving the Twin Pines pickup truck."

"Not anymore he ain't," Sheriff Clauson said. "I got a report
out of Muleshoe just before you landed. A gasoline explosion
and fire at a convenience store burned up a truck parked at the
pumps, and probably killed the store clerk and maybe a cus-
tomer or two inside the place. The VIN off the engine block
matches that of the stolen Ford 150 four-by-four from that Bible
ranch."

"Are you sure the vehicle ID numbers are the same?" Clayton asked.

Clauson took a slip of paper out of his shirt pocket and handed it to Clayton. "I had the Muleshoe police chief read the VIN off to me twice to make sure I got it right. Could well be your cop killer is now nothing more than some crispy critter body parts strewn around the wreckage of that stop-and-rob."

"We should be so lucky," Steve Ramsey replied. "Were you told the cause of the explosion?"

Clauson rubbed the tip of his nose with a forefinger and shook his head. "'To be determined' was what was said. The fire chief has an arson investigator on scene."

Clauson glanced from Ramsey to Clayton to the chopper sitting in the middle of the highway. "I guess you boys will want to take that whirlybird of yours up to Muleshoe. I'd sure appreciate it if you did so pronto. Traffic is starting to back up and I'd like to get a lane open for those vehicles."

"Sure thing," Clayton said as he looked down the highway in both directions. At one roadblock there were three pickups, one semi, and two cars waiting. At the other, two empty yellow school buses, delayed from making the morning run to pick up students, idled behind the barrier.

Clayton handed Clauson his card. "You might want to have your people look for a .22 Marlin rifle."

"We're fairly sure it's the murder weapon used to kill my officer," Steve Ramsey added, giving Clauson his card as well.

Clauson pocketed the cards and gave Clayton and Ramsey each one of his own. "I'll let y'all know if anything turns up. Bad business, killing a lawman." He glanced over at the dead boy. "This is the first homicide victim I've seen in Yoakum County since I got elected."

"Let's hope it's the last," Clayton replied.

"Amen to that, brother," Clauson intoned solemnly. "I'll let the boys up in Muleshoe know that you're on your way for a look-see."

The pilot of the New Mexico State Police whirlybird made short work of getting Clayton and Steve Ramsey up to Muleshoe, a small town of no more than five thousand people, close to the New Mexico border. From the air, it was apparent that agriculture dominated the economy. Dairy farms, with irrigated fields in sharp contrast to the checkerboard sections of brown prairie, and tall grain elevators ringed the community. Within the town limits, motels and eateries were clustered along one main drag, and smack in the middle of it were the cordoned-off, blackened roofless ruins of a cement-block building. A large hole in front of the building was most likely all that remained of the gasoline pumps. Around the perimeter were blasted-apart remnants of a vehicle, including an engine that had been severed from the chassis. From the size of the crowd kept back by police officers and firefighters, Clayton figured half the population of the town had gathered to watch events unfold.

He wondered out loud about the origin of the town's name, and the pilot, a native of an eastern New Mexico village within spitting distance of Muleshoe, told him it had come from a nearby ranch that had been homesteaded long before the town was established. He set the chopper down in a vacant lot behind the destroyed building, killed the engine, and reported their arrival by radio as Clayton and Steve Ramsey left the bird.

The man who hurried to meet them was no more than forty but almost totally bald except for buzz-cut sidewalls. He had square shoulders and one of those permanently etched, hard-nosed expressions some cops liked to adopt as their public persona. He introduced himself as Police Chief Billy Pruitt in a dour tone that matched his expression. He had smudges on his face, and gray soot dirtied his white shirt and once polished boots.

As he shook Pruitt's hand, Clayton wondered if the chief's full name might be Billy Bob. He resisted the impulse to inquire. "What have you learned so far?" he asked over the sounds of the thudding chopper rotors slowing to a stop.

"It's been a real mess," Pruitt answered as he walked Clayton and Ramsey to a panel truck with a Muleshoe PD logo on it, which served as a mobile command post. "After the explosion, the fire burned hot and long. Once the firefighters put it out, it took a while for it to cool down enough for a look-see. The only one who's been inside is the arson investigator. So far, he's found the badly burned remains of one individual. But the place is such a shambles, who knows, there may be more."

Clayton gazed at the ruined structure, looking for signs of movement. "Is he in there now?"

Pruitt nodded. "At the back of the building, where there was less damage."

"I take it you got the VIN off that engine block sitting at the edge of the crater," Ramsey said.

Pruitt nodded. "Yep, and that's the sum total of the evidence we've recovered so far." He stopped talking to answer a cell phone clipped to his belt. As he listened he got an exasperated look on his face. Finally he said, "I don't care how long it takes, dammit, find his sister."

"Whose sister?" Clayton asked when Pruitt disconnected.

"There was a new clerk working when the store blew up. According to the manager, he's an older Mexican named Bernardo Ulibarri who used to work in a local dairy until he injured his back. The manager says Ulibarri has a green card, but that could be a bunch of BS. Supposedly, he lives with his sister, but the address he gave the manager was bogus, and the manager doesn't remember the sister's name. I've got an officer out looking for her."

Pruitt paused and looked at the crowds behind the police lines. "You'd think she'd be here," he said. "Everyone else in town seems to be."

A figure emerged from the innards of the destroyed building and walked slowly toward the police van, pulling off his gloves, a pair of goggles, and his breathing mask.

"That's Eloy Miramontes, our arson investigator," Pruitt said.

Pruitt waited to make introductions until Miramontes, a man in his thirties with a weight lifter's body, pulled off his boots and tossed them inside the cab of a fire engine with his other gear.

"What have you got for us, Eloy?" Pruitt asked after handshakes all around had been completed.

"There are no other bodies inside," Miramontes replied. "I had to move a lot of debris to get into the bathrooms at the back of the structure, but they were both empty. I took a closer look at the victim and there's a bullet hole in his forehead."

"You're sure of that?" Pruitt asked.

Miramontes nodded. "Shrapnel from an explosion is messy and the entry wound is circular, consistent with what you'd normally see from a gunshot. Also, outside the building I found fingering. That's the splash effects of the gasoline being spewed around before it ignited. The fire was deliberately started away from the fuel pumps on the side of the structure. There's even some melted material from the fuel hose embedded in the paving. That tells me it was dropped on the ground prior to the explosion. We've got ourselves a felony arson and a homicide."

Ramsey glanced at Clayton and Pruitt. "Did our perp just walk away from the explosion? Larson obviously isn't driving the Bible camp pickup anymore."

"Did the clerk have a vehicle?" Clayton asked.

Pruitt shook his head. "Not one that he owned, as far as we know. That's why we're looking for the sister. The store manager said Ulibarri would either walk to work, borrow his sister's car, or get rides from her. He thinks it's an older-model Toyota, but isn't sure."

"We need to know about that vehicle," Clayton said.

Pruitt grunted in agreement.

Clayton watched a heavyset woman push her way to the front of one of the barriers and wave both hands over her head in his direction.

"Somebody wants your attention, Chief," Clayton said as he nodded at the woman.

"Wait here," Pruitt said as he hurried toward the woman.

Out of earshot, Clayton, Ramsey, and Miramontes watched. The woman said something to Pruitt as he approached, gesturing frantically at the rubble of the convenience store. He took her away from the crowd and a TV reporter holding a microphone who'd elbowed her way up to the woman and leaned close to say something. When he finished talking, the woman's knees buckled, and Pruitt grabbed her arm to keep her upright.

"It seems the sister of our vic may have arrived," Miramontes said.

"Let's hope she didn't get here in an older-model Toyota," Ramsey said. "Because if she did, we're screwed."

"So much for our compassion for the bereaved," Clayton said grimly.

"We're a sorry lot," Steve Ramsey replied as the image of Officer Leroy Ordonez's fiancée flashed before his eyes.

Several hours before dawn, on a rural two-lane state highway, ten miles beyond the village of Logan, New Mexico, the piece-of-shit Toyota died on Craig Larson. Of course, there was no frigging flashlight in the car, and no tools either, for that matter, even if he could see what in the hell needed fixing. He stayed with the car for a while, with the hood up and the parking lights flashing, hoping some good Samaritan would come along and stop. Be it a cop or a civilian, it didn't matter, Larson was prepared to blow away whoever came to his rescue for their wheels.

After an hour passed and the chill of the high desert summer night had seeped into his bones, Larson realized that the chances were slim that anyone would be out on the road until first light. He gave up on the idea of waiting for help to arrive, closed the hood of the car, turned off the flashers, and pushed the car off the shoulder of the highway, next to a tree. Hopefully, anyone passing by would think nothing of seeing a disabled vehicle at the side of the road.

He grabbed his stuff out of the car and started walking. A good mile or more down the road, he threw the .22 Marlin rifle into a culvert. Carrying the weapon in daylight would only spook any driver passing by.

From the village of Logan north, Larson was virtually on his home ground. He set a steady pace, and by sunup, he was closing in on the hills to the west and knew the tiny ranching settlement of Gallegos on Ute Creek was just ahead. The first vehicle he saw was a school bus traveling from that direction, It had to be on the way to gather up the ranch kids and take them to school farther north in Mosquero, the county seat. As a boy, he'd ridden buses with classmates who spent three hours a day or more traveling to and from school, and he knew it was no different now.

In Gallegos, ranch wives and their children waited in pickup trucks for the school bus to swing back around, and several men were out in a pasture digging what appeared to be a water line trench. Larson didn't stop, and although his passage earned him some curious glances, no one seemed disturbed to see a wandering vagrant plodding along.

A half hour outside of Gallegos, the school bus whizzed by on its way to Mosquero. He had half a mind to run after it and abduct the entire kit and caboodle, thinking it'd be fun to terrorize a bus full of children and young teenagers, especially the girls. He'd bet even money there were a couple of tasty thirteen-year-olds on it. But the bus moved quickly on, and he was too bone-weary tired to chase after it and try to wave it down.

He topped the crest of a small hill and saw the school bus stopped with lights flashing to pick up some kids. When Larson reached the ranch road where it had stopped, he laughed out loud in delight at the sight of a thirty-year-old pickup truck parked behind the locked gate.

A sign posted at the side of the gate announced that the Dripping Springs Ranch headquarters was eight miles off the pavement. The truck had to be used by the ranch kids to drive themselves to and from the school bus stop.

Larson climbed the gate and found the truck to be unlocked, just as he'd suspected. He searched for an ignition key hidden above the visor, under the rubber floor mat, or in the glove box or the ashtray, without any luck. But there was a small toolbox under the bench seat, with a couple of screwdrivers, pairs of pliers and wire cutters, electrical tape, and assorted other stuff. Larson took what he needed from it, pried the ignition lock off the steering column, and easily hot-wired the truck. The engine turned over and purred.

Larson used the wire cutters on the barbed wire fence and drove north on the highway thinking about his next move. He would have to hide this truck so it wouldn't be easily found, just as he'd done with the pickup owned by the former Lincoln County clerk and newly deceased Janette Evans.

He had the perfect place in mind. Below Taylor Springs, a few miles east of Springer on the Canadian River, stood the headquarters of the Lazy Z Ranch. The Cimarron Cutoff of the Santa

Fe Trail ran right through the center of it. Started by a man who had once owned shares in the Maxwell Cattle Company, it had been passed down to Martha Boyle, one of Larson's high school classmates.

As a teenager Larson had cowboyed on the ranch during spring and fall works, and he knew it well. It was off the beaten path, and best of all was used only as a private retreat when Martha needed a respite from living the big-city life. He could hole up there for months without raising any suspicions.

He wondered if Martha was at the ranch. If she was, he wouldn't have to go looking for a woman. If not, he'd go out trolling one night and collect one.

Either way, it was all going to work out just fine. He turned on the radio and drove down the highway listening to George Strait sing about true love and a broken heart.

Chapter Six

For three days, Jack Burke dealt with the loss of his son by working himself into a state of exhaustion. Friends, neighbors, and
relatives who stopped by the ranch to voice their sympathy, or
offer support, found Irene at home while Jack labored outside at
some task that suddenly, desperately needed doing. During those
days, from sunup to sundown, Kerney worked alongside his friend.
He showed up at the ranch house early in the morning, learned
from Irene where Jack had gone, joined him, and along with several of Jack's close buddies from neighboring ranches, pitched in
to help. Talking only when absolutely necessary, the men cut fire-
wood for the winter, repaired fence lines, patched water tanks,
greased windmills, tuned up the ranch vehicles, and replaced rot-
ted wood siding on the horse barn. It seemed that whatever needed
fixing around the ranch, Jack Burke was determined to get done
before he had to bury his son.

Not once during those days did any friend, neighbor, or family member suggest that Jack needed to get in touch with his feelings, see a counselor to deal with his grief, or have himself a
good, long cry. Everyone saw that Jack was coping the best way
he knew how.

Each day at lunch, Kerney sat with Jack and his pals at the table in the Burkes' kitchen and talked about the tasks ahead in the
afternoon, while Irene, red-eyed and hollow-looking, occupied

herself cooking food to feed all the folks who kept dropping in during the day to offer help, comfort, and sympathy.

So Jack toiled, Irene cooked, and Lynette, Riley's widow, escaped to Kerney's ranch to care for the horses her husband had been raising and training, so that she could grieve privately. One evening, Kerney came upon her in the tack room of the horse barn on his ranch, leaning against the wall, eyes closed, hands to her mouth, sobbing quietly. He backed away unnoticed, wondering why grief always seemed to be such a solitary affair, no matter how many people surrounded you. His passing inquiry into the nature of personal suffering didn't make Kerney feel one damn bit better about Riley's death. Each time he saw the spot in front of his house where Riley had been senselessly gunned down, he winced.

On the morning of Sara and Patrick's scheduled late afternoon arrival at the Albuquerque airport, Kerney worked with Jack and his friends clearing out some invasive young juniper trees in otherwise good pastureland that bordered a wide arroyo. After the last of the junipers had been chained, pulled out by the roots, and piled in mounds at the edge of the pasture, he told Jack he needed to go home, clean up, and get down to the airport.

Jack pulled off his work gloves and shook Kerney's hand. "Thanks for your help. It's meant a lot to me."

"Anytime," Kerney replied, looking at Jack's tired and empty face. "I'll see you later."

"Yeah," Jack replied. "Tomorrow, I guess."

"Tomorrow," Kerney repeated, thinking that was about as close as Jack could get to admitting that he would soon bury his son.

At the airport, Kerney learned that the connecting flight out of Chicago had been delayed by bad weather. He passed the time people watching, unscientifically proving to himself once again that the majority of Americans, as recent statistics indicated, were indeed overweight, if not outright obese.

When Sara and Patrick finally came through the security checkpoint, it was getting on to dusk. He greeted them with hugs and kisses, grabbed their carry-on luggage, and walked them to the short-term parking garage where he'd left the rental car. A hot yellow sun hung on the western horizon, lighting up a dust-laden golden sky.

After Sara strapped Patrick into the child's seat of the car, he asked Kerney what had happened to his mother's Jeep.

"A bad man took it and broke it," Kerney replied.

"Why?" Patrick asked.

"Because he does bad things, like stealing your mother's Jeep. But it's getting fixed." Kerney paid the parking lot attendant and waited for his change.

"Can I take Pablito for a ride when we get home?" Patrick asked as the attendant raised the gate and Kerney drove on.

"No, it will be dark by then," Sara replied.

"In the morning?" Patrick asked hopefully.

Sara shook her head. "Tomorrow morning we have something else to do, remember? We talked about it on the airplane because it's the reason we came home to Santa Fe so unexpectedly."

Patrick nodded seriously. "We have to go to church and say good-bye to Riley, because he died."

"That's right," Sara said.

"And he can't work with Daddy anymore."

"Right again," she noted.

"But I can help Daddy with the horses," Patrick said, brightly.

"Only until we go back to London," Kerney said as he merged into northbound traffic on I-25.

"I don't want to go back. I don't like London."

"You like horseback riding in Hyde Park," Kerney countered.

"Yeah, but . . ."

"And you like the zoo," he added before Patrick could continue, "and London is where your mother has her job. We promised that we would all stay together, remember? Not like the last time when she went to Iraq all by herself."

"I don't want Mom to be a soldier anymore," Patrick announced. "She doesn't even wear her uniform to work, so why does she have to stay in the army?"

"Let's change the subject," Kerney said, thinking his son was no slouch when it came to mounting an argument, no matter how unreasonable it might be.

"Okay." Patrick yawned in reply and fell silent. Through the rearview mirror, Kerney saw his son's eyes close and his head droop.

Sara turned her head and looked back at Patrick. "He's almost asleep," she whispered.

"Good," Kerney whispered back.

"What's happening with the manhunt for the killer?"

"Officially, it's still going full bore. Unofficially, it has stalled. Larson may have gone into hiding up in his old stomping grounds around Colfax County. That's the theory, anyway. As far as the police know, he hasn't murdered anybody since the Muleshoe, Texas, killing. Because the hunt is concentrated up north, most of the smaller departments in the central and southern part of the state have scaled back on the search. But Andy Baca is keeping dozens of his state police officers, agents, and investigators assigned to the case. He's even pulled central office supervisors away from their desks and sent them into the field hunting for Larson."

"He's lost an officer, so he'll be a bulldog on this one," Sara said. "What's Paul Hewitt's status?"

"Not good," Kerney said glumly. "I've seen him once and I've talked to Linda by phone several times. He knows that he'll never have the use of his arms and legs again, and according to Linda he's been talking a lot of negative crap about not wanting to live. Clayton's driving up to Albuquerque tomorrow from Lincoln County to see him. He said he'd call and fill me in afterwards."

"That's so sad," Sara said. "It must be scary for both of them."

"I'd hate to be facing their future," Kerney said.

"And Jack, Irene, and Lynette? How are they holding up?"

"They're coping in their own way," Kerney answered in a somber tone. "Jack works himself to a nub sunup to sundown, Irene cooks frantically in her kitchen day and night, and Lynette hides out with the horses at our place and falls apart when no one is looking."

"Have you signed on with Andy to join the hunt for Larson?"

Kerney shook his head. "Not yet. I've been sticking pretty close to Jack these last few days. Family and friends will be gathering at Jack and Irene's after the burial. They're expecting quite a crowd."

"I'll call Irene when we get home and offer to help," Sara said.

"I'm sure she'd like that. Did you tell Patrick the particulars of how and where Riley died?"

"No, I thought it best not to until he's older." Sara reached out and touched Kerney's cheek. "Are you still feeling responsible for Riley's death?"

Kerney smiled tightly. "I can't help it. I keep thinking that I put him in harm's way."

"Actually, you gave him a chance to do something he loved. He told you that time and time again."

"I know I'm being illogical."

"That's okay. I understand the feeling." Sara had lost soldiers in ambushes and firefights during her tour of duty in Iraq, and still felt she could have done more to save them. She looked out the car window at the brilliant ribbon of red sky on the western horizon. "I'd almost forgotten how big and beautiful the New Mexico sky is. I really miss it."

"Maybe you should take Patrick's advice and leave the army. Then we can all come back home to the ranch and enjoy the sunsets."

Sara poked him on the arm. "Don't you start in on me too."

"Okay, I take it back. London will be our home until you retire."

"I hope you mean that."

"I do," Kerney said, trying to sound convincing.

At the ranch, they dumped the carry-on luggage on the couch, put Patrick to bed, and sat silently at the kitchen table holding hands and talking.

"We're very lucky," Sara finally said, thinking that she would fall to pieces if anything bad happened to Kerney or Patrick.

"Let's keep it that way," Kerney replied, remembering the moment when he'd learned that Sara had been wounded in Iraq. The thought of it made him shudder.

Sara laughed.

"What?"

"Just how do you plan to keep us safe from the perils of life?"

"By managing contingencies and limiting unintended consequences," Kerney answered with a grin.

"My, my," Sara replied, raising an eyebrow. "Where were you when the administration needed help planning the war on terror?"

"Serving my country on the home front as your local chief of police."

Sara laughed again, rose to her feet, and kissed Kerney on the mouth. "I'm pouring myself a glass of wine and calling Irene," she said. "See what's in the garage freezer that I can thaw and cook up in a hurry to take with us tomorrow."

"I'm sure Irene doesn't expect you to bring anything."

"Maybe not," Sara replied, "but my mother would."

Paul Hewitt's wife, Linda, had called Clayton and asked him to meet with the sheriff as soon as he could break away and drive to Albuquerque. Clayton had promised to be there in the morning, and he left Mescalero before dawn, arriving in the city just in time to get slowed down by the last of the rush hour traffic crunch on the interstate. He had no idea why Paul wanted to see him, so as he lurched along in the stop-and-go traffic a quarter mile from the exit ramp that would take him to the hospital, he tried to avoid guessing. But it was irresistible. Perhaps Paul simply wanted to be personally briefed on the manhunt for Craig Larson, or maybe he wanted to share some encouraging news about his chances for recovery. Whatever the reason, Clayton stopped speculating as he left the interstate, drove the few blocks to the hospital, and made his way quickly to Hewitt's room, where he found the sheriff alone.

"You just missed Linda," Hewitt said as Clayton approached the bed. "She went down to the cafeteria to get something to eat."

Clayton nodded. It was still a shock to see a man who had once been so vital and active now able to move only his facial muscles and eyes. "How are you doing?" Clayton asked.

"Just fine," Paul replied with a touch of sarcasm. "As soon as I get out of the hospital and finish my rehab program, I'm gonna go skydiving without a parachute to celebrate my newfound freedom."

Clayton raised an eyebrow.

"You're not laughing at my little joke."

"It's not funny."

Hewitt grunted. "You never did have much of a sense of humor."

"Apaches believe that humor should never cause embarrassment."

"Whom am I embarrassing?" Hewitt asked.

"Yourself."

Hewitt chortled. "Damn, you've gotten uppity since I promoted you to chief deputy."

"I've always been just another uppity Indian. Is that what you wanted to talk to me about?"

"Know what I like about you, Clayton? You're the only person who comes to visit who doesn't treat me like a cripple."

"The politically correct words, Sheriff, are 'handicapped' and 'disabled.' "

Hewitt's eyes flashed with annoyance. "Neither word adequately expresses my present and permanent reality. 'Cripple' comes close. It has more clarity."

"I can tell you've given it a lot of thought, Sheriff."

Hewitt made a grumpy face. "What a polite way to tell me to stop feeling sorry for myself."

Clayton said nothing.

Hewitt grimaced. "Okay, I'll get right to the point. Linda and the doctors have convinced me that I should resign as sheriff, and they're right. With what I'm facing, I can't see myself being able to get my head around the job anytime soon. I wanted to tell you in person before I make it official. I spoke to the county commission chairman and asked him to keep you on as chief deputy."

Hewitt paused.

"And?" Clayton asked.

Hewitt snorted. "I got a lot of mumbo jumbo about how the commission wanted to leave all internal personnel and administrative decisions to the interim sheriff, whoever that will be."

"I'm sure it will be Sergeant Rudy Aldrich," Clayton ventured.

"Most certainly. It was also pointed out to me that a majority of the commissioners don't like the idea of the chief deputy living outside the county limits."

The Mescalero Apache Reservation where Clayton lived was in neighboring Otero County. "Is it that they don't like me residing outside the county, or that I'm an Apache from the Rez?" Clayton queried.

"It wasn't put that way, but feel free to take it as evidence of a combination of not so subtle racism and some political maneuvering to give Aldrich a leg up in the general election. By replacing you with a chief deputy who has some drawing power at the polls, he'll have a better chance of getting elected. However, I was assured that you would be allowed to revert to your permanent rank of lieutenant once Aldrich is installed and appoints a new chief deputy. Isn't that generous of them?"

Clayton shrugged. "Okay."

"'Okay'?" Hewitt echoed. "That's it?"

Clayton smiled at Paul Hewitt. "Don't worry about me, Sheriff. Just do the best you can to get better."

"Yeah, right. I've been told there are a whole lot of electronic gadgets I can learn to operate by using a breathing tube that's no bigger than a soda straw. Even wheelchairs can come equipped with them. Modern science. Amazing."

"You've got to stop sounding so negative," Clayton counseled, stone-faced. "It makes talking to you really grueling."

Hewitt grinned. "You *do* have a sense of humor."

Linda Hewitt stepped into the room before Clayton could

respond. She greeted him warmly, but the smile on her face was forced and tiny lines tugged at the corners of her mouth. She talked for a time about plans to take Paul home, including what needed to be done at the house to make it more accessible and comfortable for him. Paul chimed in that she'd been wanting an excuse to redecorate, and they all shared an uneasy laugh.

After a few more minutes of small talk and a farewell hug from Linda, Clayton took his leave and made his way down the brightly lit hospital corridor to the elevators and outside to his unit. Grace had asked him to call after his meeting with Paul. He sat in the unit holding his cell phone and wondering what to say. Should he tell her that Paul was the most miserable son-of-a-bitch on the planet and would gladly kill himself if he could? Should he tell her that Linda was working hard to be strong, upbeat, and supportive, but every second of her life since Paul had been shot and their world collapsed was now permanently etched on her face? Or should he tell her that by the end of the week—if that long—he'd be unemployed because he would not, could not, work for Rudy Aldrich.

He put the cell phone down and headed south toward Lincoln County, hoping that along the way he could come up with something positive to say to Grace before he called.

The fancy wrought iron gate controlled by a solar-powered electronic keypad wasn't what Craig Larson had expected to find upon his arrival at the entrance to Martha Boyle's ranch road, nor was the nearby sign behind the fence announcing that the Lazy Z was closed to unannounced visitors. On the sign was a phone number to call for permission to enter.

Larson snorted at himself for being so stupid. The last time he'd had any word about Martha must have been ten, maybe fifteen years ago. What made him think that time or Martha had stood still? He figured she must have sold the place to some rich, out-of-state cowboy wannabe, because no New Mexican raised on a ranch would ever lock a gate to keep out the neighbors and post a phone number on a sign to call for access.

He sat in the truck and considered what to do. It was too risky to go back on the highway in the stolen pickup, or even drive the dusty back county roads looking for a place to hole up. Because he knew the lay of the Lazy Z land, it made sense to stick to his plan no matter who now owned the spread.

Larson knew three different ways to get to the ranch head-quarters that bypassed the fancy solar-powered wrought iron se-curity gate. He popped the clutch and headed toward a jumbled rock outcropping, wishing he'd kept the Marlin .22 rifle. No tell-ing how many folks would need killing in order to make his plan work once he got there, and the additional firepower would have been helpful.

Just beyond the outcropping, Larson downshifted and entered an arroyo that deepened quickly as it snaked through rolling rangeland. It finally petered out at a boundary fence to the Lazy Z where a rutted track followed the tightly strung barbwire. He rattled the old truck up a shallow draw to a rickety old gate, stopped, got out, undid the chain that held the gate closed, pushed it open, and drove through. Within twenty minutes he was on top of a mesa looking down at the ranch headquarters.

The old stone ranch house, with its rounded, mission-style doors and windows under a low-pitched roof, and the matching stone barn looked pretty much as Larson remembered them. But the bunkhouse where Larson had once slept and the white clap-board foreman's cottage were gone, replaced by two fairly large flat-roofed, pueblo-style houses, separated by a wide, landscaped courtyard with a kidney-shaped swimming pool, two tennis courts, a cabana, and a freestanding veranda with an outdoor kitchen and dining area.

A short way beyond the old barn stood an enclosed circular metal structure and several corrals made of expensive steel pipes painted white. Within easy walking distance was a horse barn with stalls that opened onto individual paddocks. There were no animals in the corrals or paddocks.

Larson didn't like the changes he saw. It made him think about Melvin and Viola Bedford and their showy attempts to act and live like Westerners, when in fact they were nothing but an elderly, retired rich couple from Minnesota. He figured the Lazy Z had maybe been turned into some sort of corporate retreat or a rich bitch's equestrian fantasy come true.

Larson's thoughts wandered back to Melvin and Viola and how he laughed behind their backs when they went off to some highfalutin Santa Fe social function wearing their matching cowboy hats, shirts, and boots, and sporting expensive Indian turquoise and silver jewelry. Aside from being old, both were short, fat, and unattractive. They looked like rejects from Munchkinland. When they climbed into their pristine, never-been-off-the-pavement, extended cab 4x4 pickup truck, their heads barely showed above the dashboard. The notion to steal a chunk of their wealth and kill them had grown in Larson's mind the more he came to see them as ludicrous, undeserving posers.

He scanned the ranch headquarters for a while looking for a sign of movement. Only an older-model Subaru at the front of the ranch house and a shiny silver Hummer parked by the circular structure, which Larson took to be an enclosed horse arena, gave a clue that someone might be about. As he walked down the narrow, overgrown switchback trail, he pictured a good-looking woman wearing jodhpurs and riding boots exercising a horse in the riding arena, and that got him thinking about sex.

He held off any further thoughts about the woman as he

reached the bottom of the mesa and quickly went from house to house knocking on locked doors and getting no answers. The old stone barn was locked as well, so he made his way to the silver Hummer. It wasn't locked and the key was in the ignition.

Through the open door to the riding arena he could hear the sound of hoofs on dirt. He waited until the horse passed by before quietly slipping inside and crouching at the side of the door with the semiautomatic in his hand. He focused hard on the horse and rider cantering on the far side of the arena, but it took a minute for his eyes to adjust from the bright sunlight outside. At first he thought the rider was a young boy, but it was a woman, a skinny old hag at that, in her sixties, with leathery skin and stringy long gray hair that flopped against her face as she rode. She wore tight jeans, boots, and a loose-fitting halter top that covered a flat chest. About the only positive things about her were that she sat a horse well and seemed to have a nice ass.

Larson hid the semiautomatic behind his leg when the woman saw him. She reined the horse to a walk and rode over.

"Can I help you?" she said, looking down at him as the horse, a nervous gray mare, snorted and pawed the ground.

Larson pointed the handgun at the mare's forehead. "Get down or I kill the mare." He pulled back the hammer for effect.

The woman's hands tightened on the reins.

"Try to run and I'll kill you too," he added.

The woman dropped the reins and dismounted. She was small, not more than five foot two, but the boots made her seem taller.

"What do you want?" she asked. "Food? Money? The Hummer? Take it."

She had a prominent chin and a missing tooth just visible at the right side of her mouth. Her upper lip was heavily wrinkled.

"You work here?" Larson asked, somewhat surprised at the woman's cool demeanor.

The woman nodded. "I'm the caretaker."

"Is anyone else here?"

"Not today."

"Tell me the truth now," Larson said, pointing the gun at her eye, trying for a reaction.

"I'm not lying," she said flatly.

Larson gave it a rest. The woman seemed totally unruffled by him, like getting killed didn't matter. "Who else lives here?" he asked.

"No one, full-time. When guests are here, a wrangler takes care of the horses and stays in an apartment in the old stone barn."

"What horses?" Larson demanded. "The only horse I've seen is this mare."

"She's mine," the woman answered. "The other horses are boarded at a neighboring ranch when no one is here."

"Who owns this place?"

"A multinational corporation headquartered in Germany. It's used as an executive retreat. The CEO's wife is a horse lover."

"Do you live on the ranch?"

"Yes."

"Where?"

"I have rooms in the main house."

Larson waved the gun at the open door. "Take me there."

The woman reached for the reins. "First I need to unsaddle the mare and put her in the corral."

"Stop stalling," Larson barked. "The mare is fine as she is. Let's go."

The woman hesitated. "I have some money, if that's what you want."

Larson stepped up to the woman and bitch-slapped her. "Just do as you're told."

She rubbed her cheek and shrugged. "Whatever you say."

"That's a good girl," Larson said as he pushed her outside into the bright sunlight. "Is the old line camp on Point of Rocks Mesa still standing?"

The question caught the woman by surprise. She stopped and gave Larson a quizzical glance that slowly turned to a look of recognition.

"You know who I am, don't you?" Larson demanded.

"I don't know you at all," the woman replied.

Larson laughed. "Smart answer." He poked the gun barrel in her ribs. "I asked you about the line camp."

"Yes, it's still there, and used as a hunting lodge."

"Good deal." He pointed the handgun at the old stone ranch house. "Get moving. What's your name?"

"Nancy Trimble."

"Stay in front of me, Nancy." He walked behind her, thinking that from the backside, she didn't look that bad at all. In some ways, she reminded him of manic-depressive Jeannie Cooper in a down phase, but there was a toughness to her that Jeannie never had. "You don't rattle easy, do you?"

Nancy walked on with no comment.

"I like that in a woman," he added, touching his genitals.

She looked back at him and broke into a hard run, veering in the direction of the stables. He caught up to her and slammed her facedown to the ground.

"Get up," he ordered.

She gave him a dirty look, got to her feet, and brushed the dirt off her face. "Just shoot me," she said without emotion.

"You'd like that, wouldn't you?" Larson replied with a chuckle, trying not to concentrate on her old hag face. "No such luck, Antsy Nancy. I got plans for you."

He prodded her along to the ranch headquarters, where he hogtied her securely with electric extension cords he found in a pantry, taped her mouth shut, and left her on the kitchen floor while he did a quick look around the old house.

The place had changed a lot. The large kitchen was equipped with restaurant-size appliances; walls had been knocked out to make the living room bigger; two bedrooms had been converted into a master suite; the bathrooms were all redone. It didn't look anything like the house Martha Boyle had grown up in.

Back in the kitchen, Larson raided the refrigerator, made himself two big sandwiches, and popped open a bottle of imported German beer. He sat on a stool at the kitchen island and started eating, keeping an eye on Nancy, who was lying on her side at his feet. He decided to call her ugly instead of antsy.

After wolfing down half a sandwich, he removed the tape from the old bitch's mouth so she could talk. "Is that old Subaru yours?" he asked.

When Ugly Nancy didn't answer, Larson kicked her in the stomach. "Is it, Ugly Nancy?"

Trimble gasped out a yes.

"Good girl," Larson said, retuning to his meal. "Now, I'm gonna ask you a lot of questions, so don't piss me off and make me kick you again."

By the time he finished eating, Larson had learned that the Subaru could easily make it to the old line camp on Point of Rocks Mesa, and that the lodge was fully stocked with food, drink, bedding, and necessities. After another slightly harder kick to the stomach, Ugly Nancy also told him that no one was expected at the ranch for two weeks, that she had no appointments off the ranch in the next few days, and that he could find the key to the gun case in the living room on top of the cabinet.

Larson taped Ugly Nancy's mouth shut, left her on the floor, opened the gun cabinet, and picked out a lever-action Winchester 30.06 rifle, a six-shot .357 Ruger handgun, two nice hunting rifles, and enough ammunition to keep a SWAT team at bay for several days. He loaded everything in the back of the Subaru before returning to the kitchen, where he cleaned up the mess from his meal. He regretted not being able to take the Hummer, but everything had to appear normal if anyone came looking for Ugly Nancy.

He finished putting things away, dragged Ugly Nancy by the hair outside the house, locked the front door, carried her to the Subaru, stuck her facedown on the backseat, and drove to the horse arena, looking for the mare, but it was nowhere in sight. He'd planned to unsaddle it and put it in a corral with feed and water, but decided not to bother with it. After some playtime with Ugly Nancy, he'd come back and round it up.

The smooth gravel road to the line camp was a far cry from the set of ruts that had once snaked along the back of the mesa and climbed to the top. Larson felt pretty damn lucky. He was on his way to a well-provisioned hideout packing a decent arsenal and bringing along some company, even if she was old, ugly, and unwilling. When the line camp came into view, he wasn't surprised to see that it had been enlarged and fixed up. The solar panels and television dish antenna on the roof meant he'd have electricity, access to the outside world, and hot water for a nice long shower. Compared to camping out in the Capitan Mountains in dead Janette's pickup truck, it was gonna be Valhalla.

He parked the Subaru behind the lodge, under a small stand of old cottonwood trees that partially hid the vehicle from view, opened the back door with a key off Ugly Nancy's key ring, and carried her inside. He dumped her facedown on a bed in one of the two bedrooms, and tapped her unconscious with the butt of his semiautomatic to keep her quiet, careful not to hit her too hard like he had Kid Cuddy. He checked to make sure she was still breathing, and then took a look around the cabin. The living room had a big stone fireplace and a flagstone floor covered by some Navajo area rugs. On the walls were mounted deer, elk, and antelope heads. Flanking the fireplace were two oversize leather chairs and a couch with a thick pine wood frame. In front of the couch was a Mexican tile coffee table. Matching lamp tables were at the ends of the couch.

The kitchen was as well supplied as Ugly Nancy had promised and the bathroom had a separate shower stall that Larson couldn't wait to try out. He held off on stripping down butt naked on the spot and finished his tour. Inside a large linen closet was a washer and dryer, and on a coatrack in the mudroom by the rear door, he found a coil of good rope.

He took the rope into the bedroom where he'd left Ugly Nancy, undid the electrical cords that bound her, stripped her naked, and tied her up again with the rope, this time facedown and spread-eagled.

Larson put a pillow under her stomach to prop up her rump and gave her the once-over. Her shoulder blades were like fins in her skinny back and her arms were thin yet muscular, but from the waist down, old Nancy had a very nice, juicy-looking butt and slender, well-formed legs. From the way she looked at this angle, Larson figured it wasn't going to be hard at all to forget about her face.

He left her, went to the bathroom, and spent a good fifteen minutes in the shower. He toweled off and put his dirty clothes in the washing machine. Aroused, he padded naked into the bedroom, where he found Ugly Nancy wide awake.

"What perfect timing." Larson hopped on the bed, positioned himself between her legs, grabbed her hips, pulled her to him, and slapped her ass. "Giddyup," he said.

• • •

An overflow crowd of tearful, somber mourners packed the church for Riley Burke's funeral. Ranch families from all corners of the state were in attendance, along with family, neighbors, local friends, and Riley's old college buddies from New Mexico State University. Eulogies brought smiles and more tears to many of the mourners, and through it all Patrick sat quietly on Kerney's lap not saying a word.

After the services ended, Jack, Irene, Lynette, and Lynette's parents were escorted through a side exit, and although Jack had his head bowed, Kerney was close enough to see tears on his friend's face. He nudged Sara, who had also been watching Jack, and she whispered to him that it was a good sign.

At the graveside, Kerney, Sara, and Patrick held hands and watched and listened as Riley was laid to rest under a bright, cloudless sky. After the minister read the final scriptures and asked all in attendance to remember that Riley was now at peace with his Lord, the mourners dispersed, except for the immediate family, who lingered near the casket.

Because of the large size of the gathering, the wake was held under the shade of massive cottonwood trees outside the Burkes' old hacienda. There were tables loaded with home-cooked food and ice chests filled with beer and soft drinks. Patrick ran and played with other children while the grown-ups shared memories of Riley and recounted family stories. The Burkes were Irish-American on both sides of the family tree, and fond laughter replaced at least some of the tears that had been shed at graveside. The party continued long into the afternoon, and it wasn't until most people had left that Kerney got a chance to talk with Jack.

"Did you see me fall apart at the cemetery?" Jack asked as the two men lifted one of the tables rented for the gathering into the bed of a truck.

"I saw you cry a little before we left," Kerney replied as he slid the table all the way in. "But I'd hardly call it falling apart, although your eyes are still pretty red."

Jack smiled wanly as they folded up the last table and carried it to the truck. "I bawled like a baby after most folks had left the cemetery. Couldn't hold it in. After we got home, I had to go inside and break down a couple more times while people were here."

"Good for you," Kerney said.

Jack closed the tailgate and leaned against it. "The pain is never going to go away, Kerney."

"I expect not."

"I've just been so damn angry. I want to find the man who killed my son and break him in two with my bare hands. You know what I mean?"

Kerney nodded. "I do."

"When do you and the family go back to England?"

"I'm not quite sure, but Sara and Patrick will probably leave before me. I've got some things to take care of before I can follow along."

"If you're worried about the horses and your ranch, we can look after things."

"Let's talk about that in a day or two," Kerney replied. He still hadn't talked to Lynette about whether or not she'd be interested in taking on the responsibilities of the partnership. If not, he'd sell off most of the horses and hire a caretaker to look after the place until Sara retired and they could return home permanently.

Sara came out of the house with Patrick in tow, waved in his direction, and walked toward Kerney's pickup truck parked in front of the old toolshed.

"Seems like it's time to leave," Kerney said, nodding in Sara's direction and shaking Jack's hand.

Jack gripped Kerney's hand hard in return. "I appreciate all you've done these last few days."

"No thanks are necessary, amigo," Kerney replied as he thumped Jack on the back and stepped away, thinking it would really help them both feel better if he could catch and kill that son of a bitch Larson before he returned to London.

During the short drive home on the ranch roads, Kerney let Patrick stand between his legs on the driver's seat and steer the truck.

As they poked along at a top speed of ten miles an hour, Sara asked Kerney about Jack.

"He's had a couple of good cries."

"That's a start."

"And Irene?" Kerney asked.

Sara shook her head. "Her heart is broken, but her sisters are going to make sure she doesn't go into a state of permanent depression. They're already planning to take her to Ireland on vacation in the fall."

"Good deal."

"Wasn't Clayton supposed to call you yesterday?"

"Yep, and I haven't heard a word from him. I'm sure he's busy."

"I want another brother besides Clayton," Patrick announced, looking back at Kerney. "One that's younger than me and not all grown up."

"Keep your eyes on the road, sport," Kerney cautioned.

"How about a baby sister?" Sara asked.

With his eyes firmly fixed on the road, Patrick considered it. "Okay, just as long as we all stay at the ranch and don't go back to London."

"Aha," Sara said. "So that's your scheme, is it?"

"What's a scheme?" Patrick asked.

"Your mother means that it's a sneaky idea," Kerney answered.

"It's *not* sneaky, because I already told you about it," Patrick replied indignantly as he glanced at his mother.

"Good point," Kerney said. "Pay attention to your driving."

"Yes, sir," Patrick replied, gripping the wheel tightly with his little hands.

At the ranch, Patrick refused to take a nap, so Kerney put him to work in the horse barn helping him clean out stalls. Soon Patrick ran out of steam. Kerney spread a horse blanket on the floor of the tack room and told his son to take a little break. Patrick stretched out and within a few minutes fell fast asleep.

Kerney had just finished spreading fresh straw in the last stall when Sara appeared.

"Have you lost track of our son?" she asked as she hitched her feet on the bottom rung of the open stall gate and swung on it.

"He's sleeping soundly in the tack room."

"Good, now we can talk. If you stay behind at the ranch, will you really return to us in London?"

"What kind of question is that?" Kerney asked.

"An important one. I know you're no happier living in England than Patrick is."

"We're still adjusting," Kerney replied.

"That's a pretty slick answer, mister."

"Then I'll give it to you straight," Kerney said with a grin. "The best possible place for Patrick and me to be is with you in London. Living in Europe for three years will give Patrick experiences few children are fortunate to get. It would be tragic not to give him a chance to learn firsthand about the world outside the United States. He may complain about London now, but give him time and he'll make some good friends in his new school and start enjoying himself."

"You mean that?"

"I do, although you can count on me to occasionally bitch about missing New Mexico, Santa Fe, the ranch, the sky, the mountains, the smell of the high desert air after a rainstorm, and green chili."

Sara jumped off the stall gate and gave Kerney a hug. "I'm holding you to everything you just said."

"Including my bitching?"

"As long as you keep it to a minimum."

"I'll try."

In the tack room with Sara at his side, Kerney knelt down, gently picked up his sleeping son, and carried him in his arms toward the house. He knew he was lucky to have his family intact, knew that circumstances beyond his control could easily rip his world apart just as it had the Burkes'. That didn't stop him from making a silent vow to do all in his power to keep Sara and Patrick safe.

The day after Paul Hewitt had called in his resignation as Lincoln County sheriff from his Albuquerque hospital bed, with Linda holding the phone for him, Clayton Istee sat in his cramped lieutenant's office entering numbers into a desk calculator to discover how deep in the hole the department was for paid overtime.

He ran the totals again, just to be sure, and then began examining the fiscal year line-item budget to see where he could find $8,000 to cover the current overtime shortage and another $6,000 to pay for anticipated overtime through the end of the budget cycle. He decided the only way he could make up the difference would be to drop one of the three new police vehicles Paul Hewitt had budgeted for. He hated the idea of delaying the replacement of even one cop car, but saw no alternative.

A knock on his open office door made him look up. Steve Durbin, the chair of the county commission, a man with an ingratiating façade and a viperous personality, smiled warmly at him.

"Clayton," Durbin said by way of a greeting as he sat in the straight-back chair on the other side of the desk. He had a fleshy face and a wide mouth with thick lips. "I thought at least you would have moved into the vacant chief deputy's office after your appointment."

"I haven't had the time," Clayton replied. "What can I do for you, Mr. Durbin?"

"Please, it's Steve. I wanted to tell you personally that the commission has just appointed Rudy Aldrich to fill out Paul's term in office."

"I was expecting that."

Durbin turned on his most sugary smile. "Of course, it was hardly a secret who the majority of the commission favored for the job. However, you do understand that Sheriff Aldrich's appointment in no way diminishes our appreciation of the wonderful work you've been doing here during these difficult times."

Clayton said nothing.

Durbin kept the smile going. "In light of that, we want you to attend our commission meeting next week so that we can present you with a commendation recognizing the contribution you've made to the citizens of Lincoln County."

"That isn't necessary."

"Perhaps not, but it's well deserved nonetheless. Now, on to a more sensitive subject." Durbin's smile blossomed wider but his eyes narrowed. "Sheriff Aldrich has decided to fill the chief deputy position with someone other than yourself and has asked that we keep his choice confidential until he makes a public announcement later in the week."

"I was expecting that also," Clayton said.

"The commission unanimously asked me to tell you that we

very much want you to remain with the department at your permanent rank of sergeant."

"Sheriff Hewitt promoted me to lieutenant."

"True enough, but you are some weeks shy of completing the mandatory six months' probation period. Thus, under current personnel rules, your permanent rank is sergeant. It will be up to Sheriff Aldrich to decide if he wants you to continue to serve as a lieutenant."

Aldrich had always been weak-kneed and two-faced, but until now Clayton hadn't realized how spineless the man truly was. He reached for a writing tablet on the desktop and tore off a piece of paper. "Let's end this charade."

He wrote out his resignation effective the end of the month and handed it to Durbin, who scanned it quickly.

"I'll take annual leave until then," he added. "Tell Aldrich I'll clean out my desk by the end of the day and turn in my department-issued equipment on Friday."

Durbin waved the resignation at Clayton. "You don't have to do this, you know."

Clayton stood. "Yes, I do. Now, if you'll excuse me, I have some work to finish up."

Durbin left with no further appeal for Clayton to remain with the department, confirming that resigning had been the right thing to do.

He looked at his watch. He had half a shift to wind things up and clean out his desk. He decided not to call Grace at work with the news. It could wait until he got home.

ChapterSeven

Larson planned on several more giddyups with Ugly Nancy after he'd gotten some sleep. He left her securely tied up before raiding the well-stocked liquor cabinet in the living room and then crashing in the smaller, second bedroom. He slept twelve hours, woke up refreshed, and wrapped himself in a bathrobe before making coffee in the kitchen. While the coffee brewed, he transferred his wet clothes from the washer to the dryer and went to check on Ugly. He found her where he'd left her, spread-eagled on the bed, but lying in a smelly mess of excrement and piss.

Disgusted, Larson untied her, forced her into the shower, and had her scrub down. He marched her dripping wet and naked back to the bedroom and made her strip the blankets and sheets off the bed and put them in the washing machine.

In the light of a new day and with a clear head that wasn't groggy with lack of sleep, Larson found Ugly Nancy even more nasty and horrid-looking than he'd remembered. Her little titties sagged flat against her skinny chest, there was an unattractive fold of wrinkles across her lower abdomen, her pubic hair looked like a dirty wire scrub pad used to scour pots, and she had unsightly underarm hair.

As she poured laundry detergent into the washing machine, she asked Larson if she could dress and have something to eat and drink.

He looked for any sign of emotion in her face and saw nothing. "You're a butt-ugly old bitch," Larson said in response.

Ugly Nancy laughed between clenched teeth. "Don't you want any more giddyup with me, Mister Killer?"

Larson slapped her hard across the face. "Don't piss me off, bitch." He pushed her back into the bedroom and threw her clothes in her face. "Get dressed."

While Ugly Nancy put her clothes on, Larson considered what to do with her. The idea of more sex with her was repulsive, and if the cops found him and killed him before he could find a better-looking, young woman to play with, Ugly Nancy might wind up being his last piece of nooky. That just wouldn't do.

"What if I let you go?" he asked.

Ugly Nancy looked at him suspiciously as she sat on the mattress and pulled on her boots. "You'd do that?"

"I'm thinking about it. But I'm keeping your Subaru, so you'll have to walk back to the ranch."

"Why not just take my car and leave me here?"

"That's not what I'm thinking I want to do," Larson hissed as he pulled her to her feet. He tied her hands behind her back, found some duct tape to cover her mouth, and hobbled her legs with rope. He yanked her to the front door and pushed her outside.

"I figure you've got a three-hour walk," he said. "Get going."

She stood rooted to the ground, shoulders hunched, glaring at him.

"Want me to make it more interesting? How about I blindfold you and make you go barefoot?"

Slowly she turned and started walking.

Larson watched her for a moment, went inside, picked up the Weatherby Mark V bolt-action rifle he'd taken from the gun cabinet at the ranch headquarters, loaded it, and walked to the open front door, expecting to see Ugly Nancy hobbling along no more than fifty feet from the lodge. Instead she was nowhere in sight.

He cursed, slipped his bare feet into his boots, and went looking for her. He found her hiding behind her Subaru.

"You're stupid as well as ugly." Larson kicked her feet out from under her, pulled off her boots, dragged her back to the lodge, and used more duct tape to blindfold her. He spun her around and pushed her in the direction he wanted her to go. "Now get moving," he ordered.

He watched Ugly Nancy walk gingerly away from the lodge, zigzagging a little but keeping a fairly straight line as she hobbled slowly across the mesa. Larson giggled when she ran into an occasional cholla cactus, stumbled over some gopher mounds, and stubbed her toes on some rocks. He hollered at her to keep moving.

When she was about a hundred yards out, Larson raised the Weatherby, sighted the target through the scope, and squeezed the trigger. Ugly Nancy fell hard and didn't move. From all appearances, it was a clean kill, and Larson congratulated himself on another fine piece of marksmanship.

He went back inside the lodge, drank some coffee, dressed in his clothes fresh from the dryer, and went to check on good old Ugly. The bullet that entered her back had pierced her heart.

He grabbed the hobble rope tied around her ankles and dragged her tiny, bony body back to the lodge, where he left it under a cottonwood tree while he fixed breakfast and figured out what to do with her. He decided to walk to the stolen truck he'd left at the edge of the mesa, drive it back, load up Ugly, and take her to an old nearby water tank where coyotes could feast on her when they came to drink. Then, when it was time to leave, he would torch the truck, burn down the lodge, and drive away in the Subaru.

He waited until the cool of evening to fetch the truck and take Ugly to the water tank. He rolled her out of the bed of the truck thinking that what the coyotes didn't want the vultures and crows would consume. She'd be nothing more than scattered, picked-over bones in a day or two.

Back at the lodge with a bottle of Scotch at his side, Larson sipped single malt and watched TV until the local late-night news came on. He was pleased to see that the manhunt for him wasn't the top story, although after the first commercial break the news anchor did remind viewers that "escaped fugitive Craig Larson is still at large and armed and dangerous."

He switched channels and found the other local newscasters were also giving the manhunt story less broadcast time. Somewhat reassured that things were quieting down a bit, Larson decided to stay put overnight, but not any longer than that. Although Ugly had told him nobody was due at the ranch for some days, he didn't know if she'd been lying or not. Best not to take any chances.

In the morning, he'd work out a really good plan, maybe heading north. Since the federal government was building fences and stationing National Guard troops along the Mexican border to keep out the wetbacks, it would probably be far easier and a lot safer to sneak into Canada.

Larson had read stories about escaped convicts who'd lived normal lives for twenty years or more. They'd taken on new identities, held down jobs, and raised families. And he'd heard about guys who'd broken out of prison and never been seen or heard from again.

He had enough money and jewels to get himself set up once he got to Canada and learned his way around. But he didn't want to make a major move until the manhunt fizzled out a bit more. He needed to find another place to stay where there wasn't an old biddy caretaker to deal with or any nosy nearby neighbors.

He'd cogitate on it overnight, but the one thing he already

knew he needed to do was stop killing people for a while until things calmed down.

He poured another double shot and switched the channel to a late night movie.

It took Grace nagging Clayton for a full day about his foolish pride before he broke down, called Kerney, and gave him the news about his impending departure from the Lincoln County S.O.

"I'm meeting with Andy Baca tomorrow morning to get sworn in as a special investigator with the New Mexico State Police," Kerney replied without missing a beat. "How would you feel about coming on board to help catch this scumbag?"

"Sara doesn't mind you coming out of retirement?" Clayton asked.

"Not for this. She said she doesn't want to see hide nor hair of me until Larson is planted in the ground."

"She actually said that?"

"When it comes to the people she loves, the woman doesn't have a mean bone in her body. But if you're her enemy, watch out. How about you? Will Grace and the kids put up with you being gone for a while?"

"That's not a problem. She thinks Paul Hewitt should be inducted into a national top cop hall of fame, if one existed."

"And she's right. Get yourself up here tonight. You can stay with us. I'm scheduled to meet with Andy early in the morning. I'll let him know that you're coming on board."

"Isn't that his call to make?"

"Andy will jump at the chance to put a shield in your hand. I'll even bet you a steak dinner that, before this is over, he'll offer you a permanent position."

"We're not about to move away from the Rez. Not yet, anyway."

"That's your call to make," Kerney replied.

"You haven't asked for details about what went down at the S.O."

"I don't need to. Paul Hewitt called me, told me he'd resigned and was putting in his retirement papers, and mentioned what he thought might happen to you as a result. From what he said about the slacker the county commission appointed as the interim sheriff, I figured you'd turn in your walking papers sooner or later."

Clayton laughed. "Tell me truthfully, did you call in a favor from Chief Baca to get him to agree to hire me?"

"If that had been necessary, I might have," Kerney replied. "But you don't need a leg up; your record speaks for itself. See you tonight."

The following morning, Kevin Kerney and Clayton Istee arrived in Andy Baca's spacious office at the Department of Public Safety building on Cerrillos Road.

After greeting his visitors, Andy perched on the edge of his big oak desk, built for a predecessor years ago by convicts at the old penitentiary before it erupted into a murderous riot, and studied his visitors.

Kerney and Clayton sat on the leather couch facing the desk and waited him out.

"We have evidence of one sort or another that links Larson to a whole slew of crime scenes," Andy finally said. "From the attack on the corrections officer, to a kid on the schoolbus who saw him walking along the highway just north of Gallegos where the pickup truck was stolen from the Dripping Springs Ranch two days ago, we've got solid physical evidence, substantial eyewitness accounts, and excellent circumstantial evidence. What we don't have is a single sighting of Larson or the stolen Dripping Springs vehicle during the last forty-eight hours."

He picked up two thick case files, brought them to the large coffee table in front of the couch, and plopped them down. "That's everything we've got on Larson, including the crime scene investigations, and all the field interviews and interrogations from every participating law enforcement agency in New Mexico and West Texas. The page count is just slightly less than *War and Peace* but we're adding to it every day."

Kerney lifted one of the bulky files wrapped with thick rubber bands. "Well, by volume it certainly does show a good-faith effort to catch him."

"And isn't that just hunky-dory," Andy replied sarcastically as he sat in an easy chair at the side of the coffee table. "I have over two dozen officers and investigators spread out over the northeastern quadrant of the state, trying to get a line on Larson. As you know, once you get outside of the towns, villages, and settlements, it's remote, isolated, and largely unpopulated country up there. I could put two hundred officers in the field and it would still take months to cover all the ground. We can't really be sure that Larson is still even in New Mexico."

"What do you want us to do?" Clayton asked.

Andy nodded at the case files on the conference table. "First, read the case files and get up to speed. Second, target any gaps in the investigation needed to be filled in, people who need to be interviewed again, and do the necessary follow-up. Talk to the lead investigators on the various cases to see if there are any loose ends that might give us a clue to Larson's whereabouts. I want you two operating independently from the task force. But coordinate with it as needed and keep me personally informed of your activities."

"Okay," Clayton said.

Andy went to his desk, returned with two special investigator shields, and handed one each to Clayton and to Kerney.

Kerney weighed the shield in his hand. "From what I can see,

Larson is spiraling more and more out of control with each fresh kill. He's become totally erratic and unpredictable. I think we need to dig into his personal history to get a handle on him."

"And completely bypass the existing investigations?" Andy asked.

"Not at all," Kerney answered. "We'll analyze both the historical and the current facts."

"Okay," Andy said. "What else?"

"If we turn up anything of value," Clayton said, "I want in on the hunt."

Kerney nodded in agreement.

Andy looked hard at both men. Because of Larson, he had lost an excellent young officer, Kerney had lost a young friend and partner, and Clayton's boss, Paul Hewitt, a fine man and a super cop, was now totally dependent upon his wife and caregivers for every aspect of his continued existence. It was ugly all the way around.

"Personal vendettas cloud judgments," he cautioned.

"Don't worry about me, Chief Baca," Clayton replied. "If I find Larson, I promise to bring him back, dead or alive."

"Me too," Kerney chimed in.

Andy shook his head in mock dismay. "I've never hired a father-and-son act—I mean team—before. I hope I'm not making a big mistake. Stand up so I can swear you two in."

Kerney and Clayton got to their feet, raised their hands, and took the oath of office as special investigators with the New Mexico State Police.

At his desk, Andy signed the commission certificates and asked his secretary to send in a lieutenant who would take Kerney and Clayton to have official photo identifications made, get department weapons and equipment issued, have vehicles assigned, and qualify with their weapons at the range.

"I'll have an empty nearby office set up for your use when you get back," he added, "and my secretary will make sure you have any and all support and assistance you need."

"Let's get started," Kerney said as a young female lieutenant in a crisp uniform knocked and entered the office.

"Good hunting," Andy said as the lieutenant ushered Clayton and Kerney out.

Craig Larson woke up lying on a Navajo rug in a pool of vomit. He pushed himself to a sitting position and tried to figure out where he was, but his spinning head and fuzzy vision made it hard to focus. He rolled away from the pool of puke, closed his eyes, and tried to think. All he could concentrate on was a pounding ache in his head that made him want to scream.

Slowly he opened his eyes, sat up again, and recognized the hunting lodge living room. There were two empty Scotch bottles on the end table next to the leather couch. The bolt-action Weatherby he'd used to bring down Ugly Nancy sat on the fancy Mexican-tile-top coffee table. On the opposite side of the room, the big-screen television had a bullet hole in it. Larson tried to think of what had made him want to kill the TV, but he drew a blank. There must have been something on the tube he really didn't like.

He got to his feet, went to the kitchen, soaked his head in the sink, and sucked down water from the faucet. Partially revived, he sat at the kitchen table and tried to sort out what he'd done before he started hitting the sauce. As far as he could recollect, he'd walked across the mesa, fetched the truck, driven Ugly's body to the water tank, dumped it, and returned to the lodge.

Just to make sure he didn't dream it all up, Larson looked out the kitchen window. The truck was there all right, parked next to the propane tank, baking in the harsh light of a blazing afternoon summer sun. He mixed up a can of frozen orange juice concentrate from the freezer and started a pot of fresh coffee. The stove clock read 1:10.

While the coffee brewed, he slugged down some orange juice, gobbled some aspirin from the bathroom medicine cabinet, brought the clock radio from the bedroom into the kitchen, and plugged it in. With the TV out of commission, he'd have to rely on the radio to stay updated on the manhunt.

He poured hot coffee into a mug, sipped it, fiddled with the dial, and found five AM stations but only static on the FM band. Of the AM stations, three were playing country music, one was broadcasting a canned talk radio show, and one was a pulpit for an evangelical Christian preacher asking for money.

The noise hurt his head. Larson turned off the radio, washed down more aspirin with orange juice, and considered what to do. He'd originally planned to torch the lodge and burn the truck before leaving in Ugly's Subaru, but smoke from a fire like that would be seen for miles and draw a lot of attention in a big hurry.

As he abandoned that idea, he walked to the bathroom, stripped off his clothes, and stood under a hot shower. He needed to move on before someone came looking for Ugly, and find a place where he could hide out for a couple more days until he was sure the manhunt had fizzled out.

He toweled off. If he recalled correctly, he'd seen a laptop in Ugly's office at the ranch headquarters. One of the tricks he'd used when he first started running from the law was to research houses for sale on the Internet. Because real estate agents posted so much information about and so many photographs of properties on Web sites, it was easy to find vacant houses to case and break into for a night. He decided to drive back to the ranch house, surf the Internet, and see what he could turn up.

Larson dressed, went to the kitchen, raided the cupboards for packaged and canned food, and put it all in a pillowcase. He did the same with whiskey from the liquor cabinet and carried everything to the Subaru. He transferred his money and jewelry stash from the truck to the car, went back inside the lodge, unwrapped all the freezer food from the refrigerator, and spread it throughout the house. Then he scattered dry cereal, sugar, crackers, flour, and rice on the floors, topped it off with the contents of several cans of tomato sauce, opened the doors and windows, and removed all the screens.

By nightfall the building would be crawling with all sorts of insects, birds, snakes, and four-legged critters. If and when the police came looking for Ugly, they would find one godawful mess.

Larson put the weapons and ammunition in the Subaru and took off for the ranch house. He stopped on the mesa and did a quick surveillance on foot just to be sure no surprises awaited him below. Satisfied that all looked okay, he drove down, used Ugly's keys to open the front door, powered up the laptop in her office, and clicked on the Internet icon on the screen. Within minutes he was scrolling down a real estate agency's Web site listings for homes, land, and ranches in northeastern New Mexico.

Larson found three properties in the Springer area to his liking, but the one that stood out was a small ranch on the Canadian River east of town, off a country road with no close-by neighbors. Larson knew exactly where the property was located, figured he could get there without getting back onto the pavement, and best of all the pictures on the Web site showed the property to be vacant.

He shut down the computer and went scavenging through the house, found a top-quality sleeping bag, an inflatable air mattress, a high-powered flashlight, a camp stove, a portable battery-operated radio, and all the other gear he would need to stay comfortable for a few days. He supplemented his foodstuffs from the kitchen cabinets, and from the gun cabinet in the living room he added a .357 Colt pistol and a 9 mm Glock autoloader to his arsenal, along with a hundred rounds of ammo for each handgun.

After closing all the curtains and drapes, Larson locked up the house and left the ranch feeling upbeat. The place where he was going was remote, but not too far away from several working ranches. After settling in, he would reconnoiter the neighbors to see if he could locate a vehicle to replace Ugly's car when it was time to move on.

Two more days of hiding out should do it, Larson thought with a smile as he fiddled with the car radio and found a country station playing an old Marty Robbins tune. Larson hummed along until he remembered he'd forgotten to chase down Ugly's mare, unsaddle her, and put her in the stable. He slowed the Subaru to turn around but then decided to blow it off. Whoever found the mare and went looking for Ugly Nancy was in for a big surprise.

Since the day Craig Larson escaped from custody and started his rampage, Everett Dorsey, chief of the Springer Police Department, had gotten very little sleep. Along with his three officers, Dorsey had been putting in eighteen-hour days trying to turn up any shred of information from Larson's hometown friends and acquaintances that might help get a fix on the fugitive's where-abouts. An eyewitness had sighted Larson in and near the settlement of Gallegos, less than seventy miles from Springer as the crow flies, which had convinced Dorsey that Larson had been heading home to familiar turf to lie low for a while. But where?

Dorsey had redoubled his efforts to find out where Larson might be hiding by concentrating his attention on the twin brother, Kerry. After three intensive interview sessions he had started to break through when his efforts had been sabotaged by a contract psychologist with the state police sent up from Santa Fe to draw information out of Kerry. But what the shrink didn't know was that while Kerry looked as normal as the next person, he had a few loose screws, wasn't very bright, didn't relate well to strangers, and was as stubborn as a mule when it came to protecting his brother.

Blown off by the psychologist, Dorsey had complained to the major in charge of the state police task force, but to no avail. Condescendingly, the major had advised Dorsey to leave the head stuff to the shrink.

Dorsey eased into his desk chair and rubbed his tired eyes. Housed in a separate three-office suite of the town hall building one block off the main north-south drag, the Springer Police Department headquarters was a dismal place to spend any time. Battered old desks, ancient filing cabinets, and frayed miscellaneous office furniture filled the small rooms. Clutter added to the mess.

Dorsey liked it that way; the cramped, unattractive quarters kept him and his officers from hanging out there, which meant they spent most of their time on the streets actually policing.

Dorsey opened his eyes. If the reports of his officers were to be believed—and there was no reason to doubt them—nobody in the town of Springer had heard, seen, or had any form of contact with Craig Larson since the last sighting. On a much wider scale, the sheriff's offices in eight counties, the district state police office, area game and fish officers, the local livestock inspector, and the special state police task force out of Santa Fe were reporting the same results.

All of this meant it was possible that Larson hadn't come home to roost, but had just passed through Colfax County on the way to his next crime. But there had been no new reports of murder or mayhem.

Dorsey's stomach grumbled from lack of food, but he knew if he stopped to eat, the food combined with lack of sleep would put him into a stupor for the next twelve hours. He was about to go back out and talk again to all of Craig Larson's high school classmates who still lived in the area when the telephone rang.

Dorsey picked up and a woman with what he guessed to be a German accent asked to speak to the officer in charge.

"This is Everett Dorsey, the police chief, ma'am," he replied. "How can I help you?"

The woman explained that she was calling from Frankfurt, Germany, that she was the executive assistant to the CEO of the multinational company that owned the Lazy Z, and that she'd been trying to reach the ranch caretaker without success over the last forty-eight hours.

"A group of our corporate executives are due to arrive at the ranch from Hong Kong in three days, and various arrangements needed for their accommodations must be made," the woman added. "It's not like Ms. Trimble to be away or unavailable for several days without giving advance notice. I've left a message with the Colfax County sheriff and have not yet heard back."

"Ms. Trimble is the ranch caretaker?" Dorsey reached for a pen and a writing tablet on his disorderly desk.

"Yes, Nancy Trimble. Could you please send an officer to see if she's ill or has had an accident?"

"I'll surely do that, ma'am," Dorsey said, "but first I need to ask you some questions."

"By all means."

The executive assistant, Ms. Hannelore Schmidt, told Dorsey

that Nancy Trimble was a divorced, older woman in her sixties who lived full-time at the Lazy Z. Schmidt didn't know what kind of vehicle Trimble owned but said the company kept a silver Hummer on the premises. Dorsey also learned Trimble was the only employee and that no corporate executives or their guests were currently staying at the ranch. Schmidt supplied Dorsey with the name and phone number of a neighboring rancher who boarded the Lazy Z horses when the Lazy Z wasn't in use.

Dorsey asked Schmidt how he could reach her and she rattled off a string of numbers. He wrote them down, realizing he'd never made an international telephone call before.

"I just dial these numbers you gave me to get through to you?" he asked, feeling like a total hick.

"You must dial your international access code first," Schmidt replied.

"Okay, thanks." Dorsey wasn't about to ask if she knew his international access code. "I'll call you back."

"Thank you, Chief Dorsey," Schmidt said. "But before you ring off, let me give you the keypad code to the ranch road gate."

Dorsey wrote down the code, said good-bye, hung up, and headed for his unit, not even thinking about contacting the sheriff's office, which as far as he was concerned had dropped the ball. He'd spent nine years with the Colfax County S.O. before becoming the Springer police chief, he held a cross-deputy commission that gave him full law enforcement powers outside the city limits, and he was a good half hour closer to the Lazy Z than any deputy. Besides, if there was the slightest chance that Trimble's disappearance was in any way connected with Craig Larson, Dorsey sure as hell wanted to be in on it.

He called Ed Seward, the rancher who boarded the Lazy Z stock, and asked if he'd recently seen or talked to Nancy Trimble.

"Not since last week," Seward answered. "We stopped and visited in town for a few minutes. Is there a problem?"

"Don't know. I got a call from the ranch owner's assistant asking me to make contact with Trimble. Said she couldn't get in touch with her. Did Trimble seem like her normal self when you saw her?"

Seward laughed. "Nancy keeps to herself, so it's hard to say what's normal with her."

"What kind of car does she drive?"

"A dinged-up green Subaru. One of those hatchback models."

"What do you know about her?" Everett Dorsey asked.

"Not much. She has a grown son who lives back east. South Carolina, I think. I can go over there and check on her, if you'd like."

"I appreciate the offer, Ed," Dorsey replied, "but it's best if I do that."

"You're the law, Everett," Seward said. "Let me know if I can help out."

"Will do." Dorsey disconnected and made radio contact with one of his officers, Rick Mares, and Mitch Lowe, a local state police officer.

"I need backup on a welfare check at a ranch," he said to both men. "Care to join me?"

"You got something, Everett?" Mitch asked.

"Yeah, a cautious nature," Dorsey replied.

Mitch laughed. "Give us a ten-eighty-seven."

Dorsey told the officers where to meet up.

• • •

Larson's new hideout was perfect. The setting was remote, the unlocked barn was less than one hundred steps from the house, and the old pitched-roof house sat on a knoll that gave him excellent views in all four directions. He parked the Subaru in the barn just in case someone came wandering up the ranch road, broke into the house through a side window, and took a look around. The rooms were empty, the curtains and shades closed, and the house was spic-and-span clean. According to the real estate sales brochure he'd found on a kitchen counter, the walls had been freshly painted, the hardwood floors sanded and resealed, a new forced-air propane-fired furnace had been installed, and the one-year-old roof was still under a full warranty. Total cost for the property, which consisted of the house, barn, and shed on eighty acres, was less than the cost of a manufactured double-wide on a postage stamp–size lot in a Santa Fe trailer park.

Larson checked to see if the utilities were working. The kitchen wall phone had no dial tone, there was no juice to the ceiling lights, and the stove and furnace had been turned off. Fortunately he had water, probably from a gravity-fed well.

Larson opened the propane tank valve on his way to the barn, where he unloaded his arsenal, supplies, and gear from the Subaru. It took three trips to get everything into the house.

He set up housekeeping in the living room and kitchen, lit the stove and water heater pilot lights, and turned on the portable radio just in time for a top-of-the-hour local news summary from a station broadcasting from nearby Raton, the county seat and largest community in the far northeast corner of the state. He was still a hot topic on the news, but not the headline story. That honor went to a Raton man who had shot and killed his estranged wife at her place of employment.

The house was hot and stuffy, and Larson was about to open all the doors and windows when he heard the sound of an approaching vehicle. He took a peek though a living room window and saw a late-model GMC SUV roll to a stop at the closed but unlocked gate. A portly, older man got out of the passenger side of the Jimmy, opened the gate for the driver, and climbed back in. As the SUV drew near, Larson read the magnetic sign on the driver's door:

TAMI PHELAN
YOUR HOMETEAM REALTOR
RATON, NM

Larson shook his head in disbelief at such shitty luck, picked up the 9mm Glock, and waited for his uninvited guests to arrive. But when a leggy blonde in jeans with big hair and a stacked pair opened the driver's-side door and climbed out, Larson grinned and changed his mind about his bad luck. He watched Blondie fast-talk the old dude as he climbed the porch steps and waited for her to unlock the front door. He was another Porky like Bertie Roach, the man from Tulsa Larson had offed in the Albuquerque motel, and Lenny Hampson, the bigmouth friend of Kerry's he'd left in the desert.

"The property is in excellent condition," Blondie said as she swung the door open and moved aside for Porky to enter first. "There are thirty acres under irrigation. It would make an excellent horse ranch."

Larson shot Porky in the chest as he stepped over the threshold. Grunting, the man crumpled to his knees and fell face forward. Before Blondie could react, Larson grabbed a handful of her big, curly hair and yanked her inside.

"What did you do?" Blondie screamed, her hand flying to her mouth as she stared at the body on the floor. She had bright red fingernails.

Blood from Porky's chest wound seeped across the newly re-finished, once pristine hardwood floor, which was no longer a strong selling point for the property.

"What did you do?" she screeched again, her gaze locked on Larson's face.

"Three's a crowd," Larson explained with a smile as he wrapped his hand around her neck. "You must be Tami."

Tami averted her eyes. "Please don't hurt me."

"Hurt you?" Larson replied softly, feigning indignation. He dug the barrel of the Glock into Tami's neck and forced her to raise her pretty head so he could take a closer look at her. "Why, when I'm finished with you, sweetie, you'll be calling me your daddy and begging me for more."

He cocked the Glock for dramatic effect and ripped open Tami's blouse. She was indeed stacked.

Everett Dorsey met Officers Lowe and Mares at the entrance to the Lazy Z. The two men stood with Dorsey in front of his unit while he filled them in on his conversation with Hannelore Schmidt of Frankfurt, Germany.

"Nancy Trimble is in her sixties and lives alone at the ranch," he added, "so it's possible she might not be missing at all. She could have taken a bad fall or dropped dead."

Officer Mitch Lowe consulted his paperwork. In his late twenties, he had just completed his seventh year with the state police. A frown crossed his boyish face. "The locked gate was reported by the officer assigned to contact residents in this area. He left a phone message, but there's been no follow-up since then."

Rick Mares, Dorsey's senior officer, a thin and wiry man in his forties, shrugged a shoulder. "It's been frustrating as hell to make contact with everybody, and a bitch to track people down.

There are folks who are out of town, people on vacation or sick in the hospital, people who live somewhere else and have a second home or a getaway place out in the boonies. Hell, we've even got some Texas ranchers who own outfits just for summer grazing and there's not a soul to be found on any of those spreads."

"It hasn't been easy," Lowe concurred.

"Let's hope Nancy Trimble is alive and well," Dorsey said as he stepped over to the electronic keypad of the solar-powered gate and punched in the code. "But with Larson on the loose, we go in prepared for anything."

The gate swung open and the three officers convoyed their units slowly down the ranch road, scanning the landscape for anything that looked out of the ordinary. They arrived at the ranch headquarters to be greeted by a saddled horse that cantered over from a nearby open field, the reins of its bridle falling loose to the ground.

"Could be that Trimble did have an accident," Mitch Lowe said as he reached out and caught the horse's reins. He wiped a hand across the dusty saddle. "Nobody has been astride this animal for at least a day, maybe more."

Dorsey unholstered his sidearm. "Let's check the house before we get ahead of ourselves." He knocked on the locked front door while Lowe and Mares inspected the exterior for any sign of forced entry.

"Anything?" he asked when they returned.

Rick Mares shook his head. "It's locked up tight and the window shades and curtains are drawn."

"Do we break in?" Mitch Lowe asked.

Dorsey didn't hesitate. "Kick in the door."

Inside, they did a quick plain-view search and found evidence that the house had been ransacked.

"Do we call in forensics?" Rick Mares asked as they returned to the front porch.

Dorsey scanned the grounds. "Let's do a sweep of all the other structures first."

They forced their way into the two guesthouses, walked through the barn, the stables, the tack room, and the horse arena, looked inside the fenced paddocks and the silver Hummer, and did a field search of the immediate surrounding area. There was no sign of Trimble, her body, or her green Subaru.

Mitch unsaddled the horse, put it in a paddock, and fed it some oats. In the late afternoon light, Dorsey stood with the two officers in front of the main ranch house looking up at the mesa.

"Trimble is missing, her car is gone, the ranch house has been tossed. The gun cabinet was left unlocked, so we can presume some weapons are missing along with other items," Dorsey said. "I'm thinking there's a good chance Larson has been here. We'll call in forensics and keep looking."

He pointed to the ranch road that snaked up the mesa. "Let's see where that road goes."

The road, with fresh vehicle tracks, took them to a hunting lodge on the mesa top where they found the truck Larson had stolen from the Dripping Springs Ranch. Mitch Lowe called it in and they took a quick look inside the lodge and found it occupied by vermin, spiders, some squawking crows perched on the back of a leather couch, several flighty robins, and a coiled rattlesnake. There were bird droppings, rat shit, and coyote scat in every room, along with about a million or more red fire ants.

Outside, they followed the stolen truck's tire tracks to a water tank and found a partially eaten woman's body, which was most likely all that remained of Nancy Trimble. Almost all of her clothing had been ripped off by the coyotes that had obviously feasted on the internal organs. Rope had been used to tie her hands, she'd been hobbled around the ankles, the bottoms of her bloody, bare feet were pincushions of imbedded cactus spines, and there were shreds of gray duct tape at the corners of her empty eye sockets. The entry wound told Dorsey she'd been shot in the back by a high-powered rifle, and signs of recent bruising on her buttocks convinced him that she'd been raped.

Dorsey pictured Trimble panicked, violated, hobbled, blind-folded, and barefoot stumbling across the mesa, knowing she was about to die, and his stomach turned at the thought it. He'd seen his share of human perversion, evil, and ugliness, but this was a new, all-time low.

"Somebody needs to put a bullet in Craig Larson's head," Dorsey said as he covered the body with a tarp.

Springer had one motel and a small, ten-room hotel. The state police task force hunting for Craig Larson had filled them up and spilled over to a budget motel on the outskirts of Raton, some forty miles distant. Just after nine at night Kerney drove past the Raton motel, with its No Vacancy sign and parking lot filled with cop cars, and pulled in next door at a slightly more expensive lodging establishment. Clayton parked behind him and they registered for separate but adjoining rooms. When they finished stowing their gear, Kerney used his cell phone to call Frank Van-meter, the state police major in charge of the manhunt, and advise him of their arrival.

Just as Kerney disconnected, Clayton popped into the room and asked if there were any new developments.

"Nope," Kerney replied. "No fresh kills since the caretaker at the Lazy Z and no sightings of Larson."

Clayton nodded, turned as if to leave, hesitated, and gave Kerney a questioning glace.

"What is it?" he asked.

"I keep hoping Larson won't get caught until I find him. I haven't even being thinking about the innocent people he's been murdering while he's on the loose. Is that perverse or what?"

"No, it's human," Kerney replied with a grim smile. "I want a piece of Larson just as much as you do."

ChapterEight

In spite of her good looks, sex with Tami was a real bummer. Larson figured her to be a frigid, hysterical bitch. The only hole that worked on her was her mouth. He finished quickly, zipped up his pants, and slapped her hard repeatedly to get her to quit begging for her life. When she wouldn't quiet down, he stuck her head in the toilet and held her under until she went limp.

As he laid Tami's body out on the living room floor next to Porky, he decided it would have been more fun to send her out into the cactus patch behind the barn to use as target practice. Blindfolded and barefoot, just like Ugly Nancy, except that he wouldn't have let Tami put any clothes on. Shooting people was far more enjoyable than drowning them.

He searched Tami's purse. She carried a New Mexico voter identification card for the Republican Party and held memberships in the Toastmasters, the Rotary Club, and the Raton Chamber of Commerce. Her business card showed an address on a downtown street of Raton's so-called historic district near the train tracks and old railroad station. Her home address on her driver's license didn't ring any bells, but he'd last been in Raton half a lifetime ago, so who knew what had changed?

He leafed through Tami's day planner. The final entry for the day was a notation to meet Carter Marion Pettibone in the lobby of a Raton motel, to tour several ranch properties. The wallet in Porky's back pocket confirmed he was Pettibone, age sixty-six, of Omaha, Nebraska. It also contained a key card to a room at the motel where Tami had picked him up.

Larson looked down at the bodies he'd neatly arranged side by side. Tami Phelan and Carter Marion Pettibone. What a pair. He could just imagine them as a Bible-thumping husband-and-wife team, evangelizing the back-road, dusty villages of West Texas door to door and on dinky public access television stations.

He went to the kitchen, sipped from the bottle of twenty-year-old whiskey he'd taken from the Lazy Z Ranch, and pondered his next move. For sure, staying put wouldn't work. There was always the chance that Tami, Pettibone, or both had told somebody where they were going.

Larson retrieved Tami's cell phone from her purse, found her home number on the speed-dial list, and punched in the number. The phone rang, went unanswered, and switched over to a voice message recorded by Tami. He disconnected, speed-dialed her office number, and got another message from Tami. There was no wedding ring on Tami's finger and her business card showed her to be the broker who operated the real estate agency. Maybe she lived alone and even worked alone.

Outside, Larson searched Tami's GMC Yukon. If Pettibone had a cell phone, he hadn't brought it with him. Back inside, Larson paged through Tami's day planner and found a two-week-old entry for Pettibone showing his home address and phone number in Omaha circled in red, with a note that he was interested in ranch land of less than 320 acres.

Larson dialed the Omaha number on Tami's cell and a woman answered on the fourth ring.

"Hello," she said, in a breathless voice as though she'd run to answer the telephone.

"I'd like to speak to Mr. Pettibone," Larson said, trying not to crack up at the absurdity of his request.

"I'm sorry, my husband's not here right now. Can I take a message?"

"When would it be best to call back and speak to him?"

"He's out right now, but I can take a message for him."

"I'm just passing through town. Do you expect him back any-time soon?"

"No, he's away on business."

"For how long?"

"He'll be back in three days."

"Tell him Ted Landry called. He'll remember who I am."

"Ted Landry?"

"Yes, ma'am. Thank you"

Larson disconnected and went through Tami's day planner more carefully. There was nothing in it about picking up the kids from school or meeting the hubby for lunch or drinks. The only names that showed up repeatedly other than clients seemed to be those of a few women friends Tami would meet for dinner or a movie.

The car keys in Pettibone's pocket were for a Buick, probably with Nebraska plates, which was most likely in the motel park-ing lot. If Porky's wife wasn't going to start missing him for the next three days, the cops wouldn't be looking for the Buick any-time soon. Larson decided to ditch the piece-of-shit Subaru on the off chance that what was left of Ugly Nancy had been discov-ered, drive to Raton in Tami's GMC Yukon, and use Porky's Buick as his new set of wheels.

Back at the Yukon, he removed the magnetic real estate signs from the driver's- and passenger's-side doors. Tami had a vanity li-cense plate that read "COWGIRL." Larson discarded it in favor of the Subaru's plate, thinking that Tami the cowgirl hadn't even been as good at giddyup as Ugly Nancy. He loaded the Yukon with all the gear he'd carted into the house, figuring that under the cover of darkness he would transfer his stuff to Pettibone's Buick.

Finished with his tasks, Larson downed another couple of fingers of whiskey before returning to the living room. What to do with Tami and Porky was nagging him. His druthers were to burn the house down around them, but that would just draw quick attention and bring a slew of volunteer firefighters to the place. He could bury the bodies, but that felt like too much work. Instead, he brought the Subaru from the barn where he'd stashed it, opened the hatchback, folded down the backseats, and manhandled Tami's body into the car. To get her to fit inside, he had to pull her head up between the front bucket seats and place it on the center armrest. He spread her legs, raised her knees, dropped Porky's drawers down around his ankles and, grunting under the effort, wrestled him on top of naked Tami. Larson doubted that Pettibone, in life, had ever been on top of such a good-looking piece of tail. That was the downside. In death, however, the upside was that Porky would never know what a bum fuck she was.

He put the Subaru back in the barn, carefully closed the gate to the property, and drove away in the Yukon, with a low-hanging western sun in his eyes. Tami's cell phone, which hadn't rung once, was on the front passenger seat, along with the 9mm Glock, the .357 Ruger, and the .357 pistol. The two hunting rifles, the Weatherby and a Remington 700 Safari that fired a .458 Magnum bullet with great stopping power, were on the backseat, along with the lever-action Winchester 30.06. If the cops found him and wanted to party, the firepower he had at hand would make it possible for him to oblige them greatly.

Larson turned north toward the Sangre de Cristo Mountains, which rose up to fill the horizon from east to west. It seemed he had a knack for killing people, but so far his victims had been random folks who'd stood in his way. Maybe it was time to get more serious and up the ante.

Some years back, Larson had been mesmerized by the two

snipers who had killed all those people in Maryland and Virginia. He even remembered their names, Muhammad and Malvo. At the time they seemed unstoppable, and he'd paid close attention to the details of the manhunt and their eventual capture.

He knew they had used a Bushmaster XM15 E2S to take down their targets. Patterned after the M-16, it had a ten-shot magazine and fired .223-caliber rounds. He knew the car they'd driven, a Chevy Caprice, had been checked out by the police seven times before the pair were finally arrested, that they used a stolen laptop to navigate around the D.C. area, and that they took turns as the shooter and the spotter, sometimes firing from the vehicle and sometimes not.

Supposedly, Malvo and Muhammad had killed for money: some ten million dollars they'd hoped to get from the cops. In truth, Larson knew it had to be all about the blood sport, not the money. He was starting to feel that way about his own killing spree.

On the interstate heading north toward Raton, a state police car passed him without slowing, and Larson toyed with the idea of assassinating cops. That would be a hell of a lot more entertaining than shooting unarmed housewives at gas stations or in front of grocery stores, as Malvo and Muhammad had done. It could also be a lot more challenging too, because cops could shoot back.

Not that Larson planned to give them the chance. The Weatherby and the Remington would provide plenty of range and give him time enough to disappear, just like Malvo and Muhammad. The more he thought about killing cops, the more it appealed to him. After all, cops gave him the most grief, not Pettibone, Tami, Ugly Nancy, Cuddy the KO'd Kid, or most of the other folks he'd wasted. Those poor suckers had just been in the wrong place at the wrong time. But the Lincoln County sheriff, the cop at the roadblock, and the horde of cops looking for him were all trying to bring him down.

Maybe it was time to stop the cops.

Larson liked the sound of that. *Stop the cops.* He said it over and over. If he really went through with it, he would be bigger than Malvo and Muhammad. Way bigger.

In Raton, along the motel strip, Larson made up his mind to do it. All the cop cars parked outside a budget franchise motel sealed the deal. He passed by slowly, watching a small group of uniformed officers talking as they stood next to a patrol vehicle.

Larson felt invisible. He was no more than twenty-five feet away from them, driving slowly as he passed by, and the cops ignored him completely. And why shouldn't they? He was in Tami's Yukon nobody was looking for, and with his shaved head and new beard he now had a completely different look.

He was invisible, maybe even invincible.

Larson grinned as he wheeled into the motel entrance where Porky Pettibone, now lying dead on top of cold and frigid Tami in the back of Ugly's Subaru, had booked a room.

He'd seen a television show where the cops found a body carefully arranged on a bed and called it staging. He mulled over a way to kill a whole bunch of cops and stage their bodies in a circle jerk. He laughed out loud at the idea of it.

He parked next to the Buick with Nebraska plates and let himself into Porky's room. The bedside telephone message light was blinking. Larson followed the instructions on the placard next to the phone and dialed to retrieve the message. It was from Pettibone's wife, reporting that a man named Ted Landry had called for him, and asking if he liked the ranch he'd gone to see with the Realtor.

Larson closed the window curtains and checked the time. It was a good two hours before nightfall, when it would be safe to move his gear to Porky's car. Until then, he would stay put and do some serious cogitating about ways to kill cops.

After attending an early morning state police task force meeting, Kerney and Clayton talked privately over coffee in the motel restaurant with Major Frank Vanmeter, the task force commander. Barely in his forties, Vanmeter was a twenty-year veteran of the department. He'd been a lieutenant during Kerney's brief stint as a deputy chief of the state police.

Kerney asked him how the psychologist, Dr. John Casados, had made out talking to Larson's twin brother.

Vanmeter pursed his thin lips and shook his bald head. "Kerry Larson clammed up. But Casados thinks it likely that he could be deliberately withholding information about his brother's whereabouts."

"What makes Casados think that?" Clayton asked as he spooned some sugar into his coffee cup.

"Hero worship," Vanmeter replied. "Kerry Larson idolizes his brother, who in his mind can do no wrong. He's an identical twin and the spitting image of his brother, Craig, but slow in the head."

"Other than the psychologist's theory, is there any reason to believe that Kerry is protecting or harboring Larson?" Kerney asked.

"No, but Everett Dorsey, the Springer police chief, thinks Kerry would have a pretty good idea where his brother might go to hide out if he's still in the area."

"That makes sense," Kerney said.

"Casados is going to take another crack at Kerry today," Vanmeter added.

"We know Larson has no other blood relatives in the area,"

Clayton said, "but what about old friends and acquaintances? Would they have any ideas about Larson's whereabouts?"

"Dorsey is working a list of locals who knew the Larson brothers before Craig left town. Former friends and folks they went to school with, people they once worked for, old schoolteachers and coaches. It's a long shot."

Kerney pushed back his chair and dropped some bills on the table to cover the coffees and tip. "But worth pursuing, given the fact that the Lazy Z once belonged to the family of Craig Larson's teenage girlfriend. His familiarity with the ranch is probably one of the factors that drew him there."

He glanced at Clayton. "We need to visit with Chief Dorsey and take a look at the Lazy Z crime scene."

"Except for the vermin-infested hunting lodge on top of the mesa, there's not much left to see," Vanmeter said as he nodded at a file folder in Kerney's hand. "The briefing packet I passed out this morning brings you up to speed on what happened there."

Kerney stood. "And it does so very nicely, Frank. But I want to take a gander for myself."

Vanmeter smiled and shrugged. "According to Chief Baca, you both have carte blanche."

"We won't step on any toes unless we have to," Clayton said as he got to his feet.

Vanmeter's smiled widened. "That's not the back-channel traffic I heard about what you did when you departed the Lincoln County S.O., Agent Istee."

Clayton smiled back at Vanmeter. "Those were bruised egos I left behind, Major, not sore toes."

Vanmeter laughed as he followed Kerney and Clayton to the parking lot.

• • •

After dark, Larson had transferred his stuff to Pettibone's Buick, driven Tami's SUV to her office, left it in the reserved space at the back of the building, and put the magnetic signs on the doors. He'd forgotten to bring along Tami's vanity license plate, so he left the Subaru plate on the Yukon and walked back to the motel, where he spent the night in Pettibone's room. In the morning, he'd risen early, got breakfast at a fast-food drive-through window, and parked the Buick back in the lot at the motel so he could watch what was happening at the nearby budget lodge where all the cops were staying.

Things were quiet at first, but soon officers started coming out the front entrance and driving away in their patrol vehicles. Along with cops in civvies, there were cops in at least five or six different kinds of uniforms.

Between bites of his breakfast egg-and-bacon sandwich, Larson used his finger as a handgun and pretended he was blowing them away as they hurried to their patrol cars. He figured with a real gun, he could've taken down three, maybe four of them, before drawing any fire.

Overnight, his plan to assassinate cops had changed from an absolute thing he was going to do to a definite maybe. The plan hadn't lost its appeal; he just needed to do more headwork before taking that first shot.

A bald-headed cop in a state police uniform and two men in blue jeans and cowboy boots with semiautomatics strapped to their belts came out the sliding glass motel doors just as Larson was about to drive away. There was something familiar about the taller of the two men wearing civvies. Larson checked him out carefully as he walked toward an unmarked Ford Crown Victoria. Damned if it wasn't the cop who'd been the police chief in Santa Fe when he had first been busted. *What was his name?*

He'd never seen the other plainclothes cop, who was getting into his own unmarked car. He was younger, a few inches shorter, and definitely Indian looking, with dark hair that covered his ears. Larson didn't recognize him.

He watched the two unmarked cars enter traffic and turn toward the interstate on-ramps. Just for the hell of it, he decided to follow them for a while to see where they were going. Watching how they operated might give him some good ideas on how he should kill them.

Ever since Tami's husband had walked out on her late last year for a twenty-five-year-old bimbo barmaid who lived just across the state line in Trinidad, Colorado, Claudia Tobin had talked to her daughter on the telephone every day. Tami would mostly call in the evenings from home, but sometimes she'd call from her office or from the car on her cell phone when she was out and about.

When Tami didn't call, which happened very rarely, Claudia, a widow who now lived in Albuquerque and worked as a part-time home health aide to supplement her Social Security check, always called her. Last night, she'd tried repeatedly to reach Tami without success, and she'd gone to bed worried about her daughter.

Very early in the morning Claudia again called Tami's home, work, and cell phone numbers. After getting no response other than voice mail and answering machines, she called the Raton Police Department and reported her daughter as missing.

A polite-sounding officer gathered some basic information about Tami and, upon learning of the recent dissolution of her marriage, suggested it might be possible that Tami had gone out of town on a mini vacation or business trip, or might have spent the night with a friend.

In no uncertain terms, Claudia told him that she had a very close relationship with her only child and would have known if Tami had decided to do any of those things.

The officer promised to send a patrol vehicle to Tami's house and place of employment for a welfare check and advised Claudia not to get too worried. He told Claudia that people sometimes act out of character or impulsively after a major upheaval in their personal lives, and that Tami was probably perfectly all right. Before disconnecting, he took Claudia's phone number, said they would have Tami call her once they made contact, and once again told her not to worry.

Claudia wasn't having any of it. She called in sick, showered and dressed quickly, got into her ten-year-old imported subcompact coupe, and started the two-hundred-mile road trip on Interstate 25 to Raton.

While serving as the Santa Fe police chief, Kerney had met Everett Dorsey several times during legislative hearings on a concealed-carry bill that eventually passed and was signed into law. Kerney, along with the vast majority of top cops in the state, had opposed the bill. Dorsey had spoken in favor of it.

A brief conversation with Dorsey had left Kerney with the clear impression that the man was marking time as the Springer police chief until he could retire and pull a full pension.

He slowed to a stop in front of the Springer municipal building and in the rearview mirror watched Clayton glide in behind him. The building was a single-story structure with a brick façade, on a residential street just up from a house that had been converted into the town library. The town hall was sandwiched between the police and fire stations. A lone cop car was parked in front of a walkway that led to a windowless steel door with a Springer Police Department sign above it. With Clayton at his side, Kerney tried the door, found it locked, pushed the doorbell, and waited.

Dorsey opened up, let them in, and Kerney introduced him to

Clayton. For a moment, they stood and talked in the small, dingy front office, which was badly in need of a paint job and some housecleaning; then Dorsey ushered them into his equally shabby private office.

Kerney asked how the interviews with Craig Larson's former friends and associates were going and Dorsey shook his head.

"All the publicity has made people around here tight-lipped," he said. "Folks that knew him in the old days aren't talking. I don't think they're hiding anything from me. It's more like they don't want to admit any kind of past personal association with a cop killer who has a price on his head."

The reward for Craig Larson had started at ten thousand dollars after the shooting of Paul Hewitt and had now climbed to twenty-five thousand.

"Major Vanmeter says the psychologist thinks Kerry Larson knows something about his brother's whereabouts," Clayton said.

Dorsey perched on the edge of the dinged-up surplus desk that dominated his cramped office. "That well may be. I told Vanmeter to send that psychologist packing and leave Kerry to me if he wanted to get anywhere with it, but he wouldn't listen. Kerry suffered brain damage at birth. He looks as normal as anybody, but he isn't real bright, can be as stubborn as a four-year-old, and he's real suspicious when it comes to strangers. I don't see him opening up to a shrink, especially when it comes to his brother."

"I take it the psychologist knows all this?" Clayton asked.

"I told him so to his face."

"What if you were allowed to take another crack at Kerry?" Kerney asked. "Could you get him to open up?"

"Possibly, but not with the shrink present," Dorsey replied.

"I'll talk to Vanmeter," Kerney said. "Now, before we go out

DEAD OR ALIVE 173

to the Lazy Z, walk us through what you saw when you first arrived on the scene."

Dorsey grunted in disgust. "You've seen the crime scene photos I took?"

Kerney and Clayton nodded in unison.

"I don't ever want to see anything like that again," Dorsey said before beginning his narrative.

Parked a block away from the Springer town hall, Larson watched and waited. Following the two cops from Raton had been a breeze, and although he'd been a little uneasy about driving into Springer, people in their cars and those few ambling down the sidewalks had paid him no mind.

After watching the morning exodus of cops at the motel, he'd expected the town to be crawling with police. But there weren't any fuzz on the streets. Maybe he'd stay better hidden if he broke into some old lady's house right here in town, took her hostage, and just laid low until the pigs gave up and called off the manhunt.

Larson's attention swung back to the two plainclothes cops, who'd left the police department and were about to get in their vehicles. He remembered the older cop's name, Kerney or something like that. They drove away but he didn't follow. Best not to push his luck.

He figured the cops were keeping a close watch on his brother, Kerry, hoping he'd show up. Well, there were a couple of ways to get to Kerry's place the cops didn't know about. Maybe it was time to get his younger brother to help him out. When it came to killing, two shooters would be better than one, and he'd never known Kerry to go against his wishes. Like Jesse and Frank James, the Larson brothers would show Malvo and Muhammad how to do it.

Larson fired up Pettibone's Buick, made a U-turn, and headed for an old, seldom-used dirt road that would take him within a half mile of Kerry's digs.

Late in the morning, Claudia arrived in Raton and used her own key to let herself into Tami's house, which was located in a foothill subdivision overlooking the small city. Quickly she checked for any signs that her daughter had packed for an out-of-town trip or had left in a hurry. All her clothes were in order, the house was tidy, and nothing seemed disturbed. Stacked in the two-car garage were boxes of Tami's husband's things he'd yet to pick up.

Last month, Claudia had told Tami to have Goodwill come and take it all away. That Tami hadn't done so confirmed Claudia's suspicion that she still wasn't over the SOB.

In the kitchen, the message light on the wall phone blinked. Claudia pushed the Play button. All she heard was breathing for a few seconds before the caller hung up. It gave her an eerie feeling.

She tried hard to contain her growing anxiety by telling herself she was just being silly. Maybe the police were right and Tami had spent the night with a new boyfriend or gone to Colorado Springs or Denver for a real estate conference or some such.

Claudia dialed Tami's office and let the phone ring until the message machine clicked on and she heard her daughter's cheery voice say she was out of the office but could be reached on her cell. But she couldn't get a connection when she tried the cell phone number.

Back in her car, Claudia drove to the real estate agency Tami owned. The door was locked. Through the big plate glass window Claudia could see clearly that the front room Tami used as her office was unoccupied.

Tami had no employees, so it wasn't unusual for the building to be locked when she was out showing property or getting new listings. And in the wide-open spaces of the northeastern plains, cell phone reception was spotty at best.

At the rear of the building Claudia expected to see an empty space where Tami always parked her Yukon. But to her surprise the SUV *was* there, missing Tami's vanity license plate, "COW-GIRL," which she'd had for almost twenty years.

Claudia had seen enough. With her hands shaking on the steering wheel, she drove directly to the Raton Police Department and told the civilian receptionist that her daughter was in danger and she needed to speak to an officer "right now."

Starting with the crime scenes on the mesa, Clayton and Kerney took their time at the Lazy Z. Using the briefing document supplied by Major Vanmeter, they walked through the trashed-out hunting lodge, looked over the pickup stolen from the Dripping Springs Ranch, examined the spot where Nancy Trimble had fallen, shot dead from behind, and then drove to the site where her body had been dumped.

Fingerprints lifted from the lodge, the ranch house, and the stolen truck left no doubt that the brutal rape and deliberate murder of Trimble were the work of Craig Larson.

With the sun at high noon and a hot breeze freshening from the southwest, Kerney and Clayton stood on the porch of the hunting lodge.

"This kill was different," Kerney said. "He's changing."

Clayton squinted against the windblown sand. "I don't see it. He shot Officer Ordonez at the roadblock from a distance with a long gun."

"I would argue that his motive in shooting Ordonez was to escape capture," Kerney said. "But with Trimble, he first turned her into wounded prey. He's killing for vicious pleasure now and that's an entirely different MO."

"I figured him to be a head case right from the start." Clayton glanced at the sky. The clear blue morning had given way to a gritty, dusty afternoon.

"Agreed," Kerney said. "But I think he's about to take it in a whole new direction."

"Like what?"

Kerney shook his head. "I don't know. But let's assume he's well provisioned, heavily armed, and is obviously proficient with firearms. That combination scares me. Let's go down to the ranch headquarters and see what we can discover there."

Clayton reached down and brushed off some red fire ants that had crawled up his pant leg. The stench from the inside of the lodge was nasty. "I could use a change of scenery," he replied.

In his cubicle, Sergeant Joe Easley, a twelve-year veteran of the Raton Police Department, read the note that had been brought to him by a secretary. Claudia Tobin was in the reception area waiting to speak to someone about her missing daughter.

From the daily logs, Easley knew that officers had already gone to Tami Phelan's home and place of business. Although no contact with Tami had been made, nothing suggested any mishap had occurred.

As a longtime cop in a city of under ten thousand people, Joe Easley personally knew by sight or by name virtually every permanent resident of the community. Thus, Claudia Tobin, who'd for years operated a day-care center in Raton before moving to Albuquerque with a husband dying of cancer, was not a stranger to him. Neither were Tami Phelan and her ex-husband, Brodie.

Until Brodie had moved to Trinidad to shack up with a very

hot-looking young barmaid, he'd played second base on Easley's softball team, and Tami was a member of Easley's Downtown Rotary Club, which met monthly at Suzy's Sizzlin' Steakhouse.

Joe Easley also knew that since being dumped by Brodie, Tami had been throwing herself at every eligible male in town—and there weren't that many of them—between the ages of twenty-five and sixty, almost as an act of revenge for being done wrong. Or was it an act of self-loathing? Whatever it was, she was most likely shagging somebody in or around the area, which accounted for her being missing.

Furthermore, since the sighting of Craig Larson in the northeast part of the state, there had literally been hundreds of calls to his department reporting strangers resembling Craig Larson lurking about, hiding in the foothills, camped out at a nearby state park, breaking into vacant houses, stalking women and children, cruising by in cars, or eating in the restaurants and registering in the motels near the interstate.

Each and every call had been thoroughly checked out and found to be unsubstantiated. Easley had taken to thinking of the undercurrent of panic that gripped the community as the "Craig Larson Bogeyman Days."

A distraught-looking Claudia Tobin got to her feet when Easley came into the reception area.

"Mrs. Tobin," Easley said pleasantly. "Good to see you. I understand that you're concerned about Tami."

Tobin nodded. Easley had remembered her as once being a good-looking older woman with some flesh on her bones. Now she was skinny to the point of seeming anorexic, her dyed blond hair was thinning on top, and she was heavily wrinkled around her mouth and eyes.

"Something terrible has happened to my daughter," Claudia said. "I just know it."

"Why do you say that?"

"She's not at home, her office is locked, her car was left at work, and her license plate has been removed and replaced with another one."

Easley's interest level rose a thousand percent. Tami's "COW-GIRL" vanity plate was a common sight in Raton. She even billed herself as the "Cowgirl Realtor" in all her print advertising.

"What kind of license plate is on her car now?" he asked.

"It's a New Mexico plate." Claudia opened her purse and handed Easley a piece of paper. "I wrote it down."

Joe Easley gave Claudia an approving smile. "That's great. Wait right here. I'll be back in a jiffy." He paused at the security door. "Would you like some coffee?"

Claudia Tobin smiled weakly. "Yes, please."

After getting Claudia some coffee, Easley sat at his computer, accessed the Motor Vehicles Division database, and typed in the license number Claudia Tobin had supplied.

In New Mexico, drivers own their license plates, and when Easley got a hit that the plate belonged to Nancy Trimble, the murdered caretaker at the Lazy Z, his eyes widened. He reached for the phone and dialed dispatch.

"I want two officers at Tami Phelan's real estate office right now," he said. "Have them secure her office and vehicle, and await my arrival. Advise Major Vanmeter of the state police that I have evidence pertaining to the Lazy Z murder investigation and need his assistance at that twenty immediately."

"Ten-four," dispatch replied.

At the Lazy Z Ranch headquarters, Clayton and Kerney went through every room of the rambling house, which was filled with the sort of expensive, oversize Western-motif furnishings favored by rich people from somewhere other than the West. Looking for anything that might have been missed by the investigators and crime scene techs, they dug into nooks and crannies. From what they could tell, except for the probability that Larson had taken weapons, provisions, and some camping gear, nothing else appeared to have been stolen. A wall safe behind a painting in the master bedroom hadn't been tampered with, many valuable rifles and handguns had been left behind, and an unlocked petty-cash box in the office adjacent to the kitchen held over three hundred dollars in currency.

"I wonder why Larson didn't take the money," Kerney said as he closed the lid to the petty-cash box and watched Clayton power up the office laptop. "Aside from that," he added, "why did he feel the need to leave? Trimble was dead and out of the way. Nobody else was around. Did something or someone scare him off?"

Clayton shrugged in response as he accessed the Internet and began scanning the most recently visited Web sites. "What did the medical investigator give as Trimble's estimated time of death?" he asked.

Kerney read it off the briefing document.

Clayton smiled.

"What?" Over Clayton's shoulder, Kerney could see the home page of a northeastern New Mexico real estate company.

"This computer was used hours after Trimble died." Clayton called up all the Web pages that had been recently accessed. "He looked at three rural Springer properties posted for sale. I bet he was surfing for his next hideout."

"The question is which one he chose," Kerney said.

Clayton started printing the pages. "The vacant ranch on the Canadian River is the one I'd pick. The other two look occupied."

Kerney used the office telephone to call the real estate firm. When a man answered, he identified himself as a police officer and asked for directions to the ranch property on the Canadian River.

"It's off a county road a few miles east of Taylor Springs on Highway 56. About three miles in you'll see a ranch road on the left. Take that due west. About four or five miles farther, you'll reach the gate to the property."

"Thanks."

"Is there a problem there?" the man asked.

Kerney sidestepped the question. "When was the last time you showed the ranch?"

"About a month ago. There's a small ten-acre inholding on the ranch owned by a family member who refuses to sell, so that's been putting off prospective buyers. The place has been vacant for six months. But it's a multiple listing, so I don't know who else has been showing it."

"Okay, thanks." Kerney dropped the office phone in the cradle and said, "Let's go."

"Where is this place?" Clayton asked as he grabbed the Web pages he'd printed.

"Off the highway out of Springer that runs to Clayton, near the Texas state line," Kerney replied as they hurried to their units.

"Ah, yes," Clayton said, "that's the town that's named after me."

"I don't think it was named after you. It's been around a lot longer than you have."

"Yeah, I know that, but I like to think of it as my town. Actually, it was named for the son of Stephan Dorsey, a former U.S. senator from Arkansas. He built a mansion near the Santa Fe Trail Cimarron Cutoff. I understand it's still standing and owned privately."

Kerney veered toward his unit. "I didn't realize you were such a font of historical knowledge about New Mexico."

"I was forced to study white man's history in school," Clayton replied somberly as he climbed into his vehicle. "To further your education, you might like to know that the town of Clayton got its name in the late nineteenth century. Wasn't that about the time when you were born, old-timer?"

Kerney looked over the roof of his unit and grinned at Clayton. "Just about, wise guy. Just about."

The vehicles kicked up clouds of dust along the dirt road until they hit the pavement, and more dust flew when they left the highway and rattled their vehicles over the county road to the ranch turnoff. They stopped short of the gate to the ranch property, at the bottom of a small rise in the road that hid them from view.

Clayton joined Kerney in his unit, passed him the pages he'd printed off the real estate Web site, and pointed to the photograph of the exterior of the ranch house. "If Larson is here, he's got a clear line of fire from the house to the gate. Plus, he's got a high-ground advantage once we enter the property."

"There's not much cover going in," Kerney said, flipping to the picture of the barn. "Unless we leave the road, cut the fence behind the barn, drive through, and use the barn as cover to get within striking distance of the house."

"Then what?" Clayton asked. "Charge the ranch house with our sidearms and shotguns against his high-powered hunting rifles?"

"If he's got a rifle, that wouldn't be a good idea," Kerney said. "Better we should entreat him to give up."

Clayton opened the passenger door. "Let me take a look at the tire tracks up ahead before we decide anything."

"While you do that, I'll call for some backup firepower. Be careful."

"Always."

Bent low to stay out of sight, Clayton reached the crest of the small rise in the road, dropped prone to the ground, and belly-crawled in a circle, studying the tire tracks. He returned to Kerney's unit and brushed a layer of dust off his clothing before settling onto the passenger seat.

"Well?" Kerney asked.

"Two vehicles recently went in, but only one came out. The size of the tread marks show that the vehicle still on the property is a compact or subcompact passenger car. The vehicle that came and went is either a full-size light-duty truck or an SUV."

"When?"

"Yesterday. Blowing dust from the ranch road has barely begun to fill in the tread marks."

"Trimble owned a small Subaru that was missing from the Lazy Z," Kerney noted.

"Let's assume Larson drove it here," Clayton replied. "Have you called for backup?"

"Yep, and as a result I had an interesting conversation with a Raton PD sergeant named Joe Easley. He's ten minutes out from our ETA with a state police SWAT team and Frank Vanmeter in tow. Seems Easley found evidence that a missing female real estate agent named Tami Phelan brought a client out here yesterday, and hasn't been seen since. Craig Larson's fingerprints were found all over her vehicle."

"Let me guess," Clayton said. "The lady drives a full-size SUV."

"You got it. A Jimmy Yukon. Which vehicle entered the ranch property first?"

"The passenger car," Clayton replied.

"So what do you think we have waiting for us up ahead at the ranch—a firefight with Craig Larson, dead bodies, or both?"

"Dead bodies," Clayton replied solemnly.

"You're probably right." Kerney gave Clayton a cautionary look. "But we're still going to wait for Sergeant Easley, Frank Vanmeter, and SWAT before we go in."

Clayton chuckled. "Gee, thanks for looking out for me, Dad."

Kerney winced. "Ouch. I deserved that."

"Yes, you did."

"Sorry." Through the rearview mirror Kerney saw a dust cloud on the ranch road, signaling the impending arrival of re-inforcements. "Vanmeter and his troops are almost here."

Some number of police vehicles arrived to disgorge a heavily armed SWAT team of eight officers in full regalia, Major Frank Vanmeter, two uniforms from the Raton PD, and a short, wiry cop wearing jeans, boots, a white shirt, and a Western-cut sport coat, who introduced himself as Joe Easley.

"How did you fellows beat us here?" he asked Kerney as they shook hands.

Kerney nodded at Clayton. "Agent Istee did some cyber-tracking of Larson on the Internet at the Lazy Z. And you?"

"A missing-person report got us started. She's a woman named Tami Phelan, a real estate agent in town, reported missing by her mother. We found her vehicle at her place of business, and when we searched her office, we found an entry on her computer that she was scheduled to show this property to a prospective client yesterday afternoon."

"Have you got a lead on the client?"

"Just a name." Easley consulted a pocket notebook. "Carter Pettibone. As far as we can tell, he's not a local. I have officers contacting all the area motels to see if we can run him down."

Kerney nodded. "Very good." He turned to Frank Vanmeter, who stood nearby with the SWAT commander and his seven offi-cers. "How do you want to do this?"

Vanmeter laid out a plan that started with a plea over a bull-horn asking Larson to give himself up. If there was no response in five minutes, the request would be repeated one more time before the SWAT team was sent in.

Using the Web-page photographs of the ranch property Clayton had downloaded and printed, it was decided the SWAT team would first clear and secure the barn, place a sniper in the hayloft to lay down covering fire, and launch tear gas into the ranch house before moving on the target.

To get into position behind the barn without being seen from the house, the SWAT team would backtrack on foot down the ranch road, follow a shallow, winding arroyo to the fence line, and use the barn as cover to get into position.

"Okay," Vanmeter said, "let's do this. And remember, nobody except Larson gets killed."

The SWAT team nodded in unison and moved out. When they reached the fence line, the SWAT commander gave Vanmeter a heads-up over the radio. Vanmeter made his bullhorn pitch twice to Larson, and when there was no response, SWAT moved to the barn.

Near the assembly point on the ranch road, Kerney, Vanmeter, Clayton, and Joe Easley spent an anxious few minutes flat on their stomachs at the rim of the rise, binoculars trained on the barn, waiting in silence for either a radio report or the sound of gunfire. Finally, the radio crackled and the SWAT commander reported that the barn had been cleared.

"We've got two dead victims in the back of a Subaru," the commander said. "A male and female. The scene has been staged. Naked female on bottom, male with pants around his ankles on top. Vehicle matches the description of Trimble's car. The license plate is missing."

"Dammit," Vanmeter said. "Take the house."

"Roger that."

Just as the sniper opened up and started shooting out windows, Joe Easley's cell phone rang. He answered, listened for a minute, and disconnected.

"We've located the motel where Pettibone is registered," he said. "According to the housekeeper, the room was slept in last night."

"Well, if Pettibone and the real estate agent are in the backseat of the Subaru," Clayton said, "it sure wasn't him who stayed there last night."

"I'm thinking it might have been Larson who used the room," Easley said as he watched the SWAT team launch the tear gas canisters through the windows of the ranch house. "Because it sure doesn't look like he's here."

"What motel is Pettibone registered at?" Kerney asked.

Easley told him.

"Son of a bitch," Kerney said. "That's where we're staying."

The SWAT commander gave an all-clear over the radio.

Fuming at the thought that Larson had been so close at hand last night, Kerney got to his feet and started for the barn just as the SWAT team fanned out and started a field search of the property.

Chapter Nine

Either Larson had remembered the wrong road or it had badly deteriorated over the many years he'd been away. On a narrow, deeply rutted, rocky strip, he attempted to turn around and high-centered the Buick on some large rocks. Additionally, he'd smashed the tailpipe like an accordion and seriously damaged the muffler.

He was out in the Big Empty with nobody around for miles, and there was no way he could pack out all his gear, weapons, and valuables in one trip. He would either have to get himself unstuck, or leave most everything behind and make the long, grueling trek to Kerry's cottage in ninety-five-degree heat.

Larson crawled under the Buick for a closer look at the problem. The front tires were two inches off the ground and the transmission housing was hung up on a humongous rock. He got the jack out of the trunk and cranked it up as high as it would go. Even at the fullest extension it couldn't reach to lift the Buick off the boulder. He put some flat rocks underneath the jack and tried again, but with the Buick's nose angled in the air, he couldn't get leverage to budge it off the rock.

A second look in the trunk revealed a towing strap tucked in the spare-tire well. He wrapped it around a nearby tree, secured it to the rear axle, revved the engine, put it into reverse gear, and tried to pull the car loose, using the axle as a reel. The rear tires spun, the Buick lurched back several inches, and the towing strap broke.

Disgusted, Larson broke a stout branch off a down and dead juniper tree, crawled back under the Buick, and started loosening the soil around the rock with the stick. It was tough, dirty work, and after an hour he was breathing hard through a cotton-dry mouth.

Wishing he'd brought some water with him, he crawled out from under the car and rested his aching back against the rear bumper. His forehead throbbed from hitting his head repeatedly on the undercarriage, and his knuckles were bruised and bloody.

Groaning at the thought of being stuck in the middle of no-where all night, Larson put rocks under the elevated front tires and placed more rocks behind the rear tires to prevent it from rolling backward and crashing down on him while he was under-neath it. He dug into the rocky soil with the juniper branch again, and used the loosened dirt to build up a platform for the jack un-der the front axle. If he could raise the front end another inch or two, maybe he could push the car loose from the boulder and slide it free.

After jacking the car up, he could see just the barest clearance between the boulder and the transmission housing. Hoping that was enough, he removed the rocks from behind the rear wheels, put the transmission into neutral, released the parking brake, and pushed the car from the front end as hard as he could. Metal screeched against rock as the Buick rolled back and all four tires dropped down.

Body aching, hot and sweaty, dirt and dust embedded in every pore of his face and hands, Larson grabbed the bottle of twenty-year-old whiskey he'd liberated from the Lazy Z, took a long swig, and poured some of the liquor on his bruised and bloody fingers.

After a careful inspection to avoid getting stuck again, he got behind the wheel and slowly backed up to where he could turn the Buick around. He headed toward Springer, hoping that the broken muffler wouldn't attract any undue attention from the cops when he got there.

On the main street, two state police cars were parked in front of a small hotel that had a popular eatery favored by locals and tourists alike. Up the street, he passed by the old courthouse, which had been turned into a museum and contained as a main attraction the only electric chair ever used in New Mexico—or something like that.

It reminded him of old gangster flicks he'd seen on television where James Cagney, Edward G. Robinson, or some other screen villain called their guns gats and their women molls and vowed never to let the screws fry them.

Murderers on death row in the state pen didn't get fried anymore. Instead, they got injected with a lethal cocktail, which was supposedly a more humane way to die. Larson thought forcing the cops to gun him down by shooting some of their own would be a far better way to go.

Even though there were no cops in view, he stayed just under the speed limit as he continued down the main drag. There was one other back way to Kerry's place, but to use it he'd have to trespass across part of one of the biggest spreads in the state. He'd also have to drive right by the prison and skirt an artificial lake fed by the Cimarron River that supplied the town with water and also served as a recreation area for fishing.

There was some risk, but he was armed and dangerous like the television reporters said, so why not?

He made the turn onto the prison road, and within a few minutes the high, double chain-link fences topped with concertina wire came into view. He gave the prison the bird as he drove past, at the same time silently thanking the nameless, dumb-shit guard at the Bernalillo County lockup who'd mistakenly scheduled him to be transported to Springer in the first place.

Where the pavement gave out, the road swung toward the lake, and soon Larson was clunking over a rocky surface that wasn't much better than the route he'd abandoned earlier. With no other alternative, he pressed on. Only a few people were at the lake, two elderly couples and a family of four, all fishing from the shore. They paid little attention as he drove by. After the lake, the dirt road smoothed out some, and Larson relaxed a bit as he drove deep into lush rangeland that stretched for miles, right up to the foothill canyons and mountains beyond.

If he remembered correctly, a ranch road up ahead paralleled the wagon-wheel ruts of the historic Santa Fe Trail for a time, and then turned east toward Kerry's place. Larson doubted the pasture gates would be locked, but if they were, he would bust his way through them one way or another.

He turned on the radio when he reached the ranch road, just in time to catch a news bulletin from a Raton AM station that reported police were investigating a crime scene at a ranch in the Springer area. No other information was available.

Larson wondered if the cops were at the Lazy Z or the other place on the Canadian River, and decided he really didn't give a shit. It had been another hell of a day and he hadn't even killed anybody yet.

Kerry Larson finished installing a rebuilt starter in the ranch manager's three-quarter-ton truck and cranked the engine. It started up fine, just like he knew it would. He would drive it over to ranch headquarters in the morning and catch a ride back to his garage from one of the manager's two sons, who were home from college for the summer.

Kerry had changed the engine and transmission oil, drained and flushed the radiator, lubricated the chassis, and rotated the tires. Although the three-quarter-ton had seventy-five thousand hard miles on it, Kerry kept it running in tip-top condition, just like he did with all the ranch vehicles.

Following his normal routine, Kerry carefully cleaned the tools he'd used, cleared the debris off his workbench, and washed his hands at the small laundry sink. He stepped out of his stained and greasy overalls, hung them on a wall peg next to the barn doors, and looked up the ranch road that led to the state highway, where a police car was parked under one of the old shade trees.

He'd told the police that he didn't know where Craig was, but it didn't seem to matter. They'd sent a head doctor to talk to him, and Chief Dorsey had come around again asking a lot of questions. And now cops were up there on the road watching day and night, just in case Craig showed up. They'd never catch his older brother like that.

Kerry's last chore of the day was the one he enjoyed the most, feeding and caring for a small herd of riding and pack horses the ranch used to take paying sportsmen out on camping hunts. The herd was made up of mostly geldings and a few mares, all of them gentle and suited for inexperienced riders.

On his way to the horse barn in the bone-dry, calm early dusk, he waved at the officer in the police car, thinking that when the day was done he could do with a meal at the diner on the outskirts of town. Maybe chicken-fried steak, mashed potatoes and gravy, a big slice of apple pie, and a cup of fresh, hot coffee.

He thought about it hard as he put out feed, filled water troughs, cleaned up the manure, and spread fresh straw in the stalls. Going to town was no fun anymore. People he'd known all his life had started looking at him funny after Craig started shooting people and killing cops. It got worse when Chief Dorsey kept telling folks that Kerry had told Craig about Lenny Hampson's tipping off the cops on his whereabouts. All of a sudden it seemed like Kerry had done something bad, when he hadn't even known that Lenny had told the cops where to find Craig in California.

He'd explained to Everett Dorsey that he didn't have cause to see Lenny hurt, and didn't know when Craig came by the house that he'd escaped from a prison guard. But that part of the story didn't come out, and now he was getting the cold shoulder from just about everybody. Even folks at the ranch headquarters, who'd always treated him with respect, weren't looking him in the eye anymore.

Kerry finished up with the horses, said good night to every one of them, and walked down the hill to his house. Inside, he grabbed a beer out of the refrigerator, sat at the kitchen table, and took a long swallow. The old, squeaky plank floor in the front room made him look up just as Craig stepped into view.

Kerry took in his brother's shaved head, his beard that looked like barbwire, and his grimy, dirt-crusted face. "How come you look like that?" he asked. "What happened to you?"

Craig pulled his brother to his feet, gave him a hug, and laughed. "I did it so people can finally tell us apart. You got any more beer in the fridge?"

"That's a joke, right?" Kerry grinned and got Craig a brew. "You look like you've been rolling around in a manure pile."

"Not quite." Larson popped the top and took a swig.

"There's a cop up on the ranch road."

"I know that, little brother," Craig replied.

"People have been asking me to help find you."

"What people?"

"A head doctor that came up from Santa Fe, and Everett Dorsey, the town police chief."

"And what did you tell them?"

Kerry crossed his heart. "Nothing. I swear. I said if you didn't want to be found, to just forget it."

"What did the head doctor ask you?"

"He wanted to know about all the places we liked to go to when we were kids. Secret or special places."

"What else?"

"Folks you liked that maybe you would go and visit."

"Was that it?"

"Yeah, except for telling me that I'd be helping you if I told him what he wanted to know. But I didn't, because I didn't like him much. Did you really kill all those people?"

Craig smiled and nodded. "I surely did. Want to help me kill some more?"

Kerry twisted his mouth into a grimace and shook his head. "That's a bad thing to ask me. The police want to catch you for shooting all those people, and blowing up places in Texas, like they showed on the TV news."

Larson chuckled. "Tell me about it. I thought my baby brother liked to go hunting."

Kerry's expression brightened at the thought. "Yeah, but nothing's in season right now unless you want to go plunk at some jackrabbits. We could do that."

"People are always in season."

"That's not hunting."

Larson shook his head in dismay. "Damn, you're no fun, baby brother. I thought we'd be like Frank and Jesse James. Maybe become mountain men and live up in the high country, like we used to dream about doing when we were kids. But if you don't want to come along, I could just shoot you."

Kerry gave a forced laugh. "That's a joke, right?"

"Shoot you, take your truck, and pretend I'm you."

Kerry reached into his jeans pocket and took out his keys.

"You don't have to shoot me for that. If you need the truck to get away, take it. Tell anybody you meet that you're me."

"That's awfully nice of you, little brother, but not without a shower, a change of clothes, and a hot meal. Have you got anything you can cook up for me?"

"I've got some venison steaks in the freezer from an eight-point buck I took last year."

"In season, I bet."

"Yep."

"Get them out and fry them up for us while I jump in the shower."

Kerry hesitated. "Would you really shoot me?"

Larson shook his head, showed his teeth, and smiled. "That would just be like shooting myself, now wouldn't it, little brother?"

"I guess so," Kerry said as he reached into a cupboard for the frying pan. "I knew you were just funning around," he added, trying to sort out why he felt so scared.

With the shower spray beating on his head, Larson mulled over possible ways he could kill Kerry, assume his identity, and get far enough away before the cops figured out the switch. Better yet, what if he could get the cops to kill Kerry, thinking it was him? He couldn't hit on a good idea on how to make it work. But if he came up with a feasible plan, wasting baby brother wouldn't be a problem.

He got out of the shower, toweled off, dressed in some clean clothes from Kerry's closet, and looked at his reflection in the bathroom mirror. The scabs from shaving his head had healed over and his hair was growing back. His beard looked hobo-scraggly and it itched. He thought about shaving his head again and decided not to waste his time.

He opened the bathroom door expecting to smell venison steaks sizzling in the frying pan. But there was no scent in the air and no noise coming from the kitchen. He called out to Kerry and got no answer. In the kitchen he found the frying pan on an unlit stove burner and the venison steaks in a freezer bag sitting in the kitchen sink.

Holding the 9 mm Glock autoloader just behind his right leg, Larson called Kerry's name again. He moved quickly to the front room. Through the open door he could see Kerry's truck was missing.

"Son of a bitch," Larson said. Had little brother turned on him? Or had he been frightened away by his threat to kill him?

Larson didn't have time to wait and find out. He left the cottage, walked through a grove of trees to the horse barn, circled around the back of it, and took a quick look up the ranch road. In the fast-fading dusk the cop car was out of sight. Working as swiftly as possible, he saddled one of the geldings, put a pack frame on one of the mares, got some additional gear out of the tack room, and quietly led the animals behind the barn and back through the grove of trees to the cottage, where he filled a pillowcase with food, including the venison steaks.

He was twenty minutes away from the Buick, and if Kerry hadn't sent the cops after him, on horseback he could make it safe into the high country by daybreak. To get there, he'd have to cross open country, and even in the darkness he would need to keep to the dry washes, arroyos, and streambeds.

Larson decided to move west toward the settlement of Miami and then cut north across a big spread to avoid the huge Philmont Scout Ranch, where thousands of Boy Scouts and their adult leaders were camped for the summer. Once beyond the town of Cimarron, he would turn west again and enter the Sangre de Cristo Mountains. There was hard riding ahead, but he could make it.

At the Buick, he packed up quickly, listening for the sounds of wailing sirens in the night, but all was quiet. He mounted the gelding, tugged on the mare's bridle, and started out, feeling pumped about the trip ahead. It was like being one of the old Western desperados, like Jeremiah Johnson, or Tom Horn, or maybe Clay Allison, the gunslinger who had terrorized Cimarron back in 1870s.

He'd be like Clay Allison, Larson decided. At the old St. James Hotel in Cimarron, there was a plaque on the wall listing all the men that Allison had killed. Maybe when everything was said and done, they'd put a plaque on the wall for him. But if memory served, he'd have to kill a bunch more people to equal the number Allison had gunned down.

Although he'd thought about telling the cop parked on the ranch road that his brother was down at his house taking a shower, instead Kerry had waved and passed by without stopping. He knew there was something wrong with Craig, something bad-crazy, just from how he'd looked and talked. It was like Craig wasn't his brother anymore. Still, he couldn't bring himself to tell the police.

For the past half hour he'd been stopped in front of the marquee of the old Springer movie house, which had been turned into a church. The marquee read "NOW SHOWING: JESUS CHRIST." While he wasn't much of a churchgoer, Kerry had occasionally attended with Lenny Hampson and his family. They were trying to help him become a believer. He had thought about talking to the preacher, but the place was locked up tight and he couldn't remember the preacher's name and didn't know where he lived.

The state police substation was just a few doors up the street in what was once an old mercantile store, and a black-and-white patrol car was parked out front. Light from inside the station shone through the large plate glass window onto the sidewalk.

Kerry's stomach grumbled. Maybe a plate of chicken-fried steak and mashed potatoes would help him figure out what to do. He always did better thinking with a meal in his belly. He cranked the engine, put the truck in gear, and drove off.

The Raton Police Department was housed in an ugly mid-twentieth-century, single-story municipal building that had a series of large windows below a boxy, yellow aluminum façade. The department shared a waiting area with the municipal court, and the part of it reserved for police business consisted of four beat-up chairs, three vending machines, one side table with a stack of dog-eared, out-of-date magazines, and a one-way privacy window where you spoke through a hole in the glass to state your business to a woman who doubled as dispatcher and receptionist. Kerney doubted that it could have been made any less inviting to the general public.

After announcing themselves and showing their shields, Kerney and Clayton were passed through quickly and led down a hallway to a briefing area that also served as a conference room. There, seated at tables lined up facing a speaker's rostrum, were Sergeant Joe Easley, the Raton police chief, Everett Dorsey, Major Frank Vanmeter, three of his state police lieutenants in charge of the field search and interview teams, the regional state game and fish law enforcement supervisor, and the Colfax County sheriff. All had assembled to debrief on the Pettibone-Phelan murders and fine-tune the next phase of the manhunt for Craig Larson.

The Raton police chief nodded to Joe Easley and said, "Let's get things started."

"A BOLO on Pettibone's Buick and another armed-and-dangerous advisory on Craig Larson have been sent out nation-wide," Easley said.

"We're increasing patrols along major highways and the north-south interstate," Frank Vanmeter said. He passed around a sheaf of papers and continued, "There's a list included of the roadblocks we've got staggered throughout a four-county area."

After reporting the tentative conclusions of the medical investigator regarding the causes and times of death for Phelan and Pettibone, and noting that family members had been duly informed, Easley summarized the crime scene investigation findings at the vacant ranch, Pettibone's motel room, and Phelan's vehicle. With that out of the way, the conversation turned to the advisability of intensifying field searches, increasing close patrols of rural properties and ranches, and making house-to-house welfare checks and follow-up visits again. "That's just more of the same-old same-old," Dorsey said.

"And we'll keep doing it until something breaks or we get a brainstorm," Vanmeter replied. "That reminds me, Chief Dorsey: Did you get anything out of Kerry Larson?"

Dorsey dropped his gaze. "Nada."

"In that case," Vanmeter said, "I suggest we get back on the job with the troops." The Raton police chief nodded agreement and Vanmeter stood up. He grimaced in frustration at Kerney as he walked out the door.

As the others followed him out of the room, Kerney cornered Dorsey. "What was Kerry's mood like?" he asked.

"Not good," Dorsey said sourly. "He's just clammed up tight."

"You said you thought there was a chance he'd open up. What changed?"

Dorsey fidgeted with his car keys, but Kerney stayed planted in his way. Finally Dorsey swallowed and said, "Seems he got this notion in his head that I've been telling folks that he's in cahoots with his brother."

Kerney raised a questioning eyebrow. "Have you?" he asked, but from the look on Dorsey's face, he figured he already had the answer.

"Don't give me any crap, Kerney. Fact is, Kerry has gotten plain paranoid about all of this, to the point he thinks just about everybody in town has turned against him."

"So you thought you'd play good cop and bad cop with Kerry?" Kerney asked, unable to suppress his dismay. The room was empty except for Joe Easley and Clayton, who were having a conversation by the door.

"Jesus, you can be a real prick. I'll admit public sentiment isn't on his side right now. But that's because folks are feeling jittery about Larson running loose, and Kerry is a convenient target for their frustration."

"Such understanding souls."

Dorsey shrugged.

"How about your second go-round with Larson's old cronies and former friends?" Kerney inquired.

"It's a dry well," Dorsey replied, "and priming it got me nowhere."

Kerney nodded. "Okay. Thanks for the update."

"Not a problem. Just don't try to jack me around next time we talk."

"I didn't realize you were so sensitive, Everett," Kerney said, finally stepping aside to let Dorsey pass.

"Screw you," Dorsey said and headed for the door.

Outside, Kerney found Clayton, who was looking up at a large illuminated star, a big American flag bathed in light, and a glowing RATON sign on the peak of a hill that towered over the city.

"That's Goat Hill," Clayton said.

"It that something you learned while studying the white man's ways?"

Clayton laughed. "Nope, Joe Easley told me."

"So that's what you two were talking about."

"Oh yeah. You can learn a lot from the natives. The flag was added to commemorate 9/11. He also told me that the MI determined that Tami Phelan was raped. He'd forgotten to mention that in his briefing. What about you and Dorsey?" Clayton asked.

"Dorsey got nowhere with Larson's twin brother. I'm thinking he blew it with Kerry. He got real defensive when I questioned him about it."

"If that's the case," Clayton said, "maybe we should go and have a little chat with Kerry."

"Exactly."

"Let's leave your car at the motel and ride together."

Kerney stifled a yawn. "Suits me."

"And you can nap along the way," Clayton added as he stepped off toward his unit.

Kerney shook his head and groaned in dismay as he followed. "To quote Everett Dorsey, 'Don't jack me around.'"

"You're right," Clayton replied, over his shoulder. "Teasing one's elders is disrespectful."

On the ranch road, Clayton pulled his unit up next to the parked state police vehicle, and asked the officer if Kerry Larson was at home.

"Nope, left two hours ago," the officer replied, "but he's got a plainclothes tail on him."

"What has he been doing since he left the ranch?" Clayton.

"He spent some time just sitting in his truck outside a church a few doors down from our substation. At first, we thought he was working up the courage to talk to us, but he just sat there and did nothing. Then he went and had a meal up at the diner on the north end of town. From there he bought a six-pack of beer at the convenience store, and for the last forty-five minutes he's been at the Springer cemetery near the high school, drinking Bud Light at his mother's grave."

Clayton turned to Kerney. "Want to wait for him here?"

"Hold on." Kerney leaned around Clayton. "How many beers has he had?" he asked the officer.

"Let me check." The officer keyed his microphone and repeated Kerney's question. The reply came back that the subject had just opened his fourth brewski.

"Am I sensing a DWI stop here?" Clayton asked.

"With a good-cop/bad-cop twist to it," Kerney replied with the smile. "If I remember correctly, Kerry has one prior DWI, which means a conviction will cost him his license and some jail time. That gives us a bargaining chip."

He got on the radio to Major Vanmeter and arranged to have Kerry Larson stopped by a uniformed officer in a marked vehicle after he left the cemetery.

"Tell the officer to be hard-nosed, but to do it by the book," Kerney added. "Have him taken to the substation after he fails the field sobriety test. We'll pick it up from there."

"I have a patrol supervisor nearby," Vanmeter replied. "I'll have him stop the subject when he gets to the main drag. That way it shouldn't arouse any suspicions."

"Excellent," Kerney replied.

Inside the Springer state police substation, a low counter separated the public waiting area from several desks used by officers to do shift paperwork and make phone calls. An unhappy-looking Kerry Larson sat in a chair next to one of the desks, his hands cuffed behind his back, watching the officer who'd arrested him fill out forms. On the desktop were the empties he'd thrown in the bed of his truck before leaving the cemetery, and the one unfinished beer he had been drinking when the cop pulled him over.

The cop, a tough-looking sergeant with a nasty, pushy personality, wasn't one of the regular officers who worked out of Springer. Kerry didn't know him, but the name tag on his uniform read "Shaya." Sergeant Shaya had put Kerry facedown on the pavement before making him stand on one foot, put his finger on his nose, count backward, and do some other stupid stuff. Then he drove Kerry to the state police office and had him blow into a machine that could tell whether he was drunk or not. According to Sergeant Shaya, the machine proved that he was legally drunk. But Kerry didn't feel that way, just jumpy and worried.

"Maybe I should have come here instead of buying that six-pack," Kerry said.

Shaya looked at Kerry with interest. "Were you thinking about talking to somebody here?"

"Gary," Kerry said. "He's a state cop like you but I can't remember his last name."

"LeDoux."

"Yeah, that's right. LeDoux."

"What did you want to talk to Officer LeDoux about?"

Kerry licked his lips and shrugged. "Nothing special."

"You're sure about that?" Shaya asked.

Kerry glanced away from Shaya's stare. "Yeah, I'm sure."

"Listen, whatever you wanted to tell Officer LeDoux, you can tell me."

Kerry shook his head. "Nope. I don't like you."

"Suit yourself." Shaya returned his attention to his paperwork.

"Are you going to put me in jail?"

Shaya grunted without looking up. "That's what happens when you drink and drive."

"Can't I just pay a fine? I've got cash money in my wallet."

"No, you can't. It's not that simple."

The front door opened and two men wearing holstered handguns and police badges clipped to their belts entered. One looked like a rancher and the other looked Indian. If Kerry had seen them on the street without their guns and badges, he would have figured them to be just ordinary cow people.

"Who are they?" Kerry asked.

Sergeant Shaya got to his feet. "Stay put."

He went over and greeted the men, who talked in low voices so Kerry couldn't hear. When the jawboning stopped, the two men came around the counter, stood him up, and took off his handcuffs.

"I'm Kevin Kerney," the rancher-looking cop said. He nodded at the Indian. "And this is Clayton Istee. Let's go in that office and talk."

"About what?"

"Why you were drinking and driving," the Indian cop named Istee said.

Kerry stared suspiciously at him. "You Navajo?"

"Apache."

"I'm not gonna say anything to you about my brother."

"You don't have to," the rancher cop named Kerney said with a smile.

"Then what are we going to talk about?"

"How we can keep you out of jail." Kerney led Kerry by the arm into the office. "Did you know the law has changed since your last DWI conviction?"

"Changed?" Kerry asked, rubbing his wrists.

Clayton Istee sat him in a chair. "Jail time is mandatory now," he said. "So paying a fine won't keep you out of the pokey. Because this is your second offense, you could get six months to a year."

Kerry looked startled. "I can't go to jail for a year."

Kerney nodded sympathetically as he perched on the edge of the desk. "I understand. You'd probably lose your job at the ranch and get kicked out of your house to boot."

Kerry lowered his gaze and shook his head. "That's not good. Not good."

"No, it's not," Kerney said. "But it could get even worse for you."

Kerry looked at Kerney cautiously. "Are you trying to scare me?"

"Not at all. We believe that you didn't know Craig was on the run from the police when he came to see you."

"Well, that's the truth of it," Kerry replied hotly.

"But if you know where he is now, or where he might be, that's a totally different story," Kerney said.

"I told you I'm not talking about my brother." Kerry sounded much less emphatic.

"We're not talking about Craig," Clayton said, picking up a cue from Kerney to take the lead. "We're talking about you. Your life, your freedom."

"I haven't done anything wrong to nobody."

"We believe you," Clayton said. He pulled up an empty chair and sat close to Kerry. "But if Craig keeps breaking the law, kidnapping and killing people, stealing and destroying property like he has been, and you have helped him in any way, or even refused to tell the police what you knew about his whereabouts, that makes you guilty of all those crimes."

Kerry gave Clayton a sullen look but said nothing.

"Do you understand what I'm saying?" Clayton prodded, leaning closer.

"Yeah. That's crazy."

"No, that's the law," Kerney chimed in.

Kerry bit his lip. "Show me."

Clayton got to his feet. "Wait right here."

He left the office, got a New Mexico criminal statutes book from Sergeant Shaya, found the appropriate sections, and flagged them with pieces of paper. He returned to the office and gave the book to Kerry.

"Go ahead," Clayton said, "read them for yourself."

Kerry lowered his head, ran a finger along the page, and read, his mouth forming words as he went along.

He finished one excerpt, stopped, and looked up at Clayton. "This uses different words than you did."

"But it means the same thing."

Kerry closed the book. "What if I didn't want to help him so instead I just ran away?"

Kerney leaned forward. "Is that what happened?"

"Maybe," Kerry replied softly.

"What made you want to run away?" Kerney said.

"Nothing."

"When did this happen?" Clayton asked.

"Today, just after quitting time."

Kerney and Clayton exchanged glances. The surveillance logs on Kerry Larson, summarized at the debriefing meeting, indicated that he'd stayed at the ranch all day, spending most of his time repairing a truck.

"Come with us," Kerney said, lifting Kerry by the elbow to his feet.

"Where to?"

"The ranch," Kerney said. "That's where you saw Craig today, right?"

"I didn't say that."

"No, you didn't," Kerney replied. "And I'll make sure every-one knows that you didn't squeal on your brother."

On their way toward the front door, Clayton told Sergeant Shaya to alert the officer on surveillance duty at the ranch that Craig Larson might be on the property and to get a lot of people rolling to that twenty pronto.

"Are you kidding me?" Shaya asked, reaching for his hand-held radio.

"Not even," Clayton said.

"Do I still have to go to jail?" Kerry asked.

"Not even," Kerney echoed as he hustled Kerry out the door to the unit.

Even with every law enforcement agency in the northeast quad-rant of the state on high alert, it took a fair amount of time to put enough officers in place to surround the immediate buildings and grounds where Kerry Larson lived and worked. Once the perim-eter was sealed, a SWAT team cleared the garage, barn, stable, and corral before moving on to the main house. Once that had been cleared, Frank Vanmeter set up his command post at the top of the lane overlooking the main house and cottage, ordered the cordon tightened around Kerry Larson's residence, and brought a state police helicopter on standby in Springer to light up the exterior with its high-powered searchlight.

With the chopper rotors thudding in the night sky a hundred feet overhead, the cottage washed in harsh, white light, and sharpshooters zeroed in on every window and door, Vanmeter waited for his SWAT commander to report on any sign of visual or thermal movement.

"The only thing giving off a significant heat signature inside that structure is the kitchen refrigerator," the SWAT commander said by radio after checking with his team. "Are we good to go?"

Vanmeter turned to Kerry Larson, who stood between Kerney and Clayton. "Does your cottage have a basement?"

Kerry shook his head.

Vanmeter keyed his radio. "Go."

The SWAT commander gave the word, and the team moved in under the protection of covering snipers. Within minutes the cottage was declared clear.

Vanmeter pulled SWAT back and ordered the chopper pilot to sweep and light up the surrounding area, in the hope that Larson might be hiding nearby.

"Did you see which way your brother came from?" Clayton asked Kerry.

"No."

"Okay." Clayton motioned to a nearby uniformed officer to come forward. "Wait with this officer in his vehicle."

"Why can't I stay here?" Kerry demanded.

"You can," Clayton replied, "if you want me to forget we weren't going to bust you for that DWI."

"You said I didn't have to go to jail."

Clayton nodded at Kerney. "He said that, not me. Go with the officer."

After the officer and Kerry moved away, Clayton said, "That's twice we've come up empty."

"But now we're only hours behind him," Kerney said. "Let's take a look around the cottage."

Shining his flashlight on the ground, Clayton took the lead as they walked down the lane. When he got to the parking area in front of the cottage, he squatted down, looked closely at some tread marks and hoofprints, and quickly stood up.

"What is it?" Kerney asked.

"Ten-to-one odds our man is on horseback," Clayton said. "There are hoofprints on top of Kerry Larson's tire tracks, and they're very recent."

He followed the tracks up the backside of the hill with Kerney following. "Two horses," he said.

Vanmeter's voice came over Kerney's handheld radio. "The chopper pilot has spotted a vehicle under a grove of trees. Says it looks like the stolen Buick. I'm going in with SWAT."

"Ten-four," Kerney replied as he kept pace with Clayton, who continued to move up the hill in the direction of the horse barn. "It's likely Larson left the ranch on horseback, trailing another animal. Have Kerry brought to us at the barn."

"Will do."

At the barn, they found ten tidy, clean stalls, only eight horses, and empty spaces in the tack room for a saddle and a pack frame. Kerney met Kerry at the barn door and asked how many horses were stabled inside.

"Ten," Kerry answered.

"Two are missing," Clayton said, "along with some tack."

Kerry stepped past them. "Let me see."

Clayton pulled him back by the arm. "Only if you tell us what else is missing here and at your house."

"No jail?" Kerry asked, looking at Kerney.

"No jail," Kerney replied with a smile.

"Okay."

After a quick tour, Kerry told Kerney and Clayton that the best riding horse and pack animal were gone, along with the necessary tack to load up and travel cross-country. At his cottage, a pillowcase had been removed from his bed, and the venison steaks he'd taken out of the freezer were gone, along with a bunch of food from his pantry and refrigerator.

After reassuring Kerry once again that he wouldn't go to jail,

Kerney turned him over to a uniform, got on his handheld, and asked Vanmeter what was happening at the Buick.

"The Buick is empty and it looks like you were right about the horses. He took whatever he had in the vehicle and left. The tracks head west as far as we can tell."

"Frank, we need eyes in the sky at daybreak," Kerney said. "As many as we can get. State Police aircraft, Civil Air Patrol, State Forestry, Game and Fish—whoever's willing. Have Andy ask the governor for Air National Guard assistance. If Larson gets to the mountains before we find him, it's going to be a hell of a lot tougher to track him. Let every rancher in the area know that Larson may be traversing their property. Tell them to hunker down overnight and stay close to home tomorrow."

"I've got a lieutenant making those calls right now," Vanmeter replied.

"Can you get Kerry's boss to outfit Clayton and me with good horses and enough gear and supplies to stay on Larson's trail for a week, minimum?"

"Starting when?"

"Right now," Kerney replied. "But we want good, sturdy, endurance trail horses, not the ones for the tenderfoots that are stabled here at this barn."

"I'll see what I can do," Vanmeter said.

"Better have your lieutenant tell the folks at the scout ranch that they should mother hen all their Boy Scouts for a day or two."

"Affirmative."

"Thanks." Kerney keyed off his handheld and looked at Clayton. "Are you ready for a midnight trail ride?"

Clayton nodded. "More than ready."

•••

When Larson reached Miami Lake, he checked the time on the nice Omega wristwatch he'd taken off Carter Pettibone's pudgy dead body. It was just coming up on midnight and he was a little behind schedule, slowed down by the darkness, broken terrain, and a few locked gates he'd been forced to skirt. As he watered the horses, he kept an ear tuned to the sound of any traffic along the two-lane highway that passed by the lake, but all was quiet.

A little west of the lake, the dim outline of Kit Carson Mesa jutted into the night sky, barely lit by the Milky Way. Behind it stood the Cimarron Range, an inky black swath that Larson could feel more than see. But that would soon change, for in the east, the first hint of a rising three-quarter moon broke over the horizon. With it, Larson would have enough light to pick up the pace. He'd have to be careful of badger holes, but figuring six to eight miles per hour riding at a steady trot, he should be across Rayado Creek, beyond Hagerdon Lake, past Coyote Mesa, and entering Dawson Canyon well before dawn.

He decided to throw any trackers off by crossing the highway and heading in the opposite direction, toward the mesa south of the farming settlement of Miami before correcting course. Hopefully, if a search for him was mounted at first light, it would be concentrated there, while he would be a good twenty miles away, about to enter the high country.

Larson mounted up and spurred his horse into a trot, the packhorse following behind. For a time he'd actually be riding in the ruts of the Old Santa Fe Trail, crossing some of the most famous ranching land in the West.

He thought about the Clay Allison plaque in the St. James Hotel in Cimarron. If he remembered it correctly, along with the names of the men Allison had killed, it listed a number of unnamed Negro soldiers he'd gunned down.

While there weren't any more Buffalo Soldiers around to kill, the idea of riding over to Philmont Scout Ranch and shooting a parcel of Boy Scouts held a certain appeal. But Larson dropped the idea. He'd already racked up one kill down at that Bible-thumping church camp in Lincoln County, and he didn't like the notion of repeating himself by shooting more clean-cut all-American boys. Besides, his true calling now was to kill more cops.

All he had to do was find the perfect place and then draw them in.

Chapter Ten

Arranging for the horses and gathering all their supplies and equipment held Kerney and Clayton up well past midnight. They delayed pushing off for another twenty minutes while a just-arrived state game and fish officer briefed them on the major trails into the mountains, the best places to find good water and forage for the horses, and the location of several line camps and old cabins to use in case of severe bad weather. He gave them a set of clearly labeled keys that would get them through locked gates on private and public land, some Bureau of Land Management and U.S. Geological Survey topographical maps to guide them, and a global positioning system receiver loaded with more maps.

"The GPS should keep you from getting lost," the officer said with a smile. "Watch out for the black bears. It's the tail end of their mating season, and they get seriously irritated when interrupted."

"We'll keep that in mind," Clayton said, throwing a leg over the saddle of the roan gelding he'd picked out to ride.

Kerney mounted a buckskin quarter horse and took the reins of the two packhorses from Frank Vanmeter's outstretched hand.

"I'll have aircraft in the air before first light," Vanmeter said.

Clayton looked skyward. "Maybe not."

Both Vanmeter and Kerney looked at the clear night sky and then glanced at Clayton questioningly.

"The wind has shifted, the pressure is dropping, and we're in for a blow," he explained.

"And you know this how?" Vanmeter asked.

"At dusk, the crows were cawing, the swallows stayed close to the ground, and the hawks weren't soaring as high as usual."

"So, it's like some Apache insight into the natural world, right?" Vanmeter said.

Clayton laughed. "Actually, I learned it in a wilderness survival class I took years ago." He turned to Kerney. "Let's go. We're a good five hours behind Larson, and I want to close the gap before the rain comes."

"Lead on, Chief," Kerney replied as he waved a good-bye to Vanmeter.

Clayton shot him a look over his shoulder. "I hope you mean that in the nicest possible way."

"I do," Kerney replied as he fell in behind Clayton. "I'm sure you know it was the gringos who came up with the idea of calling the leaders of the Apache bands chiefs. They couldn't grasp the concept of a warrior society without one person holding absolute authority."

"And it's still true today," Clayton replied. "Have you been studying Apache history?"

"I figured with an Apache son, I'd better learn something about it," Kerney said.

After a pause, Clayton said, "I think my mother was wise to choose you to mate with."

"Now that's a compliment I bet a father rarely hears," Kerney replied with a laugh.

The two men fell silent as they followed Larson's trail west across the rolling rangeland. In the deepest part of the night, the wind picked up, the temperature dropped, and the short prairie grasses swirled in cross breezes that whipped through the plains.

Soon, lightning flashes were cutting the night sky, illuminating the mountaintops as cascading rolls of thunder roared down the slopes.

Massive, boiling clouds that had been hidden from view came over the peaks of the Sangre de Cristo Mountains. Clayton and Kerney broke their horses into a fast trot.

"We're going to have to take shelter before this storm comes in," Kerney said as he came up alongside Clayton.

"We can hole up in Miami," Clayton said, "but we're gonna get wet along the way."

Damp but safe under shelter in an empty barn on the outskirts of Miami, they shook the rain off their ponchos, hung them over the door to a stall, and watched the deluge start. Lightning strikes lit up the sky and wind-driven rain battered the cottonwood trees that bordered the road through the settlement.

"This weather sure doesn't help us any," Kerney said as he wiped down his horse with an old towel he'd found in a rag bin. When he finished, he got more dry rags and moved on to the pack animals.

"It shouldn't delay us that much," Clayton said as he dried his mount. "If Larson hasn't found shelter, he's been slowed way down on making tracks. When it clears, we'll circle the village, cut his trail, and follow his tracks. After this storm, fresh hoofprints won't be hard to find."

"Plus," Kerney added, "Larson didn't do a good job of loading his packhorse. The animal's left rear hoofprint is deeper than the others."

"You noticed that, did you?"

"I grew up on a ranch, remember, so I'm not a complete novice when it comes to tracking livestock," Kerney said as he spread a blanket on a bed of straw and stretched out on it. Some distance away on the open prairie a big lightning bolt struck. "Wake me when it's time to move."

"How can you sleep through this?" Clayton asked.

Kerney closed his eyes. "Watch me."

Drenched and cold to the bone, Craig Larson dug his heels into the flanks of his frightened horse and pushed on. He tugged at the reins of the reluctant packhorse and it grudgingly raised its head and picked up the pace. When he crested a small rise, he stopped and listened. Although he couldn't see it through the sheets of rain, close by he could hear the roar of the usually dry creek that wandered along the foot of Coyote Mesa.

Larson dismounted and slowly walked the horses to the edge of the creek. Four feet below him, brown, foaming water filled the creek, rising fast, carrying with it tree branches, plastic bottles bobbing up and down, and other debris. He'd have to find a better place to cross. He got back on the horse and rode away from the mesa, toward the grassland where he knew the creek forked and ran between shallow banks. Once there, he dismounted and walked the skittish horses through the knee-deep, swiftly moving water safely to the other side. If he'd arrived five minutes later, he might not have made it across and would have been stuck waiting for the water to recede.

Born and raised in the Big Empty, Larson knew better than to be out in bad weather with lightning strikes hitting all around. But there wasn't anyplace close by where he could stop and hunker down. Going into the town of Cimarron would surely get him caught or killed, and it was way too risky to head for the ranch headquarters where his brother's bosses lived. By now the cops probably had all the area ranchers on alert looking for him.

Under a piece of canvas he had fashioned into a make-do rain slick, Larson slogged on, knowing that with the creeks rising fast, the Cimarron River up ahead would be running full and angry. Although it wasn't a broad river, he could be stranded on the bank waiting for the water to drop. If the skies cleared by daybreak and he was still there, he would be easy to spot from the air.

He looked up, searching for a break in the cover, a hint of predawn light, but it was far too early and the storm was parked low overhead. If it stopped raining but stayed heavily overcast well into the morning, he might still be able to reach the mouth of Dawson Canyon undetected.

Beyond the Cimarron River, he'd have two highways and another river to cross in order to get there. That's if he made it through the storm and across the plains in one piece.

A lightning bolt seared through the cloud cover and hit the ground half a mile away. The horses shied at the thunderclap that followed, but Larson kept his seat and held fast to the reins of the packhorse.

He hadn't sat a horse in years, and his butt was sore and his legs ached. Rain ran down the brim of the cowboy hat he'd taken off the coatrack in Kerry's front room, and then it splattered against his face. Behind him the packhorse slogged through the mud of the rutted ranch road with its head lowered. This was a doozy of a storm that would have every rancher on the plains thanking the dear Lord for the moisture come Sunday morning at worship.

In spite of the piss-poor weather, his sore butt, and the obstacles he faced up ahead, Larson felt exhilarated. This was life the way the old-timers had lived it. They fought the elements and anything or anybody that got in their way, including the law. So with gumption and a little luck he just might avoid being bushwhacked, or shot by a sniper from an airplane, or surrounded by a posse of cops. And if he made it to the high country, he could do some payback shooting of his own.

A sudden tension on the packhorse's reins made him look over his shoulder. The load the animal was carrying had shifted precariously. Larson cursed, dismounted, and with cold hands tried to undo some of the knots he'd tied so he could adjust the load. But the soggy ropes were swollen shut. He tried forcing a knot to give with the tip of a hunting knife, but all he managed to do was cut through it. He tried repositioning and tightening the pack frame, but it was cinched as far as it would go. Fumbling with the loose ends of the cut rope, he managed to retie it, got back on his horse, and cursed again. He'd have to slow down his pace even more or risk seeing his provisions, weapons, and equipment strewn along the ground.

He moved on through the storm with a little less enthusiasm than before. It seemed like ever since he'd stabbed that corrections officer in the eye with a stick and made his getaway, stupid little glitches had come along to fuck things up for him.

Lightning cracked, loud and close enough above him to send a shiver of electricity down his spine. His gelding did a dizzying three-sixty twirl, and the pack animal reared, pulled the reins free from his hand, and galloped off into the gray night. He clamped his legs tight and fought to stay in the saddle as his horse spun again. The horse planted both front hoofs, bucked hard, stomped its forelegs, shook its head, and made another full circle before coming to a shaky, snorting stop.

Larson took a deep breath. With an unsteady hand he turned his gelding in the direction where he'd seen the packhorse disappear into the night, and started after it in a slow trot.

Some time after the downpour had diminished to a steady drizzle, Clayton shook Kerney awake. He sat up and looked out the open barn door. Darkness and a blanket of fog made it impossible to see more than two feet.

"I've got Frank Vanmeter bringing in people to start searching around here pronto," Clayton said. "They'll go door to door first to check on the residents, and then do field searches, including the mesas, when the fogs lifts."

Kerney stuck his head out the barn door and looked at the sky. "Which won't be anytime soon." He looked at Clayton's damp, saddled roan gelding. "What have you been up to?"

"Out cutting Larson's trail," Clayton said. "When the storm hit, he was well past the village on a straight path for Miami Lake, due west of here. You would have figured that he would have kept going directly for the mountains, but I found his tracks doubling back toward the village."

"Maybe he backtracked to seek shelter," Kerney said.

"I don't think so."

"Why not?" Kerney asked as he threw his saddle on the back of his horse.

"Because he didn't make a beeline when he doubled back," Clayton replied. "Instead he wandered partway up a mesa trail before trying to hide his tracks on some rocky ground. I found some fresh horse apples and several hoofprints from his pack animal. He headed west again."

"So it was a feint to throw us off."

Clayton nodded. "But I thought it best to have Vanmeter and his people do a sweep anyway."

Kerney cinched his saddle. "Good thinking."

He put the bridle on the buckskin and walked him to the barn door where Clayton waited, sitting in the saddle and ready to go. "So, I take it we're heading west, young man," he said.

Clayton nodded and handed Kerney the reins to the two packhorses.

"Lead on," Kerney said as he mounted up and stared out into the soupy, dense fog. "But try not to guide us into trees, buildings, barbwire fences, ditches, or any moving vehicles," he said.

Clayton pulled the hood of the rain poncho over his head. "I'll do my best."

Larson chased the pack animal into a thick fog that enveloped and disoriented him. He knew he would be in a hell of a fix if he couldn't find that animal. Already, half of his equipment, gear, and provisions was spread along the last five miles of rangeland. But as far as he could determine, several weapons and all of the ammunition were still strapped to the pack frame, and that's what he needed most.

With his head bent over the neck of his horse and his eyes glued to the tracks on the ground, Larson didn't spot the animal until he heard it whinny. He looked up to see it lying in the mud, struggling without success to rise. He dismounted and walked to the animal. It had broken a front leg and the shattered bone showed just above the fetlock.

Cursing the worthless, stupid beast, Larson put a bullet in its brain, and retrieved the weapons and ammunition, all of which had fortunately remained securely tied to the pack frame.

He put the Colt and Ruger handguns in the ammunition bags, tied them to his saddle horn, stuck the 9 mm Glock autoloader back in his waistband, and slung the lever-action 30.06 Winchester over his shoulder. He'd been carrying the Weatherby Mark V in the saddle scabbard, so the only rifle he had to leave behind was the Remington Safari.

He looked around for the satchel with the money and the jewelry, and it was nowhere to be seen. Through the fog, Larson sensed a slight lessening of the charcoal gray sky. Should he risk backtracking to find it? He checked Pettibone's Omega wristwatch, looked again at the sky, and decided against it, although the idea of losing the satchel pissed him off. It was getting on to first light and surely the cops would be out in force looking for him, even if the storm stuck around and dumped more moisture.

He mounted up and turned the horse in the direction of the Cimarron River. After twenty minutes of steady riding, he reached the banks and walked the horse to the edge of the fast-moving water. Larson guessed it was no more than five or six feet deep and twenty feet across, but if he tried to swim across on the horse they could both be swept away.

Back when he'd cowboyed on the ranch there had been a landing strip close to the highway that ran from French Tract to Cimarron. An old plank bridge on a ranch road to the landing strip crossed the river at that point. His best bet was to go there and hope that it hadn't been washed out.

Larson followed the river, found the ranch road, reached the intact plank bridge, and gave a sigh of relief. It had been rebuilt and reinforced with riprap, and native trees and vegetation had been planted along the riverbed to control erosion. He crossed over the river and rode to the gate that accessed the highway at the end of the landing strip. As he expected, it was locked.

He took the Weatherby out of the scabbard, blew the lock into a dozen metallic pieces, unwrapped the chain from around the gate, and walked the horse through. He couldn't see more than ten feet in either direction, but there was no sound of traffic on the two-lane highway. He closed the gate, led the horse across the pavement to the far fence line, remounted, and headed west, hugging the fence line, looking for another gate.

Four vehicles passed him by in a twenty-minute stretch, headlights dim and flickering in the soupy fog. But he stayed invisible in the murkiness.

The anger Larson felt about losing his equipment, provisions, and supplies lifted somewhat. He was halfway to safety, with one more river and one more road to cross. Once in the forest, he'd hunt for his food and build a shelter, if need be. But it might not come to that. People lived in the mountains. There was a resort in the high country, some summer cabins, even some mining operations, if they hadn't been shut down, which happened periodically. There might be slim pickings where he was going, but there were pickings nonetheless.

At a painstakingly slow pace, Kerney and Clayton tracked Larson through the fog until it lifted and revealed scattered provisions and gear on an open expanse of rangeland. They followed the litter to the dead packhorse.

Clayton swung out of the saddle and gave the animal the once-over. "It broke a foreleg," he said. "Larson put it down."

"It's the only killing he's done so far that makes any sense," Kerney said. "How far behind are we?"

Clayton got back on his horse. "I'd say we're no closer than we were when we started out. But he lost his provisions, and left behind a rifle."

"Well, that's something," Kerney said glumly.

"Are you all right?" Clayton asked, eyeing Kerney closely.

Kerney nodded but said nothing in response.

Above, the sky had lifted and patches of blue broke through the fast-moving cloud cover. In the distance they could hear the sound of approaching airplane propellers and helicopter rotors.

Clayton looked up. "We've got air support now. That's something to cheer about."

Kerney keyed his handheld radio and made contact with Frank Vanmeter. He gave him their location and asked to have all aircraft concentrate the search to the west, north, and northeast of their position.

"You're sure of that?" Vanmeter asked.

"I don't think there's a chance that he's going to turn around," Kerney replied. "Not this close to the foothills and canyons. Tell the pilots and spotters to look for a horse and rider only. The pack animal is dead, and most of Larson's supplies are scattered near our twenty."

"That's encouraging."

"I wish I shared your optimistic outlook. Stay in touch." Kerney fell in behind Clayton, who'd picked up the trail, heading northeast.

The breeze turned blustery. Over the mountains the sky was a cloudless pure blue. Soon a hot July sun, still blocked to the east by the remaining clouds of the vanishing storm, would begin drying out the land. But it was going to be a muddy twenty-four hours before the puddles, sinks, ditches, arroyos, and dirt roads began to firm up.

Kerney pulled up even with Clayton, who gave him a questioning look.

"What?" he asked.

"You look kind of pale," Clayton said.

"I'm just fine," Kerney said firmly.

"Okay. Never mind." Clayton pointed at the fresh tracks that showed Larson had picked up the pace, and spurred his roan into a trot.

Larson's decision not to cross the next river right away, but to follow it to the highway that ran from Cimarron to Raton, proved to be the right move. By the time he reached the highway, the torrent in the Vermejo River had subsided and he was able to cross it and the pavement as well on a railroad spur that ran deep into the canyon to several coal mines.

When the sky began to clear, he left the spur for the cover of the old cottonwoods that hugged the bank of the river, and within minutes he heard the drone of an airplane engine. He brought his horse to a stop and through the thick foliage watched a small plane fly low along the railroad spur and disappear in the direction of the Dawson cemetery.

At one time, there had been the town of Dawson, a village of 1,500 people living and working in one of the most productive coal mining districts in the Southwest. In the early 1950s it had been shut down and dismantled by the mining company that owned it. But the cemetery remained, with hundreds of grave markers of miners killed in two of the largest mining disasters in the nation's history.

As a teenager, Larson had come to several of the annual reunions of the descendants of the old-timers who had lived, worked, or grown up in the town of Dawson, and its colorful and tragic history was part of the folklore of the area.

He waited until the sound of the engine faded before continuing on, and then stopped again when the airplane returned and banked low over the river, heading east. He wondered if the cops were tracking him yet, or still searching for him on the mesas near Miami.

When it was all clear he kept riding, past the adobe shell of an old, roofless two-story ranch house, a collapsed barn, an irrigated wheat field, and a large pasture where fat cattle grazed on lush grasses. Where the spur spanned the Vermejo River again, he walked the horse through a muddy field, found a fast-running but shallow place to cross, and followed the tracks all the way to where the adjacent road ended at a locked gate posted with No Trespassing signs. A fork in the road allowed visitors to tour the cemetery, but access to the old town site was denied.

Larson returned to the railroad spur until it bridged the river once more. He remounted his horse, dropped down into the grassy valley, and splashed through the water and up a muddy bank. Since his last visit many years ago, the old smokestacks to the coke ovens had been torn down, but through the trees near the base of a small mesa he could see the outline of the two or three structures still standing. In the past, one had been used as a line camp by cowboys during summer months when cattle were in the high country. If the line camp was still in use, maybe he'd be able to resupply his provisions before moving on.

At the sound of an approaching helicopter, Larson spurred his horse to a gallop. He reached cover under a stand of trees in front of one of the old buildings just as the whirlybird swooped low on the other side of the river and hovered for a moment over an old weather-beaten cabin close to the bank, before continuing up the canyon. When it flew out of sight, Larson circled around the line camp looking for any sign of recent occupation. There were fresh tire tracks in the road at the front of the house, but no vehicle. All the window shades were drawn, so he couldn't see inside. The front door was padlocked.

Larson figured the padlock meant no one was home. He led the horse up on the porch, used the Glock autoloader to destroy the padlock, and got himself and the animal inside with a minute to spare before the chopper returned and hovered overhead.

When the chopper left, Larson let out a big sigh of relief and looked around. The front room had a small propane cookstove on the counter, next to a sink with an old-fashioned hand pump. There was an ice chest on the floor, but it was empty. However, the pantry held a variety of canned meats, beans, soups, crackers, dried food, and bottled water. A twin bed in the back room was made up with sheets, a pillow, and a lightweight blanket, and the closet held a couple of changes of jeans and long-sleeved cowboy shirts on hangers.

Larson walked his horse into the back room, unloaded the ammunition bags, grabbed the Weatherby from the scabbard, and closed the door on the animal. Hungry, he set about fixing a meal, figuring he'd stay put at least until he ate, maybe longer if the chopper or the airplane kept coming back. He opened a can of meat, put it in a skillet, turned on the camp stove, and let it simmer while he poured a can of beans into a pot and put it on the second burner.

While the food warmed, he positioned the small dining table directly in front of the open door, arranged all the weapons he had on the table, made sure every gun was fully loaded, and put additional ammunition close at hand. Should people come calling, he was ready.

When the meat and beans were warm, he sat behind the table looking out toward the river valley, gobbled the food down, and mopped up the bean juice with some crackers. The chopper came back twice more while he ate.

Larson knew he couldn't stay long; the cops had to be on his trail by now. Hopefully the chopper would move on to other canyons that wound up the mountains, especially the one with a Forest Service road that could take you all the way to the Colorado border.

He waited thirty minutes, and when the chopper didn't return, he went and retrieved the horse from the back room, where it had dumped a load of fresh horse apples on the floor.

Larson thought that was a hoot. As he packed food he'd raided from the pantry into his saddlebags, he heard the sound of a vehicle approaching on the dirt road. He picked up the Weatherby, stood back from the open door, and waited. Soon a pickup truck pulling a horse trailer came into view. Larson used the rifle's scope to look into the cab. Only a driver was inside the vehicle, an older man with a droopy mustache, wearing a sweat-stained straw cowboy hat.

Larson sighted in on the driver and followed him with the Weatherby as he drew closer. Just when the man noticed the open door to the line camp and started to turn the truck around, Larson shot him through the windshield.

The truck careened into a tree and the horse trailer skidded over on its side and slammed into the bed of the pickup. Larson first checked the driver, who was dead with a big hole in his chest that spurted blood. He dug the man's wallet from his hip pocket and read the name on his driver's license. One day, Truman Goodson's name would be added to the plaque at the St. James Hotel that listed the people killed by Craig Lee Larson, "Last of the Western Desperadoes."

Larson pried open the rear doors to the horse trailer. Two fine-looking cow ponies were inside, both busted up pretty bad. It was a damn shame, as either one of them would have been a far sight better than the horses he'd taken from the stables at the ranch. He put them both down, walked his gelding out of the line camp, gathered his weapons, mounted up, and rode off.

He started counting up how many kills he had made, and decided he should have finished off the prison guard and that scumbag Lenny Hampson who'd squealed on him to the cops. Also, he should have iced that young couple with the baby. Maybe the sheriff he'd shot and crippled had died. Add up all his kills, throw in the ones he let get away, and it would have been a damn impressive list. Too bad he hadn't thought it through before he got in the groove.

Looking back, he should have written down their names for posterity so when the commemorative plaque went up at the St. James Hotel, nobody was left off. But since the cops would ID all the victims anyway, that wasn't a problem. His big mistake was not thinking to leave instructions about the plaque with his brother, Kerry.

Thinking he needed to kill more cops to add to his luster as a badass bandito, Larson headed for the base of the mesa behind the line camp, where he could easily find cover if the chopper came back.

Following Larson's trail under a blue sky in full sunlight proved easy enough to do. By noon, Clayton and Kerney had reached Dawson Canyon, and when they got to the melting shell of an old two-story adobe ranch house, they stopped to water and feed their horses.

Standing over the hoofprints of Larson's animal, Clayton scanned the low mesas that squeezed the narrow valley. "If Larson was going to skip over to the next canyon, he would have had to do it right about here."

"His tracks keep following the railroad spur," Kerney said, "so I don't think he's trying to outfox us quite yet." He opened one of the maps the game and fish officer had given them and studied it. "Besides, the most reliable water source in the area is right here on the Vermejo River. The map shows that the canyons on either side of us drain the runoff from the high country by occasional streams and dry creek beds."

Clayton nodded as he bit into a sandwich, chewed, and swallowed. "How far into Dawson Canyon does the railroad spur go?"

"About fifteen miles from where it crosses the highway, and ten miles or so from the old Dawson town site."

Clayton took another bite and chewed it down. "It would make sense that Larson would use the spur line as the fastest route into the tall pines. Once he's in the dense forest, it's going to be damn hard to find him and flush him out."

Kerney put the map away and swung into the saddle. "Let's get moving."

"Aren't you eating?"

Kerney shook his head. "Grumpy gut."

"That's why you look so pale. You got a fever?"

"Mount up and let's go."

Clayton pulled himself up on his horse. "You didn't answer the question."

Some years back, Kerney had been gut shot by a drug dealer during a gunfight, which had forced him to be more careful than most people when it came to what he ate and drank. "I haven't been doing a good job of minding what I eat," he explained.

Clayton eyed Kerney with concern. "Let me know if you need to stop or something."

Kerney handed the reins to the packhorses to Clayton and took the lead. "I'll be just fine."

"I knew you'd say that," Clayton called out. "You're such a tough guy."

"Give it a rest," Kerney called back as he slowed the buckskin to a walk across a muddy patch.

Within the hour, they entered the Dawson town site and came upon the crashed pickup truck and overturned horse trailer under a canopy of trees that had blocked any view from above. The driver and the two horses he'd been hauling in the trailer were dead.

"This guy Larson just doesn't stop," Clayton said, cursing as he speed-dialed Frank Vanmeter to give him the news and request assistance.

Kerney looked at the old house, which must have surely been a residence for a mine manager or superintendent back when Dawson was truly a town. He walked over to the truck and horse trailer and studied the skid marks. "I bet Larson shot the victim from inside the house, through the open door."

Clayton snapped shut his cell phone. "The poor guy never saw it coming."

Kerney walked across the remnants of an old sidewalk, went up the dirt path, entered the house through the open front door, and gave the interior a quick once-over.

"Are there any other victims?" Clayton asked when Kerney stepped back outside.

"No," he replied, "but he's reprovisioned himself, although it's hard to tell how much he took. I'd guess he's got two or three days' worth of food. What's Vanmeter's ETA?"

"Thirty minutes, maximum." Clayton put his foot in the stirrup and looked at Kerney. "We're not going to wait for him, are we?"

"Nope." Kerney swung into the saddle. "Let Vanmeter know we're pushing on."

"I already did."

Kerney shook his head in mock disbelief. "Then why in the hell did you ask me?"

"I read somewhere that it's important to give retired people a sense of empowerment."

Kerney grunted. "You know, I'm starting to think that maybe it's the company I've been keeping lately that's giving me my grumpy stomach."

Clayton shook off the barb and gritted his teeth before smiling. "Touché."

"You're damn right, touché." Kerney dropped the reins against the buckskin's neck and the horse stepped out nicely, showing Clayton its rump.

Figuring it was time to throw off whoever might be following him, Larson left the railroad spur far below where it dead-ended. The canyon had narrowed considerably and the tracks squeezed through tapered gaps where the thick pine forest dropped down to the rocky roadbed.

He paused for a few moments to let the gelding graze on bunchgrass along the side of the spur. Then he walked it through the overgrown forest, winding his way around stands of trees too dense to penetrate and making slow progress as he moved up the side of a mountain. The tree canopy cut the bright sunlight down to a dusklike glimmer, and except for the scurrying of squirrels and an occasional birdcall, the forest was quiet.

He reached the crest of the mountain hoping for a fix on the horizon so he could get oriented, but all he saw before him was another steep, thickly forested incline. Winded, he sat under a tree and tried to convince himself that he wasn't lost.

There was no way he could go back to the railroad spur. If there was a posse on his trail, that would be just plain foolish. He checked the time on Pettibone's Omega and looked up, trying to use the sun to get a general sense of direction, but the light was too diffused.

He decided to follow the ridgeline for a while before climbing the next crest in hopes of finding a break in the forest that would give him a better sense of direction. The ground underfoot was a hazardous combination of moist, rocky soil covered by a thick layer of pine needles, and he'd already turned his ankles several times on some loose stones.

Larson searched for a route between the two crests, gave up after twenty minutes, and started up the next steep incline. The woods were so thick that no matter how hard he tried to avoid low branches, his face stung with welt marks and there were scratches along the shoulders and flanks of the horse.

He topped the next crest and grunted in disgust at the wall of tall pines on a steep slope that greeted him. The slight tinge of panic that had been growing in his gut turned to bile in his throat. He turned on his heel and did a three-sixty, hoping for a view of anything that would give him a hint of which way to turn, but found nothing.

Larson found himself sweating and laboring for breath in the thin mountain air, his throat dry and his body aching. He could go no farther without resting. Even his jaded horse looked ready to drop. He unsaddled the animal, tied it off to a nearby tree, and stretched out, using the saddle as a pillow.

How long had he gone without sleep? Two days? More? Killing that old cowboy at the line camp felt like it had happened days instead of hours ago. What was the cowboy's name? Larson couldn't remember.

He reached into his shirt pocket and took out the cowboy's wallet. Truman Goodson, that was his name. Before he dozed off, Larson decided he needed to make a list of all his kills before he forgot their names completely.

Where Larson's trail left the railroad spur, Clayton and Kerney paused, rested their animals, studied maps, and considered their next move.

Kerney ran his finger over a map. "If Larson doesn't get disoriented, and keeps traveling northeast, he'll be in mountain wilderness until he reaches the paved highway that runs from Raton to the York Canyon coal mine."

"If he makes it through the mountains to the highway, which is iffy, I doubt he's going to ride his horse into Raton," Clayton replied.

Kerney nodded in agreement.

"And if he doesn't make it through the mountains," Clayton added, "chances are slim we'd ever find his body."

"That's unacceptable," Kerney said. "Let's have Vanmeter saturate the road to the coal mine with uniforms. Constant 24/7 patrols, plus officers stationed at every mile marker along the length of the pavement."

Clayton nodded. "And if he changes direction?"

Kerney pointed on the map to where the spur line ended. "If he cuts back, eventually he'll intersect the river somewhere above the end of the railroad tracks. At that point I'd guess he'd follow the river north to the York Canyon coal mine."

"We won't know what he does unless we follow him," Clayton said, "and I suggest we don't. At least not right away."

Kerney looked up from the map. "Explain yourself."

"Where Larson is headed, it's all up and down, except for two major north-south drainage ravines. Unless he gets totally lost and confused, he'll reach one or the other of them sometime tomorrow. But if we stay on the spur right-of-way, we can gain a hell of a lot of ground on him and, with an early start in the morning, cut across both ravines if necessary and pick up his trail that way."

Kerney folded the map. "Let's get game and fish to put some people on horseback behind us to keep Larson from sneaking down the mountainside."

"We should keep some planes in the air over our sector during the daylight hours to cover any breaks in the tree cover," Clayton said. "That should keep Larson on the move."

"Call Vanmeter, give him our coordinates, tell him what we want, and ask him to get the ball rolling," Kerney said.

Clayton hesitated before keying the handheld. "You do know with all this, we could still lose him out there."

Kerney shrugged. "Larson's luck can't hold forever. It's time for us to catch a break."

The sound of an airplane overhead woke Larson. He sat up, looked skyward, and listened as the sound of the engine receded and then returned again. He told himself that it was nothing to worry about, but decided to get moving anyway while he still had enough light to see by. He saddled the horse, led it to the ridgeline, and found a game trail that wound under old-growth trees to a rock outcropping. There he discovered a pool of fresh rainwater in a shallow stone basin.

Both Larson and the horse drank from the pool. When he finished and looked up, he could see through the undergrowth a large burn area of blackened trees that extended to the top of the next summit. Above was blue sky. Staying hidden under the canopy, Larson made his way to the burn area. The shadows cast by dead trees told Larson the direction of the sun.

He checked the time on Pettibone's Omega. Toward dusk, when the planes stopped flying for the night, he'd cross to the next ridgeline, make camp, get his bearings in the morning, and move on.

Larson took a deep breath and let it out slowly. Maybe his luck was still holding. His good spirits returned. This might turn out to be fun again after all.

ChapterEleven

Frank Vanmeter called by radio just as Clayton and Kerney finished setting up camp for the night.

"Have you caught him yet?" Vanmeter asked.

"You'll be the first to know when we do," Kerney snapped.

"Didn't mean to make you testy," Frank said, not sounding the least bit apologetic. "Thought you'd like to know that a rancher turned in a satchel he found near the Cimarron River when he was out checking his cattle after the storm. It came from the barn at the ranch where Larson's brother works and contained at least a hundred thousand dollars in jewelry and cash."

"Has Larson pulled a robbery that we've somehow missed?" Kerney asked.

"I wondered the same thing. So far the answer is negative. But that aside, if Larson was planning on using the jewelry to disappear, he's now up a creek."

"And all the more dangerous because of it," Kerney said.

"Amen to that," Frank said. "Everything you and Agent Istee asked for is in place. Uniforms are at every mile marker along Route 555, three game and fish officers are moving into the foothills to cover your back, and all aircraft are ready to go again at first light."

"I'll talk to you then," Kerney said.

"Ten-four."

Kerney filled Clayton in as they fed and watered the horses.

Then, on the off chance that Larson might be in the vicinity, they had a light dinner in the growing darkness with no campfire.

Although his stomach still hurt and he had no appetite, Kerney hadn't eaten all day. So he sat on a fallen log and forced himself to swallow some soup Clayton had mixed up from a packet and warmed over a small propane camp stove, and nibble on some cheese and crackers, hoping to keep it all down. When he couldn't stand the thought of another bite, he buried the remains of his meal in a pit and covered it, so the smell wouldn't attract any passing bears or other hungry critters.

"You're still not feeling good, are you?" Clayton asked as he hoisted the bag of foodstuffs up to a high tree branch and tied it off.

"I'll be fine after a good night's sleep," Kerney replied as he took off his boots and slid into the sleeping bag.

He spent the early part of the night awake, leaving the warmth of his sleeping bag once to vomit and returning to swelter in the cool air. When sleep came, he dreamed bizarre images of Craig Larson's murder and mayhem, and woke up several times in a sweat. Finally the fever broke, and he fell into an exhausted, dreamless sleep.

In the morning, Clayton woke him up with a hot cup of tea. "I heard you in the night," he said. "You look awful."

"I bet I do." Kerney sat up and took the tin mug from Clayton's hand. "Thanks."

"I put some honey in it. That should settle your stomach down some."

Kerney nodded and sipped his tea.

Clayton looked Kerney over with worried eyes. "We can always pull back and have Vanmeter send in replacements."

"No way. I'm fit enough to continue."

"You're sure of that?"

"Yeah." Kerney smiled. "Whatever got to me has passed."

"Do you mean that literally?"

"It's gone one way or the other."

"How about some dry toast and a bowl of instant oatmeal?"

"Sounds about right."

"I'll get to it." Clayton rose, went to the camp stove, and got busy with breakfast.

As he drank more of his tea, Kerney watched Clayton, a son he never knew he had until a few short years ago. He thought he was damn lucky to have the man as his son and his friend.

After breakfast, they broke camp and were starting out to cut Larson's trail when Frank Vanmeter called again. This time, to tell Clayton that Paul Hewitt had died in his sleep overnight.

Clayton stiffened in shock and gave Kerney the news, the expression on his face a mixture of agonized sadness and pure rage.

After thanking Vanmeter, he climbed off his horse, silently handed Kerney the reins, and walked into the forest until he was out of sight. Fifteen minutes later, Clayton returned. His eyes were dry and features composed, but he had hacked off his long hair with his hunting knife. Kerney figured it was Clayton's way of mourning the loss of Paul Hewitt. It was more eloquent than any spoken words.

"Let's go," Clayton said with a hard edge to his voice. He took the reins from Kerney's hands, got on his horse, and started up the slope of the wooded canyon wall.

Kerney said nothing and followed him.

Throughout the morning, Craig Larson stayed lost until the distant sounds of heavy machinery reached him in the thin mountain air. He followed the sound for hours, winding his way up and down canyons and across the ravines wet with standing pools of murky rainwater from yesterday's storm. He let his horse drink from them before gulping down the gritty water himself, and although it smelled like burned ash from the recent forest fire and tasted muddy, it didn't seem to do him any harm. He stayed under the trees with his jittery horse for a good half hour, upwind of an adult bear wallowing in a large pool of water, until it ambled away.

He climbed toward the top of the next ridgeline as the growing sound of engines told him that human activity was close at hand. On the crest, he stayed hidden and looked down into a large valley at an open-pit coal mining operation. It had cut into the earth a good hundred and fifty feet below the surface soil and shale-like substrate. He guessed a good thousand acres were being actively mined while another thousand had been reclaimed with native grasses and shrubs.

There were two monster electric shovels loading ore onto gigantic trucks, and at the far end of the pit, massive front-end loaders were excavating coal from what looked like a blast area. A gravel road left the valley in a direction Larson reckoned hooked up somewhere with the railroad spur. He was glad to be well north of it.

He climbed down from his horse, tied the reins on a tree branch, got some canned food out, and ate it for lunch as he watched the machines and considered his next move. Above him, a single-engine airplane dipped into the valley and flew back and forth across the mining operation.

Finished with his food, he threw the empty tin away, grabbed the Weatherby out of the saddle scabbard, and for the fun of it, sighted the weapon on the big, low-moving electric shovels, the front-end loaders, and the trucks hauling the coal. He zeroed in on the shovel operators, wondering if he could take them out.

With the distance to the targets, the constant movement of the machines, and the breezes that were kicking up in the thin mountain air, it would be awesome marksmanship.

Larson decided not to bother. He put the Weatherby away and set out to ride the perimeter of the valley mine under the tree cover. Hopefully, something would turn up to give him a sense of what to do or where to go next.

As he circled, his view of the valley expanded to include another part of the operation where the coal was crushed before being transported to the railhead. He continued the loop, riding for a good hour before arriving on the opposite ridgeline overlooking the valley. From there he headed north until the sound of rubber on pavement made him get out of the saddle.

He tied off his horse to a tree and walked through the forest until he could see a strip of blacktop. It had to be the highway that ran from Raton, past the coal mines and up to the Vermejo Resort Ranch and its fancy lodge, where millionaires came to hunt big game during the day and drink martinis at the bar at night.

He spotted a state police car parked at the side of the road. Within minutes another black-and-white passed by heading toward Raton. He walked on until he could see the access road to the mine, where a state cop car was parked next to a black SUV. A state police officer and a security guard stood talking between the vehicles.

Larson returned to his horse. The cops had figured out exactly where he planned to go and had set a trap for him. There were probably more stationed along the highway waiting to cut him off, with a posse of cops likely coming up behind him on horseback. It was time to make a new plan.

He heard the repetitive thud of a chopper overhead coming up the narrow canyon the highway snaked through. More cops most likely. In his mind it sounded like *Stop the cops* being played over and over again.

That's what he needed to do, but he had to be smart about it. Run and gun, gun and run, might be the best way. Take a cop out and move on. Then take another and another and another. Make them pay to the max for all the shit they'd put him through. But first, he needed to scope out what he was up against before he pulled the trigger on the first one.

He mounted up and disappeared into the forest, thinking he and not the cops would call the shots.

After hours of riding, Clayton and Kerney cut Larson's trail at a wildfire burn area that had destroyed a good four thousand acres of timber, sterilized the thin layer of topsoil, and exposed the washed gray granite, hardened quartz, and sandstone rock of the mountainside. They found a disturbed area where Larson had camped overnight, called it in, and kept moving, dropping into the ravine where tracks and sign showed Larson had paused to drink. In the next ravine, they found fresh bear scat and recent hoofprints that traveled even higher, until they topped out on a crest that overlooked an huge open-pit coal mine.

Kerney and Clayton looked down at the raw, gaping wound in the land.

"Well, we all like our cars and electric lights, I guess," Clayton said.

"Don't we, though," Kerney replied, thinking resource extraction could be a whole lot less wasteful. "At least they're making an effort to reclaim the land. That didn't use to happen."

Clayton grunted and moved off to inspect the area for more signs of Larson. Kerney's gut wrenched and he scurried into the woods and promptly lost all the food in his stomach. Most of the morning he'd been feeling all right, but in the last hour or so the sweats and the chills had returned along with a gut that felt like it was about to explode.

"I've called in a chopper to take you to Raton to be looked at," Clayton said when Kerney returned to the horses.

"I'm not going."

"Don't be stubborn. You're sick. We'll drop down into the mine so the chopper can pick you up."

"I don't want you going up against Larson alone," Kerney said.

"I won't be. We've got a picket line of uniforms spread out along the length of the highway, so I've got all the backup I need."

"Uniforms sitting in squad cars aren't the same as someone in the saddle next to you."

"I'll be careful," Clayton said.

Kerney shook his head in protest. "I'm staying."

"You're going," Clayton said flatly. "A sick partner doesn't do me any good and could get us both killed."

Clayton was right and Kerney knew it. "Okay," he said. "I'll get myself checked out."

They picked their way carefully down to a cut that took them to a gravel road where monster ore trucks rumbled by, kicking up dust so thick it stung the eyes.

"You know," Clayton yelled over the sound of a passing truck, "if you eat food during a storm supposedly you either lose your teeth before you get old or your stomach stays cranky."

"Who told you that?" Kerney yelled back.

"Moses Kaywaykla, my uncle by marriage. In fact, if you're eating and there's a lightning flash, you're supposed to spit the food out right away."

"Why are you telling me this?"

"To further your continuing education about Mescalero traditions and beliefs."

"Oh, and I just thought you were telling me I had a cranky stomach to make me feel better."

"Your sarcasm is duly noted. Actually, I thought it would take your mind off it."

Kerney laughed in spite of himself. Up ahead, a state police helicopter came over the tree line and landed on reclaimed flats planted in clover, saltbush, and side oats grama grass.

Clayton broke the roan gelding into a canter and Kerney followed suit on his buckskin, the packhorses loping behind. They reached the chopper to find a lady paramedic standing by. She ordered Kerney off his horse, checked his pulse, listened to his heart and lungs, took his temperature and blood pressure, prodded his gut with her fingers, and told him to get in the chopper.

Kerney hesitated. "What's the verdict?"

"Don't know," the paramedic replied with a smile. "Your heart's strong and your blood pressure is okay. Maybe food poisoning or some intestinal bug, but we'll let the doctors decide."

Kerney gave Clayton a dirty look and got in the chopper with the paramedic. Clayton smiled broadly, backed the horses away, and waved as the pilot fired up the rotors. When the helicopter was airborne, he called Vanmeter and told him Kerney was inbound to Raton from the coal mine. "Has anyone sighted Larson?" he asked.

"Negative," Vanmeter replied.

"That means he's probably discovered we've been waiting for him and he's either doing an end run or moving laterally. I'm going back to pick up his trail."

"You shouldn't do it on your own," Vanmeter cautioned.

"I'll keep my distance," Clayton replied, lying through his teeth.

As he trotted the horses down the gravel road, loud, shrill whistles blew, the heavy equipment stopped moving, and all was quiet for a moment before an explosion ripped open an exposed coal seam at the far end of the pit. The dust from the blast formed a dense cloud that floated over the valley and coated the stately mountain evergreens above the pit.

Clayton covered his mouth with a handkerchief and rode away from the mine.

All morning long, radio stations in Raton had broadcast half-hour bulletins about the police manhunt for Kerry's brother. People were warned not to open their doors to strangers, pick up hitchhikers on the roads, or let their children out unsupervised. Listeners also heard that the reward for information leading to Craig's capture had reached fifty thousand dollars.

On one of the hourly news shows, a newsman interviewed Truman Goodson's widow, who broke down crying, demanding Craig be brought to justice. Kerry looked up Mrs. Goodson's address in the phone book and took the fifteen hundred dollars cash he'd held back from his brother to buy a new deer rifle and put it in an envelope without a note or return address, put four first-class stamps on it to make sure it got there, and dropped it in the mailbox on the highway.

On a talk radio show, a trucker called in to say there were dozens of cops concentrated along Highway 555. He cogitated on the idea that they were flooding the high country looking for Craig. Another caller reported a rumor that the police had recovered out on the prairie a fortune in jewels and a pile of cash that Craig had stolen from a bunch of people he'd killed that the cops didn't know about.

All the police would say officially was that the manhunt for

Craig had intensified and the public would be advised as soon as he was apprehended.

Kerry had gone to work in the morning only to be interrupted by a state police investigator accompanied by Everett Dorsey, who for the umpteenth time questioned him about where Craig was heading with his stolen horses and supplies. For the umpteenth time Kerry played dumb.

When he did get to working again, he was bothered by an Albuquerque television news reporter who barged in asking for an interview while a truck with a satellite dish on top of it idled outside. Kerry clammed up, closed the barn doors, and wouldn't open them until the reporter and his truck left.

When he was finally alone except for the cop on the ranch road watching him, he locked up the garage, walked back to his house, gathered up a coat, a rifle, and some ammunition, and put it all in his truck along with some bottled water, crackers, and a jar of peanut butter in a small backpack. By force of habit, he checked his oil, coolant, and tire pressure before climbing into the cab.

One summer long ago when they were kids, they had been loaned out by the rancher they worked for as summer help to fix up a corral at the Vermejo Resort Ranch. It was on a high-country pasture deep in the forest an hour off a jeep trail by horseback. They'd camped out at the corral for two nights, and in their free time had found a small cave in the mountainside hidden by thick underbrush. It had all kinds of Indian paintings on the walls and ceiling, and from the looks of it nobody had used it for years.

Kerry figured if Craig was really in the high country and the cops were all around him like the radio said, he would head for the cave to hide out because that's where they had talked about what fun it would be to live like the old-time mountain men.

He would go there to look for him. Maybe he could talk Craig into giving himself up. Then people would stop thinking bad things about him.

He fired up the truck and took off. Half a mile down the highway one of those unmarked state police cars came up behind him, but Kerry didn't mind. Where he was going, the cop couldn't follow.

He turned off at the first ranch-road gate along the highway, locked it behind him, and kept going. In his rearview mirror he saw the car stop, turn around, and head back toward town.

As he drove Kerry wondered what had happened to make Craig so bad-sick in the head.

Craig Larson stuck to the trees for cover and followed the highway for several miles in both directions just to check things out. There were cops everywhere watching and waiting for him. He faded deeper into the woods and traveled in the general direction of the Vermejo Resort Ranch. Back when he was a kid, the ranch catered in the fall and winter months to rifle and bow hunters looking to bring home a trophy-size elk, bear, or deer. In the spring, the bird hunters came for the wild turkey season. During the summer, the lodge operated as a dude ranch and nature study center for wealthy vacationers. Guests could go on fake cattle roundups complete with campfire sing-alongs at night, take horseback camping trips into the wilderness, go on guided nature and wildlife hikes, or just stay put at the ranch headquarters, where they could play tennis, swim in the Olympic-size pool, get spa treatments, and drink martinis in the bar. He doubted anything had changed.

Larson had only been there once, years ago, when he and Kerry had fixed up an old corral in a bad state of repair. At the time, the owners were planning to buy a small herd of buffalo and graze them on a broad high valley tucked between two peaks. A sturdy fence had been built to keep the buffalo from straying, and the repaired corral would be used to cull a few head every now and then for slaughter so the lodge could serve up gourmet buffalo steaks, burgers, and roasts to the paying guests.

Larson wondered if he could find his way to that valley. It would be a hell of a lot of fun to stampede the animals and shoot them down just like the old buffalo hunters used to do. He wondered how many he could kill in an hour or so.

As he continued toward the ranch, the canyon narrowed. Staying out of sight of the highway became more and more difficult. Time and again he had to dismount and climb upslope at a steep angle to avoid being seen. About the only traffic on the road was cop cars going back and forth and some dump trucks traveling down the canyon toward Raton.

At the high point of one crest, Larson found himself looking down at a rock quarry where gravel and stone were being mined and loaded on the dump trucks. He eyeballed the grade at the back end of the mine and decide it was too steep to traverse with the horse. But if he backtracked, he would be in sight from the road when he went around the entrance to the quarry. That wouldn't do.

The Omega wristwatch Larson had inherited from Pettibone by way of murder told him the quarry would probably shut down for the day in another hour. He decided to wait. He found a fairly level area under a big pine tree that had been hit by lightning some time back, and stretched out for a nap. It had been another draining day.

Other than a bad gut stemming partly from an old gunshot wound that had cost him a few feet of his small intestine, a persistent cold and sore throat with postnasal drip, and an accompanying fever, the doctors at the hospital couldn't find anything wrong with Kerney. They asked questions, had a nurse draw blood, checked his vitals, and tried to keep him overnight for observation. Kerney wasn't having any of it.

They let him go with a prescription for antibiotics, told him to get some over-the-counter meds to deal with the gut and nasal symptoms, and gave him a referral to see a specialist in Santa Fe for a colonoscopy. The thought of it held little appeal.

After picking up his meds at the hospital pharmacy, Kerney met Frank Vanmeter in the parking lot next to the empty helicopter landing pad.

"Where's the chopper?" he asked. "I need to get back up the mountain pronto."

Vanmeter shook his head. "You're not going anywhere tonight; Chief Baca's orders. Even if the chief was inclined to let you return to duty, Agent Istee said he wouldn't be able to meet up with you until morning."

"Have you and Clayton snookered me?"

"You could say that," Vanmeter said with a smile as he opened the passenger door to his unit. "I'll give you a ride to the motel. Take a hot shower, call your wife, get a good night's sleep, and if you're better in the morning, maybe Chief Baca will let you return to duty."

Kerney settled into the seat. "What else did Agent Istee have to say for himself?"

"Seems our boy Larson is leading him on quite a merry chase. He's doubling back and stopping frequently to cover his tracks. Clayton says he's no closer to him than he was when you got airlifted from the coal mine. But now things are a bit more complicated."

"How so?" Kerney asked.

"Kerry Larson is on the loose," Vanmeter replied. "Going

where, we don't know. He left the ranch, passed through a locked pasture gate with a key, and slipped his tail. If he's not careful, he could get shot by somebody who thinks he's his brother."

"Great," Kerney said as they pulled up to the motel.

In his room, Kerney followed Vanmeter's advice and took a hot shower before calling Sara.

"Where are you?" she asked.

"In a motel room in Raton."

"It's not like you not to call."

"Sorry about that. I've been tracking Larson on horseback with Clayton the last two days."

"Have you got him?"

"Not yet, but he's almost surrounded. Does that sound as lame to you as it does to me?"

"I'm trying not to scoff."

"We'll get him."

"You sound all stuffed up and congested. Are you okay?"

"Just the sniffles, nothing more."

"You're sure?"

"Absolutely."

"I was on the phone with Grace earlier. She's worried about Clayton. You do know that Paul Hewitt died in his sleep?"

"We heard. Clayton took it pretty hard, but he's coping."

"He needs to call home."

"I'll let him know in the morning."

"Isn't he with you at the motel?"

"No, he's camped out on Larson's trail, and Larson's hiding somewhere on a resort mountain ranch that stretches to the Colorado state line. We've got over two dozen officers up there with him."

"Patrick and I are leaving in the morning for London."

"So soon?"

"My emergency leave is up, Kerney. Jack and Irene are driving us to the airport."

"How are they doing?"

"A little bit better. When you get back to the ranch, Lynette wants to talk to you about taking over the breeding program."

"Did she say anything more about it?"

"No, but two days ago she found out she's pregnant."

"That's heartbreaking," Kerney said.

"In a way. But in another way she's delighted. So are Jack and Irene. When will you be joining us in London?"

"As soon as this gets wrapped up."

"You're sure?" Sara asked.

"I'm sure."

"Hold on, there's a young man here who wants to talk to you."

Sara turned the phone over to Patrick, and Kerney spent a few minutes reassuring his son that he'd see him in London. He promised to take him riding in Hyde Park soon after he got home. He said good night to Sara, took his meds, set the alarm clock, and went to bed, determined to be rid of what ailed him by morning.

Clayton made camp at dusk, fed the horses, fixed a big meal, and settled in for the night. He remembered his conversation with Paul Hewitt in the hospital and the comment the sheriff had made about going skydiving without a parachute as soon as he finished his rehab. He couldn't shake the thought that somehow Sheriff Hewitt had found a way to kill himself. Maybe he'd just willed himself to stop breathing. He wondered what the autopsy would reveal, and if it would ever be made public.

Clayton worried about Kerney until Frank Vanmeter called

him on the handheld to say the illness wasn't serious, and that unless Kerney's symptoms worsened, he would rejoin the search in the morning. He'd missed Kerney's company. The last two days with him chasing Larson to hell and gone had been the best time he'd ever spent with his father. The man who only a few short years ago had been a stranger was now a true friend.

He tried to call Grace on his cell phone but couldn't get a signal. He raised Vanmeter on his handheld and asked him to relay a message to Grace letting her know he was okay.

"Anything else you'd like me to pass on?" Vanmeter asked.

"Tell her I'll call as soon as I can," Clayton replied.

"Ten-four."

Clayton ended the transmission, spread open a map on his sleeping bag, and used a flashlight to study it. Except for one drink in a streambed, the horses had gone without water since afternoon. In the morning, he needed to get them to the nearest water source before setting out on Larson's trail. He noted the closest water to his position, judged it to be less than two miles away, folded the map, and turned off the flashlight. He'd skip breakfast and get started before daybreak. That way he'd be back on Larson's trail early.

Where the rangeland ran against the foothills, a Forest Service road cut through a canyon and traveled deep into the mountains before ultimately hooking up to a state road that led to the tiny village of Costilla, just south of the Colorado border. There were some primitive campgrounds along the way, up around Ash Mountain, but for the most part the area was mainly wilderness.

For all his adult years, what Kerry Larson loved to do best with his free time was hunt, and time and again he had gone into the backcountry looking to take his annual buck during deer season. In the last twelve years he'd rarely failed to bring a big one home for the freezer.

Kerry knew every jeep trail, game trail, old abandoned mining road, footpath, and backcountry trace in those mountains. And by nightfall he was five miles beyond where he'd hidden his truck, sitting next to the bank of a crystal-clear stream that fed into the Vermejo River, wrapped in his coat to keep away the chill, eating peanut butter and crackers for his supper.

He figured to be north of the lodge at the ranch by midmorning, and no more than two hours away on foot from the valley where he and Craig had found that cave so long ago. If Craig wasn't already there, he would wait for him. And when he came, Kerry would make him give himself up to the police.

Kerry washed down his peanut butter and crackers with some water, curled up on a bed of pine needles he'd fashioned next to the streambed, and let the sound of rushing water lull him to sleep.

Craig Larson slept well but woke hungry. Hiking up and down ravines, canyons, and mountains, sometimes having to almost drag his horse to come along behind him, had given him quite an appetite. He checked the supply of food he'd taken from the pantry at the line camp in Dawson where Truman Goodson had caught his bullet. He was down to one can of sardines. He ate it quickly and saddled his horse. It was time to get more provisions, and that meant paying a visit to the ranch lodge. But first, he needed to find water and grass for the horse.

After two hours of difficult riding over rocky ground and through dense tree cover, Larson broke clear into a long finger-like meadow ringed by tall pines, causing a startled doe and her fawn to bolt for the woods. He dismounted and walked the horse to a stream where they both drank before he turned the animal loose to graze on the tall grass.

Larson wasn't exactly sure of his location, but he knew he was beyond the coal mine and the gravel pit and more or less parallel to the pavement that dead-ended at the ranch. Eventually he would top out on a summit that overlooked the valley where the lodge nestled. Once there, he'd stop and make a plan on how to conduct his attack.

He thought about Truman Goodson and decided to give him the moniker of "Good Old Truman." That way he could join Kid Cuddy, Ugly Nancy, Cowgirl Tami, and Porky Pettibone as victims firmly entrenched in Larson's mind. And how could he forgot *la cucaracha,* Bertie Roach, whose neck he'd snapped in that Albuquerque motel? An idea surfaced that he needed to come up with nicknames for all the people he'd killed. It would make the memorial plaque that much more historically interesting.

Larson let the horse graze for a good long time before riding on. Underneath a tall pine, he looked back and saw a rider trailing three horses come into view at the far end of the meadow. He pulled the Weatherby from the scabbard and looked through the scope. It was the Indian-looking cop he'd seen coming out of the Raton motel with the state police officer.

He sighted in on the cop and squeezed off a round. Horse and rider went down in the tall grass and neither got up. The three riderless horses, one saddle mount and two pack animals, scampered back into the trees.

Larson dismounted and fired five more rounds at the spot where the horse and rider had fallen. From his vantage point he couldn't tell if his shots had hit the mark. He waited a good ten minutes for any sign of life before scrambling partway up the slope to see if his quarry was down.

He cautiously peered around a tree and a bullet almost took

his ear off. Larson blind-fired rounds before retreating to his mount and riding away. He figured the cop's horse was dead. If the cop was unharmed, he'd have to round up his scattered animals before he could continue the chase.

Larson decided to get to higher ground, find a good spot, and pick the cop off if and when he closed the gap.

Cradling his rifle in his elbows, Clayton belly-crawled through the tall grass. He made it to the tree line, found cover, called in a 10-55, officer under fire, gave his location, and inspected the leg his roan had fallen on. From what he could tell it was maybe a pulled ligament and not broken. Standing behind a thick pine tree for protection, he stood up and put some weight on the leg. It didn't buckle.

He keyed his handheld and reported he was limping a bit but otherwise unhurt, then went looking for the buckskin and the two packhorses, and found them one by one. He returned to the edge of the meadow, secured the horses, and crawled back to the dead roan. It had taken all six rounds meant for Clayton. Keeping his head down, he removed the animal's saddle and bridle, secured the saddle on his back, and crawled to where the horses waited.

Kerney's voice came over the handheld as Clayton was about to circle the meadow and attempt to get behind Larson.

"Are you all right?" he demanded.

"Affirmative."

"I'm in a chopper five miles out. Give me your exact GPS coordinates."

Clayton did as asked. "I'm at the near edge of a narrow meadow," he added. "You can't miss it."

"Ten-four."

"If you're planning to come along with me," Clayton said,

"eighty-six the idea. The roan is dead and I'm riding the buckskin."

"You're not getting shot at again without backup," Kerney countered. "Put your saddle on one of the packhorses and stay off my buckskin. How far ahead is Larson?"

"No more than an hour if you hurry and he isn't perched somewhere up high waiting to pick us off."

"Is the meadow big enough for a safe landing?"

"It is." Clayton could hear the approaching chopper.

"Cover us if it's a hot LZ."

"Ten-four."

The bird came over the ridgeline, dropped fast into the meadow, and made a quick pass from one end to the other before delivering Kerney, who tumbled out the door and zigzagged to the trees.

Clayton walked to him and handed the reins to the buckskin. "Hold this while I saddle the packhorse," he said.

"You're limping," Kerney replied, eyeing Clayton's leg.

"Yeah, I'm limping and you've got a crabby gut." Clayton unhitched the frame from a packhorse and wrestled it to the ground.

"I'm better."

"That's good to hear," Clayton answered. "As soon as I'm on horseback I'll be better too, because I won't be limping."

Kerry Larson hiked through a thinned-out stand of trees at the edge of the valley where the Vermejo River gurgled clear and cold in a rocky streambed. He was well north of the ranch lodge, with one tall summit left to climb to reach the secluded valley where he and his brother had long ago rebuilt the old corral.

Kerry had been back several times since then on solo elk hunting trips. He always took some time to visit the hidden cave with the Indian drawings and watch the small herd of buffalo that roamed the fenced-in valley.

Although he had no way to prove it, Kerry knew for certain that his brother would come to that valley, and it wasn't just the mountain man comment that made him know it. In the past, he'd have hunches Craig was about to call him or had sent him something in the mail, and it would happen just like he thought.

He started up the mountain, his thighs aching from the effort, his calves still sore from his steep descent into the valley. He paused for a drink of water from the canteen in his backpack. What could he say to Craig to make him stop running? He had always bossed Kerry around, but not this time. Not this time.

Kerry concentrated his thoughts as he climbed, trying hard to put together words he could use to get Craig to do the right thing and give himself up.

Craig Larson heard the chopper and changed his mind about lying in wait to bushwhack the cop. He'd already passed beyond the meadow and didn't want to return and risk the possibility that the helicopter had landed and disgorged a half dozen more cops who were already scrambling up the hillside to run him down. He guided the horse through the trees as fast as it would go, stopping occasionally to listen for the sound of pursuit. Except for the wind in the trees and brief bird songs all was quiet behind him.

Larson walked the horse sideways down a steep gully where the tree cover parted enough to give him a glimpse of the highway below. Beyond the slight curve in the road he caught sight of a stretch of grassland, and hurried the gelding along to take a better look. He broke free of the trees on a rock shelf that gave him an unobstructed view of the valley and the ranch lodge with its many outbuildings, barns, stables, and corrals.

The lodge was an old timber-frame building with a pitched shingled roof, deep verandas, and massive stone chimneys. The guest parking lot adjacent to the building held a dozen expensive passenger cars and SUVs.

The barns and outbuildings sprinkled through the sheltered valley were of the same design as the lodge. A rectangular building set well back behind the stables had a gravel lot at the rear where an assortment of much less expensive vehicles were parked. Larson figured it to be staff housing.

In a large paddock in front of the stables were several sleek, fine-looking horses. Larson decided to bypass the lodge, see what kind of food he could grab in the staff quarters, and get a fresh mount from the paddock.

He doubted he would be able to get in and out without being spotted, so he checked the magazine in the Glock autoloader to make sure it was full before backing the horse off the outcropping and following a well-worn trail down to the valley.

Once on the valley floor, Larson spurred his horse toward the staff quarters, expecting to be seen and challenged. But nobody came to intercept him. He made it safely to the stables only to be greeted by a young freckle-faced woman who stepped outside to meet him.

"Can I help you?" the young woman asked.

Larson smiled as he slid off the horse, stuck the Glock in the young woman's face, and hustled her back inside the stables.

"Why, yes, you can, Cutie Pie," he said. "Tell me, where is everyone else beside you?"

"You're that man," the woman replied, almost screeching. "That man."

Larson put her in a headlock and pressed the Glock against

her eye. "I've got no time for small talk, Cutie Pie. Where is everybody?"

Cutie Pie swallowed hard before answering. "Most of the guests are out on a trail ride with our wranglers. The others are on a birding walk with our wildlife manager. And the lodge staff are getting ready for an early evening wedding reception."

"That's good, Cutie Pie," Larson said, easing the pressure on her neck. "The building behind the stables is where the staff lives, right?"

The woman nodded. She had pretty blue eyes filled with tears.

"Who is there right now?"

"Nobody. Everyone's at work."

"What about the gardeners who keep the grounds ship-shape?"

"There's only one gardener and he's helping set up for the wedding party."

"Is there food at the staff quarters?"

"Yes, we have our own kitchen."

"Good. Let's go." Larson released his grip and poked her in the kidney with the Glock. "Act natural. Try to run, and I'll kill you. Scream or shout, and I'll kill you. Understand?"

"Yes."

Inside the staff quarters, Larson found the refrigerator and cupboards well stocked. He ordered Cutie Pie to fill a pillowcase with food and carry it back to the stables.

He walked behind her, prodding her along with the Glock. "What's your name, Cutie Pie?" he asked.

"Celia Calvin."

"I'm gonna make you famous."

"How? By murdering me?"

Larson laughed as he pushed her into the stables. "I probably should. No, I'm gonna let you live so you can tell people Craig Larson didn't hurt you much."

"How much is not much?"

Larson slapped her. "I hate a smart mouth on a woman. Don't make me change my mind about killing you. You tell them I didn't violate you. No rapine, as the old-timers used to call it. You tell them Craig Larson was a gentleman. That he tipped his hat to you and thanked you for the food and the loan of a horse. You got that?"

"Okay."

"Say it!" Larson ordered with a snarl.

"No rapine," she replied in a shaky voice. "You were a gentleman who treated me like a lady."

Larson bared his teeth and smiled. "That's good. Real good. Bring that chestnut mare in here and saddle it for me."

Celia did as she was told. When she finished, he clubbed her on the side of the head with the Glock, laid her facedown on the floor, hogtied her with rope, and stuck a rag in her mouth. He packed the food from the pillowcase into saddlebags, transferred the sheathed Weatherby to his fresh horse, and mounted up.

Behind the stables and the staff quarters, the forest underbrush had been cleared and the trees thinned, creating a parklike setting. There were several well-marked trails that led to vantage points above the valley, complete with signs giving the mileage to each destination. Larson followed the trail that took him in the general direction of the buffalo pasture and the cave hidden in the mountainside.

He was about to leave the trail and strike out cross-country when a man packing a sidearm and leading a group of four sturdy-looking boomers, two men and two women, came into view. They all had binoculars around their necks and wore floppy hats, hiking shorts, and hiking boots.

When the man with the *pistola* held up his hand and told Larson to stop, he shot him with the Glock. The boomers looked on in stunned silence for a minute until one of the women started to scream.

He pointed the Glock at her but didn't pull the trigger. "Shut the fuck up!" he yelled.

She covered her mouth and gagged for air.

"I should kill you all," Larson announced, "but I won't. Because I want you to tell the law it was a fair fight. You tell them he was gonna draw down on me. Understand?"

The foursome nodded in unison.

Larson waved the Glock at the dead man. "What was his name?"

"Wade Christopher," one of the men replied, his gaze fixed firmly on the ground.

Larson smiled. "Wade. I like that name. It's a good Western name. I'm proud to have shot him down." He pointed the Glock in the direction of the lodge. "Get going, before I change my mind."

The foursome moved quickly around the body, sidestepped Larson on the chestnut mare, and scurried down the trail. He fired a couple of bullets in the air to hurry them along and continued up the mountain.

Chapter Twelve

Clayton and Kerney arrived at the ranch and learned that a young woman, sobbing in the arms of the resort manager, had been knocked unconscious and tied up by Larson. Four very distraught lodge guests who'd witnessed Larson shoot down the ranch wild-life manager on a hiking trail huddled nearby. They didn't know if the victim was alive or dead.

Clayton called it in as they rode hard to reach the spot where the man had been gunned down. Before they were out of sight of the lodge, the first of a string of wailing squad cars could be heard coming up the canyon.

At the crime scene Kerney advised Vanmeter by radio that the victim was dead.

"According to the resort manager, there's a large group of guests out on a guided trail ride," he added, "and a wedding re-ception is scheduled for this evening at the lodge. Let's get the re-ception canceled, a roadblock set up on the ranch road to keep people out, the trail riders found and brought in, all guests and staff accounted for, and everyone under police protection, ready to be evacuated quickly if need be."

"Ten-four."

"We're moving on," Kerney said.

"Best to wait for backup," Vanmeter replied.

"There's no time to wait. We're closer to Larson than we've ever been. Put some SWAT sharpshooters on the chopper, bring them to the ranch, and have them ready to go airborne at a moment's notice. That's our backup. I'll call for it if and when we need it."

"Affirmative. Be careful out there."

"Let's all be careful," Kerney replied.

Up ahead, Clayton waited impatiently. When Kerney joined up, Clayton pointed at trampled bunchgrass under some trees.

"He's traveling cross-country," Clayton said as he turned his horse to go up the trail. "I checked one of the maps the game and fish officer gave us. The only logical place he can be heading is to a small mountain valley above us. There's a notation on the map that it's home to a small buffalo herd owned by the ranch. Other than that, it's rugged, uninhabited country."

"Why in the blazes is he going there?" Kerney asked as he came abreast of Clayton's horse.

Clayton shook his head. "Don't know, but if we stay on the trail for another mile or so, we'll intersect a jeep track that will take us right to the valley. If we push it, we may even be able to get there before him."

"Then let's ride." Kerney spurred his horse and left Clayton, who was astride a less than speedy packhorse he'd drafted as his mount, in the dust.

Kerry Larson reached the valley where the buffalo, enclosed by a high fence, were clustered on three hundred acres near one of the streambeds that drained out of the higher peaks and coursed through the basin. The land never got a break from the animals, and the tall grassland and wildflower meadows that had once filled the valley had been grazed and trampled into hardpan. The shallow, wandering, clear streams had been turned into deep, fast-running gullies bounded by eroded banks.

Kerry thought the cattle down on the short grass prairie ranches lived better than these poor animals, who survived on feed brought in by ranch hands on the jeep track. He'd learned somewhere that these were domestic buffalo. Dangerous, as any big animal on the hoof could be, but not wild. They still needed to roam though, maybe not like the truly wild ones up north somewhere in a national park, but enough so the land could heal and not be ground to powder under their hoofs.

Kerry circled the fence, looking for sign that Craig had arrived. Finding none, he climbed the side of a mountain that rose almost vertically from the valley floor, and went directly to the mouth of the small cave he'd discovered with his brother that summer long ago. It was hard to spot the opening through the thick branches of an ancient mountain mahogany, but once there, he threw some stones inside just in case some critters had taken up residence. The stones caused no ruckus, but to be make sure it wasn't home to a rattlesnake nest, he shined his flashlight around before crawling in.

For a few minutes he sat and looked at the Indian drawings that were still visible on the cave walls. There were deer and bear figures and one of a hunter with a bow and arrow. But his favorite was a warrior wearing a headdress. Down in one corner of the back wall, he and Craig had carved their initials in the rock, along with the date. Kerry ran his hand over the letters, remembering the good times with his brother.

He wrapped his small backpack containing his remaining supply of food and water in his coat and went outside to find a good place to wait on Craig's arrival. With his back against a big old pine tree and a clear view of the whole valley, he settled in, his rifle close at hand.

He still hadn't come up with any good words to use on his brother. He was slow all right, just like Craig always said he was.

But he wasn't a bad man, and he didn't want his brother to be bad anymore.

Not long after leaving the trail where he'd met up with the pistol-packing guide and his flock of bird-loving tourists, Larson found himself on a well-used jeep track that traveled straight up over a summit and down some switchbacks to the valley. At the crest he stopped and looked over the buffalo herd clustered behind the high post-and-wire fence at the far end of the basin. He counted twenty animals, including four calves. That wasn't as many as he'd hoped for, and they looked none too wild and woolly, but if he could get them stampeded, it still might be fun to see how many he could bring down with the Weatherby Mark V.

A rifle shot from the far side of the valley cut through the air. Larson jumped off the chestnut mare, pulled the Weatherby, and hit the dirt, looking frantically for the shooter. Another shot echoed through the peaks, followed by the sound of his brother's voice calling him.

Cursing, Larson stood, used the scope of the rifle to scan the mountainside across the valley, and spotted Kerry clutching a long gun and waving at him with his free hand. He hollered, waved back, got on the chestnut, and started down the switchbacks, totally mystified. How could Kerry have possibly known where to come looking for him? More than that, what in the hell was he doing here?

He kept his gaze fixed on his brother as he dropped down the mountain, watching Kerry scramble to the fence line and run along the perimeter toward a gate a good half mile distant. Seeing no horse or vehicle, Larson figured Kerry had hiked into the valley. But why?

A wave of paranoia unexpectedly hit Larson. He pulled the

chestnut to a quick stop. What if Kerry had brought the cops here to ambush him? Or barring that, what if the cops had been smart enough to follow his dumb-ass brother? He did a tight three-sixty on the chestnut, looking for any movement or glint of a reflection off a gun barrel or sunglasses. Heart racing, he scanned high and low, half expecting to feel the sudden impact of a slug take him down. After a long ten seconds, nothing had happened. He hurried the chestnut to the valley floor and galloped to his brother, who was still a good quarter mile away from the gate to the high fence.

"What in the hell are you doing here?" Larson shouted as he closed the gap. He slipped out of the saddle, tied the chestnut mare to a fence post, and watched his brother jog the final fifty yards.

Winded, Kerry slowed to a walk and caught his breath. "I came to take you home," he said with an apologetic smile.

"Do what?" Larson replied incredulously. "What the fuck are you talking about?"

Kerry stopped three feet away from his brother, his hand tight on the stock of his rifle. "Take you home so you can stand up for me and make it right."

"Make what right?" Larson demanded.

"That I'm not the cause of you killing all those people."

"What is that supposed to mean?"

"People say I told you about Lenny Hampton turning you in to the police and that's what started you off being a killer. If I hadn't said anything, you just would have gone away."

"But you did tell me about Lenny, didn't you?" Larson said with a short laugh.

Kerry hung his head. "Not to get him hurt. Or those other people either."

Larson smiled. "Well, let me ease your pain, little brother. I started killing people long before I left your pal Lenny Hampson begging for his life in the desert. Does that make you feel any better? Or do you need a note to take back to all your friends explaining that you're not to blame for the notches on my gun?"

"Don't make fun of me."

"I wouldn't think of it," Larson snapped. "But now that I turn the situation over in my mind, it comes to me that you could be an accessory after the fact."

"What's that?"

"Somebody who helped me get away from the police."

"Because you lied to me."

"The cops aren't going to believe that."

Kerry squared his shoulders, both hands locked on his rifle. "That's why I need you to come with me and give yourself up. To tell the truth."

Larson laughed in his brother's face as his hand found the grip of the Glock autoloader. "Never gonna happen, younger brother. And if you point that rifle at me, I'll shoot you down, brother or not."

"So you can pretend to be me, right? Just like you said the other day."

"It's an idea with some merit," Larson allowed. "How did you know I'd be here?"

Kerry shrugged. "I just thought on it for a spell and figured this is where you'd come."

Larson laughed. "Well, isn't that something? And here I didn't even know I was headed this way myself. Are you sure you weren't followed?"

"I know I wasn't, but you were."

"You're right about that, little brother. Are you gonna stay and help me when the cops get here?"

"I'll help you give yourself up."

Larson groaned in mock disappointment. "That's not it. I want you to help me shoot the sons-of-bitches."

Kerry shook his head. "I won't do that."

"Then you're worthless to me." Larson tilted his head in the direction of the buffalo herd at the far end of the valley. "But that's okay. You always have been."

Larson and Kerry locked eyes. *It's like looking in a mirror, but it's not,* Larson thought. "Let's you and me shoot those buffalo before the cops get here," he said. "Then you can skedaddle."

"What?" Kerry asked, mystified.

"I've heard that when they're running, the ground shakes. And when you shoot them while they're at a full gallop, the thud when they fall sounds like a small explosion. Man, I'd like to see that."

Kerry looked at his brother as if he were a stranger. "That's a bad-crazy idea. It's just more killing for no cause."

"You think so?" Larson snarled. "I'll tell you what a bad-crazy idea is. Firing your rifle twice in the air was really bad-crazy. Now the cops know exactly where I am, even if they're five miles back."

He stepped up to Kerry and pushed him hard in the chest with the flat of his hand. "Just walk away from me. Get the hell out of here before I shoot you. Go home. Go back to your spark plugs and grease gun, and your simpleminded life. Get going."

"You're gonna get yourself killed," Kerry said.

"Maybe so. But if you stay, I'll probably get you killed too. Go on now."

Kerry dropped his gaze and hesitated.

"Get," Larson ordered sternly. "Do as you're told."

Kerry turned, stepped away, stopped, and looked back, his expression like that of a crestfallen puppy.

"Go," Larson repeated, more severely.

Reluctantly, Kerry walked away, headed back the way he'd come. Larson watched him for a few minutes before mounting up. He turned the chestnut toward the mouth of the valley, where he had spotted a ledge about two hundred feet up the side of the mountain that would give him cover and a great vantage point. That was where he would make his stand.

He looked back once in Kerry's direction. He was nowhere to be seen. Maybe he was hiding in the woods waiting to see what happened and would still manage to get himself killed before the day was out.

Larson decided he couldn't worry about Kerry anymore. For a time, he had honestly believed that killing him would have been as easy as pie. But when he'd tried to work himself up to pulling the trigger, he'd realized that it just wasn't in him.

Must be brotherly love, Larson thought with a snicker as he guided the chestnut to the ledge.

The sound of a rifle shot brought Kerney and Clayton to a full stop. The second shot got them out of their saddles and moving cautiously on foot up the jeep track. Just shy of the crest, they dropped down and belly-crawled to a mountaintop shelf shaded by the broad branches of a tall pine tree. They scanned the valley floor and surrounding peaks using binoculars. Below, a small herd of buffalo moved slowly inside a fence that ringed the confined basin. Above, a pair of ravens floated on thermals in the cloudless midday sky.

"See anything?" Kerney whispered.

Clayton shook his head. "Other than a bunch of buffalo in a used-up dust bowl, nothing."

"Me neither. He could be right below us, or off to one side or the other."

Clayton put his binoculars aside and turned over on his back. "So other than us becoming targets for him to shoot at, how do we get him to make his play?"

"We could ask him pretty please to give up," Kerney said as he turned on his side to face Clayton. "Or better yet, we could ask Kerry to ask him to give up. That's assuming Kerry is still alive after finding his brother."

"And here I thought you missed those fresh footprints we passed on the jeep track," Clayton replied with a hint of approval in his voice.

"Not likely." Kerney returned to scanning with his binoculars. "Let's assume Kerry has joined up with his brother. That might not be the case, but I'd rather err on the side of caution."

"Agreed." Clayton flipped back on his stomach. "So how do we smoke them out?"

"You stay here while I move to the other side of the valley. Once I'm on the ridge across from you with a good line of sight into the basin, I'll have the chopper bring in the SWAT team. That should get both brothers' attention."

"There's no cover down there," Clayton said.

"I'll tell Vanmeter to have the team treat it as a hot LZ." Kerney pointed to a small clearing outside the fence line, near a stand of trees. "If the pilot lands the bird there, the team can get to cover quickly. Once they flush our targets or draw their fire, we can take our best shots."

Clayton nodded. "Ten-four. You stay here. I'll head over to the other side."

"No, you won't," Kerney said as he started to crawl back away from the shelf. "I've seen the way you've been walking, and don't tell me it doesn't hurt like hell. You probably tore a ligament when that horse fell on you. Maybe you even cracked a bone. Stay put and stay alert."

• • •

At the mouth of the cave, Kerry Larson removed the scope from his rifle, stretched out behind the branches of the mahogany bush, and quickly spotted Craig working his way up the mountainside riding the chestnut horse. The trees rose straight up on the rocky, steep slope, and twice the chestnut slipped badly and sunk to its haunches as it scrambled around a tall pine.

Finally, Craig got out of the saddle and led the horse up to a ledge where they disappeared for a minute into heavy timber. When Craig came back on foot, he was carrying two long guns and a bag. He leaned the rifles against a large, jagged rock and took boxes of ammunition and two handguns out of the bag. Kerry couldn't see Craig anymore after he settled down behind the rock, but he could see the faint swishing of the horse's tail in the trees behind him: a sure giveaway sign for anyone with a pair of binoculars and a keen eye.

Kerry used the scope to search either side of the jeep track that dropped over the crest to the valley below. It was the only way in, short of breaking a new trail, which would be pretty much impossible to do without chain saws, bulldozers, and a crew of twenty men. When the cops came, they would come that way.

For a moment Kerry thought he saw a quick movement on a shelf off to one side of the track. He held the scope steady on the spot but the only things moving were tree branches in the gusty wind.

The question of what he should do when the cops came pounded through his head, over and over. Help Craig? Help the cops?

Sometimes, when he couldn't get something figured out, he used a trick he'd learned as a child to clear his mind. He put the scope back on his rifle, crawled into the cave, sat, folded his arms across his chest, closed his eyes, and rocked back and forth.

• • •

It took Kerney more than an hour to hike through the forest and find a good location with a sweeping view of the valley. He scanned for Craig Larson and his brother before plugging his headset into his handheld radio and reporting his position to Clayton.

"Okay," Clayton replied after a brief pause. "I've got your twenty. Any sign of our targets?"

"I thought I saw some movement in among the trees behind an outcropping, but I can't be sure."

"What if Kerry Larson didn't come here to join up with his brother?" Clayton asked. "And if he is here, how are we going to tell the twins apart?"

"Good questions. Once SWAT lands and finds cover, we'll have the team leader broadcast an appeal asking Kerry to stay out of harm's way. I'm calling SWAT in now. Stay alert. Put down suppressing fire if one or both of them go after the chopper."

"Ten-four."

Kerney made the call and Vanmeter gave him a five-minute ETA. When he heard the approaching chopper, the sound of the rotors and the threat of Craig Larson out there somewhere, armed and dangerous, put Kerney back into the Vietnam jungle for an instant. He shook off the flashback just as the bird crested the mountain and dropped quickly toward the LZ.

Larson fired twice at the helicopter before Kerney spotted him on the outcropping he'd scanned a few minutes earlier. He zeroed in his Browning rifle and squeezed off three quick rounds. Across the way, Clayton, who had no line of sight, held his fire.

"Where is he?" Clayton asked.

Larson fired again at the descending chopper and ducked behind the large boulder. Kerney's bullets ricocheted and splintered into shrapnel off the rock face.

"He's about a quarter mile on your right and two hundred feet down. He's on a rock outcropping behind a boulder."

"I can't see it from here. I'm moving."

Larson's next bullet cut the air six inches above Kerney's head before it tore into a tree trunk. Kerney scooted back to cover.

"Keep in sight," Kerney answered, "and I'll guide you into position. Larson can't see you."

"Any sign of Kerry?"

"Negative."

Larson rose up and fired once more at the chopper as it landed, and Kerney's bullet creased the boulder next to his head. Larson answered with a shot that blew rock fragments off the spot Kerney had just vacated. He responded with suppressing fire that kept Larson's rifle silent while the SWAT team made it to the cover of the trees.

Spooked by the helicopter and the gunfire, the buffalo herd began to stampede away from the chopper. When Larson started firing again, it was at the buffalo. Two big animals went down before he quit shooting. As the herd thundered by Kerney's position, kicking up a cloud of dust from the hardpan valley floor, he saw a flash of movement behind the boulder.

"Stand fast," he radioed Clayton as he focused on the outcropping with his binoculars. "I think Larson's on the move."

"I'm holding," Clayton replied.

Kerney kept the glasses locked on Larson's position. There was a quick movement in the trees and then nothing. Below, under the tree cover at the edge of the basin, the SWAT commander's voice came over the bullhorn, asking Kerry Larson to lay down any weapons he had, make his whereabouts known, keep his hands in plain sight, and remain calm until an officer reached him.

"Well?" Clayton demanded.

Kerney saw the backside of a horse with a man hunched over

a saddle flash between two trees. "He's on horseback but I can't tell whether he's traveling up or down the mountain." He slung the binoculars around his neck, retreated farther into the forest, and started down the slope. "I'm heading to the valley floor."

"Roger that," Clayton replied. "I'll stay up high and track him from here."

"Ten-four." Kerney passed the word by radio to the SWAT commander, told him to have his people concentrate the search on the south side of the valley, and continued down the mountain, slipping on the steep slope and fighting his way through thick underbrush.

Once again, the sound of the SWAT commander's voice rang out over the bullhorn, telling Kerry Larson to disarm himself, keep his hands in plain view, remain calm, and await the arrival of an officer to take him into custody.

Kerney hoped Kerry would do as he was told and avoid getting shot.

Twice Kerry Larson heard somebody calling his name and saying to stay put and remain calm, or something like that. He couldn't catch it all inside the cave, but from the sound of the arriving helicopter and the shooting, he knew the cops were in a gunfight with his brother.

He collected his thoughts for a moment. He could either stay hidden until the shooting stopped or go out and see what the cops wanted with him. He worried that maybe he would be arrested for that "after the fact" thing Craig said he'd done, being an accessory or something. That Indian cop had said the same thing at the state police station in Springer and showed him the writing in the law book.

He couldn't stand the idea of going to jail. It scared the beje-sus out of him. He needed to put into words that he'd come here to get his brother to give up, not to help him, and that he hadn't been in cahoots with Craig to help him get away.

He grabbed his rifle and crawled out of the cave into the blind-ing sunlight. Clutching the weapon, he blinked to clear his vi-sion, scampered down to the flats, and started walking along the fence line. He passed two dead buffalo and shook his head at the idea that Craig had killed them for the fun of it. At the gate, he paused and looked through his rifle sight at the ledge where he'd last seen his brother. All the ammo and weapons Craig had arranged on the outcropping were gone, a sure sign he'd moved on.

"Drop the rifle," a voice behind him said, "then raise your hands and turn around slowly."

Kerry turned. Twenty feet away stood the policeman who had partnered up with the Indian cop to track his brother down. He had a nasty-looking semiautomatic rifle pointed at Kerry's chest.

"Don't shoot me."

"Drop the rifle," Kerney repeated.

"I wasn't going to hurt anybody," Kerry replied, as he laid his rifle carefully on the ground.

"I believe you. Step away from the weapon and back up to the gate with your hands raised."

"Okay." Kerry walked backward to the gate, his hands high above his head.

Kerney approached, kicked the rifle away, and quickly cuffed Kerry to a gate railing. "You'll be okay. No one will hurt you. Someone will be here shortly."

Kerry nodded, and then looked up at the rock ledge.

"We know where he is," Kerney said, following his gaze.

"He's bad-crazy," Kerry whispered, half-afraid Craig might hear him.

"I know," Kerney replied as he started a zigzag run across the narrow valley, hoping bad-crazy Craig wasn't looking at him through the scope of his rifle, about to gun him down.

Clayton hugged the ridgeline, traveling as fast as his bum leg would carry him, the pain shooting through his kneecap with each step. He slipped on a loose rock, and the jolt to his knee made him pause and catch his breath. He couldn't tell if he'd cracked a bone in his leg, but the fibula felt real sore. Maybe it was just a bruised bone.

He pushed on, dipped below the ridgeline twice and clambered back up, before finding some fresh hoofprints. He followed them for a while before checking in with Kerney by radio.

"He's moving laterally, deeper into the forest," he said into his headset.

"Give me your twenty," Kerney responded.

Clayton described what he could see of the mountainside beneath his feet.

"Got it," Kerney replied. "I'm coming up. How's your leg?"

"Fine," Clayton responded as he started out again, wincing at the pain.

"Don't give me that. Stay where you are."

"Negative. He's no more than five minutes ahead of me."

"Is that based on traveling with two good legs or one?" Kerney shot back.

"I'm moving," Clayton answered flatly.

Kerney spied a narrow ravine that coursed down the mountain about a hundred yards from Clayton's summit location. He ran to the mouth of the ravine and began scrambling up, at times pulling himself over large rocks, the Browning slung on his back and his binoculars bouncing on his chest.

Halfway up, a small rockfall cascading through the trees caused Kerney to stop. He looked just in time to see Clayton tumble down a steep slope and land hard, his rifle flying through the air and clattering a hundred feet below.

Kerney called out but got no answer. He climbed the ravine as fast as he could, repeatedly shouting Clayton's name. It took ten minutes of hard going to reach him, alive but unconscious with what appeared to be a broken leg. With a pocketknife, Kerney cut Clayton's pant leg. There was bruising and swelling around the lower leg but no visible sign of fracture. Discoloration marked the side of Clayton's skull and Kerney felt a knot above his left ear.

But his color was good, his skin dry to the touch, his pulse regular, and his breathing strong. Because of the possibility of a head injury, Kerney didn't elevate Clayton's feet. He contacted the SWAT commander and asked if there was a medic on the team.

"Affirmative. Officer Hurley was a combat medic in Afghanistan."

"Send him to me," Kerney said. "I have an officer down with a broken leg and a possible head injury. He's unconscious."

Hurley's voice came over Kerney's headset. "Is he in shock?"

"Not so far as I can tell."

"Give me your location."

Kerney told him where to look and pitched some baseball-size rocks over the treetops, as a visual cue for Hurley.

"I have you."

"Larson's brother is cuffed to the fence gate," Kerney added.

"We have him in custody," the SWAT commander replied.

"Send the rest of your team east of my position, and put the chopper up for aerial recon. Larson is moving away from the valley."

"Ten-four."

Kerney used his shirt to make a pillow for Clayton's head and stayed with him, hoping he would wake up, but he didn't. Every few minutes he checked Clayton's pulse and respiration while he guided the SWAT team medic to him over his headset.

When Officer Hurley arrived, he quickly inspected Clayton's skull. "No major swelling around the knot on his head. That's good."

He took Clayton's vitals before inspecting the leg. "No signs of shock, and the break isn't a compound fracture. All good news."

Relieved, Kerney nodded.

Clayton opened his eyes, and before Kerney could say a word, Hurley quizzed him to make sure he wasn't disoriented, sick to his stomach, or agitated.

"How's the leg feel?" he asked.

"It hurts. Who are you?"

"Pat Hurley. I'm going to immobilize the leg and give you a painkiller, which should help. But it's gonna take a while to get you off this mountain. I'll stay with you."

"That's okay, I'm not going anywhere." Clayton smiled apologetically at Kerney. "Sorry to have slowed you down."

Kerney squeezed Clayton's hand. "Not a problem. I'll check back on you in a while."

"Okay. Be careful."

Kerney picked up his Browning, told the SWAT commander over his headset he was rejoining the hunt, and started climbing.

•••

Craig Larson didn't like being shot at. *Stopping the cops* only made good sense if he could kill them when they weren't expecting it. Better yet, it was best to kill them when they were unarmed and not expecting it. The cop who had been shooting at him from across the valley had nearly killed him twice, dammit.

He hadn't gotten very far into the forest when the chestnut lost its footing, spooked, and almost scraped a ponderosa. Larson ducked to avoid a branch, but the tree limb took him out of the saddle anyway and left him sitting on the ground with a throbbing head.

The horse skedaddled before Larson could reach up and grab the reins, and he was left with only the Glock autoloader and one spare magazine. He got on his feet and started walking. If he was going to survive, he needed to catch that chestnut and retrieve the Weatherby and the rest of his ammo.

Up ahead, the sound of a deep, short blow by the chestnut, followed by a loud whinny, got Larson's attention. He found it with the reins hung up in some thick underbrush, still carrying the Weatherby and the ammo bag. He got it untangled, mounted up, and headed in a direction that would take him around the valley and into higher, rougher country closer to the Colorado state line.

Off in the distance, Kerney heard the whinny of Larson's horse. He broke into a steady jog toward the sound of it. In the dense, overgrown forest, Larson had little advantage over a man on foot. In pursuit, Kerney dodged trees and skirted groves of mountain mahogany bushes until he came upon a faint game trail. He followed it, running faster, pushing aside the branches of new-growth pine trees that crowded the trace. After about a quarter mile, the trail widened and became more distinct. There, he found fresh hoofprints.

Kerney slowed to a walk, his heart pounding and his chest heaving from running in the thin mountain air. There were tail hairs from the horse in some of the pine branches that overhung the trail, and up ahead a warm pile of dung. He stopped, put a fresh clip in the Browning, switched off the safety, and started moving, treading lightly, breathing as quietly as he could, his eyes scanning for the slightest movement.

The chestnut was completely done in. It walked with its head lowered, mouth open, and showed bared teeth as though prepared to bite. It lashed its tail in irritation and slowed to a stop even after Larson spurred it. He slid out of the saddle, took the Weatherby and ammo bag, turned the animal loose, and watched it wander slowly down the trail.

He was about to follow along on the trail when he heard a sound behind him. He turned to find the cop who used to be the Santa Fe police chief holding a Browning semiautomatic rifle on him.

"How many more cops are there?" Larson asked.

"Enough," Kerney said, "and they all want to kill you."

Larson dropped the Weatherby and ammo bag. "So, I give up. That way none of you can kill me."

"Why spoil all the fun?" Kerney asked, pointing the Browning at the Glock semiautomatic stuck in Larson's waistband. "Are you sure you don't want to go for that Glock?"

"Against your Browning?" Larson shook his head. "No way."

"I'll lose the Browning. Fair enough?"

Larson considered the offer. Maybe he had a chance if he could pull the Glock and get a round off while the cop was losing the Browning. He needed time to think about it. But adding another cop's name to the plaque of his kills at the St. James Hotel would be really bitching.

"Did you guys kill my brother?" he asked.

"Don't change the subject," Kerney replied. "Do you want a chance against me, or a lethal cocktail mixed up especially for you at the state penitentiary?"

The cop looked like a dangerous mother. All of a sudden the idea of prison didn't seem so bad to him. He raised his hands over his head. "I know you. You used to be the police chief in Santa Fe, right?"

"Right." Kerney shot him in the midsection with the Browning.

Larson sunk to his knees and clutched himself. "You weren't supposed to do that."

Kerney walked up, pulled the Glock from his waistband, and tossed it aside. "Why not?"

The first wave of shock hit Larson hard. "Rules," he sputtered. "You're supposed to follow the rules."

"In your case, I made an exception."

Larson shivered. "Get me help. Please."

"You're liver shot, Larson. You'll be dead in under twenty minutes."

"Please," Larson begged. "Help me."

Kerney backed away from Larson and waited for him to lose consciousness. Then he called Clayton and told him the hunt was over.

"Larson's just about dead," Kerney added.

"How dead is that?" Clayton asked.

"Ninety-five percent dead."

"Ninety-five percent. That's good."

"I think so. How are you doing?"

"Officer Hurley says if the rescue team doesn't drop me when they haul me off this mountain, I should survive with no permanent damage to my leg or my thick head."

"I like your odds."

"Yeah, me too," Clayton said. "Thanks for making Larson mostly dead."

"I had no choice," Kerney replied.

Chapter Thirteen

Kerney stayed with Clayton as the rescue team carried him safely down the mountain and put him on a helicopter for a short flight to the Raton hospital. The remainder of the day he spent wrapping things up. Convinced that Kerry Larson had not deliberately or knowingly colluded with his brother, Kerney released him from custody and had an officer drive him to where he'd hidden his truck. He took statements from the young woman Larson had battered and the guests who'd witnessed the murder of the ranch employee on the trail. He debriefed with the SWAT team, made arrangements to return the borrowed horses and equipment used to track Larson, and talked to the ranch owner about compensation for the roan that had been shot out from under Clayton.

Late in the afternoon, Andy Baca flew in from the Santa Fe headquarters with his boss, the governor's cabinet secretary for public safety, and the state police captain in charge of internal affairs. The trio stopped by the Raton hospital to check on Clayton before making the short hop to the lodge, where the resort manager turned over his office for Kerney's use. Although Pat Hurley had reassured Kerney that Clayton's injuries were not serious, he was relieved to hear Andy report that Clayton was alert, fidgety, and eager to go home.

Kerney spent a good hour briefing Andy and his boss on the conclusion of the manhunt and the shoot-out. After the brass left to talk to Vanmeter and the SWAT team leader, the IA captain came in. He advised Kerney that any official statement he might wish to make regarding the use of lethal force in the shooting death of Craig Larson would be viewed by the department as a pro forma exercise. He turned on a small tape recorder and asked Kerney to describe the events leading up to and during the shooting. Kerney took the cue and said that he'd come upon the heavily armed subject in the forest and had been forced to shoot him to stop the action and protect his own life.

The captain nodded, turned off the tape recorder, told Kerney he would report to Chief Baca that it had been a righteous shooting, shook his hand, and went off to take statements from Vanmeter and the SWAT team leader. As far as Kerney knew, it was possibly the shortest official investigation ever into a deadly shooting by a police officer.

In Raton, Kerney went to visit Clayton at the hospital while Andy Baca, the cabinet secretary for public safety, the county sheriff, and the local police chief held a press conference on the steps of the county courthouse to officially announce that Craig Larson had been killed during an intense gunfight in a remote mountain valley. Television reporters from stations in Colorado, Oklahoma, West Texas, and New Mexico were on hand sending live feeds to all the broadcast networks and cable news channels.

The ER staff had put Clayton in a wheelchair and parked him in a room where he could watch the proceedings on television.

"The brass are making some big political hay out of this one," he said as Kerney entered the room, "big-time."

"As well they should," Kerney replied. "It's a gripping story with a good ending. Justice prevails. Order is restored, and folks are once again safe in their homes. Have you called Grace yet?"

"Yep." Clayton pushed the Mute button on the TV remote. "She knows I have a sore head and a broken leg. She knows it, but doesn't like it."

Kerney laughed. "I wouldn't think so. You're officially on medical leave. Andy has arranged to have you sent home by ambulance tonight. He also wants to talk to you about staying on with the department once you're fully recovered."

Clayton shrugged a shoulder. "I'm not sure about that."

"I know, but it's quite a compliment nonetheless. The state police don't often bring officers from other departments into their fold without making them start at the bottom of the ladder."

"It's not a decision I can make alone."

"Call Grace and tell her you're coming home."

After Clayton called Grace, the two men watched the tail end of the news conference until a male nurse stuck his head inside the open door to announce that Clayton's ride was ready. Outside the entrance to the ER, Kerney helped the driver load Clayton into the ambulance, said good-bye, closed the rear doors, and told the driver to run with his emergency lights on all the way to the Mescalero Apache Indian Reservation.

At the motel, he stood under the shower for a good ten minutes, letting the hot water wash away some of the tension in his muscles and bones. He hadn't eaten all day, but he was too tired to care and really didn't feel all that hungry anyway. He swallowed some of the over-the-counter medicine the doctor had told him to take for his gut, rolled into bed, and was asleep within minutes.

A week into Clayton's convalescent leave, Andy Baca paid him a visit at home while Grace was at work and Wendell and Hannah were at their grandmother's house for the afternoon.

"How soon do you get off the crutches?" he asked.

"Another two weeks. The doc says I'm healing up nicely."

"Have you thought any more about staying on with us?" Andy asked. "I have an investigator slot open in Las Cruces, but I could transfer the position to the Alamogordo office. It would shorten the work commute for you. And the pay is a hell of a lot better than what you were making with the sheriff's department."

"It's tempting," Clayton said as he walked to an easy chair, leaned his crutches against the armrest, and eased himself onto the cushion.

Andy settled on the couch. "What's holding you back?"

"If the Capitan police chief gets elected sheriff in November, and his chances are pretty good, he wants to bring me back at my old rank of lieutenant in January."

"Does that possibility appeal to you?"

"I'm not sure."

"How about this idea until you do decide," Andy said. "Finish your convalescent leave and continue to work for me in the Alamogordo office. If you feel you must rejoin the Lincoln County S.O. when the new sheriff gets sworn in, so be it."

Clayton's eyes widened in surprise. "You'd do that?"

"Yep, for selfish reasons only."

"Such as?"

"Well, aside from the fact that you're a hell of a good detective, it would be bad PR if you weren't working for me when we pin the departmental Medal of Valor on your chest."

Clayton looked stunned. "What?"

"We're giving one to Kerney also."

"He deserves it." Clayton shook his head. "But me . . ."

"Do you have a problem with this?"

"Giving me a medal for getting my horse shot out from under me, breaking a leg, and knocking myself unconscious doesn't make much sense."

"That's not quite how the citation will read," Andy replied with a chuckle. "Don't be so modest. The cabinet secretary wants to present the medals to you and Kerney at a Santa Fe ceremony."

"When?"

"We haven't set a date yet. It depends on when we can get Kerney back from London."

"Does he know about this?"

"Not yet, but I suspect he'll be just as cantankerous as you about it." Andy rose and stepped over to Clayton. "Do we have an agreement?"

"It's an offer I can't refuse," Clayton replied with a grin. He pulled himself upright, stuck the crutches under his arms, and gave Andy his hand. "Thank you, Chief."

Andy patted Clayton on the shoulder. "I'll let the Alamogordo office know to start making room for you. Call me as soon as you have a date when you can return to work. We can put you on light duty for a while, if need be."

"Yes, sir," Clayton replied.

He walked Andy to the door, watched him drive away, and returned to the easy chair. Clayton hadn't told Chief Baca that the tribal council had approached him to take over as police chief. But as he'd discussed with Grace, he planned to let the tribal administrator know before the end of the day that he was declining the offer.

He'd worked for the tribal police for over five years before joining the Lincoln County Sheriff's Office, and the chief's position was a job he didn't want to tackle, at least not yet. Perhaps when he had a full law enforcement pension that could buffer him from all the intricate tribal politics, he would consider taking it on. Or maybe then he might run for election to the tribal council.

He knew turning down the tribal council's offer would make his mother unhappy. Ever since he was a kid, she had harbored ambitious plans for him. She had never approved of his decision to get a degree in criminal justice and go into law enforcement. But it was Clayton's life to live and his mother's dream of wanting to see her only child installed as a tribal leader would have to wait.

He reached for the phone to call Grace and decided against it. He would talk to her about all of the important news of the day after dinner, when the children were asleep.

Lynette Burke, Riley's pregnant widow, had agreed to take over the cutting horse enterprise with the understanding that the animals owned jointly by the partnership would be moved to Jack and Irene Burke's spread. None of the Burkes was ready to spend a lot of time at the ranch where Riley had been gunned down.

Kerney leased some pastureland to a local organic beef producer, who wanted to finish a few head each month on native grass before taking the animals down the road to a small slaughterhouse in Moriarty, a short distance away. He offered State Police Sergeant Russell Thorpe free rent to stay in the guest quarters in return for looking after his remaining horses and keeping an eye on the place. Thorpe jumped at the chance.

Back in London, Kerney was not only glad to be reunited with Sara and Patrick, he also felt surprisingly more at ease in the city than he had before. A growing familiarity had something to do with it, but he also found himself enjoying all the amenities that one of the world's most important cities had to offer.

After recovering from jet lag and spending a weekend running errands and grocery shopping with Sara and Patrick, Kerney pulled Patrick out of preschool for a week to make up for all the time they'd missed together while he'd chased down Craig Larson. During a glorious run of sunny, mild weather that had Londoners out in droves, the two of them rode horses in Hyde Park, took hikes along the river Thames, visited the children's zoo at Battersea Park, watched an impromptu softball game played by expat Americans living in London, went boating in Regent's Park, and explored neighborhoods adjacent to where they lived.

At the end of one afternoon jaunt, they met up with Sara and shopped for the required school uniforms Patrick needed when he entered private school in late August. Running a little late, Sara came rushing into the clothing store to join them, dressed in a black pantsuit and looking strikingly beautiful. Passersby on the street and shopgirls in the store would have never guessed her to be a highly decorated, combat-wounded career military officer.

Patrick didn't like the summer uniform of rust-colored corduroy shorts and beige short-sleeved shirts, arguing that he should be allowed to wear blue jeans and cowboy boots like he did back at the ranch. Ganged up on by both parents, he quickly lost the squabble.

Because he was growing so fast, they decided to wait until fall to buy his winter school uniforms. Kerney paid the bill, still a bit shocked by what things cost in England compared to the States.

Packages in hand, they took a bus to within a short walk of the embassy for a prearranged tour and visit to Sara's office. Kerney and Patrick had seen the building only from the outside, during one of their safaris around the city. It was a starkly functional structure except for a huge gilded eagle perched on the parapet and a statue of General Eisenhower anchoring a corner plot outside the building.

According to the embassy staff, in the aftermath of 9/11, the building had been surrounded by portable wire fencing with concrete-and-marble bollards to keep car bombers away. Armed police foot patrols had roamed the grounds and a temporary guard shack served to process visitors.

It had all rather offended the locals, who resented an armed fortification set in the middle of tranquil Mayfair, and they lampooned it as a failure of American aesthetics. Now the embassy was no less well protected, but the portable chain-link barrier was gone, replaced by an attractive iron fence, the closed-off road in front of the building had been nicely landscaped, and new entry pavilions had been created to process the steady stream of visitors and visa seekers.

Sara took them through the pavilion reserved for American citizens, where Kerney and Patrick presented their passports and military dependent identification cards to a security clerk who checked their names against a list of authorized visitors. They walked through a formal reception area with a soaring ceiling and walls of bronze plaques to a bank of elevators and went up to a suite of offices housed behind a locked door.

Holding Patrick's hand, Sara gave them a tour and introduced them to the one-star navy rear admiral who was her boss, and a few of her army, Marine, and air force colleagues. Her own large, handsome office overlooked the lush lawn and majestic trees in Grosvenor Square.

Patrick immediately climbed into the chair behind the big desk and started asking his mother questions about the maps and pictures on the walls, the books and papers on the desk, all the people he'd just met, and what they did.

Sara sat with Kerney on the couch and patiently answered Patrick's questions as he swiveled in the leather desk chair. When he stopped swiveling, he admired the framed desk photograph taken at the ranch, of himself on his pony, and asked his mother where the glass jar filled with seashells had come from.

"Your father and I gathered those seashells on beaches in western Ireland when we were first married," she replied, remembering a honeymoon that now seemed so distant, given all that had happened over a few short years.

Patrick eyes widened. "I'd like to go to the beach and see the ocean again."

"How about next weekend?" Sara proposed as she squeezed Kerney's hand.

Patrick waited for Kerney's response.

"The beach and ocean it will be," Kerney replied.

Patrick beamed and resumed swiveling.

Kerney turned to Sara. "I got a call from Andy Baca today."

"Really? What did Andy have to say?"

Sara's telephone rang and she took the call before Kerney could reply. A concerned look quickly crossed her face as she reached for pen and paper and scribbled notes.

After thanking the caller, she hung up, gave Kerney a glum look, and said, "I'm going to have to cut our visit short."

"Problems?"

"You could say that." Sara scooted behind the desk and plucked Patrick out of the chair. "In the words of the Royal Army major who just called, one of my chaps has gone missing."

Kerney raised an eyebrow as Sara passed Patrick to him. "That's not good news."

"No, it's not," Sara said in agreement. She gave Patrick a kiss on the tip of his nose. "I'll walk you out. What did Andy want?"

Kerney set Patrick down on the floor. "Nothing that can't wait," he said.

Michael McGarrity is the author of twelve acclaimed Kevin Kerney novels. In addition to receiving the prestigious New Mexico Governor's Award for Excellence in the Arts, he has been nominated for an Anthony Award and for the Western Writers of America Spur Award. A Hillerman–McGarrity scholarship at the University of New Mexico recognizes both writers' contributions to the literary arts. A former deputy sheriff for Santa Fe County, McGarrity served as an investigator for the New Mexico Defender's Office and taught at the New Mexico Law Enforcement Academy. He lives in Santa Fe. Visit his Web site at www.michael mcgarrity.net.

Everyone Dies

"If you have never read Michael McGarrity, then do yourself a favor and read *Everyone Dies*." —Harlan Coben

Santa Fe police chief Kevin Kerney is called to the crime scene of a prominent attorney gunned down by an unknown assailant. With few clues and no motive for the killing, Kerney directs his detectives to delve into the victim's personal and professional life. But the killer's work has just begun. A second victim with ties to the criminal justice system is found with her throat slit, along with a warning: EVERYONE DIES. Next on the madman's list: Kerney, his wife, and their unborn son.

Slow Kill

"Combin[es] realistic police procedures with well-drawn characters . . . [a] crisply told story." —*USA Today*

While visiting a California ranch, Santa Fe police chief Kevin Kerney stumbles upon the murder of hotel magnate Clifford Spalding. Spalding was definitely a marked man, considering the sordid characters in his life: his conniving wife, her shady lover, and a deranged and bitter ex. But when the case is apparently solved, Kerney's investigation leads him to believe it's not the end of the story at all, just the beginning of a mystery rooted in the strange disappearance of Spalding's son thirty years before—and a secret that the old man may have taken to his grave.

Nothing but Trouble

"One of the best books in the Kevin Kerney series . . . a police procedural filled with action, intrigue, and a touch of romance. . . . Michael McGarrity writes his usual realistic and entertaining crime thriller."
—The Best Reviews

At the urging of his old friend Johnny Jordan, Santa Fe police chief Kevin Kerney takes a job as a technical adviser on a contemporary Western being filmed near the Mexican border. Joining him on his working vacation are his wife, Lieutenant Colonel Sara Brannon, and their three-year-old son, Patrick. And before long, a dead man on a road near an isolated border crossing, a federal undercover investigation into immigrant smuggling, the search for a fugitive from military justice hiding somewhere in Europe, and Jordan's troublesome behavior will embroil them in circumstances that will forever change their lives. . . .

Death Song

"A terrific police procedural with double the fun."
—Midwest Book Review

The bushwhack killing of a deputy sheriff in Lincoln County and the brutal murder of the deputy's wife in Santa Fe County bring Chief Kevin Kerney and his Mescalero Apache son, Sergeant Clayton Istee, back together. The double-homicide investigation is soon linked to a major drug-trafficking scheme and the cold-blooded slaughter of two women in Albuquerque. Due to retire at the end of the month, Kerney calls upon Clayton to find the slain officer's son, discover what triggered the killings, and give him the ammunition he needs to bring a multiple murderer to justice.